D1800017

BECKETT'S DEDALUS: DIALOGICAL ENGAGEMENTS
WITH JOYCE IN BECKETT'S FICTION

P.J. MURPHY

Beckett's Dedalus:

Dialogical Engagements with Joyce in Beckett's Fiction

UNIVERSITY OF TORONTO PRESS
Toronto Buffalo London

ISBN 978-0-8020-9796-5

Library and Archives Canada Cataloguing in Publication

Murphy, P. J. (Peter John), 1946–
  Beckett's Dedalus : dialogical engagements with Joyce in Beckett's fiction /
P.J. Murphy.

  Includes bibliographical references and index.
  ISBN 978-0-8020-9796-5

  1. Beckett, Samuel, 1906–1989 – Criticism and interpretation. 2. Beckett,
  Samuel, 1906–1989 – Fictional works. 3. Joyce, James, 1882–1941 – Influence.
  4. Joyce, James, 1882–1941. Portrait of the artist as a young man. I. Title.

  PR6003.E282Z7834 2008   848'.91409   C2008-904623-4

University of Toronto Press acknowledges the financial assistance to its publishing program of the Canada Council for the Arts and the Ontario Arts Council.

This book has been published with the help of a grant from the Canadian
Federation for the Humanities and Social Sciences, through the Aid to Scholarly Publications Programme, using funds provided by the Social Sciences
and Humanities Research Council of Canada.

University of Toronto Press acknowledges the financial support for its
publishing activities of the Government of Canada through the Book
Publishing Industry Development Program (BPIDP).

For my great-nephews Samuel and James Bryce, identical twins, born London, England, 30 July 2003

Must we wring the neck of a certain system in order to stuff it into a contemporary pigeon-hole, or modify the dimensions of that pigeon-hole for the satisfaction of the analogymongers?

Samuel Beckett, 'Dante ... Bruno . Vico .. Joyce'

Contents

Acknowledgments

Beckett's Dedalus grew out of a Social Sciences and Humanities Research Council (SSHRC) grant I received for a projected study of Beckett's aesthetics. This quickly turned into a study of Joyce's influence on Beckett, which remains one of the great unanswered questions in Beckett studies. My article 'Portraits of the Artist as a Young Critic: Beckett's "Dante ... Bruno . Vico .. Joyce" and the Rewriting of Joyce in "Assumption"' in the *Journal of Beckett Studies* (1999) staked out this territory by showing the extensive degree to which Beckett was influenced by Joyce at the very beginning of his career. The chapter version is half again as long as the original article, moving beyond the descriptive identification of particular Joycean allusions and echoes to an encompassing argument about how to reread Beckett's prose works in light of an abiding Joycean influence that progressed through a number of distinctive phases over Beckett's lifetime of writing.

Above all, I have to acknowledge a special debt to the students in my English 416 class, Topics in Modern Irish Literature: Joyce and Beckett. I devised this course in order to test out whether or not there would be enough material to extend my *JOBS* article to a full-scale investigation of Joyce's impact on Beckett's prose. Several students made particular contributions to points in this study and deserve special acknowledgment: Jessica Michell for Mr Kelly's folding and unfolding of his crimson kite, just as the crimson flower unfolds in Stephen Dedalus's theory of artistic creation; Keith Haughton for locating Watt's chair in *Portrait*; Jenna McManus for focusing on Arsene as a feathered biped whose epiphany can be compared to that of the birdgirl in *Portrait*; and Jean Nelson for noting parallel images in Davin's tale in *Portrait* and in Molloy's recounting of his stay at Sophie Lousse's. I would also like to thank David

Melnyk for his suggestion to me at a University of Reading Beckett Seminar (2003) that Beckett's 'It is not' of 'Dante and the Lobster' fame had its source in Stephen's aesthetic speculations in *Portrait*.

Jill McConkey, my editor at University of Toronto Press, supplied encouragement, much astute advice, and professional guidance as this study worked its way through the publication review process. The anonymous reviewers offered perceptive and challenging insights, especially with regard to maintaining the distinction between Stephen Dedalus's aesthetic theories and those of his creator; further development of this fundamental difference proved critical in my revisions. Charles Stuart's careful copy-editing was also greatly appreciated. Colleagues at Thompson Rivers University encouraged me in various ways during the work on this project. Nick Pawliuk was a most patient and tolerant sounding board for many of the ideas developed in this study, as well as a valuable source for bibliographic references on particular topics I was engaged with. Bruce Baugh pinpointed the exact reference in Hegel for Moran's famous 'It is midnight'/'It was not midnight' conundrum. Robert Kroetsch was a source of inspiration when he was writer-in-residence at TRU several years ago. He remembered for me how each new Beckett book had acted as a kind of liberation for him, sanctioning how things could now be done in a new way (he was also pleased to have someone recognize his Beckett allusion in 'Voice/ in prose: effing the ineffable'). My colleague Will Garrett-Petts's discussion of the 'frozen word' trope in Kroetsch and other Canadian postmodern writers in *PhotoGraphic Encounters* offered alternatives to the rhetorical device of *ekphrasis* and counterpointed my own efforts to show how Beckett reconstructed and reconfigured the modernist revelation in order to allow for a sense of the temporal. Likewise, my colleague George Johnson's *Dynamic Psychology in Modernist British Fiction* was a stimulating counterpoint to my discussion of the importance of kinesis in Beckett's aesthetic. Finally, thanks to my friend and colleague Alex Forbes for his much appreciated encouragement over the years of my work on Beckett. And – as always – to Jennifer for her abiding support.

Abbreviations

Beckett Editions

CP	*Collected Poems in English and French.* New York: Grove, 1977.
CSP	*The Complete Short Prose 1929–1989*, ed. S.E. Gontarski. New York: Grove, 1995.
Dis	*Disjecta: Miscellaneous Writings and a Dramatic Fragment*, ed. Ruby Cohn. New York: Grove, 1984.
Dr	*Dream of Fair to Middling Women*, ed. Eoin O'Brien and Edith Fournier. Dublin: Black Cat, 1992.
HII	*How It Is.* New York: Grove, 1964.
MC	*Mercier and Camier. New York: Grove, 1974.*
MPTK	*More Pricks Than Kicks.* New York: Grove, 1972.
Mur	*Murphy.* New York: Grove, 1957.
NO	*Nohow On (Company, Ill Seen Ill Said, Worstward Ho)*, intro. S.E. Gontarski. New York: Grove, 1996.
Pr	*Proust.* New York: Grove, 1957.
Tr (M, MD, Un)	*Trilogy (Molloy, Malone Dies, The Unnamable).* New York: Grove (Evergreen dition), 1991.
W	*Watt.* New York: Grove, 1959.

Joyce Editions

FW	*Finnegans Wake.* New York: Viking, 1969.
JJP	*James Joyce: Poems and Shorter Writings*, ed. Richard Ellmann, A. Walton Litz, and J. Whittier-Ferguson. London: Faber and Faber, 1991.

P   *A Portrait of the Artist as a Young Man*, ed. R.B.
                       Kershner. New York: Bedford Books of St Martin's
                       Press, 1993.
PJJ   *The Portable James Joyce*, intro. Harry Levin. New
                       York: Penguin Books, 1976. (Referred to for *Dubliners*,
                       Collected Poems, Exiles)
SH   *Stephen Hero* (part of the first draft of *A Portrait of the
                       Artist as a Young Man*), ed. T. Spencer, rev. ed. J.J.
                       Slocum and H. Cahoon. London: Jonathan Cape, 1956.
U   *Ulysses*, the 1922 text, ed. Jeri Johnson. Oxford UP
                       (World's Classics), 1993.

Biographies

DF   James Knowlson, *Damned to Fame: The Life of Samuel
                       Beckett*. London: Bloomsbury, 1996.
JJ   Richard Ellmann, *James Joyce*, new and rev. ed. New
                       York: Oxford UP, 1982.

BECKETT'S DEDALUS

Prolegomenon to Any Future
Beckett Criticism

Beckett's Dedalus was conceived as both a complement and a supplement to my earlier study of the post-*Trilogy* prose, *Reconstructing Beckett: Language for Being in Samuel Beckett's Fiction* (1990). It is a complement in so far as the emphasis now is upon an in-depth discussion of Beckett's early works from 'Assumption' through to *The Unnamable*, encompassing the first twenty years of his writing career (1929–49); only the final chapter now deals with the period that was the primary focus of the earlier work. More importantly, *Beckett's Dedalus* is also supplementary in that it pursues a very different route towards the same set of revisionist readings that I put forward in *Reconstructing Beckett*. Foremost among these was the view that radically new interpretations of Beckett's prose would be possible if we proceeded upon the ultimately more defensible assumption that Beckett is trying to devise new means of integrating self and fiction and word and world, rather than being fundamentally guided by the need to deny the power of words to express – the so-called art of failure that has enthralled so many Beckett critics. More specifically, I argued, via Peter Bürger's theory of the avant-garde, that rather than directly trying to integrate art with life, Beckett sought, particularly in the post-*Trilogy* works, to bring life to his art, to 'let being into literature' through what he calls the 'proper syntax of weakness.'[1]

That other route is by means of an aesthetic debate concerning Beauty which Beckett engaged at the very beginning of his writing career through his critical investigation of the theory of art promulgated by Stephen Dedalus in *A Portrait of the Artist as a Young Man*. This dialogical engagement with Joyce over such traditional aesthetic questions as the nature, form, and significance of Beauty may indeed sound strangely out of place in a Beckett criticism that has almost solely emphasized

Beckett's aesthetics of negation in various formulations, thereby largely excluding any serious consideration of alternative dimensions of his work of a more affirmative nature. This more traditional aspect of Beckett's aesthetic theorizing has been largely neglected and generally unrecognized in critical readings, which is hardly surprising in that it is a commonplace judgment that twentieth-century art no longer concerns itself with the question of Beauty. In a comment on avant-garde art in his *History of Beauty* (2004), Umberto Eco stresses that such 'art is no longer interested in providing an image of natural beauty, nor does it aim to procure the pleasure ensuing from the contemplation of harmonious forms.' Instead, art is designed 'to teach us to interpret the world through different eyes';[2] or – as might be said with more particular reference to Beckett – it raises questions regarding how such worlds are brought into being and their ontological status. Wendy Steiner from a feminist perspective states the case in even more dramatic terms in *Venus in Exile: The Rejection of Beauty in Twentieth-Century Art* (2001): whereas in the nineteenth century female subjects symbolized artistic beauty, 'the twentieth-century avant-garde, by contrast, could barely bring itself to utter "woman" and "beauty" in the same breath.'[3] The same trends are evident in literary art, but not in such extreme terms. In Joyce's *Portrait*, whose very title suggests a linkage between the pictorial and literary arts, the questions about Beauty and the roles of Venus are prominently foregrounded in Stephen Dedalus's theorizing. Similarly, the title of Beckett's very first novel, *Dream of Fair to Middling Women* (written 1932; published 1992), highlights a preoccupation, no matter how ironically phrased, with just such central matters of more traditional aesthetic speculation. The disrupted sequence of publication for Beckett's prose works has perhaps made it more difficult to see such obvious starting points, a situation admittedly made more complex by the emergence of Beckett as a major writer in the 1950s at a time when existentialist readings were in vogue and the subsequent development of his career throughout a period generally dominated by various post-structuralist interpretations of his work.

Beckett's Dedalus will trace in detail how Beckett's critical encounter with Joycean aesthetics plays a heretofore unrecognized and vital role in the development of his own theories. We will see that *Portrait* is the most important and influential Joycean text for Beckett, who, of course, also possesses a thorough knowledge of *Dubliners, Ulysses,* and *Finnegans Wake*. While there are some important references to these works, the most telling reference points in terms of the structuring of key ideas in Beckett's own fiction are to *Portrait* (with the final story of *Dubliners*, 'The Dead,' a transitional work marking Joyce's new style in *Portrait*, also a recurrent focal point). The critical point of our investigation concerns Beckett's reservations about the modernist moment of revelation, what Joyce termed in *Stephen Hero* the 'epiphany.' In his first published work of fiction, 'Assumption' (1929), Beckett very carefully delineated what he regarded then as the fundamental distinctions between his approach and Joyce's to matters aesthetic. Beckett's approach proceeds from the premise (or 'assumption') that it is the 'pain of Beauty' (*CSP*, 4) that should now concern the modern artist: 'Before no supreme manifestation of Beauty do we proceed comfortably up a staircase of sensation, and sit down mildly on the topmost stair to digest our gratification: such is the pleasure of Prettiness' (4). The full-scale discussion of 'Assumption' in the first chapter of this study will detail how it is a cento, a complex interweaving of references from *Portrait*, with special reference to the final episode of the second chapter, Stephen Dedalus's encounter with the prostitute. In the reference to Beauty cited above, Beckett rewrites a key aesthetic passage of *Portrait* in which Stephen Dedalus refers to the 'supreme quality of beauty, the clear radiance of the esthetic image' (*P*, 186) as the 'supreme manifestation of Beauty.' 'Manifestation' is indeed carefully chosen: the epiphany was explicitly defined as a 'sudden spiritual manifestation' in *Stephen Hero* (215).[4] From 'Assumption' to 'What is the word' (1989), Beckett's development of his own aesthetic theory repeatedly targets his rejection and subsequent revision and rewriting of Stephen Dedalus's more traditionalist view that the supreme manifestation or quality of Beauty is 'the luminous silent stasis of esthetic pleasure' (*P*, 186). For Beckett the aesthetic experience is from the very beginning characterized as kinetic in nature: it is the pain and disorder of lived life that art must somehow accommodate. His first major prose work, the greatly undervalued 'Assumption,' suggests key points of departure from such Dedalian theorizing at the same time that it makes clear to just what degree and just how very detailed these echoings and revisions of *Portrait* often are. Beckett has chosen Joyce as his starting point. From the very beginning, Beckett has displayed a complex relationship with Joyce (a veritable Joyce complex), one whose twofold nature is perhaps best described by Linda Hutcheon's definition of modern parody as combining a critique of as well as a homage to the targeted literary reference point.[5]

Beckett's choice of Joyce as a means of initiating his own writing focuses primarily on one figure, namely, Stephen Dedalus, would-be author-hero of *Stephen Hero* (surname replete here with diphthong),

Portrait, and, even more problematically, *Ulysses*. In Beckett's first published piece of criticism, 'Dante ... Bruno . Vico .. Joyce' (1929), commissioned by Joyce for *Our Exagmination ... defence of Work in Progress*, Beckett writes as if Stephen Dedalus's views were indeed somehow conterminate with his creator's. Kevin Dettmar in 'The Joyce That Beckett Built' comments pointedly on this very questionable assumption: 'Elsewhere in the essay we find Beckett inaugurating what was to become a frequently repeated fallacy in Joyce criticism: he was perhaps the first critic to use the system of aesthetics set out by Stephen Dedalus in *A Portrait of the Artist* as a yardstick by which to measure the success of Joyce's later fiction, and certainly the first to apply it to *Finnegans Wake*, then *Work in Progress*.'[6] Dettmar concludes that Beckett's failure to recognize Joyce's attempts to distance himself from Stephen's views is 'disingenuous at best.'[7]

There are two very different aspects to Beckett's misprision of Stephen Dedalus for Joyce that warrant further comment. First of all, Beckett most likely read *Portrait* in 1927, when he was twenty-one, the same age as Stephen at the conclusion of the novel. James Knowlson points out that in the same year Beckett was enthusiastically promoting Joyce's delicately lyrical and earnestly self-important *Pomes Penyeacb* (*DF*, 98). These first readings of *Portrait* (as will be extensively corroborated) made a very powerful and lasting impression on the young Beckett, and, as with many readers of the same age, he would have naturally enough identified more closely with Stephen than with his ironically detached narrator or creator. As a prototypical artist-figure, Stephen Dedalus would have at least resided within Beckett's own realm of possibilities. Such a point of comparison was reinforced by the fact that Beckett from the very beginning also adopted a highly critical attitude towards Stephen's theories of art, even as he adapted these ideas to his own writing. Regarding Stephen's theories as if they were equivalent to Joyce's own was then perhaps not so much 'disingenuous' as a rhetorical and psychological strategy necessary for Beckett to undertake his own writing. The heavily ironized depiction of *Portrait* pointed towards one James Joyce, master novelist of modernist experimentation circa 1927, whom Beckett would meet the following year and with whom any such comparisons must have seemed then to be virtually unimaginable. In 1989, the last year of his life, Beckett told Knowlson that he 'admired Joyce's *Portrait of the Artist as a Young Man*. There was something about it.'[8] The following discussions will try to explicate just what this indefinite pronoun entailed and how its significance revealed itself over a lifetime of writing.

The second aspect of Beckett's misreading of Dedalus-Joyce relations is more complex in so far as it implicitly does admit what Dettmar claims Beckett had intentionally overlooked: that Joyce's theory of art had quite clearly progressed by the time of *Portrait* to a point well beyond those views that Stephen so laboriously formulates. To some degree, Beckett could not help but be aware of how Joyce is aesthetically distancing himself from his own past by fictionalizing it through Stephen Dedalus. Paul Jay, who has explored in depth this complex issue of distancing in *Portrait*, proposes that Joyce gave birth to himself as the author of *Portrait* by exploiting the deconstructive reversals, gaps, and discontinuities between an earlier version of his former self (Stephen) and his mature authorial self.[9] Inscribing his own authority through the representation of Stephen's failure to become an artist in his own right is the definitive instance of Joycean *différance*: the identification of Daedalus the 'fabulous artificer' with Dedalus the would-be modern artist will indeed be indefinitely deferred. As a virtuoso logodaedaliast, Joyce uses Stephen for his own ends and then abandons him; on the other hand, Beckett will take up in a complex fashion Stephen's cause at a number of key junctures in his own writing. As I argued throughout *Reconstructing Beckett*, the fundamental dynamic in Beckett's fiction is the struggle between an 'author' and his 'other' (whether depicted as fictional or otherwise) and the search to find ways of accommodating their competing interests. To this power struggle now needs to be added Beckett's relationship with Joyce and the seminal implications of his contestatory adoption/adaptation of Stephen Dedalus's theories of art.

Beckett's only extended critical study, *Proust* (1931), probes much further into the various aporias inherent in the modernist aesthetics of revelation that are highlighted in 'Assumption.' We will see that Beckett is also extending his critical engagement with Joyce in conjunction with his discussion of Proust, this Joycean subtext being indirectly announced in Beckett's choice of one of Joyce's favourite lines from Leopardi as his epigraph.[10] Most of Beckett's discussions focus on the vexed status of the symbol and the question of direct expression of the moment of privileged insight. Jacques Aubert in a rigorous and illuminating critique of the development of Joyce's aesthetic makes a number of telling points that virtually coincide with Beckett's extended critique of Stephen Dedalus's theories as we will trace it throughout this study. Foremost among these points is the recognition that there are a number of contradictions Joyce 'failed to negotiate and upon which his aesthetic was to founder: image versus symbol, nature versus grace, essence versus object, ethics versus ontology.'[11] Beckett's points of departure for his own aesthetic investigations are effected by means of what might then be refreshingly termed Joyce's 'art of failure,' the *dissonantia* inherent in his founding principles. To begin with such a critical perspective would indeed be liberating for Beckett studies, which have developed for the most part under a number of stereotypical assumptions about Beckett's own so-called art of failure. Aubert's final judgment is that Joyce was compelled to admit the failure of his artistic theory and to move from it to the realm of ethics; 'the final emphasis is on the love of life, of living, mortal, and erring beings.'[12] Joyce came to 'an acceptance of his own contradictions and necessities' and this included his realization and acceptance of 'the real as multiplicity, fragmentation, difference, that only art can adequately grasp.'[13] Joyce's aesthetic by the time of *Portrait* is, to be sure, difficult to characterize – most certainly his views cannot be equated with those of Stephen Dedalus; the 'acceptance of his own contradictions' entails a mature acceptance of the world that is well beyond Stephen's level of insight as depicted in *Portrait*. It is crucial to recognize that Beckett begins his writing with a critical awareness of the various theoretical impasses inherent in modernist aesthetics. A generation after Joyce, Beckett takes up the challenges posed by the same set of very powerful ideas found in Stephen's theorizing in *Portrait*, testing out the limitations of these theories as well as trying to find ways to overcome the aporias upon which Joyce's aesthetic 'foundered.'

Turning from criticism to his first novel, Beckett declared that his intention was to write something more 'genuine' and 'direct.'[14] Any reader of *Dream of Fair to Middling Women* is initially bound to be bewildered by such terms since this novel is so very heavily riddled with allusions from sources of all sorts, many of the obscure variety, as John Pilling's studies in this area have so thoroughly tabulated. Beckett's strategy for dealing with this apparently self-contradictory situation entails a complex extension of his deployment of parodic structures as first evidenced in 'Assumption.' Linda Hutcheon's discussion of modern parody has shown that it can be 'a source of freedom' in so far as its repetitions with a difference allow the newcomer to deal with the 'anxiety of influence' by working through the words of others to find his own.[15] Moreover, I will argue that this extensive network of allusions in *Dream* functions in many respects to camouflage the fact that Beckett is here still fundamentally engaged with a critique and assessment of the aesthetic theory formulated in *Portrait* and that these ideas are decisive in determining the structure and actual development of Beckett's novel. Central again here is a debate over Beauty: Beckett's principal character Belacqua is in some defining respects a latter-day version of Stephen Dedalus, his nickname 'Bel' making this thematic linkage even more obvious. His pursuit of his various 'fair to middling women' serves to underline these analogies. There is a scene in *Dream* in which the Syra-Cusa (the model for whom was Lucia Joyce) loses a copy of Dante given her by Belacqua; the text she mislays might have even more appropriately been Joyce's *Portrait*. Although this would, of course, have been much too obvious, it would certainly have been poetically fitting in that this is indeed the 'purloined novel' at the heart of so many of Beckett's aesthetic deliberations, not only in the early works but, in varying degrees, throughout his writing career, if in less obvious and pervasive ways. In this regard, Beckett could be added to those 'few people' for whom Ezra Pound said *Portrait* 'has become almost the prose bible.'[16] This is particularly ironic since Pound was openly contemptuous about Beckett's real-life imitation of Joycean mannerisms and dress, the rudeness reaching such proportions that Joyce felt compelled to 'constrain' his friendship with Pound.[17] The decisive point, however, is that when it comes to his writing, Beckett's imitations of Joyce are of a much more complex and contested nature. If *Portrait* is indeed a sort of 'bible' for Beckett, the host of critical revisions of it throughout his career results finally in *parodia sacra*,[18] as Bakhtin employed the term to refer to 'doublings' of various sacred works that can become canonical in their own right.

In Beckett's last two novels in English, the testing out of Stephen Dedalus's aesthetic system is brought to a critical turning point. *Murphy* (1938) is structured around a tug-of-war between the eponymous hero and Mr Willoughby Kelly, a surrogate version of Joyce himself, with Celia the prostitute/Venus figure caught in the middle. This aesthetic debate over the role of Beauty is developed throughout the work by means of a number of specific correspondences in the parodying-travestying mode with Joyce's *Portrait* again supplying the primary reference points. This more traditional dimension of the novel has been consistently overlooked in favour of the much more highly touted 'nothings' of Geulincx and Democritus pointed to by Beckett himself as privileged points of entry.[19] But Beckett, like the 'whispering prestidigitator' (4) of 'Assumption,' is misdirecting his readers: the real sleight of hand takes place as Beckett rewrites in complex ways key scenes from *Portrait* that deal with aesthetic matters of a much more traditional sort.[20] Most strikingly, chapter 13 is a complex revisioning of one of the most famous epiphanies in all of Joyce:

the birdgirl encounter that comes near the end of chapter 4 of *Portrait*. The ending of *Murphy* is 'Joycean' and also 'Beckettian' in so far as Beckett's parodic doubling generates its own distinctive poetry. And this conclusion we will later see is carefully set up at the beginning of Beckett's novel and developed throughout in ways that have not thus far been fully appreciated.

Beckett wrote *Watt*, his 'war novel,' in Roussillon in southern France, where he had fled to escape the German occupation of Paris. The novel was begun shortly after Joyce's death in 1941 and can perhaps best be regarded as Beckett's hail (homage) and farewell to his friend/father-figure and literary mentor. In *Watt* the connections with Joyce are much more obvious than in *Murphy*, so obvious indeed that like Poe's 'purloined letter' they escape recognition because they are, as it were, hidden in the open. Watt's very name and his contingent problems with words and things are cognate with *Portrait*'s foundational tenet of *quidditas* or 'whatness.' For Watt, however, there is no accompanying sense of *claritas* or 'radiance,' rather only a series of unnamable entities (including himself) that issue forth only as a series of negative epiphanies; in short, it is the very absence of any modernist revelation that is at the core of Beckett's investigation here. Such an 'epiphany' is reserved for Watt's predecessor at Mr Knott's, Arsene, a composite figure of one James Joyce, whose so-called 'short statement' about his experiences of transcendence is the key to the first part of the novel and the subsequent sections that underline (painfully so) Watt's failure not only to duplicate such moments of visionary insight but even to hold on to mundane reality.

Mercier et Camier (completed in 1946) and the sequence of *Nouvelles* (*Stories*) that preceded and followed it are still greatly undervalued in terms of their role as decisive transitional works between the evacuation of meaning in *Watt* and Beckett's imaginative breakthroughs in the *Trilogy* and his emergence as a major contemporary writer. Behind these developments reside Beckett's statements about his own 'revelation': the sudden realization that the 'dark' which he had previously tried to suppress was in fact his real subject matter and that somehow or other he had now to find ways to accommodate its expression.[21] Neither Beckett's biographers nor his critics have made much of this experience, which Beckett has persistently maintained was the turning point in his career. I will argue that Beckett's 'dark' revelation is nothing less than his own version of Joyce's epiphany and that Beckett's artistic vision is in many ways complementary to Joyce's rather than being diametrically opposed to it.

If there is one area in which criticism has singularly failed to rise to the challenges posed by Beckett's works, it is the refusal to acknowledge fully the visionary quality of his writing. In *Watt* and the other earlier works, Beckett's engagement with *Portrait*'s theory of Beauty and its 'supreme manifestation' has also focused on Kant's other type of beauty, the Sublime, which transcends any 'bounding line' and offers a vista of the immeasurable as inhuman and annihilating (witness *Murphy*'s 'flux of forms' and Watt's reaction to the broken circles in Erskine's room). Beckett's vision of the 'dark' as his true subject matter is evident in *Mercier and Camier* and entails a revisioning of one of the most imaginative scenes in the Western canon: Dante's ascent of the Purgatorial Mountain on his own after Virgil has guided him as far as he can. Joyce played a similar role in guiding Beckett to this new vantage point. For Beckett this new perspective affords ways of critically and imaginatively exploring how a newly emergent authorial figure within the text takes responsibility for connecting the world of the imagination with the world outside through the illumination of the 'dark' to probe the nature of this new reality. 'The Calmative' will be the major focus of our discussion here, for of all the *Stories* it is the one most directly engaged with the process whereby the perplexing issue of a fictional being and its relationship to various worlds or realities is brought to the forefront of Beckett's writing. 'First Love' ('Premier Amour'), the last of the *Stories* to be published, focuses on the question of what is the beautiful as it offers a revisionist history in literary terms of Beckett's relationship with Lucia Joyce and the rift with her, which resulted in his banishment for a period from the Joyce household. This story ends on a note of 'distant cries' that reflect Beckett's own fundamental aesthetic concern with pain and suffering, abiding issues that he has in various ways set in opposition to Joycean 'distant music' as most famously formulated in 'The Dead.'

Most Beckett criticism has pre-emptively determined that Joyce's influence as a significant factor ended well before the famous *Trilogy*, even if there is considerable disagreement over when exactly such 'influence' need no longer be regarded as important in the development of Beckett's writing. But Beckett's level of engagement with Joycean aesthetics is far too complex by the time of *Molloy* to be so simplistically and prematurely dismissed. The most obviously foregrounded reference to Joyce in *Molloy* is to the 'distant music' the eponymous narrator hears when he is stopped by a policeman who demands to see his papers. A comprehensive contextualization of this particular Joyce allusion as well as a network of other references that critics have not noticed will show that Beckett's echoing of Joyce is indeed much more complex and reconstructive in nature: the Joyce references function as a significant means of counterpointing and hence of advancing Beckett's own aesthetic investigations. *Portrait* is (again) the key textual counterpoint: it supplies Beckett with touchstone references for determining what an artist is and is not. The discussion of *Molloy*'s Joyce references will reveal that they are used in part *I* to show how Molloy is becoming an artist in his own right and in part *II* to show how Moran fails to attain such status. Such Joycean counterpoint should not be lost sight of in the midst of the perplexing and convoluted discussions of authority, origins (and 'originality'), the fictional versus the real, not to mention the most striking and challenging factor of all, the radical questioning of language itself as an expressive medium. From the very beginning of his writing career in 'Assumption,' Beckett has proposed a critical investigation of such aesthetic-philosophical issues; the various conundrums and impasses should not in themselves be regarded as the desired result of the confrontation with such theoretical exigencies. *Molloy* is Beckett's climactic encounter with Joyce; here, however belatedly, we have Beckett's first full-length portraits of the artist. Given the very rich allusive texture of Beckett's writing, it is easy to overlook the obvious, such as *Watt*'s 'whatness' (or *quidditas*) and Molloy's 'portraiture' of the artist-figure. The Joycean counterpoint is vital to our critical understanding of *Molloy*, the rest of the *Trilogy*, and those remarkable prose works of his last forty years (1949-89), in which Beckett finds a way out of the linguistic impasses of *The Unnamable*'s conclusion and works towards finding new ways of letting being into literature.

In the post-*Trilogy* prose, Beckett has incorporated Joyce in a number of ways that are decisive in determining the structure and development of particular texts; even more importantly, Beckett at certain junctures collaborates with Joyce as 'ghost writer' to produce remarkable *parodia sacra* such as 'Enough,' 'Still,' and *Ill Seen Ill Said*. Tracing Joyce's influence in these later works complements my earlier readings and speculations in *Reconstructing Beckett*, reinforcing my argument for the fundamentally critical and more affirmative nature of Beckett's experiments with language. 'L'Image' ('The Image'), the first separately published piece of what became *Comment c'est* (*How It Is*), is greatly indebted to a passage of *Portrait* that it extensively rewrites; 'All Strange Away' arguably takes its very title from references in *Stephen Hero*, as well as a number of particular doublings of Joycean images; and, perhaps most strikingly in terms of structural correspondences, the fifteen sections of 'The Lost Ones' (1970) can be compared with the fifteen stories of *Dubliners*, with particular emphasis upon Beckett's long-delayed final section and Joyce's late addition of 'The Dead' to complete his collection. 'Enough' is a hauntingly beautiful hail and farewell to Joyce, who might be regarded as the prototype of the 'old man' in this short story. 'Still' reveals in a very brief space how Beckett has finally managed in his own way to work the miracle of the Joycean epiphany. Through a fine-tuning of syntax and the music (now no longer so distant) of certain collocations of words, this text reconciles kinesis and stasis, the spatial and temporal inherent in 'still' as a Janus-word that incorporates both these dimensions. Beckett's masterwork of his later prose is, in my opinion, *Ill Seen Ill Said*, which explores the life and afterlife of the hovering vulturine eye as it tries to grasp hold of the spectral old woman whose actions constitute the destabilized ontology of this work. Miraculously, a sense of being – however tentative for both perceiver and perceived – is at times glimpsed. On another plane, this is arguably Beckett's fullest realization over a lifetime of writing of his relationship with Joyce. In his own way, Beckett has gone beyond the ending of 'The Dead' to explore the conclusions and implications of those final great paragraphs in order to create an original work only he could conceivably have written, but one which he could not possibly have attained without his contestation and collaboration with Joyce. This work is written under the sign of Venus – literally so: the text opens with 'from where she lies she can see Venus rise.' And Beckett's text possesses a moving beauty that, again, would not have been possible without Beckett's lifelong engagement with this concept, which is so alien to most of contemporary critical theory but which Beckett never fully lost sight of.

Such an encompassing argument is radically at odds with the tradition of Beckett criticism, which has – with a couple of notable exceptions to be examined later – essentially dismissed at various points in the pre-*Trilogy* period the Joyce connection in terms of having any significant influence. Knowlson in the authorized biography basically dismisses the Joyce question before it can even become a factor, regarding 'Assumption' as proceeding on the premise that Beckett saw that he needed to turn away from Joyce's influence from the very beginning. Pilling in his two studies of sources in *Dream of Fair to Middling Women* argues that Beckett purges himself of Joycean influences by turning to and embracing a host of other literary and cultural references; C.J. Ackerley's annotated *Murphy* does not see Joyce as a major influence on Beckett and fundamentally regards Beckett's strategy as one of resistance to Joyce's writing; hence, by the time of *Watt*, virtually all critics agree that Joyce is no longer relevant to the Beckettian enterprise. (Ackerley's recently published annotated *Watt* notes a number of Joycean echoes and allusions, but he no longer feels the need to argue that Joyce is not central to Beckett's thought after *Murphy*.) It is hardly surprising, then, that in *The Grove Companion to Beckett*, which Ackerley co-authored with S.E. Gontarski, whose *Intent of 'Undoing'* had notably advanced the 'resistance' theory of Beckett-Joyce relations, there is a general dismissal of Joyce's influence by the time of the *Trilogy* and an outright rejection of Stephen Dedalus's theories of art and the artist being of the least relevance at this point, since romantico-modernist renditions of the artist's grand calling are of no import within the post-structuralist paradigms that now generally hold sway for writers and their critics.[22] All of the above position statements have in common a desire to close off much too soon a complex and challenging question that is central to our understanding of Beckett.

The three studies solely devoted to the Beckett-Joyce relationship highlight in different ways some of the major obstacles to be overcome when dealing with the difficult question of influence. Barbara Gluck's *Beckett and Joyce: Friendship and Fiction* (1979) never fully engages its topic since its founding premise is that Beckett's prose is struggling always to escape from Joyce's theory of circular time, as if *Finnegans Wake* were to be regarded as Beckett's fundamental reference point. The question of circular time is so vaguely and generally framed that it lacks any real critical value. Nor are 'friendship' and 'fiction' brought into any revealing critical alignment: we get the usual potted summaries of Beckett's meeting with Joyce in 1928 (via the good graces of Thomas MacGreevy), Beckett's various roles in the Joyce circle, his temporary banishment due to the Lucia Joyce imbroglio, and the various tidbits of their relationship, for which Beckett was the main source in Richard Ellmann's Joyce biography. One can then certainly appreciate Beckett's opening words in his 'Foreword' to *Proust*: 'There is no allusion in this book to the legendary life and death of Marcel Proust'; there will be allusions in *Beckett's Dedalus* to the 'legendary life and death' of Samuel Beckett, but only in so far as they are connected with his writing. In this regard, Gluck's study does deserve more credit than it is usually given for its extensive tabulation of Joycean echoes and allusions in Beckett's work.[23] This documentation does at least point us towards the area where critical energies need to be focused in terms of influence: the recognition of particular and precise references to Joyce in Beckett, so that we can move beyond vague generalizations that might happen to appeal to certain critics.

On the other hand, in the final essay in his co-edited collection *Re: Joyce 'n Beckett* (1992), Ed Jewinski advances a sophisticated argument about the Joyce-Beckett nexus, one that, albeit in elliptical fashion, anticipates provocative arguments by Dettmar and Daniel Katz. Jewinski believes that 'the "influence" of Joyce on Beckett can best be understood by studying how these two writers have helped to "author" the postmodern desire to "rewrite" the very notion of "literature."'[24] Jewinski combines this notion of postmodernist rewriting with Harold Bloom's *The Anxiety of Influence* and its guiding principle that great writing is dependent upon strong 'misreadings.' This does lead to some challenging conclusions; for example, Beckett's well-known views on Joyce as modernist master of his medium as found in the Israel Shenker 'interview' (1956) – his preferred 'misreadings' – are in turn deconstructed by the various post-structuralist readings that now dominate Joyce criticism. For Jewinski this leads to a 'curious paradox' in which the more Beckett 'separates himself from his precursor the more he brings his writing closer to Joyce's.'[25] This does indeed possess a certain theoretical symmetry: a postmodernist Joyce is neatly brought into conjunction with a postmodernist Beckett.

However, as the preceding summary of my argument in *Beckett's Dedalus* was at pains to make clear, what is now needed in terms of exploring the Beckett-Joyce question is a very thorough grounding in specific textual realities from which theoretical positions can then be inductively drawn in a more convincing fashion. Jewinski's seductive theorizing of the Joyce-Beckett relationship is detached from such textual groundings and instead proffers a number of aperçus that, even if suggestive and sometimes insightful in themselves, do not form part of a continuous argument. The problem, put simply, is that 'Joyce' and 'Beckett' are such complex entities that critics, in order not to be overwhelmed, tend to pick certain aspects of each that appeal to them and then set up comparatist models that often do not really tell us much about either author. Hence the refocusing in the present study from 'Beckett *and* Joyce' in order to concentrate on 'Beckett's Joyce,' via Stephen Dedalus's aesthetic theories; this narrowed focus will allow us to think our way through Beckett's relationships with Joyce, without relying on the imposition of theoretical models upon the discussion. The Beckett who emerges in my readings is still concerned with issues of authorship, of authors and their roles, and over a lifetime of writing does, I believe, find his own ways of validating the modernist revelation or epiphany in terms of the ontology of the fiction and our relationship with such word-worlds. Moreover, despite the overlay of contemporary critical theories in so much Beckett criticism, the fundamental shaping of many critics' views of Beckett appears to be largely predetermined by the ideology of negativity that underlies this tradition of scholarship from its very beginnings; the title of Jewinski's essay, for example, is 'James Joyce and Samuel Beckett: From Epiphany to Anti-Epiphany.'

The third study devoted exclusively to Beckett and Joyce, the collection edited by Friedhelm Rathjen, *In Principle, Beckett Is Joyce* (1994), takes the 'anti-' position to an extreme. According to Rathjen, Beckett's efforts to avoid Joyce constitute an indirect Joycean influence:

> The Joycean influence does not manifest itself in direct Joycean traces that can be found in Beckett's work but rather in the absence of any superficial traces: Joyce was Beckett's starting point not in the sense of Joyce's showing Beckett where to go but in the sense of Beckett's realising what to avoid: he had to avoid the Joycean 'apotheosis of the word' in order to create something of his own. Beckett's work therefore is reciprocally connected with Joyce's: the greater the impact of Joyce, the more it is left blank in Beckett's work, and this is why there are relatively few allusions to Joyce in Beckett's allusion-packed texts.[26]

We will see that there are indeed 'direct Joycean traces that can be found in Beckett's work,' and, yes, we will see that in many ways Joyce did initially 'show Beckett where to go,' and that Joyce's influence is not left 'blank' the greater its impact on Beckett. Beckett's knowledge of Joyce's work, particularly *Portrait*, is so detailed and thorough that we simply have not in many instances recognized these references. Such instances support Stephen James Joyce's assertion that Beckett knew more about his grandfather's work 'than any person living or dead.'[27]

This strategic deployment of imitative allusions entailing detailed rewriting of a predecessor text should definitely not be mistaken for some self-serving game of literary 'hide-go-seek.' Allusions do imply 'a common knowledge between reader and writer,'[28] with the qualification, in terms of Beckett's references to Joyce, that the reader has to work at the acquisition of a close reading knowledge comparable to that of the writer. Beckett's primary intention in this regard is certainly not to withhold knowledge of what he is doing with Joyce from the reader. A certain opacity is, of course, to be expected in regard to such personal issues of ontogenesis, particularly in light of modernist anxieties about influence.[29] Nevertheless, building in such specific textual references Beckett would have expected them at some point to be recognized. That it has taken so long to see the extent of these connections has more perhaps to do with the guiding assumptions of Beckett studies than it does with Beckett's intentions in this regard. Since the prevailing view is that Beckett came to terms with Joyce's influence at an early point in his career, most certainly well before the *Trilogy* in most estimations, critics could not see what they did not believe could be there. Nor should the extensive echoing of Joyce be misconstrued as some jejune game of literary cryptography. Beckett chose Joyce's work as his starting point and returned to it again and again throughout his career for the decisive reasons mentioned at the beginning of this introduction: reading early Joyce, *Portrait* in particular, and then meeting Joyce led Beckett to work out his relationship with Joyce's work through a complex relationship between himself and Joyce's would-be artist figure Stephen Dedalus. Beckett appropriated and rewrote Joyce's version of Dedalus primarily as a means to work towards his own aesthetic formulations. This relationship with Joyce via Stephen Dedalus is fundamentally dialogical in nature, a contestation that is in some ways also a collaboration. And the consequences of this rewriting can be recognized by readers without being privy to this Dedalian pattern of references; however, an awareness of this dimension should significantly expand our understanding of Beckett's development through a reassessment of his relationship with Joyce.

Of the three studies devoted to Beckett and Joyce, the most suggestive remarks are found in Jewinski's essay, none more so than those on Beckett's often-cited statements to Shenker about the relationship of his writing to Joyce's:

> With Joyce the difference is that Joyce is a superb manipulator of material – perhaps the greatest. He was making words do the absolute maximum of work. There isn't a syllable that's superfluous. The kind of work I do is one in which I'm not master of my material. The more Joyce knew the more he could. He's tending toward omniscience and omnipotence as an artist. I'm working with impotence, ignorance. I don't think impotence has been exploited in the past. There seems to be a kind of esthetic axiom that expression is achievement – must be an achievement. My little exploration is that

whole zone of being that has always been set aside by artists as something unusable – something by definition incompatible with art.

I think anyone nowadays who pays the slightest attention to his own experience finds it the experience of a non-can-er. The other type of artist – the Apollonian – is absolutely foreign to me.[30]

Dettmar might be exaggerating for rhetorical effect when he says 'these are perhaps the most influential 150 words in all of Joyce criticism,'[31] but they certainly do constitute the single most influential statement on Beckett's supposed relationship with Joyce in all of Beckett criticism. Such 'maps of misreading' must be critically assessed when working out the perplex of Beckett's relationship with Joyce. *Beckett's Dedalus* will show that Beckett's characterizations of Joyce as modernist master are carefully formulated to divert attention away from any consideration that his own work might more rightly be regarded as complementary in a roundabout way to Joyce's. This is a far cry from the mainstream view that takes its cue from Beckett's own remarks (most often those to Shenker) that the contrasts between the two writers are most decisive.

Nor is my complementary-yet-different thesis to be confused with the argument proposed in Katz's *Saying I No More* (1999), which is premised (as was Jewinski's) on a number of would-be similarities between post-structuralist versions of both Joyce and Beckett. Such a comparison relies on a number of generalizations of a deconstructive nature rather than any specific network of textual echoes. Moreover, there still resides the persistent and unexamined assumption that somehow Beckett is still 'secondary' to Joyce, consigned to being an echo of an echo. Witness, for example, the last two sentences of Katz's study that centres on Joyce and Beckett, even if only two of its six chapters are explicitly so designated: 'No less than Joyce, Beckett gives us an inventory of the detritus from which we write ourselves, but without the lure of a circling, winding list, ever spiraling back toward itself as it curls away. Beckett instead offers variations of the possible rhythms of these possible inscriptions, as they extend, replace, and preserve themselves and us in their wake.'[32] In so far as this conveys an argument, it is strangely *déjà lu*: Hugh Kenner's view of the 'inventory' from *The Stoic Comedians* and Gluck's view of the circular in Joyce as the key to defining the relationship to Beckett are now read deconstructively.[33] However, the new critical paradigm adds little to the earlier approaches, except for the 'coda,' which underscores musical variations on a theme ('possible rhythms of these possible in-scriptions'). But we will see in *Beckett's Dedalus* the startling degree to which Joyce's texts are intertwined with Beckett's, the truly surprising number of instances in which Joyce's verbal 'music' is appropriated and rewritten by Beckett so that it is no longer so 'distant' but incorporated into original works of his own devising. 'Original' here signifies that it is via the very nature of Beckett being the most derivative of writers that he 'reinscribed' himself as arguably the most innovative and distinctly recognizable of contemporary writers following after Joyce.

A recent study directed – nominally, at least – to the Beckett-Joyce relationship also focuses on 'absence as the chief condition (and therefore parallel) of Beckett's and Joyce's literary worlds.'[34] Colleen Jaurretche, editor of *Beckett, Joyce and the Art of the Negative* (2005), categorically asserts, however, that her collection of essays most definitely 'does not seek to draw comparisons between the authors' (and indeed only one of the twelve essays deals with both Beckett and Joyce), declaring that 'neither has a greater or lesser relationship to negation.'[35] We need to come to terms in a much more encompassing sense with Beckett's negative capabilities, and this entails a fully detailed rethinking of the Beckett-Joyce relationship from its very beginnings. Such an approach could help point the way towards an integration of new developments in Beckett studies to which the centenary celebrations of 2006 give an added urgency. Knowlson's groundbreaking *Damned to Fame: The Life of Samuel Beckett* (1996) has supplied the inspirational impetus for two of the most promising advances in Beckett studies over the last decade. These are an enriched understanding of Beckett within a number of specific historical contexts and a concentrated focus upon Beckett's manuscripts, notebooks, and the various sources for his writing. Two recent issues of the flagship journals of Beckett studies neatly exemplify these new directions: 'Historicising Beckett,' edited by Seán Kennedy in *Samuel Beckett Today/Aujourd'hui* (2005), and 'Genetic Beckett Studies,' edited by Dirk Van Hulle in the *Journal of Beckett Studies* (Spring 2004). These approaches afford an opportunity for rethinking and perhaps even reconfiguring the ways in which we have framed our discussion of Beckett. Propaedeutics should precede further hermeneutics. Reassessing Beckett's relationship with Joyce is one way of rethinking our first principles whereby we have read and interpreted Beckett's fiction. Beckett's dialogical engagement with the aesthetic theory of *Portrait* and his very detailed rewritings of Joycean materials constitute, in my estimation, one of the most extensive and remarkable instances of literary influence in the twentieth century.

1 Portraits of the Artist as a Young Critic: Beckett's 'Dante … Bruno . Vico .. Joyce' and the Rewriting of Joyce in 'Assumption'

To apprehend the complex and vexed underpinnings of the Joyce-Beckett relationship, we need to go back to Beckett's first two published works, the essay 'Dante … Bruno . Vico .. Joyce' and the short story 'Assumption,' and read them anew; that is, with a hitherto unrecognized awareness of the extent to which these two so ostensibly very different texts are complementary. These two works need to be read together, as companion pieces, as a sort of palimpsest (keeping in mind, however, that 'the danger is in the neatness of identifications,' *Dis*, 19). [1] Both of these pieces appeared in the double issue of *transition*, numbers 16/17, June 1929, an ironically fitting conjunction in a number of ways, for we will see that there are a number of doubling effects that draw them together intertextually. The first point to make about Beckett's double-headed debut as writer is that we do not know the order in which these first two works were composed. James Knowlson in his Beckett biography states what appears to be a straightforward chronology: 'Inspired by Joyce and MacGreevy, Beckett started to write in Paris, first the essay on Joyce, then "Assumption"'(110). In conversation and correspondence with Knowlson, it was, however, made clear that we do not know in what order the works were actually composed. Knowlson's sequencing seems to be based simply on the fact that in the double issue of *transition* the Joyce essay precedes 'Assumption.' This is a point Beckett critics have not belaboured since there seemed little to be gained by even posing the question; both works were obviously composed within the same brief period in 1929, so let's just leave it at that. However, if we recognize that these first two Beckett texts reveal radically different ways in which Beckett approached Joyce at the very beginning of his career, then the question certainly is at least worth posing.

And this is, in fact, the case: in 'Dante ... Bruno . Vico .. Joyce,' a piece commissioned and overseen by Joyce as part of *Our Exagmination ... defence of Work in Progress*, one of Beckett's strategies, as pointed out by John Pilling in his close reading of the work, seems to involve putting off as long as possible his 'duty of writing in praise of Joyce';[2] moreover, when that praise does duly appear, it seems implicitly qualified by the suggestion that Beckett doesn't really know what to make of Joyce's so-called 'direct expression' and that perhaps he harbours with respect to Joyce some of the same critical reservations initially voiced about Vico, namely, that concerning 'hoisting the real unjustifiably clear of its dimensional limits, temporalizing that which is extratemporal' (19). Beckett's circling about the relevance of Vico to Joyce – for over half the essay – appears designed to avoid direct engagement with the job at hand. The impact and significance of this strategy are doubled when we realize that 'Assumption' has not yet been recognized by Beckett critics for what it essentially is: a text that is supersaturated with Joycean references from *A Portrait of the Artist as a Young Man*, that at its centre is a quite incredibly detailed rewriting of the last two and a half pages of section 5, chapter 2, of *Portrait*, Stephen's visit to the prostitute. But the degree of Beckett's indebtedness to *Portrait* is much more extensive than a reliance on this one scene. In fact, 'Assumption''s five rather eccentric paragraphs might be regarded, to borrow a phrase from Beckett's 'Dante ... Bruno . Vico .. Joyce,' as a 'quintessential extraction' (28) of the five chapters of *Portrait*.[3] Basta! Joyce and Beckett are here, and more substantially than would appear from this swift survey of the question.

What we have then at the very beginning of Beckett's career is the very odd conjunction, virtually simultaneous, of a critical essay on Joyce, the topic for which was, as Beckett said, 'suggested' by Joyce,[4] even though the structuring of the piece was left to his own devising, with Beckett's first published creative piece of writing, the very short story 'Assumption,' which is riddled with Joycean references, to such an extent that one might again be tempted to adapt one of the chestnut phrases of Beckett's Joyce essay to the effect that the commissioned piece is merely *about* Joyce whereas the short story '*is that something itself*' (27). Yet to do so would be to fall prey to the 'danger' of the 'neatness of identifications.' The reality of the situation is much more complex and untidy. Faced with the 'obligation to express' in the Joyce essay, employing a critical terminology with which he is obviously ill at ease (or unsure of), Beckett, it would seem, released his 'spirits of rebelliousness' in a more direct way by writing a sort of pastiche/parody,[5] however condensed and elliptical, of *Portrait* in his 'Assumption,' a rewriting of Joyce that is also a rewriting, in part, of Beckett's own views as imparted in 'Dante ... Bruno . Vico .. Joyce.' It could be speculated that Beckett's 'Assumption' in fact grew out of his resistance to the dutiful act of required homage to a literary master that the *Our Exagmination* piece demanded and that 'Assumption' was in some ways a type of subversive literary game-playing, a sort of hoax or joke, whereby Beckett, by pushing Joyce's ideas in *Portrait* to extremist positions, would begin to find the direction his own voice might take. These first two works of Beckett are intimately intertwined, and unravelling these interrelationships is vital to our rethinking of Beckett's early views on art and his relationship with Joyce.

A central characteristic shared by both of Beckett's first published works is their highly derivative nature, their dependence upon the works and ideas of others (acknowledged or not), in conjunction with a highly original restructuring of those ideas in ways that allow Beckett, in varying degrees, to appropriate these as his own. Terence McQueeny in his unpublished dissertation 'Beckett as Critic of Proust and Joyce' (1977) has brilliantly brought to light the extent of Beckett's 'borrowings' in 'Dante ... Bruno . Vico .. Joyce.' He details the extent to which Beckett has relied on secondary sources, often translating from various critics with little or slight modification (and without any scholarly apparatus whereby this might be credited), namely, Croce and Michelet for Vico, McIntyre for Bruno, and De Sanctis for Dante. What might today with a less charitable eye be termed simple plagiarism, McQueeny generously overlooks by terming the essay 'primarily an assignment written quickly with a good deal of help from Joyce' and by concluding that it is a 'brilliant mosaic of secondary sources done by a rushed apprentice,' one which, nevertheless, is 'valuable in spite of defects' as it does supply the 'basic needs for even a rudimentary understanding of *Work in Progress*.' In short, McQueeny regards the work as exhibiting 'weakness in composition, not comprehension.'[6]

Be that as it may, when one comes to read this essay anew, some seventy years after its publication, it is indeed what McQueeny terms 'obvious defects in composition' that are, in fact, most revealing about Beckett's attitude to an ostensibly academic exercise on Joyce's *Work in Progress*. These 'defects,' in addition to the essay's 'derivative' nature, would obviously include its highly elliptical nature, delaying tactics in terms of an actual engagement/commentary on Joyce's work, and the interpolation of various vehement denunciations of a philistine audience that fails to recognize and appreciate Joyce's 'direct expression' in

Work in Progress – all of which serves to draw attention to the writer, that all this is 'by Samuel Beckett.' Beckett is indeed anything but direct himself in his exposition in 'Dante … Bruno . Vico .. Joyce,' though the use of the first-person pronoun in the first paragraph might initially mislead a reader to think so: 'And now here am I, with my handful of abstractions, among which notably: a mountain, the coincidence of contraries, the inevitability of cyclic evolution, a system of Poetics, and the prospect of self-extension in the world of Mr Joyce's *Work in Progress*' (19). And now here are we, rereading Beckett's first published paragraph, a paragraph, moreover, that, in the huge mountain of Beckett criticism does not appear to have been read critically so much as glossed over. Something is very strange here in terms of the sequencing of the items in the thesis statement ('handful of abstractions'). We all know that the title of the essay, with its eccentric use of ellipses, is meant to schematize the historical order of the principal authors to be dealt with, and not the actual order in which they are discussed. But Beckett's 'handful of abstractions' would, with one notable and striking exception, seem to outline the actual order of the key ideas in his essay (just as a student in a freshman composition course might learn to set up an outline for his 'pensum'). That is to say, with the exception of the striking and perplexing first entry, 'a mountain,' Beckett does give us the actual order of his essay's development: 'the coincidence of contraries' of Bruno is dealt with (albeit very briefly) in paragraphs two and three, almost en passant, as Beckett begins his discussion of Vico as 'a practical roundheaded Neapolitan' (paragraph 2, topic sentence) and as a 'scientific historian' (paragraph 3, topic sentence). [7] No wonder Joyce found Beckett 'short on Bruno'! And the rest of the essay, in an even more clearly signposted way, does then, in turn, deal with the remaining three items – 'the inevitability of cyclic evolution, a system of Poetics, and the prospect of self-extension in the world of Mr Joyce's *Work in Progress*.'

Everything is neatly tucked away in academic pigeonholes, except for the mountain. But the whole 'handful of abstractions' makes sense and indeed is in the proper order if we realize that Beckett's approach in this ostensibly academic piece is based on an incredible assumption of poetic licence: when Beckett states disarmingly 'And now here am I,' he can only mean that he is *already* on Dante's purgatorial mountain, at the point of the Terrestial Paradise, which, as I have documented in *Reconstructing Beckett*, is Beckett's determining trope for that zone of the imagination and critical intelligence where the writer must work out the complex interrelationships of the real and its dimensional limits, while avoiding temporalizing that which is extratemporal. In other words, the very first paragraph of Beckett's first published work has not been read aright so much as 'skimmed' over: we have theorized *about* it, but have not seen that '*it is that something itself.*' Why have we missed this? Most obviously because of a sort of intentional fallacy – we do not expect a would-be scholarly elucidation in its opening gambit to subvert the very conventions of its discourse. Yet this first paragraph and, in particular, the 'And now here am I' sentence, with its 'poetry' and its 'logic,' is, if read anew from the perspective I am putting forward, the most successful embodiment of Vichian 'poetic logic' in the whole essay. John Pilling in *Beckett before Godot* has commented, with reference to the concluding paragraphs of 'Dante … Bruno . Vico .. Joyce,' which deal with Dante's Purgatorial Mountain and a comparison of it with Joyce's Purgatory, 'But in the final paragraph of the essay Beckett wants, in his "last word about the Purgatories" – of which he is only too conscious that it is actually his first word on the subject – to drive a wedge between Dante and Joyce.'[8] However, Beckett's 'last word about the Purgatories' does make good sense if we have recognized the duplicitous poetic logic of his opening paragraph. The two sentences preceding the final sentence of the fourteenth and final paragraph of Beckett's 'essay' on Joyce begin with 'And,' perhaps a doubling that is meant to return us to the first paragraph's 'And now here am I.' The cycle, in a sort of Vichian fashion, has been completed, beginning and ending telescoped across the intervening discussions. 'Prospects of self-extension,'[9] namely, Beckett's own, are suspended in any direct way after the opening paragraph; nevertheless, it is clear from the concluding discussion of Dante and Joyce that Beckett is, behind the scenes as it were, using them to clarify his own views. We will see later how these ideas are adapted to the ending of 'Assumption,' how key terms such as 'a flood of movement and vitality' and 'the partially purged' take on significance for Beckett within his own first published work of fiction.

The line of ellipses (or suspension points) that marks off Beckett's first paragraph from the rest of the essay is a typographical means of underlining how the topography of this opening is at once separate from yet connected to what follows. Joyce employed such lines of demarcation in *Dubliners*, most often in order to foreground the transition to the epiphany in the story's conclusion. A last word then about the structure of Beckett's 'Dante … Bruno . Vico .. Joyce.' What Beckett calls his 'painful exposition of Vico's dynamic treatment of Language, Poetry, and Myth' (26) occupies the first eight paragraphs; the concluding six paragraphs are made up of two long paragraphs on Joyce's *Work in Progress*, followed by four final paragraphs that develop the Dante-Joyce comparison. Beckett's fundamental point in this essay is to argue for an idea of form and structure that is not merely a frame on which to hang metaphysical generalizations such as Vico's, which Beckett says were used by Joyce only 'as a structural convenience – or inconvenience' (22). Beckett endorses instead throughout this first critical venture a flexible, dynamic view of structure that is an 'interior intertwining [...] a decoration of arabesques' (22). In short, an anti-'neatness of identifications' argument as announced in the very first sentence and echoed throughout the discussion. Beckett's own structure for 'Dante ... Bruno . Vico .. Joyce' would seem, as with his first paragraph on the 'mountain,' to attempt to embody these very principles. Bizarre as it might sound, the essay is structured along the lines of an Italian (Petrarchan) sonnet, a form possibly suggested by the Italianate context of Dante, Bruno, and Vico, with Giacomo Joyce thrown in for good measure.[10] The conventions of this form dictate that the octave states a problem (or expresses an emotional tension) that the sestet then answers or relieves. The two-part division is neatly marked by the topic sentence of the very short eighth paragraph, 'Such is the painful exposition of Vico's dynamic treatment,' followed by the turn to the 'sestet' in the topic sentence of the next paragraph, 'On turning to the *Work in Progress* we find the mirror is not so convex.' Of course, this literary game playing could be taken as Beckett's ironic way of reminding us that literary criticism is not mere bookkeeping (though mathematics is prominently displayed and is commented upon as an important means of accounting and recounting). The danger is indeed in the neatness of identifications; after all, taking into account the line of ellipses after the first paragraph, do we have thirteen or fourteen paragraphs making up 'Dante ... Bruno . Vico .. Joyce'?[11]

Another of the very odd features of Beckett's Joyce essay – and a feature that is directly relevant to Beckett's rewriting of Joyce in 'Assumption' – is that references to *Ulysses* are conspicuous only by their absence whereas there are four direct references to *A Portrait of the Artist as a Young Man*, two paraphrases and two quotations. The first paraphrase comes in the midst of a diatribe against those 'Ladies and Gentlemen' who are 'too decadent to receive it' (namely, Joyce's 'direct expression'): 'The title of this book [*Our Exagmination ...*] is a good example of a form carrying a strict inner determination. It should be proof against the usual volley of cerebral sniggers: and it may suggest to some a dozen incredulous Joshuas prowling around the Queen's Hall, springing their tuning-forks lightly against finger-nails that have not yet been refined out of existence' (26–7).[12]

The second paraphrase of Joycean terms from *Portrait* carries on Beckett's opening remarks in paragraph 11 on the Joyce-Dante comparison: 'They both saw how worn out and threadbare was the conventional language of cunning literary artificers, both rejected an approximation to a universal language' (30).[13] The first direct quotation (and the very first reference to *Portrait* in 'Dante ... Bruno . Vico .. Joyce') is used to buttress Beckett's point that Joyce only adapts the Vichian 'system' as a 'structural convenience' and that it is in 'no way a philosophical one': 'It is the detached attitude of Stephen Dedalus in *Portrait of the Artist...* who describes Epictetus to the Master of Studies as "an old gentleman who said that the soul is very like a bucketful of water"' (22).[14] The second quotation from *Portrait* is from the aesthetics section of chapter 5 and is by far Beckett's most extensive and significant use of Joyce's first novel and a foreshadowing of things to come in Beckett's handling of the host of *Portrait* echoes, borrowings, and paraphrases in 'Assumption.' Beckett's reference is to the opening remarks by Stephen on the 'phases of artistic apprehension,' via Aquinas's 'Three things are needed for beauty, wholeness, harmony and radiance.' The excerpt Beckett chose for 'Dante ... Bruno . Vico .. Joyce' deals with the first of these only, 'wholeness' or *integritas*: 'Perhaps "apprehension" is the most satisfactory English word. Stephen says to Lynch: "Temporal or spatial, the esthetic image is first luminously apprehended as self-bounded and selfcontained upon the immeasurable background of space or time which is not it ... You apprehend its wholeness." There is one point to make clear: the Beauty of *Work in Progress* is not presented in space alone, since its adequate apprehension depends as much on its visibility as on its audibility' (27–8).[15]

What is most telling here is that Beckett has, of course, got it wrong; he has reversed Stephen's terms, as is made clear by citing the sentence in *Portrait* immediately preceding the passage Beckett uses in his essay: 'What is audible is presented in time, what is visible is presented in space' (*P*, 184). Either Beckett has simply made a mistake (McQueeny's 'rushed apprentice') or he has intended the miscue as an indirect critique of Joycean aesthetics, perhaps a further probing, however circuitous, of his opening critique of Vico (and, by association, possibly Joyce himself) and of the need to resist the temptation for 'neatness of identifications,' of tidying things up – 'hoisting the real unjustifiably clear of its dimensional limits, temporalizing that which is extratemporal.' Or perhaps Beckett is simply registering a critique of Stephen Dedalus's theory of art (which is not, of course, equivalent to that of Joyce himself), one which clearly is much too 'static' for Beckett's liking; for example, 'Beauty expressed by the artist cannot awaken in us an emotion which or a sensation which is purely physical. It awakens, or induces, or ought to induce, an esthetic stasis' (*P*, 180). This discussion, as we will soon see, is elaborated upon by Beckett in 'Assumption' with a much more violent wrenching of Joycean terms, about which there can be no doubt that they are indeed intended. The four detailed references to *Portrait* in 'Dante ... Bruno . Vico .. Joyce' also supply some intertextual support for my view that 'Assumption' is essentially a rewrite of key aspects of Joyce's first novel and is coterminus with Beckett's first critical venture in the essay commissioned by Joyce; we cannot fully read one without reading the other in conjunction with it.

Beckett's fundamental strategy in 'Assumption' is lodged ironically in its title, and it has much more to do with the common usage of presumed 'arrogance' (literary or otherwise) than with the feast in honour of the raising of the Virgin Mary to the heavens. Beckett's literary tactics here involved him pushing to the extreme a whole series of ideas about 'esthetic philosophy' as found in *Portrait*. First and foremost is the situation portrayed of a 'he' who is struggling to contain the 'other' within him (his 'prisoner') and who is also struggling to escape, to find expression in sound, a quest which is only finally realized through the mediations of a 'Woman' (and her sexuality) and then only at the price of a final 'splendid drunken scream' that destroys the host 'he.' This is indeed anything but that 'neatness of identifications' promulgated by young Stephen Dedalus as the basis of the aesthetic subject, 'selfbounded and selfcontained.' With 'he' and 'other' in deadly conflict, there cannot, of course, be any 'wholeness' (*integritas*), 'harmony' (*consonantia*), or 'radiance' (*claritas*); the very *quidditas* or whatness of the deeply divided protagonist figure is that very dilemma to which this short story has no answer.

The syntactical and logical impasse of the very first sentence underscores the problem to be somehow dealt with, or at least to be delineated in its major components, so that an aesthetic image might at least be projected: 'He could have shouted and could not.'[16] Here Beckett has pushed to the point of absurdity a phrasing that Joyce employs pervasively in *Portrait*: the 'He could' pattern, with a qualifying negative. For example, towards the end of chapter 1 of *Portrait* (the one chapter to which there is no explicit reference in 'Assumption,' by the way), [17] Stephen is on his way to state his case against his unfair punishment by Father Dolan to a higher authority, the rector. Stephen feels that he will not be able to utter the required words: 'It was impossible: he could not' (59). Of course, he does manage to negotiate this little ethical dilemma; he is temporarily 'Stephen hero,' until the deflationary irony of the next chapter, at least. Beckett's dilemma is, however, quite different: it is a linguistic and ontological one. In short, Beckett is, in his opening move, challenging the central assumption of Stephen Dedalus's aesthetic theory (and that of traditional aesthetics itself): Aristotle's principle of non-contradiction, in which 'the same attribute cannot at the same time and in the same connection belong to and not belong to the same subject' (*P*, 181). Beckett's first sentence therefore develops an explicitly anti-Aristotelian stance that abandons any reliance on the 'neatness of identifications' of conventional aesthetic theorizing.

The next two sentences of 'Assumption' attempt to explain the nature of the problem Beckett has set for himself, via Joyce, or more accurately via Joyce's depiction of Stephen Dedalus's theories. In *Reconstructing Beckett*, I employed the second cryptic sentence of 'Assumption' – 'The buffoon in the loft swung steadily on his stick and the organist sat dreaming with his hands in his pocket' – as a veritable refrain throughout my discussion of the later prose. The sentence neatly encapsulates the author ('organist') other ('buffoon') dilemma and the complexity involved in working out a modus vivendi between the two, something that is well beyond the reach of young Beckett in this early effort. But the central players are now at least onstage: the narrator of the work; the 'he' whose travails he records; that mysterious 'other' within the 'he' who is struggling for some type of expression; and the Woman, who detaches herself from the social context of the outside world to join the 'he' in his room. Here the principals are not fully in action – one swings 'steadily,' treading time metronomically almost, while the other 'dreams'; the constituent elements have, however, been annunciated.

The third sentence of the first paragraph of 'Assumption' contains a 'buried' allusion to *Portrait*, one so obscure – or apparently so commonplace – that the only person who could even have had a chance of recognizing it in the June 1929 double issue (16/17) of *transition* would have been James Joyce himself. The sentence deals with how the 'he'

speaks ('little') and with what tone ('low-voiced timidity') and characterizes him as one 'who shrinks from argument, who can reply confi-
dently to Pawn to King's fourth, but whose faculties are frozen into
bewildered suspension by Pawn to Rook's third' (all of this qualified, if
not contradicted, by the beginning of the next sentence, which states:
'He indeed was not such a man, but his voice was of such a man').
Beckett is here echoing, however distantly, the scene towards the end
of chapter 5 of *Portrait* when Stephen enters the library in search of
Cranly and finds him having a chess problem read to him by a medical
student: 'Pawn to King's fourth' (196). This hardly ranks as an 'allusion' since it is a standard opening move. That Beckett is broaching
an in-joke with Joyce, however, is further supported by the ironic
counterpoints in Joyce's scene vis-à-vis what Beckett describes in his
first paragraph of 'Assumption.' The rule-breaking talking of Dixon,
the medical student, and Cranly has irritated another reader who has
gone to complain. Cranly certainly doesn't shy away from argument
and doesn't speak timidly; he pauses on the stairway and shouts:
'Pawn to King's bloody fourth' (197). He clearly does not have the faculty of 'whispering the turmoil down' that the 'he' of 'Assumption' is
said to possess. What Beckett seems to be saying to Joyce (via his critique of Stephen Dedalus's theories of art) is this: when I begin to
write, I won't be bound as your alter ego was by precepts of an Aquinas or an Aristotle, and I won't make the standard opening gambit of
Pawn to King's fourth, but the much more unorthodox opening of
Pawn to Rook's third, the verbal equivalent of which is, 'He could have
shouted and could not' (metaphorically a sort of 'endgame' before the
game even properly gets under way).

The heart of the first paragraph concerns a commentary by the narrator
of the story on the various psychological strategies employed by the 'he'
in social contexts whereby he can subtly impose his will on others and
hence 'whisper the turmoil down.' This is done in an academic style or
tone – one that, in fact, might be more appropriate for a would-be scholarly essay such as 'Dante ... Bruno . Vico .. Joyce' was intended to be. We
are cautioned by the narrator 'not to imply that the least apostolic fervour
coloured what was at its worst the purely utilitarian contrivance of a man
who wished to gain himself a hearing, and at its best an amused experiment in applied psychology' (4).[18] The last part of the first paragraph
does, however, return to the dialogical encounter with Stephen Dedalus's
speculations in *Portrait*, though in a game of one-upmanship he takes it a
step further: 'To avoid the expansion of the commonplace is not enough;

the highest art reduces significance in order to obtain the inexplicable bombshell perfection' (4). Compare this with Stephen's comments as he sits down to begin a youthful attempt at artistic distillation: 'Now it seemed as if he would fail again but, by dint of brooding on the incident, he thought himself into confidence. During this process all those elements which he deemed common and insignificant fell out of the scene' (*P*, 71). Then there follows a passage that employs Dantean imagery of the Purgatorial Mountain (as found in the first and concluding paragraphs of 'Dante ... Bruno . Vico .. Joyce'): 'Before no supreme manifestation of Beauty do we proceed comfortably up the staircase of sensation, and sit down mildly on the topmost stair to digest our gratification: such is the pleasure of Prettiness. We are taken up bodily and pitched breathless on the peak of a sheer crag: which is the pain of Beauty' (4). Beckett is specifically targeting here Stephen's interpretation of *claritas* (radiance) in chapter 5: 'The instant wherein that supreme quality of beauty, the clear radiance of the esthetic image is apprehended luminously by the mind which has been arrested by its wholeness and fascinated by its harmony is the luminous silent stasis of esthetic pleasure, a spiritual state' (185). Beckett is endorsing a crucial point he has already implied in his critique of Stephen's aesthetics: that it is based on an adolescent case of arrested development, a state in which the aesthetic image is made safe and conventional as an emissary of a Beauty that is 'static.' In 'Dante ... Bruno . Vico .. Joyce,' Beckett identified 'hell' and 'heaven' as such lifeless realms, to be dramatically contrasted with purgatory and its art of pain and suffering. (Certainly, as I have discussed in *Reconstructing Beckett*, Beckett is fond of painfully catapulting his characters – *in medias res* – to the 'peak of a sheer crag'.)[19] The art of hunger is much more complex and untidy than such an effete aesthetics, which Beckett contemptuously dismisses as one that allows us 'to digest our gratification.' Such would be merely Hallmark greeting card 'Prettiness.'

To summarize, then, in the very first paragraph of 'Assumption,' Dante is thus obviously present; so is Bruno, whom Joyce found Beckett 'short on' in the essay on *Work in Progress* (Bruno is here with a vengeance in terms of the story's basic structure of maxima coinciding with minima – the 'whisper' and the 'great storm of sound'); so too is Vico, at least in the way that Beckett presented him (or rather misread or distorted) in the Joyce essay,[20] that is, as a thinker who emphasized the primitive hieroglyphics and their 'terribly real' powers; and so of course is James Joyce's *Portrait*, in a host of ways that we have only begun to enumerate. Beckett stated at the end of the first paragraph of

'Dante ... Bruno . Vico .. Joyce' that 'literary criticism is not book-keeping' and should not succumb to the desire of the 'analogymongers' to modify a 'certain system' (here read Joyce's *Portrait*) to suit the critics' own ends. By the end of the first paragraph of 'Assumption,' Beckett seems to be rewriting himself as well as Joyce; his first creative venture in this very short story seems, in large part, to consist of 'book-keeping' and 'analogymonger[ing].'

The second paragraph concentrates on the lonely struggle of the 'he': 'In the silence of his room he was afraid, afraid of that wild rebellious surge that aspired violently towards realization in sound.' This is the archetypal dilemma of Stephen Dedalus in *Portrait*, though Beckett, following his critique in the first paragraph of Stephen's aesthetic, has made his situation much more 'kinetic' or violent. And the situation in Beckett's parable is one of life and death, not the angst of an adolescent who seeks to 'transfigure' his sexual desires so that they merge with his ideal love object (e.g., Mercedes-Emma). Beckett's literary lexicon, however ironically twisted, is in nearly every respect Joycean à la *Portrait*, namely, key words such as 'wild,' 'rebellious,' 'murmurs,' and 'floodwaters' of various types (an image so pervasive in *Portrait* it is virtually intertwined with its very telling, since it is identified with sounds and articulations of all sorts, for example, 'His unrest issued from him like a wave of sound and on the tide of flowing music,' 75). It is the image of flooding, of an overwhelming urge to at once let the caged prisoner free and to dam up the 'flesh-locked sea of silence,' that generates the sense of an incredible and irresolvable tension that was announced in the very first sentence ('He could have shouted and could not') and then lost sight of in the psychologizing and aesthetic lecturing of the rest of the opening paragraph. The second paragraph of 'Assumption' in its opening and its conclusion shows Beckett fragmenting Joyce's sentence, which describes Stephen's encounter with the prostitute at the end of chapter 2: 'As he stood silent in the middle of the room she came over to him' (95). Beckett's paragraph begins with the phrase 'In the silence of his room' and concludes over three hundred words later with 'At this moment the Woman came to him ...' (5).

Beckett's main focus in his rewriting of *Portrait* is the last two and a half pages of the final part five of chapter 2, when Stephen visits the prostitute. Like the 'he' of 'Assumption,' Stephen 'had tried to build a 'breakwater,' to 'dam up' the 'powerful recurrence of the tides within him' (94). Stephen's efforts fail – 'From without as from within the water had flowed over his barriers: their tides began once more to jostle fiercely above the crumbled mole' (94) – just as do those of the un-named protagonist of 'Assumption' – 'By damming the stream of whispers he had raised the level of the flood, and he knew the day would come when it could no longer be denied. Still he was silent, in silence listening for the first murmur of the torrent that must destroy him. At this moment the Woman came to him ...'[21] The climax of this cluster of shared imagery in Joyce's *Portrait* occurs just prior to Stephen's actual encounter with the prostitute – a type of complex, ver-bal foreplay – and needs to be cited in detail so that Beckett's rewriting of it can be gauged and evaluated in terms of its differentiations from it in the central and decisive third paragraph of 'Assumption.'

Stephen is 'listening eagerly for any sound' (95), just as in the first sentence of paragraph 3 Beckett's 'he' 'was listening in the dusk when she came, listening so intently that he did not hear her enter.' First, the experience that ensues for Stephen Dedalus:

> He felt some dark presence moving irresistibly upon him from the dark-ness, a presence subtle and murmurous as a flood filling him wholly with itself. Its murmur besieged his ears like the murmur of some multitude in sleep; its subtle streams penetrated his being. His hands clenched convul-sively and his teeth set together as he suffered the agony of its penetration [...] and the cry that he had strangled for so long in his throat issued from his lips. (95)

Then, the experience as narrated about the 'he' of 'Assumption':

> He clenched his hands in a fury [...] She turned on the light and advanced carelessly into the room. An irruption of demons would not have scat-tered his intentness so utterly. She sat down before him at the table, and leaned forward with her jaws in the cup of her hands. He looked at her venomously, and was struck in spite of himself by the extraordinary pal-lor of her lips, of which the lower protruded slightly and curled upwards contemptuously to compress the upper, resulting in a faintly undershot local sensuality which went strangely with the extreme cold purity stretching sadly from the low broad brow to the closed nostrils. He thought of George Meredith and recovered something of his calm. The eyes were so deeply set as to be almost cavernous; the light falling on the cheekbones threw them back into a misty shadow. In daylight they were strange, almost repulsive, deriving a pitiless penetration from the rim of white showing naturally above the green-flecked pupil. (5–6)

Beckett's revision of Joyce's passage in *Portrait*, as with the previous re-writings we have foregrounded in this discussion, involves pushing things to an extreme point at which there seems to be no possibility of solution, except that of dissolution. Stephen does get to 'sin with one of his kind,' however ironically qualified the prostitute scene is in terms of his search for an ideal. There is a sense that Stephen might, finally, grope his way towards some balancing of the imaginary and the real. Joyce presents Stephen's dilemma as an ethical and aesthetic one that the religion of art might, in modernist terms, mediate.

But Beckett's protagonist faces a starkly ontological perplex: how can he coexist with that other struggling for an outlet, his 'prisoner' locked within? Stephen's fragments somehow suggest at least the pos-sibility of a whole, whereas Beckett's hero is fundamentally divided in half (not to mention the third-person narrator who won't let the 'he' speak in his own words, just as 'he' vainly tries to suppress the voic-ings of the 'other' whose 'struggle for divinity was as real as his own, and as futile').[22] That this is fundamentally an aesthetic (literary) prob-lem is acknowledged by Beckett in one of his most pointed and direct rewritings of Joyce. In the midst of 'he"s discomfiture by the Woman, he talks of a brief respite: 'He thought of George Meredith and recov-ered something of his calm.' Compare this with Stephen's self-reflection in the prostitute scene, when he pauses sentimentally over lost images of Mercedes and how 'At those moments the soft speeches of Claude Melnotte rose to his lips and eased his unrest' (94). Meredith, whose stylistic influence on Joyce is well established, is a much more appro-priate adult reference than Stephen's rather immature reliance on a Bulwer-Lytton melodrama;[23] moreover, the substitution might also be an acknowledgment that Beckett is indeed essentially invoking Joyce – not Meredith – to recover something of his 'calm,' even if he has pushed the Joycean terms to the breaking point.

The references to Joyce via Meredith are, ironically enough, anything but examples of that 'direct expression' for which Beckett so lavishly, al-beit problematically, praised Joyce in 'Dante ... Bruno . Vico .. Joyce.' The beginning of the third paragraph of 'Assumption' (in which the explicit reference to Meredith appears about a third of the way through) con-tains an allusion to 'The Young Sir Willoughby,' chapter 2 of Meredith's *The Egoist: A Comedy in Narrative*. The Woman's worshipping praise of the 'he' of 'Assumption' – 'the usual story, vulgarly told: admiration for his genius, sympathy for his suffering, only a woman could understand. ...' (5) – echoes the summary evaluation of the adulation of a woman admirer of Willoughby – 'welcome if you like, as a form of homage; but common, almost vulgar.'[24] And in the sentence that precedes the calming 'He thought of George Meredith' there is a detailed description of the Woman's face that focuses upon 'the extraordinary pallor of her lips, of which the lower protruded slightly and curled upward contemptuously to compress the upper,' a portrait sketch which is an adaptation of the very last sentence of *The Egoist*: 'But taking a glance at the others of her late company of actors, she [the Comic Muse] compresses her lips.'[25]

Just how the reference to Meredith in this instance enables the protagonist of 'Assumption' to regain 'something of his calm' is, however, very much open to questioning. One could speculate that there is some critical self-awareness implied here since the ending of *The Egoist* is a portrait of vanity and pretentiousness chastised. For, to quote from Meredith's 'An Essay on the Idea of Comedy and the Uses of the Comic Spirit', whenever men's actions 'wax out of proportion, overblown, affected, pretentious, bombastical' (characteristics that could indeed be justly applied to the 'he''s encounter with the Woman), the 'Spirit overhead will look humanely malign, and cast an oblique light on them.'[26] This paradoxical image of the 'humanely malign' brings to mind the compressed lips of both the Comic Muse and the Woman in 'Assumption.' Beckett's short story is admittedly much too slight and elliptical to bear the full weight of these suggestive analogies, which are carefully embedded in the text, even if they are by no means fully developed. Hence it might be more judicious in the context of 'Assumption' to return to the central point that it is a complex revisioning of Joyce's *Portrait*. Stephen Dedalus is calmed by the thought of Bulwer-Lytton, just as Beckett's 'he' is calmed by the thought of Meredith; and within the context of 'Assumption' and its extensive borrowings from *Portrait*, the Meredith reference could most profitably be read as a very roundabout reference to Joyce. Nevertheless, it must also be kept in mind that the 'Prelude' to *The Egoist* clearly gave Beckett the very rationale for his 'digest' version of *Portrait*. Meredith there comments on how 'wise men' tell us how the Comic Spirit 'condenses whole sections of the book in a sentence, volumes in a character.' There are fifty chapters plus the 'Prelude' in *The Egoist* and fifty-one sentences in 'Assumption.' Creative writing as well as literary criticism would seem to entail for Beckett a type of 'book-keeping.'

Stephen and Beckett's nameless hero both experience a sense of loss as a result of their encounters with women. Stephen at the beginning of chapter 3 comments that 'at his first violent sin he had felt a wave of vitality pass out of him and had feared to find his body or soul maimed by excess' (97); instead, Stephen later feels 'a dark peace' and 'cold lucid indifference.' Beckett's 'he' is, in dramatic contrast, figuratively torn to pieces: 'When at last she went away he felt that *something had gone out from him*, something he could not spare' (my emphasis). The last part of the third paragraph piles up images of pain, suffering, and destruction until the 'he,' 'in contemplation and absorption of this woman,'[27] seems to reach a state of apotheosis: 'he was released, achieved, the blue flower, Vega, GOD' (6). The conclusion to this strange story, in which Beckett relies so heavily on Joyce and yet so radically alters the context or structure of the original, begins 'Thus each night he died and was God, each night revived and was torn, torn and battered with increasing grievousness, so that he hungered to be irretrievably engulfed in the light of eternity, one with the birdless cloudless colourless skies, in infinite fulfillment' (6–7), followed by a two-sentence fourth paragraph in which, finally, 'he' does 'shout' and the 'great storm of sound' destroys him and 'fused into the breath of the forest and the throbbing cry of the sea.' The one-sentence fifth and final 'paragraph' consists solely of a post-mortem bulletin that returns us from the isolation of the room to the social realm: 'They found her caressing his wild dead hair' (7). Beckett's ending with its explosion of energy also reminds us of his ending to 'Dante … Bruno . Vico .. Joyce' and the 'flood of movement and vitality' that Beckett says characterizes Joyce's Purgatory.

The first conclusion of 'Assumption,' the vision that ends the third paragraph – 'one with the birdless cloudless colourless skies' – would seem to be the climax of Beckett's revisions and rewritings of Joyce in this, his first published short story (and by far the most condensed and elliptical). These phases of transcendence, rephrased as they are as a lessness, are a negative version of one of the most striking epiphanies in *Portrait*, the birdgirl scene that ends chapter 4 and is clearly set in opposition to the prostitute scene that ends chapter 2, and which was the core of Beckett's rewriting in 'Assumption.' At the end of 'Dante … Bruno . Vico .. Joyce,' Beckett, possibly thinking of this scene in which Stephen is transported by his sighting of the girl 'in midstream,' a 'wild angel,' stated: 'Mr Joyce's Terrestial Paradise is the tradesmen's entrance onto the sea-shore' (33). Stephen's epiphany – hedged heavily with irony, as he 'sing[s] wildly to the sea to greet the advent of life that had cried to him' (152) – is filled with numerous references to clouds, colours, and, of course, the birdgirl herself (depicted in blues and whites as a Virgin Mary figure who does not need to be 'assumed,' since her home is here on earth). Indeed, it was 'A day of dappled seaborne clouds' (147): '[Stephen's] throat ached with a desire to cry aloud, the cry of a hawk or eagle on high, to cry piercingly of his deliverance to the winds. This was the call of life to his soul' (150). For Beckett's 'he' the 'cry' that is released is a death cry and the Woman is an odd mixture of sensuality and purity, a kind of Whore-Madonna. Beckett at this point would seem to be rejecting Joyce's mediation between art and life and religion, and having set a no-win situation for himself – 'He could have shouted and could not' – for which he has no answers can only destroy his protagonist. Hence what transpires in 'Assumption' is the presentation of a vain dream of the reality that lies beyond the boundaries of art. As I wrote in *Reconstructing Beckett*, 'this very short story has, nevertheless, set out the essential conflict inherent in artistic genesis for Beckett: a life and death struggle between the self and the other.'[28] To that judgment now needs to be added the complex texturing of the Joyce-Beckett relationship as part of that struggle between self and other. Before we go on to add to the number of critical readings we already have of 'Assumption,' such as the Unanimist ones of Phil Baker and John Pilling, the Manichaean one of Laura Barge, the Surrealist one of Lois Gordon, or indeed the Orphean one of P.J. Murphy, we need to take into careful consideration the very foundations of Beckett's engagement with Joyce as evidenced in 'Dante ... Bruno . Vico .. Joyce' and its companion text, 'Assumption.'[29]

To be sure, the most difficult and confusing aspect of Beckett's first published short story is determining whether or not it affords a critical perspective whereby the reader can make informed judgments of value about the story's development and thereby ascribe significance to it. Here the Joycean elements are crucial to such aesthetic and critical deliberations. Beckett's very detailed references to *Portrait* throughout 'Assumption' all seem to focus upon a critique of the epiphany, that sudden revelatory moment of insight that Beckett and his narrator-surrogate in this story clearly see as a false assumption, so long as it is restricted by terms that would deny the kinetic and physical dimensions and instead promote only an aesthetic apprehension characterized by a 'luminous silent stasis' (185). Throughout 'Assumption' this critique is consistent and effectively developed in terms of the imagery of an armed struggle – at least until the final few sentences of the pivotal and decisive third paragraph. Here Beckett's 'he' and by implication his narrator abandon such a critique and the attendant quest for a new aesthetic fitting for this more complex reality and instead, in a remarkable volte-face, move towards the realms of the mystical and transcendental and away from the 'pain of Beauty.' And, in effecting this retreat, the attack on Stephen Dedalus's theories of art is abandoned.

Beckett's short story now ironically appears to endorse uncritically some of those very positions Stephen had successfully worked his way through in order to reach a series of modernist tenets for his future artistic production. When Beckett's 'he' is said to hunger 'to be irretrievably engulfed in the light of eternity, one with the birdless cloudless colourless skies, in infinite fulfillment,' this mystical quest would seem to fly directly against Stephen's own version of *claritas*, which, after a self-confessed long period of bafflement, he affirmed in no uncertain terms as having nothing to do with 'symbolism or idealism,' a version in which he strongly rejected the idea of the 'supreme quality of beauty being a light from some other world, the idea of which matter is but the shadow, the reality of which it is but a symbol' (185). Stephen Dedalus can then go on to reject categorically any interpretation of Aquinas that would suggest 'that *claritas* is the artistic discovery and representation of the divine purpose' (185). The 'he''s apotheosis during his nocturnal vigils ('each night he died and was God') and his desire 'to be irretrievably engulfed in the light of eternity' would seem to be Beckett's way in this story of underlining how, at this starting point, while he is able to offer a critique of some of the perceived weaknesses and omissions in Stephen Dedalus's aesthetic theory, he doesn't know what to do next, that the only way out of the impasse of 'He could have shouted and could not,' for the time being, is annihilation and a mystical desire for a transcendence that must perforce lie outside the boundaries of artistic discovery and representation. In other words, the critique peters out in the ending of this story as the 'he' (perhaps with the silent complicity of the narrator) would seem to endorse a 'symbolism or idealism' that Stephen had already quite rightly rejected as one that denied full significance to this world of ours and instead pointed to a 'light from some other world.' The turning towards a mystical reality beyond the boundaries of art (and language) at the end of 'Assumption' could be taken as Beckett's own critical self-reflection that even though he has been able to isolate for himself a number of key questions that his art will have to investigate further, he doesn't at this starting point have any answers about how to proceed beyond dramatizing such impasses.

Until the emergence of these transcendental elements, the most striking feature of the work in terms of its rewriting and recasting of elements from *Portrait* has been how they are restructured within an encompassing context of warfare imagery, which adds a kinetic dimension that differentiates Beckett's views from young Dedalus's. J.D. O'Hara points out how in the first paragraph of his story Beckett mistakenly refers to a 'Vimy Light' instead of a Very Light, a flare named for its English inventor and employed to supply a brilliant illumination of battlefields during the Great War.[30] The Vimy (Very) Light reference comes into play as a means of advancing Beckett's attack on Stephen's aesthetic theory, targeting its key concept of *claritas* (radiance) as developed in chapter 5 of *Portrait*: 'The instant wherein that supreme quality of beauty, the clear radiance of the esthetic image, is apprehended luminously by the mind which has been arrested by its wholeness and fascinated by its harmony is the luminous silent stasis of esthetic pleasure, a spiritual state' (185). The 'sudden brilliance' (3) of the Vimy (Very) Light could be regarded as an ironic debunking of Stephen's highly intellectualized aestheticism.[31] What it allows to be 'apprehended luminously' are scenes of destruction and mutilation, discord and fragmentation; in short, the Vimy (Very) Light functions as a sort of negative epiphany.

In a revision of a passage from *Portrait* cited earlier, Beckett adds the kinetic image of warfare and the paradoxical formulation of an aesthetic based simultaneously on composition and decomposition: 'the highest art reduces significance in order to obtain the inexplicable bombshell perfection' (4). These images of war and destruction begin innocuously enough in 'Assumption' as a sort of comedy of manners associated with the unnamed central character, who is disconcerted by an unorthodox opening move in a game of intellectual combat. Against the 'noisy violence' of social discourse, he possesses the 'remarkable faculty of whispering the turmoil down' (3). It is this 'whispering' that is originally likened to 'all explosive feats of the kind,' in particular the Vimy (Very) Light that calls attention to itself by its 'sudden brilliance.' This ironic play with social mannerisms does, however, transform itself over the rest of the opening paragraph into a much more serious engagement with issues of war and combat. The ironic overkill of likening the 'he''s various social manipulations as 'all finely produced and thrown into the heat of the conflict, so that the most fiercely oblivious combatant could not fail to be neatly and intolerably irritated' gives way to a much more powerful statement of an aesthetic no longer dependent on such social trifling: 'Before no supreme manifestation of Beauty do we proceed

comfortably up a staircase of sensation [...] We are taken up bodily
and pitched breathless on the peak of a sheer crag: which is the pain
of Beauty' (4).

Within the very structure of 'Assumption' there is a dramatic contrast
between a great victory gained at great risk and a series of humiliating
and demoralizing defeats. Within 'Assumption,' the 'he' whose story the
narrator recounts is totally incapable of scaling the lofty heights of any
such dizzying victory. This 'he' has retreated from such engagements to
seek refuge in his room as he tries to quell the 'other' presence/self
within him and its 'wild rebellious surge that aspired violently towards
realization in sound' (4). The imagery now switches in focus to the more
personal domain, away from the pitched battle of the set kind in the first
paragraph to internecine warfare in which the carceral image is now
foregrounded. The 'he' feels his prisoner's 'implacable caged resent-
ment, its longing to be released in one splendid drunken scream' (4); it
is, however, prevented from such, being encompassed by a 'flesh-locked
sea of silence' (5). The profound ambiguity of this struggle, more accurately termed a 'civil war,' is put this way by the narrator: 'he dreaded
lest his prisoner should escape, he longed that it might escape; it tore at
his throat and he choked it back in dread and sorrow' (5). The essential
confusion turns upon whether the 'he' regards this 'other' within himself as 'friend' or 'foe.' By the end of the second paragraph, the erection
of various defensive barriers (the damming images derived from *Portrait*
and Stephen's struggle to find expression for himself in the prostitute
scene) has only resulted in increasing the pressure of the forces tearing at
him: 'he felt he was losing, playing into the hands of the enemy by the
very severity of his restrictions' (5).

The encounter with the Woman makes it clear that sexuality as embodied by her is the fundamental means whereby the 'it' locked within
can hope to achieve more than the previously mentioned 'miserable
consummation in driblets of sound.' From this point on the imagery of
warfare is reintroduced as the dominant pattern as the 'he' sees himself
now in a pitched battle with the 'it' and 'the Woman,' who are somehow in alliance against him. In this demented comedy of manners,
even the most casual and colloquial of expressions now take on a mili-
tary bearing as a campaign of sexual warfare is waged. For example,
the 'noisy intrusive curious enthusiasm' of women is likened to the
'spontaneous expression of admiration bursting from American hearts
before Michelangelo's tomb in Santa Croce' (5), with its buried reference to the American national anthem – 'the rockets' red glare/the

bombs bursting in air.' And the Woman's voice itself would seem to be likened to the stuttering stall of a reconnaissance plane surveying a battlefield: 'The voice droned on, wavered, stopped.' The 'he' prepares to *withdraw*; 'she turned on the light and *advanced* carelessly into the room' and '*scattered* his intentness' (italics mine). No revelatory 'radiance' or *claritas* is in evidence here; her eyes 'were pools of obscurity.'[32] Thanks to her 'visitations' he 'lost part of his essential animality, so that the water rose, terrifying him.' The war image is now of an ineluctable defeat, tediously drawn out, to be sharply distinguished from 'we are taken up bodily and pitched breathless on the peak of a sheer crag': 'Still he fought on all day, hopelessly, mechanically, only relaxing with twilight, to listen for her coming to loosen yet another stone in the clumsy dam' (6). Then there occurs a revelation of sorts as, after nightly bouts of being 'torn and battered,' the 'he,' alone in his room, would transcend the battle with both the human and the 'it' or 'other self' of an unknown nature within himself – a veritable doppelgänger – and 'be irretrievably engulfed in the light of eternity, one with the birdless cloudless colourless skies, in infinite fulfillment' (7).

The last two very short paragraphs describe the denouement: 'Then it happened.' The 'it' is 'a great storm of sound' that 'swept aside' the Woman, who was 'contemplating the face that she had overlaid with death.' The opening impasse of 'He could have shouted and could not' is now broken by a battle cry that is also a death cry, 'shaking the very house with its prolonged, triumphant vehemence, climbing in a dizzy, bubbling scale, until, dispersed, it fused into the breath of the forest and the throbbing cry of the sea' (7). The 'triumphant vehemence' is, of course, at best a Pyrrhic victory in which the prisoner caged within the 'he' is released and 'fused' within nature and the host himself annihilated. The final one-sentence fifth paragraph reads 'They found her caressing his wild dead hair.' The bizarre image of a shout emanating with such earth-shattering force that it literally 'swept aside' the Woman as a bomb would is indeed an 'explosive feat', but one very different from that which 'whisper[ed] the turmoil down' within the social contexts delineated in the opening paragraph. Here the 'turmoil' is such that it cannot be suppressed but must be let out. Throughout Beckett's strange parable about the warring elements within his views of the aesthetic experience, the encompassing question that incorporates Beckett's critique of Stephen's theorizing in *Portrait* is the problematical relationship of inner and outer realities and the means of somehow authentically representing them.

This point is implicit in the Joycean reference that is built into 'Assumption''s final sentence. 'They found her caressing his wild dead hair' echoes Joyce's final sentence in his play *Exiles*; Bertha's last words there are an appeal to her 'husband,' the artist Richard Rowan: 'O, my strange wild lover, come back to me again' (*PJJ*, 626). That Beckett intends an allusion to Joyce's play is reinforced by the verbal correspondence in the stage direction leading up to her final theatrical declaration, '*again caressing his hand*' (my underlining). Whereas in Joyce's scenario the artist-figure has received 'a deep wound of doubt which can never be healed' (due to his doubts about his wife's fidelity in her relationship with his friend Robert), in Beckett's 'closet drama' the artist-figure is utterly destroyed and totally incapable of mediating the menage à trois of self, Woman, and that other being within characterized by a 'wild rebellious surge that aspired violently towards realization in sound.' Written immediately after *Portrait*, *Exiles* extends the investigation of Stephen Dedalus's fundamental dilemma: how can the artist come to terms with personal relationships and the restraints and restrictions imposed by his society, yet somehow maintain his integrity? Beckett cannot escape the contingencies of inner and outer realities – indeed, it is the engagement with these issues that drives his artistic undertaking; however, the most pressing task at hand is to find a way of first ensuring the very survival of the self since Beckett in 'Assumption' has pushed the dilemma to a point of no return, an apparent dead end. From the very beginning Beckett has likened this to a battlefield, a literary campaign.[33] The first two sentences of 'Assumption' have strategically cut off any possibility of a return to the imagined safety and security of a status quo ante bellum.

'Assumption' is a major Beckett text in that it reveals Beckett's studied and concentrated engagement with Joyce at the very beginning of the young artist's career, initiating a line of development that is extended and elaborated in surprisingly detailed ways in Beckett's next three novels in English. 'Assumption' is truly Beckett's 'first important work,' not the poem 'Whoroscope' (1930), which was so designated by Lawrence Harvey and echoed in a number of subsequent critical appraisals.[34] Indeed, as we have seen, 'Assumption''s primary focus is upon a rewriting of Stephen's visit to the prostitute at the end of chapter 2 of *Portrait*, thereby making it the first in a series of 'whoroscopes' in Beckett's writing. In her recent summary evaluation of the Beckett canon, Ruby Cohn states: 'Peter Murphy is virtually alone in viewing it ['Assumption'] as a key Beckett text.'[35] Cohn's pronouncement does not, however, take fully into account my point that it is a key text only in so far as Beckett rewrites it in a host of innovative ways in later works; taken by itself, 'Assumption' is all too obviously marked by a number of stylistic and conceptual inconsistencies, as the present discussion has taken pains to acknowledge. With reference to my argument about the Joycean sources in 'Assumption,' Cohn concludes: 'In fiction, however, feelings are only as deep as the words that convey them, and Beckett's words are shallow through staleness, however they may echo Joyce.'[36] This evaluation does not account for the literary properties of the text as an assemblage of Joycean allusions, a veritable cento, for this first Beckett fiction is a parody of the postmodern sort described by Linda Hutcheon in which the rewriting is both a critique of and a homage to the original,[37] in this instance Joyce's *Portrait*. Beckett's primary focus is then first and foremost on coming to terms with the aesthetic principles put forward in *Portrait*; this critical exercise takes precedence over the more conventional assessment proposed by Cohn. In my own reading, the expanding recognition of the full extent and complexity of Beckett's referencing of *Portrait* brought the text to life in new and illuminating ways. In the concluding paragraph of his *Allusion: A Literary Graft*, Allan Pascoe affirms that allusion has indeed a 'virtually limitless potential': 'As long as the text exists, someday a reader may come with the proper fertile background and permit a new efflorescence. When this happens, the seed sinks new roots and the reader's mind gives birth to a living text.'[38]

Most readers of 'Assumption' have understandably been bemused by its apparent lack of any indications about how to go about reading it. Is Beckett simply indulgently amusing himself in the exaggerated depictions of romantic angst, or is there a more concerted critical effort being exercised here? Above all else, the preceding discussions of the Joycean elements in 'Assumption' make it clear that Beckett's intention at least was to pursue the latter option, even if the work itself is simply not developed at enough length and depth to resolve this issue satisfactorily. Nevertheless, the detailed Joycean references do raise the encompassing question of parody as a corrective form of mimicry and, more generally, the comic function of a critical rewriting. Two possible sources for the title of the story reinforce these points. The first is from George Meredith's 'An Essay on Comedy and the Uses of the Comic Spirit.' Beckett's reference in 'Assumption' – 'He thought of George Meredith and recovered something of his calm' – echoes a key statement in the essay where Meredith explains how those persons of the 'exalted variety' (a case in point being the unnamed hero of 'Assumption') necessarily 'come under the *calm*, curious eye of the Comic Spirit' (my emphasis); in this instance, it is the Comic Spirit that '*assumes* the saving grace' (my emphasis).[39] The second source is, fittingly enough, from *Portrait*, the master text behind 'Assumption.' In response to the director's probing query as to whether he has a 'vocation,' Stephen acknowledges how he heard in 'this proud address an echo of his own proud musings,' adding: 'In that dim life which he had lived through in his musings he had *assumed* the voices and gestures which he had noted with various priests' (my emphasis, 141). In other words, Stephen's efforts to assert his own voice necessarily involve an 'assumption' of a special sort as he takes on ('assumes') the identity of various priests he has encountered. When he turns away from this 'vocation' to embrace instead that of a 'priest of the eternal imagination' (192), he will again 'assume' the voices and identifying traits of the various literary figures he has 'noted.'[40] And Beckett, following in Joyce's footsteps, will appropriate in his own right aspects of his master's voice. Reading Joyce, most especially *A Portrait of the Artist as a Young Man*, was – undeniably – based on the overwhelming textual evidence, one of the major literary revelations of Beckett's early years and warrants being considered in tandem with his early reading of Dante as instances of lifelong influence. 'Assumption' reveals some of the principles behind Beckett's assumed identity as a Dedalus redux, some of which admittedly are problematical, if not contradictory, in nature. In this regard, Beckett's first published work of fiction bears an uncanny resemblance to Joyce's essay 'A Portrait of the Artist' (1904), which has been described as 'an extraordinarily dense piece of writing' that foreshadowed 'the difficulties of Joyce's later work,' albeit 'on a reduced scale' (*JJP*, 203–4).[41] Beckett must have felt both flattered and disconcerted by Adrienne Monnier's characterization of him upon the publication of his two very different Joycean works in *transition* 16/17 as 'the new Stephen Dedalus.'[42]

2 Dreams of a Fair to Middling Critic-Artist: The Nature of Symbol in *Proust* and the Role of *Portrait* as 'Structural Convenience' in Beckett's First Novel

All of Beckett's major productions in the early period of 1929 to 1945, from 'Assumption' to *Watt*, reveal in progressively more complex and detailed ways attempts to come to terms with and move beyond the aesthetic theory formulated in *A Portrait of the Artist as a Young Man*. 'Assumption' establishes the basic pattern that will be repeated with variations in the other works of this period: an initial assumption that the modernist moment of revelation is fundamentally inadequate as an authentic means of mediating and expressing the full complexity of contemporary life and art; hence Beckett's starting point is a dramatization of the aporias of a modernist aesthetic, such as his opening gambit of 'He could have shouted and could not.' The initial series of critical reservations about the theory of the epiphany is not developed in any viable fashion and quickly terminates in an impasse of one sort or another: the nameless 'he' of 'Assumption' is torn asunder; Belacqua is inconclusively abandoned at the 'conclusion' of *Dream of Fair to Middling Women* (what *is* the point of going on pointlessly?); the tiresome Murphy is blown up, hoist by his own petard, so to speak; and Watt, who fails to fathom his own 'whatness,' or that of anyone or anything else for that matter, ends up in an asylum. The last words of *Watt* – 'no symbols where none intended' – can also stand as a judgment on all these early works in which a critical probing of modernist aesthetics as exemplified by Joyce and Proust and their handling of the symbol as a means of expressing various realities is the crux of Beckett's own speculations.

Another characteristic of Beckett's writing throughout this early period is announced in 'Assumption': the recourse to a mystical transcendence of some sort that would absolutely cancel out the perplexing question of determining what is indeed real and the search for the means of expression for the same. Beckett's own position is quite clearly self-contradictory in terms of that put forward in *Portrait* where Stephen Dedalus, after a 'long period of bafflement,' determined that *claritas* could not be taken for a 'light from some other world,' could not be regarded as a 'symbolism or idealism' pointing towards or standing for transcendent spiritual realities. Beckett's desperate manoeuvring from one extreme to the other is dramatically foregrounded in 'Assumption' with the assertion 'the highest art reduces significance' being later replaced by the protagonist's apotheosis whereby 'he was released, achieved the blue flower, Vega, GOD ...' Here we have an encapsulation of the major theoretical dilemma Beckett confronts in a number of increasingly complex and pressing ways throughout these early works: the competing claims of 'sign' and 'symbol' for the field of expression in a literary 'text' or 'work.' To reduce significance is to move towards words as 'signs' in a semiotic configuration in which they have only formal relationships with each other, as distinct from any referential connections with the commonplace or, for that matter, a transcendental beyond. The other strategy is to invoke a cluster of 'symbols,' beginning with the talismanic 'blue flower' of Novalis's distillation of Romantic idealism, moving through Vega, the brightest star in Orpheus's constellation of Lyre and hence a most fitting symbolic expression of the artist's other-worldliness, thereby leaving only – and in capital letters at that – 'GOD' as the ultimate expression of literary transcendence and deification.

Such extremist formulations allow for a 'literary' way out in Beckett's first short story, but they do not advance any rigorous probing beyond the recognition of the central problem itself in terms of the competing claims of 'sign' and 'symbol.' Nevertheless, from the very beginning, in prototypical fashion, Beckett has placed himself in the midst of the defining literary debate of our time, engaging in the 'sign' versus 'symbol' debate as an inherent feature of modernism itself and as a preliminary version of the 'linguistic turn,' which has constituted the most influential paradigm shift within contemporary thought. This shift has taken place so thoroughly that in a representative textbook such as *Studying Literature: The Essential Companion* (2001), edited by Paul Goring et al., one will find in the 'Glossary of literary and theoretical terms' under SYMBOL the entry: 'See SIGN.' Cross-referencing yields: 'A *Symbol* is anything which stands for something apart from itself.'[1] What distinguishes Beckett's literary enterprise over the sixty years of his writing life is how his avant-garde experimentalism inhabits a middle position of sorts: his writings, both theoretical and creative in this early period, are driven by an in-depth critique of modernism itself as most prominently embodied by Joyce's writing, and, to a lesser degree, by that of Proust. But Beckett never completely allows for the subsumption of the possibilities of larger claims to signification by the play of signs, and it is this 'middling' position that sets his writing apart, thereby challenging the orthodoxies of both modernism and postmodernism.

Both Beckett's *Proust* (1931) and his *Dream of Fair to Middling Women* (1932; published 1992) explore in quite different ways the question of symbolism as a means of conveying certain inescapable and essential realities of the human and literary conditions. Indeed, the key word in Beckett's monograph is 'real,' with its many cognates, such as 'reality,' 'realisation,' 'realisable,' etc. Thirty-odd references of this sort strive to sort out what can be deemed the authentic reality, to be sharply distinguished from the mock or pseudo-reality of the naturalists 'worshipping the offal of experience' (28). Throughout *Proust* a whole series of value-added adjectives are at work to underline this distinction between the genuine realities and other ersatz substitutes: for example, the repeated emphasis upon 'the essence – the Idea' (11), the numerous variations of an 'essential statement of reality' (22), as afforded by the 'mystic experience' of Proustian involuntary memory that breaks through the defensive barriers erected by habit. At one level Beckett's declared opening focus on Proust's 'dualism in multiplicity' (1) comes down to a vision of human creatures trapped in time as 'victims and prisoners' (2) being dramatically contrasted with their liberation as miraculously vouchsafed in a totally unpredictable way by the mysterious workings of involuntary memory. Another variant of this dualism casts the human dilemma in terms of a fundamentally melancholic spectacle in which we are imprisoned and 'deformed' by 'yesterday,' and such pleasures as remain can only rarely be experienced via the Proustian revelation of involuntary memory, which 'for a moment' (a repeated modernist phrase throughout Beckett's discussion) allows a glimpse of 'freedom.' This is the forlorn spectacle Beckett describes in his first two explicit references to the 'reality' that will be his topic throughout *Proust*: 'we are other, no longer what we were before the calamity of yesterday. A calamitous day, but calamitous not necessarily in content. The good or evil disposition of the object has neither reality nor significance. The immediate joys and sorrows of the body and the intelligence are so many superfoetations. Such as it was, it has been assimilated to the only world that has reality and significance, the world of our own latent consciousness' (3).

In *Proust* there is a sense at times that Beckett is still primarily engaged with Joyce and that the ostensible subject under discussion is in some instances a circumlocution for this. Even the brief commentary above on Beckett's passage in *Proust* on 'we are other, no longer what we were' foregrounds Beckett's critical distinction between Joyce's and Proust's aesthetic premises. Beckett regards Joyce as dealing fundamentally with the 'whatness' of the real, as accepting a conflux of realities as already present, whereas for himself ('Assumption' made this clear) and for Proust the antecedent question is, more problematically, 'what is real?' Hence Proust's recognition and depiction of the multiplicity of selves that coexist throughout the workings of time does allow Beckett to extend his own critical probing of a series of fragmented and oppositional selves as posited in his opening sentences of 'Assumption.' But it is also worth noting that Beckett often pointedly invokes Joycean terms in his discussion of Proust's aesthetic. For example, in the final paragraph of the opening section of *Proust*: 'At the best, all that is realised in Time (all Time produce), whether in Art or Life, can only be possessed successively, by a series of partial annexations – and never integrally and at once' (7). *Portrait*'s first stage in aesthetic apprehension, the recognition of wholeness or *integritas*, is thus dislocated in Proust, only to be miraculously not so much reinstated as at last brought into being by the alchemy of involuntary memory, specific incidents of which Beckett lists in the fourth section of his study: 'It appears for the first time as the episode of the madeleine, and again on at least five capital occasions before its final and multiple investment of the Guermantes Hotel at the opening of the second volume of *Le Temps Retrouvé*, its culminating and *integral* expression' (22–3, my italics). Moreover, such a sacred moment or peak experience '*clarifies* the most humble incident of its ascent' (22, my italics), which sounds indeed as if Beckett is paraphrasing *Portrait*'s concept of *claritas* rather than focusing solely upon Proust's own terminology. *Claritas* as 'radiance' is explicitly identified with Beckett's description of Marcel's first sighting of Albertine by the Sea, 'absorbed in the radiance of the "little band" at Balbec' (31). Nevertheless, Beckett's commentary on the nature of Proustian moments of revelation emphasizes their kinetic nature – they are 'intensely violent' (24) or, in Proust's own words, 'carved, as by a thunderbolt, within me' (28) – thereby distinguishing them in kind from the 'luminous silent stasis' of Stephen Dedalus's theory of the final stage of aesthetic apprehension.

Beckett clearly found aspects of Proust congenial in that he is able to use them to extend his critique of *Portrait*'s 'static' presentation of 'Beauty,' which he emended in 'Assumption' to the 'pain of Beauty.' A critical qualification is in order here, however; once again, as in our discussion of 'Assumption,' it needs to be emphasized that there are two distinct Beckettian approaches when it comes to his engagement with Joyce's work. Beckett realizes, of course, that Stephen Dedalus's aesthetic pronouncements in *Portrait* cannot be taken as fully equivalent to Joyce's own views. This is made abundantly clear in 'Dante ... Bruno . Vico .. Joyce' when Beckett, employing the key word that underlies the aestheticizing of *Portrait*, states categorically that 'the Beauty of *Work in Progress* is not presented in space alone': 'There is a temporal as well as a spatial unity to be apprehended' (28). Beckett is obviously aware that Joyce's vision in *Portrait*, and all his work for that matter, cannot be reduced and vastly oversimplified by seeing it as existing in essentially spatial terms only, an argument which possesses certain persuasive powers, to be sure (see, for example, Joseph Frank's influential argument about the defining spatial dimensions of modernism). [2] But there is also the other Beckett, the would-be writer as distinct from the critic, who, in order to get started, needs leverage, both critical and creative, to set himself apart from the overwhelming presence (and influence) of the master, the portrait of the artist as a fully fledged creator. Hence, as we have seen in 'Assumption,' Beckett wilfully 'misreads' Joyce à la Harold Bloom's description of the ephebe's struggle to resist, challenge, and alter his master's voice.[3] This does not exclude the fact that Beckett also raises legitimate concerns about Stephen Dedalus's trinity of aesthetic principles (*integritas*, *consonantia*, and *claritas*), but to identify such criticisms with Joyce himself is obviously more a rhetorical strategy on Beckett's part than a serious critical assessment. Nevertheless, it is by means of this misprision that Beckett begins to work his way through and finally beyond Joyce to his own aesthetic theories, and, as *Proust* exemplifies, Beckett has also adapted specifically Joycean terminology in order to develop his exposition of the Proustian moment of revelation, thereby allowing Beckett to deal with the subject at hand, as well as by indirection with Joyce (just as, for example, Beckett had circuitously engaged Joyce via Meredith in 'Assumption').

The climax of Beckett's critical investigation of Proustian aesthetics through the filter of Joycean terminology is the penultimate, sixth section of his *Proust*, what Ruby Cohn has termed 'The Epiphany in the Guermantes Library' (without, however, focusing on any particular parallels with Joyce in her brief discussion of this episode).[4] This section is much anticipated and is almost as well advertised as its more famous successor, the sixth section or chapter of *Murphy* which deals with the portrait of the eponymous hero's mind, so-called. The narrator of that novel is quick to point out: 'Happily we need not concern ourselves with this apparatus as it really was – that would be an extravagance and impertinence – but solely with what it felt and pictured itself to be' (107). In other words, symbolic expression is the central issue in both of these sixth sections. The vexed and problematical nature of the symbol as a means of expression as highlighted in *Proust* and soon after in *Dream of Fair to Middling Women* will lead to the narrator of *Murphy* ironically distancing himself from any such discussion, and in even more ambiguous and self-contradictory fashion the last words of *Watt* caution, 'no symbols where none intended.' In section six of *Proust* the symbols are, however, definitely intended in a particular way as Beckett finally delivers his exposition of the Proustian moment of revelation, which was announced as early as the topic sentence of the second paragraph of his monograph in the tantalizing reference to the narrator's experience in the library of the Princesse de Guermantes. Section six of *Proust* critically engages the role of the symbolic as the means of expressing, of conveying that sense of the integration of various temporally dislocated realities and the concomitant radiant vision. In other words, the symbol is the proposed means of identifying, and of harmonizing, the realities and idealities of the aesthetic experience.

The unifying thesis behind Beckett's necessarily somewhat fragmented approach to Proust's massive work is 'dualism in multiplicity.' The two explicit references to symbol (and cognates thereof) before section six draw out a certain dualistic, if not contradictory, situation: the first emphasizes the use of symbol as a means of conveying a heightened and expanded significance of the actual when Marcel hears his grandmother's voice over the phone – 'this strange real voice is the measure of its owner's suffering. He hears it also as the symbol of her isolation' (15); the second points in quite a different direction, towards the spiritual realm, as Marcel tries to harmonize, as it were, the various Albertines who all fulfil in some way his sense of her 'reality' – 'And the pleasure he takes with Albertine is intensified by the reaching out of his spirit towards that immaterial reality that she seems to symbolise, Balbec and its sea' (33). How can such very different meanings of the word 'symbol' be reconciled, harmonized? Indeed, it is just such a question that constitutes the fundamental aporia of modernism.

Beckett's *Proust* is a *locus classicus* of a number of theoretical impasses inherent in modernism itself. It is revealing and illuminating – even if only negatively – to see how Beckett describes this enterprise and to note the degree to which at this very early point in his career he is willing to accept or reject the implications of such theorizing in which the very nature of the symbol itself is of central importance. The decisive turn in Beckett's deliberations comes in the middle of the tenth page of section six as he presents a theoretical description of the various syntheses brought about by involuntary memory and then follows with his interpretation and critical reservations about this 'model of duplication':

> The identification of immediate with past experience, the recurrence of past action or reaction in the present, amounts to a participation between the ideal and the real, imagination and direct apprehension, symbol and substance. Such participation frees the essential reality that is denied to the contemplative as to the active life. What is common to present and past is more essential than either taken separately [...] But, thanks to this reduplication, the experience is at once imaginative and empirical, at once an evocation and a direct perception, real without being merely actual, ideal without being merely abstract, the ideal real, the essential, the extratemporal. But if this mystical experience communicates an extratemporal essence, it follows that the communicant is for the moment an extratemporal being. Consequently, the Proustian solution consists, in so far as it has been examined, in the negation of Time and Death, the negation of Death because the negation of Time. Death is dead because Time is dead. (At this point a brief impertinence, which consists in considering *Le Temps Retrouvé* almost as inappropriate a description of the Proustian solution as *Crime and Punishment* of a masterpiece that contains no allusion to either crime or punishment. Time is not recovered, it is obliterated ... (55–6)

Beckett's summary of various Proustian syntheses via the miraculous workings of involuntary memory climaxes at the end of the first sentence in the passage cited above with the pairing 'symbol and substance' (yet another example of Beckett's central thesis of Proust's 'dualism within multiplicity'). But how can 'symbol and substance' really be said to be *integrally* connected if *both* elements in this 'communion' are regarded as somehow *directly* apprehended (as Beckett throughout *Proust* has painstakingly emphasized)? When Beckett lists the various Proustian epiphanies in section four of *Proust*, he prefaces his tabulation this way: 'the elements of communion are provided by the physical world, by some immediate and fortuitous act of perception. The process is almost one of intellectualised animism' (23). As with the discussion of Joyce's language in 'Dante ... Bruno . Vico .. Joyce,' Beckett here also endorses a primitivist strain in high modernism whereby a direct, *unmediated* vision is touted as the only real and authentic goal of the artist.

That Beckett is not fully satisfied by the 'symbol and substance' pairing is made abundantly clear in the seventh and final section of *Proust*, where he has cobbled together a whole series of comments about Proust and art without any convincing or unifying argument; indeed, the reason for the eclectic grouping of various aperçus about Proust's art and the role of the artist may be due to Beckett's uneasy gyrations around how 'symbol' should be regarded in Proust's world. Proust is said not to deal in concepts: 'he pursues the Idea, the concrete. He admires the frescoes of the Paduan Arena because their symbolism is handled as a reality, special, literal and concrete' (60). And further to the point: 'For Proust the object may be a living symbol, but a symbol of itself. The symbolism of Baudelaire has become the *autosymbolism* of Proust' (60). This is a sleight of hand as Beckett juggles words to mask the fact that he doesn't really know how to make sense in a coherent critical fashion of Proust's use of symbols, and it leads to a final throwing up of his hands in failure, as he, in self-cancelling fashion, places Proust's 'point of departure' in Symbolism 'or on its outskirts,' quickly following with: 'he recedes from the Symbolists – back towards Hugo. And for that reason he is a solitary and independent figure' (61). So much for would-be old-fashioned source and influence study approaches – they are clearly no more forthcoming in terms of a genuine clarification of where Proust stands and what his symbols stand for than Beckett's preceding attempts at literary theorizing.

In some strangely appropriate ways, the concluding movement of Beckett's only major extended critical work echoes ironically the ending of Joyce's *Portrait*: the voices of Stephen Dedalus's 'kinsmen' call out to him to join their 'company,' and he answers back in his last words with a prayer that such father figures would 'stand me now and ever in good stead.' For Beckett in 'Assumption' and *Proust*, his two major literary forebears, 'kinsmen,' are found seriously wanting in terms of aesthetic theory and practice. In the final analysis, Beckett seems progressively more perplexed about the critical issue of Proust's 'symbolism' (whether the capitalised variety or not), and for reasons that we will later examine more closely he clearly does not buy into the mystical transcendence of Proustian-type modernism as he depicts it in his *Proust*. And Joyce as ghost-presence is invoked by Beckett as a sort of framing device for the key passages of section six under scrutiny. Section six opens with a litany of negatives as Beckett describes Marcel's sense of irrevocable losses, which have rendered his life 'devoid of reality' (59); foremost among these losses is Marcel's sense that even art, which he had regarded as 'the one ideal and inviolate element in a corruptible world' (59), is also part of the encompassing world of null and void. Additionally, the materials of art are dismissed 'as vulgar and unworthy as Rachel and Cottard, and pale and weary and cruel and inconstant and joyless as Shelley's moon' (50). Beckett is here pairing his two great modernist predecessors – Proust directly with the reference to two of his characters of *A la Recherche du Temps Perdu*, Joyce much more indirectly, as is often the case with Beckett: the moon of Shelley's fragment plays an important role in Joyce's *Portrait*, and Beckett's choice of adjectives in *Proust* to describe it is directly indebted to Joyce's commentary in *Portrait*.[5]

The Shelley fragment is first invoked in *Portrait* at the time of an overt rivalry between young Stephen and his father.[6] The second Joycean reference is not so much 'borrowed' from Joyce as simply expropriated and comes at the end of the long passage cited above, which draws an analogy between the appropriateness of the titles for Dostoyevsky's *Crime and Punishment* and Proust's *Le Temps Retrouvé*. Beckett was, in fact, Richard Ellmann's source for another instance of father-son rivalry of the ostensibly literary sort, this time between Giorgio Joyce and his father James: 'Giorgio liked to display in argument an obstinacy of the same weave as his father's, informing him for example that the greatest novelist was Dostoevski, the greatest novel *Crime and Punishment*. His father said only that it was a queer title for a book which contained neither crime nor punishment.'[7] A 'brief impertinence,' indeed; Beckett adopts/adapts as his own Joyce's words on Dostoyevsky in order to effect a transition via analogy to an outright rejection of Proust's climactic title for the decisive revelations whereby the writing of *A la Recherche du Temps Perdu* itself becomes possible: *Le Temps Retrouvé*.

Before examining the implications of Beckett's judgment in this instance, it is worthwhile summarizing his position as it stands just prior to delivering his 'brief impertinence.' Beckett is, to adapt the words of Shelley's fragment on the moon, 'wandering companionless': his 'kinsmen's voices have beckoned but their 'company' rejected for various reasons. The Shelley reference in section six of *Proust* is identified with the failure of artistic vision and allows Beckett to distance his aesthetic views from both Proust and Joyce – these 'Old father[s], old artificer[s]' will not stand in good stead the emerging portrait of Beckett himself as the artist as a young man, not 'now' and not 'ever,' since the nature of being in time is itself the crucial issue. In 'Assumption' the unnamed protagonist is left for dead in the final sentences, which recount the escape of the 'other' within him, his 'prisoner.' Stephen Dedalus's theorizing in *Portrait* is shown to be sorely inadequate for the Beckettian vision of a divided self. The vision of a potentially endless series of epiphanies is greeted with a thoroughgoing scepticism for Beckett is preoccupied with the more fundamental question – in a philosophical sense – of determining the very grounding or foundation whereby such modernist moments of insight might be determined to be even a possibility. Neither Beckett nor his first protagonist in the short story has any sense of how such moments of revelation might be validated. The only solution, as we have seen, is one of dissolution, of a mystical transcendence that vainly mimics such epiphanies and ends in death, in self-annihilation. And Beckett proposes a similar reading of Proust's peak modernist moment in the epiphany of the Guermantes Library. Beckett argues that this 'mystical experience' must logically imply 'that the communicant is for the moment an extratemporal being.' But what words could convey an 'extratemporal essence'? None, of course, would be the logical answer. However, as we have seen, Beckett's vexed but fruitless critical oscillations around the term 'symbol' (particularly as writ large in the Symbolist Movement) try to make sense of this fundamental questioning of the means of expression by seeing the symbol as primarily focused on a supposedly 'higher' and 'deeper' and 'more authentic' *spiritual* reality, yet somehow still connecting with its material manifestations.[8] The fluctuation veers wildly between the 'GOD' of 'Assumption' – all letters in upper case – and the later formulation of a diminished 'God' – definitely consigned to a suffixed diminutive case: a veritable 'Godot.'

This is a decisive moment in Beckett's early thinking on aesthetics, one which is crucial for his later development. In 'Dante ... Bruno . Vico .. Joyce,' Beckett underscored how he regarded Vico as anything but a mystic, negotiating the extremes of the transcendental and the materialistic by means of what Beckett termed the 'rational.' A variation on this middle position is implicit in *Proust*, perhaps best recast as the 'critical.' Beckett subjects the symbol, Symbolism, and the modernist moment of revelation in *Proust* to a thorough scrutiny, in an effort to evaluate its validity in terms of its own 'poetic logic,' to adapt Vichian terminology. Beckett recounts how after Marcel leaves the Guermantes Library 'Time is recovered and Death with it' (57), thereby acknowledging how both dimensions of time need to be taken together if justice is to be done to Proust's vision of man's temporality. But there is a fundamental contradiction in Beckett's argument in *Proust*: although Beckett does acknowledge Proust's 'dualism in multiplicity,' he also exhibits an underlying tendency in *Proust*, via Schopenhauerian Idealism, to short-circuit this complex vision by giving ultimate priority to a Transcendental realm of Platonic Ideas. This philosophical dimension of Beckett's *Proust* in many ways ends up endorsing that mystico-spiritual dimension of the symbol, thereby going against the very grain of Beckett's avowed critical reservations about such literary judgments. Beckett's key aside in the decisive section six of *Proust* in which he terms *Le Temps Retrouvé* a most 'inappropriate' title is a case in point. As Rupert Wood has pointed out, in this instance 'Proustian involuntary memory becomes Schopenhauerian aesthetic experience,' proceeding then to show how the analogy is inaccurate in so far as for Proust 'time in its pure state is regained through involuntary memory, whereas for Schopenhauer time is merely obliterated in the rapture of the aesthetic experience. Beckett, therefore, admits that he cannot understand the title of Proust's final book, *Le Temps Retrouvé.*'[9] Beckett is deemed 'more of a Schopenhauerian than a Proustian' and hence 'filters the whole of Proust's theorizing on time, memory and habit through the aesthetic system of his favourite philosopher.'[10] But not all of Proust's theorizings are filtered through Schopenhauer; as we have seen, Beckett does strive to see Proust's work within its own terms of reference in so far as he does justice to the 'dualism in multiplicity' thesis. Schopenhauer might be regarded as Beckett's 'favourite philosopher' in that certain images and aspects of his philosophy appealed to him, perhaps above all his stylistic elegance; but Schopenhauer was not the most important of philosophers for Beckett. That designation would, as I have argued elsewhere, belong to Immanuel Kant, to whom Beckett returned for careful rereadings throughout the thirties, in large part, I believe, because of his dissatisfaction with the Schopenhauerian elements superimposed upon his argument in *Proust* and which were not assimilated with the other more rigorously examined aspects of his study.[11]

Schopenhauer's unfettered Idealism collapses the Kantian categories upon which the distinctions between what is known and what cannot be known are established. No wonder Beckett was so dissatisfied with

Proust and regarded its argument as stillborn and fundamentally inauthentic – a particularly scathing term of dismissal since *Proust* was to have been about determining the authentic reality rendered by Proust's aesthetic. An uncritical imposition of Schopenhauerian readings in *Proust* at key junctures is what undoubtedly led Beckett to dismiss his first major critical study as betrayed by the use of a 'cheap flashy philosophical jargon.'[12] Beckett's choice of terminology is particularly striking here since the heart of *Proust* is a would-be critical investigation of modernist moments of being; the abstractions of 'philosophical jargon' are the antithesis of an authentic aesthetic reality communicated with an inspired and original language of one's own.

Such instances of 'philosophical jargon' are easy to tabulate in Beckett's *Proust* for they are presented in such a way as to stand out:

(i) 'Unfortunately Habit has laid its veto on this form of perception, its action being precisely to hide the essence – the Idea – of the object in the haze of conception – preconception' (11).

(ii) 'the essence, the Idea, imprisoned in matter' (57).

(iii) 'his contempt for the literature that "describes," for the realists and naturalists worshipping the offal of experience, prostrate before the epidermis and the swift epilepsy, and content to transcribe the surface, the façade, behind which the Idea is prisoner' (59).

(iv) 'When the subject is exempt from will the object is exempt from causality (Time and Space taken together). And this human vegetation is purified in the transcendental aperception that can capture the Model, the Idea, the Thing in itself' (69).

In the first three examples, the Idea – writ large – is proposed as a Platonic 'higher reality,' à la Schopenhauer, pointing towards a transcendental beyond. Its definition is translated by means of its antithesis, the carceral world below in which the 'essence' is immured by matter, habit, naive mimetic theories of art, and so on. Such vaguely formulated concepts of an avowedly mystical nature constitute that Romantic legacy which modernism attempted to put in some type of critically focused order. Beckett, as we have seen, has fundamental reservations about the aesthetic premises of both Joyce and Proust; however, since he has no answer as yet of his own whereby he might find his own way, he, ironically enough, ends up invoking in a naive and critically unexamined way a number of positions that key modernist innovators such as Joyce and Proust had made a concerted effort to move beyond (the prime example being Stephen Dedalus's rejection in *Portrait* of *claritas* having any suggestion of an idealist-symbolist' interpretation). The fourth example cited above is a classic instance of Schopenhauer's collapsing of the Kantian categories (here of Time and Space), with the result that a 'transcendental aperception' leads to 'concretizing Kant's thing-in-itself,' which Beckett spoke so strongly against in the last sentence of his spoof lecture 'Le Concentrisme' (1930).[13] Beckett might indeed be correct when he says the influence of Schopenhauer on Proust's views regarding the significance of music is 'unquestionable' (70); however, the conclusion to this discussion as it issues forth in the very long last sentence of *Proust* is nevertheless open to serious questioning: 'the ideal and immaterial statement of the essence of a unique beauty [...], the "invisible reality" that damns the life of the body on earth as a pensum and reveals the meaning of the word: "defunctus"' (72). Schopenhauer does get the last word, and this is the crowning example of what Beckett later acknowledged as an 'overstated' emphasis on Proust's pessimism.[14]

No wonder critics such as Nicholas Zurbrugg have been drawn into a highly polemical rejection of Beckett's many distortions of Proust's world. There is no convincing way that it can be argued that Beckett has written a balanced appraisal of being and time in Proust's universe of *A la Recherche*. No reader of even parts of that massive work can feel that Beckett has done more than offer, in the final analysis, a very abbreviated albeit lyrical evocation of the Proustian moments of revelation in his study's sixth section, while raising some probing questions about the communication of such mystical experiences; but the argument thereafter is sidetracked by an ever-increasing reliance on Schopenhauerian views that seem imposed on the argument and prevent its full engagement with the critical issues thus far raised. No wonder Beckett felt that his *Proust* as it stood was incomplete and that an eighth section should. be added;[15] that this was never written is hardly surprising: how could Beckett hope to synthesize his critique of the symbol and Symbolism with the Schopenhauerian elements that, in essence, support a Transcendental reading?[16]

A final assessment of *Proust* involves a debunking of a number of myths that have persisted throughout the history of Beckett criticism. Nicholas Zurbrugg was indeed justified in stating that it is one of the most puzzling enigmas of twentieth-century criticism that critics have for the most part accepted so uncritically Beckett's *Proust*.[17] We know, just as was the case with 'Dante ... Bruno . Vico .. Joyce,' that Beckett pays scant attention to scholarly conventions such as acknowledging secondary sources. John Fletcher and Terence McQueeny, along with others, have shown how Beckett 'borrows' freely from Arnaud Dandieu's 1930 study of Proust; primary sources are also undocumented, Beckett often paraphrasing Proust's own words as if they were his own, thereby further blurring critical perspective.[18] Nevertheless, certain myths have persisted and are neatly exemplified in Ruby Cohn's summary judgment that '*Proust* remains talismanic reading for those interested in either Beckett or Proust.'[19] *Proust* could, however, only be regarded as a 'template' if this idea is regarded in a deconstructive manner; the development of Beckett's subsequent work is, in many decisive and critical ways, a working towards a refutation of the idealist aesthetics of *Proust*. For example, 'Assumption' and *Proust* are filled with references to the Idea imprisoned in matter, to the soul being imprisoned by the body. Through his developing critique of idealist aesthetics, Beckett moves by the time of *L'Innommable* (1949) towards the Foucauldian inversion of *Discipline and Punish*: 'the soul is the prison of the body,'[20] as various discourses would impose their 'systems' on a self that is linguistically as well as historically determined. *Proust* is definitely not a template for Beckett's future work; almost immediately Beckett saw its fundamental weaknesses, a potentially promising critique of modernist aesthetics and the role of the symbol undermined by a 'cheap flashy philosophical jargon.'

Beckett's profound dissatisfaction with *Proust*'s confused and contradictory aesthetic speculations regarding what is the real and how it might be expressed led to his avowed declaration to write next 'something more genuine and direct.'[21] Beckett's first novel, *Dream of Fair to Middling Women*, written in Paris in 1932, but not published until 1992, three years after his death, was to have fulfilled this goal, though the results, as we will see, were of a very different import, to say the least. 'Genuine and direct' also harks back to Beckett's 'Dante ... Bruno . Vico .. Joyce,' in which Joyce is lavishly praised for his 'direct expression,' although what this might mean in terms of how language itself functions is left largely unexamined in any serious critical fashion. Beckett contents himself there with polemics against readers who are too benighted to appreciate what Joyce is up to, namely, that the words themselves embody their very meaning so that 'form *is* content, content *is* form'; the words are 'alive' in that, to use Beckett's examples, if the sense is 'drunk,' so, correspondingly with the words, ditto for 'sleep' – 'when the sense is sleep, the words go to sleep' (27). Every word of *Work in Progress* is in this regard a potential epiphanic moment – or moments, for in Joyce's great final work words are 'alive [...] glow and blaze and fade and disappear' (28), ready for another recycling. In *Proust* Beckett encountered a variant modernist aesthetic in which the moments of revelation were few and far between, vouchsafed only by the miraculous intervention of involuntary memory. Nevertheless, despite the obvious differences between Proust and Joyce, some of which we have already examined, the crucial and vital common factor they share is for Beckett a sense of *immediate* and *direct* communication of the visionary insight. What might, however, seem somewhat surprising is Beckett's own rather naive declaration of intent to write 'something more genuine and direct' at the very point at which he had to confront in the impasse of his argument in *Proust* that such terms are indeed highly problematical, particularly if the question of language itself as mode of communication is rigorously investigated.

Another factor to take into account is Beckett's identification with primitivist dimensions of modernism via his association with the avant-garde journal *transition*, in which he made his authorial debut and which published and promoted excerpts from Joyce's *Work in Progress*. In the March 1932 issue of *transition* (at the time he was working on *Dream*) appeared the manifesto 'Poetry Is Vertical,' with Beckett as one of the nine signatories. Its central theme is that the function of a truly creative personality is 'the delineation of a vitalistic world'; a 'living imagination' must supersede the merely pragmatic and mundane conceptions of the nature of creativity: 'Esthetic will is not the first law. It is in the immediacy of the ecstatic revelation, in the a-logical movement of the psyche, in the organic rhythm of the vision that the creative act occurs.'[22] Several of the key points in the manifesto echo views that we have already heard Beckett express in *Proust*, particularly with reference to the fetishized animism of involuntary memory and its 'magical' operations, which lie outside any operations of the intellectual or creative will. This is the only such public document ever endorsed by Beckett, and it deserves to be taken seriously for that reason alone; read in the context of Beckett's early works to this point, it is also clear that in broad general terms what the manifesto professes is what Beckett has just been affirming, developing, and investigating in his own writings.

Most definitely, the determining common identification of Joyce and Proust in Beckett's mind is their commitment to an aesthetic of direct expression, of immediacy of expression. Confirmation for this is found in Beckett's reply (14 June 1967) to Sighle Kennedy's letter enquiring whether 'Dante ... Bruno . Vico .. Joyce' with its praise of Vico's 'ratio-nal' thought could be regarded as 'a valid yardstick for measurement of your later work' (her focus is on *Murphy*). Kennedy was nonplussed by Beckett's response in which he politely, almost apologetically, states that his answer to her question is a negative: 'I simply do not feel the presence in my writing as a whole of the Joyce & Proust situations you evoke.'[23] She was nonplussed less by his negative response than by the fact that her query letter to him had made no mention of Joyce except in so far as his name appeared in the title of Beckett's 1929 essay, and Proust's name was not even raised. Yet, as Kennedy astutely points out, the two authors' names are presented as if they were one entity: '"Joyce & Proust" they are paired, as if forming a single firm name.'[24] In *Proust* we saw how Beckett associated the enterprises of Proust and Joyce, but the Kennedy letter is the only example of Beckett not only mentioning them explicitly but presenting them as virtually an incor-porated entity. Kennedy cannot make sense of this and finally settles, unsatisfactorily it must be said, upon the 'solution' to Beckett's per-plexing response as residing in his rejection of the works of Proust and Joyce in which the 'craftsmanship' was 'at all times controlled and ra-tional.'[25] Beckett's ostensibly unwarranted 'Joyce & Proust' coupling is really his acknowledgment of the implicit identification of these two great modernist predecessors throughout his *Proust* monograph, and the cues for such a joining together of these two authors are indeed to be found in Kennedy's own letter to Beckett: in her first paragraph she refers to Vico's 'division of human expression into gesture, animism and abstraction,' as discussed by Beckett in his Joyce essay, and in the third and penultimate paragraph she mentions 'direct expression, of man's successive visions of the universe' in *Murphy*.[26] Beckett couples together 'Joyce & Proust situations' because, as we have seen in our commentary on his Joyce essay and the Proust monograph, 'direct ex-perience' and immediacy of revelation are the two guiding and essen-tial points under discussion.

In reaction against his Proust study, Beckett sought in *Dream* to achieve 'something more genuine and direct.' Beckett's efforts to attain this de-clared goal in his first novel bring home in a much more pressing man-ner the theoretical impasses of *Proust* that we have examined. The key issue that surfaced there and in his earlier essay on Joyce is that of an ideal of direct expression; the complex, convoluted (and, to be sure, sometimes confused) gyrations around the issue of what is real and the competing claims of the imaginative ideal and the empirically perceived return again and again in *Proust* to the modernist moment of revelation in which the quest for what is real, authentic, true is fulfilled through a supposedly pure representation, the direct sensuous intuition of reality. In short, the ideal to be realized might be termed the 'unmediated vision,' as used in Geoffrey Hartman's 1954 study of modern poetry. The following summary description in Hartman neatly encapsulates the underlying theoretical dilemma encountered by Beckett in *Proust*, and which he proposed to resolve in *Dream*: 'The mind, therefore, being most keenly aware through the dominant eye of that which is the cause of perception, pure representation will, at base, be the urge to construct that ideal system of symbols which relieves consciousness of the eyes' oppression but assures it of the eyes' luminosity.'[27] Such was also the 'ideal real' as presented in *Proust*: the symbolic expression thereof is intended as an illumination, a means of accessing a luminous clarity. Hartman's argument then develops the idea of pure representation as 'the imageless vision': 'for poetry is at one with the other arts in seeking, though by varying means, visibility without image, audibility without sound, perception without percepts.'[28] These ideas are much more in evidence in *Dream* than in *Proust* and are particularly identified with Belacqua's theorizing in which there is an emphasis upon an 'aesthetic of inaudibilities' (141) and of imageless ideal expression such as is found 'between the flowers that cannot co-exist' (137).

Belacqua might be the central character of *Dream*, but he is by no means the central or abiding presence in the novel. That role is played by the narrator-figure, who is referred to at several junctures as a 'Mr Beckett,' who is an associate, if not sometime friend, of Belacqua, and who is perforce as the demiurge of this fictional universe also engaged in an aestheticizing effort to determine the very nature of what is going on in terms of his relationships with Belacqua and the other characters, in particular the 'fair to middling women' who embody and stand for various types of Beauty and are therefore central to any aesthetic debate. Above all, this is a *mediated* series of realities, and the narrator as would-be author in his own right is in the midst of things as the middleman, the intermediary who draws together the various characters and groupings within the novel as a whole. (Whether indeed the novel could be said to constitute a 'whole' rather than a chaotic series of lacunae or 'holes' is *the* question which the work proposes.) This unsettling conjunction of immediacy versus mediated, of authors versus characters, to name only two of the competing dynamics of *Dream*, foregrounds a dilemma that Hartman focuses on in the conclusion of his argument, that the modern poet who has committed himself to understanding experience in its immediacy or directness, and indeed as a result of this very commitment, 'comes to know the need of mediation only the more strongly.' The double-edged conclusion of Hartman's argument about the modern artist's commitment to an 'unmediated vision' is that 'it is the artist who, acknowledged or not, pretends to the role of mediator,' adding as corollary that 'his real mediation is to accept and live the lack of mediation.'[29]

Here then is the fundamental perplex of Beckett's *Dream*, simultaneously affirming and denying the opposing forces of order and disorder, immediacy and mediation. The narrator's self-conscious commentary on his art most often employs musical imagery to convey his inability to control his characters and hence to shape them into the accepted forms of the so-called well-written novel. They are no longer 'pure, permanent liŭs' or pings' but 'the most regrettable simultaneity of notes' (45). The novel is ostensibly out of control because the characters cannot be assimilated to any other system than their own: 'But they will let us down, they will insist on being themselves as soon as they are called upon for a little strenuous collaboration. The music comes to pieces. The notes fly about all over the place, a cyclone of electrons' (50). The narrator-author waxes rhapsodic over the poetic labours of the 'ecstatic mind' that would give expression to the 'demented perforation of the colander' of the 'night firmament' (51). The narrator, Mr Beckett, is torn between the desire to express this vision in its natural form, that is, incoherently, and a countervailing urge towards 'architechtonics.'

More to the point, in terms of the actual composition of this 'decomposition,' how can so-called direct experience – literary or otherwise – be authentically conveyed when, as the text of *Dream* makes all too painfully obvious, its vision is filtered through and set in contrapuntal opposition to a host of other literary texts? John Pilling's *Beckett's 'Dream' Notebook* (1999) allows us access to Beckett's more obscure allusions as a complement to the host of overt references to literary and artistic figures and their works that riddle the text, often in vertiginous name-dropping fashion. With the publication of his *Companion to 'Dream of Fair to Middling Women'* as a special issue of the *Journal of Beckett Studies* (2004), we now have an annotated vade mecum that details in over a thousand discrete entries how Beckett applied and exploited his very extensive and eclectic reading in his first novel. There is, however, the concomitant danger of the annotations obscuring rather than illuminating the structure of *Dream*, unless we bring to bear a critical assessment whereby we can keep in creative balance the multifarious source details and the encompassing vision evoked by the work as a whole. 'To free himself from the overwhelming influence of Joyce,' Pilling maintains that Beckett put himself 'in thrall to a multiplicity of writers and writing in a desperate attempt to demonstrate it was not mastery he was after, but quite the opposite: weakness.'[30] But, as we will see, *Dream*'s very complex structure is in fact determined by an in-depth engagement with Stephen Dedalus's aesthetic as elaborated in *Portrait* (in this regard *Dream* is 'Assumption' writ large). *Portrait* functions here 'as a structural convenience – or inconvenience,' to adapt the words Beckett used to describe Joyce's employment of Vichian ideas in *Work in Progress*. For Beckett in *Dream* such an adaptation is clearly more 'convenience' than 'inconvenience' in so far as Stephen's ideas serve again and again as the starting points for the aesthetic investigations of *Dream*, not to mention particular narrative sequences and innumerable stylistic turns of phrase. Beckett is not 'in thrall' to the host of other writers mentioned in *Dream*; far from this being the case, such references function, in the main, to mask and camouflage the extensive and pervasive engagement with *Portrait* that, as we will see, is so decisive in the very formulation of *Dream*.

How then can such a modus operandi lay claim to its own authenticity, its own 'genuine' and 'direct' nature? The answer lies in the parodic structures whereby the extensive Joycean influences in *Dream* are transformed into complex appropriations that validate the authority of the materials 'borrowed' at the same time that their authority is brought into question. Or, as Linda Hutcheon puts it: 'Parody is fundamentally double and divided: its ambivalence stems from dual drives of conservative and revolutionary forces that are inherent in its nature as authorized transgression.'[31] Hutcheon distinguishes modern parody of the twentieth-century variety from earlier types dependent solely upon an ethos of ridicule that would mock into oblivion the original target material. Parody as employed in Beckett's *Dream* employs a much more complex set of strategic manoeuvres; its simultaneous acceptance and rejection of the primary 'source' material points towards innovative ways of dealing with the 'anxiety of influence' and, as Hutcheon proposes, might even effect a 'paradoxical strategy of repetition as a source of freedom.'[32] Modern parody as a particular type of repetition that foregrounds differences holds out the possibility of critically working out one's own views by working through the ideas and words of another. This is, in effect, the strategy Beckett began with in 'Assumption,' and such parodic manoeuvres are taken to a much more sophisticated level in *Dream* as Beckett through his dialogical encounter with Joyce begins to formulate his own aesthetic principles. Underneath the polyphony of references to other writers, the basic structure and development of *Dream* are determined by the 'double-voicing' of Beckett rewriting Joyce.[33]

The very brief *ONE* of *Dream* consists of only two short paragraphs (the first composed of 66 words, the second of 29). If Schopenhauer gets the last word in *Proust* ('defunctus'), Joyce, who as we have seen is indirectly addressed at key junctures in that study, is accorded the first word of *Dream*: 'Behold Belacqua an overfed child' (1). Beckett's very first move echoes Joyce's poem written in 1932 on the birth of his grandson, an event which followed soon after his own father's death, 'Ecce Puer' ('Behold the child'). Here the child presented for our viewing is Beckett's first major literary offspring. And just as the last word of *Proust* contained a pun, Ruby Cohn pointing out that 'defunctus' implies both 'completion' as 'perfection' and as 'death,'[34] the first word of *Dream* also suggests a doubling of meaning. The allusion to Joyce's very moving poem about death, (re)birth, and guilt also brings to mind the definition of the epiphany as a 'sudden spiritual manifestation' or, to invoke Harry Levin's memorable description, epiphanies conceived of as 'mystical visions which link the beholder to the object beheld.'[35] Beckett's 'Behold' can, of course, only be regarded ironically within this context; nevertheless, this invocation of Joyce cannot be dismissed outright as merely parody in the negative sense of the word: Beckett is obviously also 'beholden' to Joyce in the sense of being indebted to him. Beckett's opening 'Behold' raises a whole series of problematical issues about literary filiation/affiliation: to what degree can the reader take up the challenge of identification with Belacqua; to what degree is the narrator-cum-author of *Dream* to be identified with Belacqua; and to what degree is Beckett's enterprise to be identified with Joyce's? The seven 'Beholds' invoked at various points in *Dream* make clear enough (painfully so) that there is indeed no ideal (mystical) union of beholder and beheld. The second reference – 'Behold how he loved her' (103) – concerns the Mandarin (the Smeraldina's father) trying, unsuccessfully, to convince Belacqua that his 'Beatrice in the brothel' perplex – the ideal and the real in irreconcilable opposition – is actually due to a naive misunderstanding of the issues at stake. The next two references involve the Alba, the most fair of the fair to middling women of Belacqua – 'Behold it is she'; 'Behold her gliding ahead of schedule' (151) – but Belacqua, of course, fails to achieve any 'union' with her, mystical or otherwise (and when she beholds him it is decidedly as 'puer' not 'homo'). The last cluster in this series neatly inverts the opening 'Behold Belacqua': '"Behold, Mr Beckett" he said, whitely, "a dud mystic"' (186), thereby adding more variations on the author/narrator's relationship with Belacqua. Here Belacqua, now a martyred 'ecce homo' of sorts, gets to address the author/narrator who had first introduced him to us using the self-same word. But the running theme of a failed sense of any mystic union of beholder and beheld on the various levels referred to above makes it clear just how *un*-Joycean these proceedings are, at the same time that Beckett is beholden to Joyce for the very terms in which these proceedings are being framed, even if the name for his central character was purloined from Dante's *Purgatorio* and smuggled into Dublin.

The degree to which Beckett is indebted to Joyce in *ONE* of *Dream* is, ironically enough, made clearer by those very references that would seem designed to supply alternatives or 'antidotes,' as it were, to Joyce's influence. The opening scene of the first paragraph pictures Belacqua on his bike pedalling madly after Findlater's van, cruising alongside and then hectoring the driver to beat his horse: 'Whip him up, vanman, flickem, flapem, collop-wallop fat Sambo' (1). From John Pilling's *Beckett's 'Dream' Notebook* we know that two references to William M. Cooper's *Flagellation and Flagellants* are combined here.[36] Yet these references (as well as the horse's defecation) still 'stink of Joyce.' In Joyce's play *Exiles*, Richard Rowan's son Archie, who is 'daft on horses,' tells his mother that when he goes on deliveries with the milkman 'I'll make him go quick. You'll see from the window, mamma. With the whip. *He makes the gesture of cracking a whip and shouts at the top of his voice: Avanti!*'[37] The 'gush of mard' in *Dream* affords the only identification of beholder and beholden in *ONE*: an empathetic 'Ah …!' follows the horse's excretion. This one-word phatic sentence signals perhaps the closest identification of narrator and narrated – and via a horse's rump at that! – in all of *Dream*. The one-sentence final paragraph of *ONE* suddenly jumps ahead several years to an image of Belacqua 'climbing the trees in the country and in the town sliding down the rope in the gymnasium.' The opening of *Dream* with its five sentences may mirror ironically the five chapters of *Portrait* and as microcosm the five very uneven parts of *Dream* itself (uneven both stylistically and in terms of length); in effect, Beckett's opening simultaneously announces an engagement with Joyce (the initial injunction: 'Behold') and a disengagement from a direct competition with Joyce at the same time since no one could for a second mistake these two opening aperçus as a serious rival to Joyce's first chapter of *Portrait* or even to the opening baby tuckoo section. Whereas Joyce's 'Ecce Puer' revises and draws upon the 'Ecce Homo'/'Behold the man' tradition of Christian iconography, Beckett's 'Behold Belacqua' might be more appropriately regarded as in the alternative Nietzschean tradition of *Ecce Homo* in which a comic and ironic self-appraisal is at the heart of the critical enterprise.[38]

TWO deals with the relationship of Belacqua and the Smeraldina-Rima, from their meeting in Dublin to the break up of their relationship in Kassel on New Year's Eve. From the very beginning, their relationship is framed by a number of correspondences with Joyce's *Portrait*, all of which turn on the critical issue of somehow working out an accommodation between the ideal and the real. As the novel proper opens with Belacqua seeing off the Smeraldina-Rima at the Carlyle Pier, on her way to Vienna to study music, he thinks back to when they first met. He 'encountered one evening' what he took, mistakenly, to be a most 'fair' woman, whose face shone 'with an unearthly radiance' (3), which echoes Stephen Dedalus's *claritas*; but in this instance the 'unearthly' qualification distinguishes it from the vision that Stephen made a point of identifying with *this* world. The meeting with the Smeraldina would seem, nevertheless, to be a fulfilment, however ironic, of young Stephen's desire 'to meet in the real world the unsubstantial image which his soul so constantly beheld. He did not know where to seek it or how, but a premonition which led him on told him that this image would, without any overt act of his, encounter him' (*P*, 66).

Stephen's sense of his grand destiny becomes Belacqua's more down-to-earth 'as luck would have it' (3). For now he sees her as a 'slob of a girl' with whom he is in love only 'from the girdle up' (3). But on that fatal evening encounter he had fallen under her charming aura and imagined her to be an embodiment of the ideal in her absolute devotion to the music of Bach and her plans to go to Vienna to study. Hence beholding the Smeraldina's face led the awestruck Belacqua to 'moor in the calm curds of her bosom,' and 'the result of this was that the curds put forth suckers of sargasso, and enmeshed him.' Two particular Joycean images – two of the most famous in all his work – are present here in variant form. Smeraldina's departure is a recasting of *'Distant Music'* of 'The Dead' fame – literally so, since she is leaving 'almost at once' for Vienna.

In short, she is a symbol writ large of ideal femininity; but – alas – Belacqua will soon have his eyes opened to her actual, complex being (just as Gabriel Conroy in a more serious vein learned of his wife Gretta's love for Michael Furey and their 'distant music'). The other reference is to the sighting of the birdgirl in the epiphany that concludes chapter 4 of *Portrait*. In that scene the girl's legs were 'pure save where an emerald trail of seaweed had fashioned itself upon the flesh as a sign' (151). In Beckett's version in *Dream*, this situation has been grossly exaggerated – 'the curds put forth suckers of sargasso, and enmeshed him' – for Belacqua is actually involved with this woman, whereas young Stephen Dedalus simply projects a number of idealized, soulful visions upon his birdgirl. Fair dream visions set off by the encounter with the birdgirl are ironically and realistically brought down to earth, to the realm of the 'fair to middling' in Beckett's revision.

After the Smeraldina's departure, Belacqua goes through a complex series of mental gyrations that he hopes will issue forth in a 'positively transcendental gloom' (16). The climax of this opening scene telescopes a number of images from the beginning and ending of *Portrait* that underline the degree to which Joyce's novel is the key reference work in structural terms in Beckett's first novel. That night Belacqua prayed, we are told, 'for no particular reason before getting into bed.' His prayer repeats that taught to him and his brother by their mother: 'That was their prayer' (8). And this, of course, echoes baby tuckoo's appropriation of his father's story in the opening of *Portrait*: 'That was his song' (19). In *Dream* Beckett combines this syntactical pattern with a reference to the scene of Stephen praying in the dormitory at Clongowes school. But what is most interesting here is how Beckett in the same night scene makes a less obvious reference to the ending of *Portrait*. Belacqua talks himself out of a so-called 'nice state of affairs when the son of Adam could quash the lover of the Smeraldina-Rima or any other girl for that matter and if that was all being in love with a girl from the girdle up meant to him the sooner he came off it the better. Thus he was crowned in gloom and he had a wonderful night' (9). Compare this with the ending of the fourth last diary entry (15 April) on *Portrait*'s closing page. As Stephen rethinks his encounter that day with E–C– and his sharing of his plans for departure from Ireland, he rejects all his earlier convoluted thoughts about her and, self-mocking – for once – advises himself: 'O, give it up, old chap! Sleep it off!' (218). Both Belacqua and Stephen do then literally sleep it off, but the chiastic nature of their situations is much in evidence as well: in the opening of *Dream* Belacqua's 'beloved' leaves him for her art, whereas at the ending of *Portrait* Stephen in quest of his artistic destiny leaves his 'beloved' behind, and with somewhat more generosity of spirit, it must be said, than that evidenced by the self-serving Belacqua. This larger pattern of reversal is mirrored in the micro-syntactical formulations of 'came *off it*' and 'sleep *it off*' (italics mine).

Particular issues, of both the major and minor variety, get invoked in *ONE* and the opening sequence of *TWO* because Joyce has already done so, said so, and Beckett is now repeating them with variation in order to test them out for himself via a parodic doubling that entails both emulation and emendation. After the invocation of these Joycean references that supply the momentum for the opening section of *TWO*, the narrator/author confesses to us that 'we do not quite know where we are in this story' (9). For *Dream* is indeed not 'that story' told by the father which opens *Portrait*, though Beckett has clearly gone out of his way to set up various analogies between the two. The most obvious and decisive difference between Joyce's story and Beckett's concerns the role of the narrator, how the question of point of view is handled. Joyce's surrogate figure is rendered invisible, virtually 'refined out of existence,' even if his irony is at times palpable, whereas Beckett's narrator is most definitely of the hands-on variety as he comments overtly about the metafictional status of his would-be story, which has barely got underway but already threatens to go no further. The proceedings are threatened since the narrator acknowledges that some of his 'creatures' will simply not allow themselves to suffer gladly a role as a 'symbol' in someone else's story or to be coerced into adopting such a role ('be made to stand for something').[39] While Nemo is, of course, as his name implies, acknowledged as one of the intractables from the very beginning, this narrator will in short order have to admit that even those creatures he believes he can control more or less (such as the principal divas – the Smeraldina-Rima, the Syra-Cusa, and the Alba) are, in fact, anything but docile minds and bodies at his disposal. This overt metafictional speculation is, however, designed in *Dream* to broach from two very different perspectives the question of the role and status of the symbol itself, which is indeed a central Joycean question and one that Beckett theoretically wrestled with in *Proust*. In 'A Painful Case' and 'The Dead' in *Dubliners*, for example, and at key junctures in *Portrait*, especially in Stephen's aesthetic theorizing, Joyce argues against turning complex human entities into soul-companions, idealized intellectual portraits, or merely reflections of a transcendental beyond. The whole business of creatures/characters as 'pings' or 'liŭs' (terms derived from Chinese music) in *Dream* is indeed a *'Distant Music,'* to adapt Gabriel Conroy's would-be characterization of his wife Gretta.

On the other hand, Belacqua is identified from the very beginning as fixated by an idealizing characteristic; his women – fair or middling – are somehow or other expected to shine forth with 'an unearthly radiance.' Hence his view could be regarded as the symbolic writ large (as Symbolist). No wonder things go 'kaput' when he is 'raped' by the Smeraldina. The 'tiffs' escalate to the point that Belacqua finally has to make good his escape. But absence, as he says, would indeed seem to make the heart grow fonder; in fact, the Smeraldina-Rima in absentia is an even more powerful presence in the 'young thought of Belacqua' (34). And his 'young thought' is similar to that of another young man, namely, Stephen Dedalus, who as a would-be artist has to figure out what Beauty entails and means for him. Belacqua is not content merely to worship various embodiments of 'unearthly radiance'; he must, it seems, compare them. The comparison of the Smeraldina-Rima with the Syra-Cusa is pursued in aid of determining 'the quintessential kernel and pure embodiment of the occult force that holds me up, makes me wax pagan and static, the kernel of beauty if beauty it be, at least in this category (skirts)' (34). The soaring quest for Beauty is cast in ironic Daedalian-Icarian terms; 'holds me up,' 'wax pagan,' and 'static' bring to mind Stephen Dedalus's view that the 'esthetic emotion' is 'static': 'The mind is arrested and raised above desire and loathing' (*P*, 179). For such a 'static' and fixated view of Beauty the young Belacqua is roundly chastised by the narrator/author: 'Unfortunate Belacqua, you miss our point, *the* point: that beauty, in the final analysis, is not subject to categories, is beyond categories. There is only one category, yours, that furnished by your stases. As all mystics, independent of creed and colour and sex, are transelemented into the creedless, colourless, sexless Christ, so all categories of beauty must be transelemented into yours' (35). Poor Belacqua does not, however, heed such critical commentary and ends up in an even more convoluted argument when he tries to reconcile the contrarieties of 'the Beatrice in the Brothel' problem via a series of mental acrobatics. Behind this strategic rationalization resides the fact that Belacqua is engaged in acts of symbolization, making the Smeraldina 'stand for' a number of idealized propositions. Belacqua's initial assumption is that of regarding his beloved as only a 'thought' or 'vision.' Employing these idealized versions of her, Belacqua could then satisfy himself, in the usual way, in the brothel – the consequences for him being an experience of 'peace and radiance' (40). As for her: 'She simply faded away' (40).

The following description/summary of Belacqua's duplicitous process of symbolic identification strongly echoes in parodic fashion that key passage in section 6 of *Proust* in which there is a 'participation between the ideal and the real, imagination and direct apprehension, symbol and substance' that 'frees the essential reality' (55): 'The rare miracle of fulfilment that had been ascribed and referred to her, exclusively to her, with which she in his mind had been identified, the gift of magic from her, real and ideal, to the soul, about which his entire preoccupation with her was organised, whose collapse as an imminent recurrence, had that been thinkable, would have involved automatically the collapse of that preoccupation, this miracle and this magic, divorced from her and from thought of her, were on tap in the nearest red-lamp' (40–1). Even Belacqua cannot swallow wholesale this symbolic rationalization because the brothel has sullied his pure conception of Beauty and violated his sense of his beloved's integrity:

> It was intolerable that she should break up into a series of whores simply because he, cursed by some displaced faculty of assimilation, by this demented hydraulic that was beyond control, found himself obliged to extract from the whore that which was not whorish, but, on the contrary, the fee-simple of the Smeraldina-Rima, who, as it seemed then to him, had either to remain one and indivisible, or else disappear altogether, become a neglible person. And the more intolerable as he was already braced against her disintegration, if not into the multiple whore, at least into the simple whore. One and indivisible. The booby would insist on that. (41–2)

Compare this with *Portrait*'s scene in which Stephen's jealous anger leads to a disintegration and degradation of his beloved Emma's 'static' beauty: 'It broke up violently her fair image and flung the fragments on all sides. On all sides distorted reflections of her image started from his memory' (*P*, 191).[40] Moreover, all these images are 'hoydenish' or whorish in nature. In both instances, the fragmentation is a temporary and intolerable situation since both lovers are committed to the ideal integrity of beauty to which their homage is directed.

Even the ostensible digressions in *Dream* take a Joycean turn at this point. The narrator/author wonders out loud: 'Why we want to drag in the Syra-Cusa at this juncture it passes our persimmon to say' (49). One conditional response is that the Syra-Cusa is indeed the 'middling' woman and thereby allows for speculations on her relationship to the two 'capital divas,' the Smeraldina and the Alba: 'From the extreme Smeraldina and the mean Syra you could work out the Alba for yourselves, you could control our treatment of the little Alba'(49). Knowlson's biography has clarified the ways in which *Dream* is a roman-à-clef: Smeraldina is Beckett's cousin Peggy Sinclair (also the model for the Woman in 'Assumption'); the Alba is Ethna MacCarthy (of whom we will hear a great deal later on – and the 'treatment' of her is by no means so neatly prescribed); and the Syra-Cusa is no other than Lucia Joyce, daughter of one James Joyce, renowned paterfamilias. Knowlson informs us that Joyce was very anxious when he saw a character named Lucy in Beckett's 'Walking Out,' one of the stories of *More Pricks Than Kicks*, the collection that was in part salvaged from the then unpublishable *Dream*. Joyce reassured himself that there was no attempt to fictionalize his daughter who had indeed 'thought she had a lech on Belacqua [read Beckett in this regard]' (50).[41] What would have happened if *Dream* had been published and Joyce had recognized the satirical portrait of the Syra-Cusa as originating in his daughter? The earlier rupture of relations over Lucia's obsession with Beckett would undoubtedly seem very minor when considered with the possible ramifications of Beckett's characterization of Lucia in *Dream*. Joyce could have broken relations off completely, and who knows what this would have meant for the development of Beckett's own work. The narrator/author announces the Syra-Cusa 'digression' with the belief 'A paragraph ought to fix her' (49) and ends up devoting three pages to her before he wishes her adieu ('Be off, puttanina, and joy be with you'). In this context, the very non-literary Syra-Cusa/Lucia Joyce who carelessly misplaces Belacqua's present of 'a beautiful book' (Dante's *Divine Comedy*) could appear, however physically attractive, as a 'cursed nuisance.'

Be that as it may, *Dream TWO* is indeed saturated with Joycean references in the sections following the Syra-Cusa 'paragraph.' This is especially so in the section published separately as 'Sedendo et Quiescendo' (64–73 of the Black Cat Press edition of *Dream*), which describes Belacqua's train journey to join the Smeraldina as requested in her mother's letter to him. The formal introductions of the central characters here – Smeraldina and Belacqua, in indented capital letters at that – does indeed make this episode sound as if it were the original starting point of what became *Dream*, what Beckett referred to at this time as the 'German comedy.'[42] Appropriately enough, then, *Dream* begins, as it were, in the 'middling' parts of *TWO*. What is most interesting here is that 'Sedendo et Quiescendo' is essentially conceived of as a burlesque version of 'Assumption.' Hence the spectacle afforded the reader might be characterized as Beckett rewriting Beckett rewriting Joyce. 'Assumption' we now know was a veritable cento, a stitching together of Joycean elements from *Portrait* in order to focus critically on Stephen Dedalus's aesthetic theory and Beckett's reactions and reservations about it; in short, a parody in both senses of the term as applied to modern literature by Linda Hutcheon: at once a homage and a burlesque. This parody of a parody might also be regarded as a form of 'self-plagiarism' on Beckett's part since he is rewriting himself at the same time he is rewriting Joyce.[43]

The elements recycled from 'Assumption,' but now in an overtly comic manner, include the reference to the Smeraldina as his 'douce Vega' and 'darling blue flower' (70), the climax of these allusions being Belacqua's love sonnet of the Shakespearean variety in which the two lovers are now 'One with the birdless, cloudless, colourless skies,' the martyred hero of 'Assumption' displaced by these comic caricatures who carry to ridiculous extremes romanticized views of a 'rapturous strange death' whereby they will be made 'entire' (71). Most of *TWO* may be regarded as a comic revision of 'Assumption': much earlier on in it we encounter the Belacqua-Vega connection mediated by the Smeraldina (16); the reference to Meredith as a calming influence after Belacqua's 'rape' by the Smeraldina, 'alla fioca lucerna leggendo Meredith' (18);[44] and characteristic stylistic features of 'Assumption,' as derived from the prostitute scene at the end of chapter 2 of *Portrait*: 'He would not go out, though the girl still came, unscathed, from without' (*Dr*, 26). This passage then goes on to elaborate as a veritable conceit the images first appropriated from Joyce's *Portrait* in 'Assumption.' The first sentence, 'He stood in the courtyard, doomed,' echoes 'He stood still in the middle of the roadway' (*P*, 95), just before Stephen is 'detained' by the prostitute's hand. Then Beckett takes the 'breakwater' imagery of the same passage and he rewrites it in comic hyperbole:

> The fragile dykes were caving in on him, he would be drowned, stones and thickets would flood over him and over the land, a nightmare strom of timber and leaves and tendrils and bergs of stone. He stood amidst the weeds and the shell of the Hof, braced against the dense masses, strained out away from him. Over the rim of the funnel, when he looked up, the night sky was stretched like a skin. He would scale the inner wall, his

head would tear a great rip in the taut sky, he would climb out above the deluge, into a quiet zone above the nightmare. (26–7)

Beckett's use of Joyce here via his rewriting of his earlier rewriting in 'Assumption' hardly constitutes allusion in the traditional sense of the word as a specific reference to a particular text; its source becomes ever more elusive as it undergoes the metamorphoses of multiple rewritings and appropriations.

With reference to the 'Sedendo et Quiescendo' section of *TWO*, John Pilling argues that Beckett is attempting 'to excrete the Joyce of *Work in Progress* from his system' in an 'explosion of narrative colic designed to eliminate from the body of this book the waste matter Beckett had accumulated from his close association with Joyce.' Pilling goes on to add that this section 'stinks with Joyce as the master who can be parodied to extinction' and that after this 'evacuation' *TWO* 'flows as if the dead weight of Joyce had been lifted from Beckett's shoulders.'[45] While some of the more superficial stylistic influences of *Work in Progress* might be so eliminated, the underlying reality of *Dream* is that its very structure draws upon *Portrait* for its leading ideas of 'beauty' and 'radiance' and 'stasis.' No, Joyce is very much alive and well throughout *Dream*, and Beckett is really only still in the preliminary stages of figuring out how to come to terms with Joyce, and this for Beckett will necessarily entail a much more complex process of assimilation and incorporation. 'Parodied to extinction' deals with the traditional role of parody; on the other hand, modern parody as Hutcheon has demonstrated involves an affirmation, however problematical, of the original target material. Far from having been killed off, Joyce's key determining presence in the very conception of *Dream of Fair to Middling Women* is actually being further strengthened here. Far from having 'excreted' Joyce's influence, 'Sedendo et Quiescendo' confirms just how deeply Joyce's influence is embedded in Beckett's thinking as the necessary starting points or assumptions for his own literary investigations. This is, in effect, only an early toilet-training exercise, to adapt Pilling's metaphor.

The Belacqua summoned by the Smeraldina's mother to a joyful reunion with her daughter is a veritable portrait of the artist as a colicky baby. Beckett's admission that the 'Sedendo et Quiescendo' section does indeed 'stink of Joyce' is, of course, redolent of Joyce's own 'true scholastic stink' of *Portrait* fame.[46] The bout of colic that precedes this episode (Belacqua is suffering from it when he receives the letter from her mother) and persists throughout it in terms of the byplay about the 'collywobbles' and what this means for the Smeraldina and her family leads back, yet again, to Joyce and *Portrait*, in particular the scene in the infirmary where Brother Michael comforts young Stephen over his case of the 'collywobbles' (*P*, 32). These are still early days in the Joyce-Beckett relationship, one which is, at this point, more mimetic than emetic in nature, since it entails a complex parodying and travestying approach. Moreover, Joyce had long ago anticipated such tactical manoeuvres against himself; in 'The Holy Office' (1904) Joyce casts himself as Katharsis-Purgative, who sets himself up as a target of those who are less honest and talented than himself:

> But all these men of whom I speak
> Make me the sewer of their clique.
> That they may dream their dreamy dreams. (*PJJ*, 658)

The narrator's very first words in the paragraph that follows the ending of the 'Sedendo et Quiescendo' section are the self-mocking 'All that sublimen of blatherskite just to give some idea of the state the poor fellow was in on arrival' (74). Certainly, the foolish chatter of Beckett's tale of Belacqua's journey to his Smerry's arms can't hold a candle to Joyce's 'O blazerskate!' of the Anna Livia Plurabelle section of *Work in Progress*.[47] The major Joycean presence in the rest of *TWO* is evident in one paragraph of about two hundred words, which, along with 'Sedendo et Quiescendo,' is the other extant piece of *Dream* to be published in Beckett's lifetime, under the title 'Text.' John Pilling has argued that while these pieces could not have come into being without Joyce's example, they also try to hold off Joyce's influence or even to challenge it. In particular, Pilling sees 'Text' as 'a semi-parody of the final chapter of *Ulysses* – Molly Bloom's soliloquy,' concluding that Beckett has indeed wisely chosen: 'better the difficult *Ulysses* than the "impossible" *Work in Progress*.' Pilling then goes on to show that Beckett in 'Text' is in fact weaving together a series of arcane references from the drama of John Ford and that this material 'has nothing to do with Joyce and very little to do with Joycean practice.'[48] Nevertheless, it must be pointed out that in this instance even as Beckett tries to circumvent Joyce he still ends up sounding *as if* he were imitating him. And this phenomenon is itself a case of *déjà lu* in that the opening of *Dream* (*ONE*), as we have seen, operates on the same principle (whether inadvertently or intentionally is a moot point): acknowledging Joyce's influence at the very point that such influence is ostensibly being countered.

It is Joyce's presence and influence that have supplied the driving force behind *Dream* to this juncture, as well as a coherence of sorts in terms of its investigation of certain aesthetic issues. It is when Joyce's influence is not operating in this formative manner that the writing in *Dream* deteriorates most markedly and confronts the reader with some truly awful writing that seems to go on endlessly with very little in fact being achieved. Such is the painful case in the last twenty-five pages or so of *TWO*. For just as Belacqua feels sick at the end of *TWO* because of the messy nature of his break-up with the Smeraldina on New Year's Eve and catches his last glimpse of her through 'a veil of nausea' (109), many readers of *Dream* (this one acutely so) cannot help feeling themselves to be in an unpleasantly similar situation. Beckett's prose over the expanse of the last drawn-out episode of *TWO* is indeed now operating as an emetic of sorts. Without the benefit of Joycean reference points, the prose is virtually pointless – self-indulgent and self-aggrandizing. It skirts around personal and private matters that Beckett has clearly not yet assimilated emotionally, such as the break-up with his cousin Peggy Sinclair, upon which this 'unsanitary episode' is based, and thus he cannot find the combinations of words to imaginatively and critically shape the raw material. Beckett/Belacqua is on his own here, embarrassingly so, and it is not a pretty sight. When Beckett in *Dream* is engaged in the complexities of a dialogical encounter with Joyce that is essentially parodic in nature, there is, consequently, an energy, focus, and concentration that animates his writing; when, as in the last twenty-five pages of *TWO*, this critical dimension is almost totally absent, the result is a highly allusive style that seems to be striving to avoid any semblance of critical self-appraisal and understanding. As Linda Hutcheon has pointed out, there are many more reasons for alluding than there are for parodying: to parade one's knowledge (a desultory spectacle in this section of *Dream*, even with respected champions of 'discontinuity' – Beethoven, Dostoyevsky, and Rimbaud – present); to circumvent criticism by citing various authorities (the name-dropping in this section of *Dream* is especially tedious); and to hint at painful subject matter without directly stating it (the inability to deal with the highly personal aspects of the break-up with the Smeraldina). A highly allusive prose also allows for the filling of pages, the killing of time, without exposing oneself to the possibilities of painful ridicule.[49] No wonder the Smeraldina, who feels the brunt of most of these strategies of emotional and intellectual circumvention, intuitively counters the *ad feminem* attack by a form of parody of her own, one which would at least engage the issues in a more authentic fashion: '"He wants to look at my face" she mimicked' (94). In short, the final episode of *TWO* is quite nasty, pretentiously brutish, and anything but short.

The thirty pages of *UND* function as an interlude on aesthetics in which the complex nature of the author-narrator's relationship with his 'characters,' including his special relationship with Belacqua, is in the forefront, thereby supplying a coherence and critical focus sorely lacking in the concluding movement of *TWO*. These ideas have, of course, been foregrounded from the very beginning of *Dream*, but here in *UND* a critical-creative essay on the topic in more depth sets up the connecting link between the two major structural divisions of *Dream*, *TWO* and *THREE*, with *ONE* and the final few pages of *AND* acting as 'bookends' for the work as a whole. This postmodernist underlining of the competing interests of the author and the characters, as first foregrounded in the second sentence of 'Assumption,' is arguably the most distinctively 'un-Joycean' characteristic of Beckett's early prose, particularly when compared to Joyce's handling of narrative point of view in *Portrait*. For example, the narrator tells us that he has no faith in 'the members of the Dublin contingent to perform like decent indivisibilities' (113). And, he adds, the 'taproot of the whole tangle' is 'our principal boy's precarious ipsissimosity.' Here the founding aesthetic principle of Stephen's theory in *Portrait*, *integritas*, or wholeness, is being ironically evoked, as is the final revelatory experience of *quidditas* or whatness; but Belacqua's 'selfness' is indeed multiple, 'trine' at least, so that there is 'no real Belacqua' (121).

The narrator-cum-author is of two minds: on the one hand, he casts aspersions on those 'characters' who will not behave as nicely disciplined 'pings'; on the other, he advocates on behalf of the multiplicity of various selves who will rightly refuse to perform on cue the traditional expectations of well-ordered fictional existence. This abiding ambiguity is nicely caught in the phrasing of 'But if at any time it happen that a passage does call for a different term, for another Apollo or another Narcissus or another spirit from the wombtomb, and if it suit and amuse us [...] to use it, then in it goes' (125). All the options here, whether of a formalistic or a nihilistic nature, depend upon a potential exercise of imperial power (hardly surprising in a section that opens with a reference to the Empress Wu extirpating rebellious peonies – shades of Belacqua as 'taproot' of a rhizomic multiplication – and, in the above reference, to Queen Victoria). However, in the disjointed world of *Dream* such musings are themselves bemused by the intransigence and inexplicability of the various characters, and with such unseemly goings-on the narrator is clearly not amused (invoking also his royal 'we' as 'extenuate concensus of me' [112]).

Belacqua is also presented as of two minds, a veritable bundle of contradictions. Putting aside the narrator's theory of Belacqua as 'trine,' the underlying and defining antinomy is that at times Belacqua is (as we saw in *TWO*) parodied and pilloried by the narrator as a failed imitator of Stephen Dedalus's theory of Beauty and at other times, such as here in *UND*, presented as an advocate of an avant-garde theory of art that would, ostensibly, appear to coincide with that at times advanced by the narrator when his musings have fluctuated from the Apollonian towards the Dionysian realm. Both of these opposing tendencies are foregrounded in *UND*. The following summary description of Belacqua (though, of course, we have just been told that such a summing up is not possible) presents him as the virtual second coming of one Stephen Dedalus, would-be artist: 'The fact of the matter is, we suppose, that he desired rather vehemently to find himself alone in a room, where he could look at himself in the glass and pick his nose thoroughly, and scratch his person thoroughly what is more wherever and for as long as it chose to itch, without shame' (128). Compare this with Stephen's reaction after his efforts to write a love poem about his missed kiss with E–C– on the tram: 'he went into his mother's bedroom and gazed at his face for a long time in the mirror of her dressing table' (*P*, 71) and, later, with his mortification of his senses – especially touch – following his confession attendant upon the hellfire sermons when he 'suffered patiently every little itch and pain' (*P*, 135), only to indulge fully such desires after he had rejected the Church's teachings. But then, contradictory to the core, Belacqua, as Beckett's portrait of the artist as a young man, proposes a type of writing that is markedly *not* of the Stephen Dedalus mode: 'If ever I do drop a book, which God forbid, trade being what it is, it will be a ramshackle, tumbledown, a bone-shaker, held together with bits of twine, and at the same as innocent of the slightest velleity of coming unstuck as Mr Wright's original flying-machine that could never be persuaded to leave the ground' (139–40). To which, the narrator responds: 'But there he was probably wrong.' Most definitely, Belacqua does seem to be haywired together as a would-be artist figure who cannot reconcile his views on Beauty in life with those he holds about art; he insists upon certain 'stases' whereby his 'fair to middling women' will fit into *his* categories as *his* 'symbols,' while simultaneously and contradictorily advancing a more liberating aesthetic: 'The experience of my reader shall be between the phrases, in the silence, communicated by the intervals, not the terms, of the statement' (137).

The portrait of Belacqua is indeed a botched one, perforce: 'Yet, various though he was, he epitomised nothing. Sallust would have made a dreadful hash of his portrait' (126). And so does the narrator of *Dream* in *UND*: after a six-page excursion dealing with shoes and Belacqua's feet (his 'pedincurabilities'), the narrator confesses that, whereas he had planned to give us the full portraiture ('to speak of his belly [...] his loins, his breast and his demeanour, and spell out his face feature by feature and make a long rapturous statement of his hands' [133]), he has now tired of his task and simply refuses to deliver the promised goods: no habeas corpus, no fully figured Belacqua for the reader to behold. The self-justifying phrase is substituted instead: 'Cacoethes scribendi, the doom of the best of penmen' (133). Joyce, as the best of penmen, did however complete his *Portrait* in style; here, Beckett, via his narrator/author, can only admit his inability to try even to do so and thereby admirably fulfils the tag phrase that all writing is indeed 'a gush of mard.'

But if there is a waning interest in Belacqua, there is obviously a corresponding increase in interest in the beautiful Alba, the fairest of them all in *Dream of Fair to Middling Women*. Her embodiment of an ideal Beauty has been announced since the introductory sections of the novel, and thereafter a number of tantalizing anticipations of her actual presence on the scene titillate the reader. We finally get to 'Behold' her in *THREE*, which she dominates in a number of decisive and definitive ways that are crucial for a reading of *Dream*. First of all, it is obvious that the narrator is just as enthusiastic about Alba as is Belacqua, and this mutual admiration society does indeed change the very ethos of *Dream*, which many readers have read as a misogynistic diatribe of sorts. The Alba is, however, most decidedly the exceptional exception; in fact, it could be argued that in the concluding sections of *Dream* (*THREE* and the final and very brief *AND*) Beckett is, in part, engaged in writing a palinode, a recantation of many of the views of women expressed earlier in the work. In this regard, the novel's epigraph, drawn from Chaucer's *Legend of Good Women*, is indeed appropriate for that work is one of the foremost examples of this genre.[50] The fanfare around the Alba's entry is presented in mock-chivalric and mock-epical terms as both narrator and Belacqua, in their different ways, compete for her 'gage,' for the right to champion her cause.

THREE is full of poems of praise for Alba by both her champions. For example, consider this 'Ode' by the narrator to 'Alba-ness': 'She reviled the need, the unsubduable tradition of living up to dying, that forced her to score and raid thus the music of days. The heavy gloom of carnal custom. To extirpate the need and remain light and full of light, to secede from the companies of the dutifully dying and go with them no more from heaviness to heaviness and from darkness to darkness according to their law, to abide, light and full of light, caught in the fulness of this total music of days ...' (166). As the embodiment of a timeless light, the Alba possesses a quality of wholeness unto herself that strongly echoes the radiance or *claritas* of supreme Beauty. Indeed, in the very next sentence that follows the above-cited rhapsody by the narrator, particular parallels between Alba and Stephen's vision of the birdgirl that ends chapter 4 of *Portrait* are implied: 'She was a rock, dayless, furled in a water that she was not doomed to harness. Alone, unlonely, unconcerned, moored in the seethe of an element in which she had no movement' (166). Here is Stephen's first sighting of the birdgirl: 'A girl stood before him in midstream: alone and still, gazing out to sea' (*P*, 151). Beckett's revision here does, typically, two things: it echoes Joyce so that the very attentive reader will have both texts in mind and then inserts a number of changes and alterations in emphasis. In this instance, Beckett's vision is once again much more kinetic in nature than Joyce's (compare the Alba fixed amidst the 'seethe' with the birdgirl 'gently stirring the water with her foot hither and thither' [151]) and Alba's sense of self-contained 'alone'-ness is much more pronounced, since in *Portrait* the birdgirl, at least according to Stephen's point of view, 'long, long she suffered his gaze' (151). Herein lies the key difference between Beckett's presentation of Alba and Joyce's of the birdgirl: an epiphany, according to Stephen, has indeed occurred – a mystical identification of beholder and beheld: 'Her image had passed into his soul for ever and no word had broken the holy silence of his ecstasy. Her eyes had called him and his soul had leaped at the call' (*P*, 152) – whereas in Beckett's revisioning the narrator-cum-author can only admire Alba from afar and can never be one with her. And, as for Belacqua, Alba remains intact as an impenetrable mystery, except for one most notable occasion when, as we will see, he is vouchsafed a visionary encounter with her, albeit a thoroughly 'terrifying experience' (182).

THREE is essentially structured around a complex revisioning of the birdgirl epiphany that concludes the fourth chapter of *Portrait* (and *THREE* is, of course, actually the fourth section of *Dream*). Beckett's controlling strategy here seems to be a series of delaying tactics whereby he continually puts off the actual Silver Strand episode with Belacqua and Alba. For, although the narrator tells us fairly early on in *THREE* (twenty-four pages in, to be exact) that 'we are more or less all set now for Belacqua and Alba to meet at least, make contact at least and carry along for a time side by side' (167), we do not, however, actually see them in such a position until much later (though the narrator had earlier boasted that nothing is simpler to arrange than a 'collision' of his various 'characters'): 'Side by side, touching, they recline in the shadow of a great rock, chosen by him for the shadow it gave, on the Silver Strand' (187). And the narrator only finally 'bring [s] down the curtain on this episode' another eleven pages later.

The narrator's original declaration, 'it is now or never the time to sidetrack and couple those two lone birds,' is followed immediately by a passage that really only makes sense when the reader realizes that it is an indirect critique of the birdgirl episode in *Portrait* wherein the narrator, 'Mr Beckett,' makes it clear how he is going to present his much more realistic version of Stephen's self-induced sense of rapture:

> would it not be idle on our part to temporise further and hold up the happy event with the gratuitous echolalia and claptrap rhapsodies that are palmed off as passion and lyricism and the high spots of the creative ecstasy [...] and which, as a matter of fact, are nothing more or less, if any dear reader would care to come in on a good thing, than padding: the fall-back and the stand-by, don't you know, of the gentleman scrivener who has no very near or dear or clear ideas on any subject whatsoever [...] in the interests of whose convulsions clouds of words condense to no particular purpose. (168)

This harsh criticism of Stephen's birdgirl epiphany would seem to make explicit what Joyce has only implied ironically in the *Portrait* scene; certainly, Beckett is even harder on that young man than Joyce said he had been when he came to reflect back on his treatment of Stephen Dedalus. 'Clouds of words' is an apt summary statement by Beckett's narrator for a scene that is framed initially by clouds 'drifting above him silently' (*P*, 151) and ends with an inner vision of 'some new world, fantastic, dim, uncertain as under sea, traversed by cloudy shapes and beings' (*P*, 152). Instead of 'temporising' in these so-called 'poetic' ways, Beckett's version nevertheless does 'temporise' (as we have already pointed out). Beckett's revision of what is arguably the most famous scene in all of *Portrait* is carried out in terms of a realistic portrayal; instead of the silent, mystical communion of Stephen Dedalus with his birdgirl, we get a more adult version in which the participants actually engage in a series of critical dialogues about art and life and love. Compare these two scenes: as Stephen Dedalus deals with the aftermath of his long-awaited encounter with ideal Beauty incarnate, he sings 'wildly to the sea' (*P*, 152); as Belacqua settles in beside the Alba, he is said by the narrator to have 'proceeded wildishly' (*Dr*, 170) in his floundering attempts to explain his visionary theory of poetry à la Rimbaud to the Alba, whose critical intellect at least equals his own and does not let him get away with any of the 'claptrap' nonsense that this parody of *Portrait* has highlighted.

Neither Belacqua nor Stephen Dedalus is allowed to escape from a critical and ironic authorial scrutiny. Stephen can indulge narcissistically his vision of the birdgirl, but he also notes the 'emerald trail of seaweed,' 'a sign upon her flesh' (*P*, 151) as a reminder that this particular version of Irish Beauty might be entangling – another of those 'nets' he will have to find means of soaring above. In Beckett's more realistic recasting of this situation in *Dream*, the Joycean image is transformed into a much more down-to-earth series of entrapments: for example, 'about them rises the marsh of granny's-bends that is their relation' (176); 'bogged beside the royal Alba he wallows caught in the reeds of their relation' (177). Indeed, what is a mere passing 'sign' in *Portrait* is transformed into a veritable conceit in *Dream* as the image expands through various metaphorical variations in order to describe a 'relation' (whereas in *Portrait* the only 'relation' that could actually be said to exist is in Stephen's head alone). The critique is, again, of a double-edged nature: a parodying reassessment conveys a series of critical reservations as it also acknowledges as well those very qualities that make the original passage worthy of such attention (after all, the passage cited above in which Beckett's narrator mocks the birdgirl scene focuses upon Stephen's 'cloudy' views, not Joyce's rendition of it through his invisible narrator's free indirect style).

Beckett's 'Silver Strand' episode, while referring to an actual Dublin locale, also takes its inspiration from a phrase in the last sentence of *Portrait*'s fourth chapter, 'like the rim of a silver hoop embedded in the grey sand' (152), conjoined with the earlier reference to the 'long rivulet in the strand' (151). The poetic nature of this 'echolalia' is commented upon by the narrator since the real name of the venue where Alba and Belacqua meet is finally identified as Jack's Hole.[51] Then,

suddenly, in the midst of the temporizing over the Silver Strand episode, Beckett's text surprisingly delivers the goods: at Frica's mention
of the name 'The Alba,' Belacqua is vouchsafed an epiphany of sorts
that transports him from the here and now to a timeless realm. The description of this experience as a 'miracle' brings to mind Beckett's description of the modernist revelation in *Proust*, and the particularities
of phrasing are also directly related to *Portrait*. Just prior to Stephen
Dedalus's encounter with the girl 'changed into the likeness of a
strange and beautiful seabird' (151), he thinks of how his soul has now
abandoned its 'faded cerements'; Belacqua's 'miracle' transports him
downwards, 'sheathing him in the cerements of clarity' (181) – the last
phrase explicitly associating the death-rebirth imagery with *claritas*.
This epiphanic revelation is, however, composed of a radiance that is a
blanking out or voiding of reality rather than an illumination of it: a
negative epiphany, in other words. The description of this state of idealized non-being is a prose version of Beckett's poem 'Alba': 'Plane of
white music, warpless music expunging the tempest of emblems, calm
womb of dawn whelping no sun, no lichen of sun-rising on its candid
parapets, still flat white music, alb of timeless light. It is a blade before
me, it is a sail of bleached silk on a shore, impassive statement of itself
drawn across the strata and symbols, lamina of peace for my eyes and
my brain slave of my eyes, pressing and pouring itself whiteness and
music through blindness into the limp mind' (181–2).[52] Here is a way
out of the theoretical dilemmas encountered in *Proust* about the nature
and referential status of the symbol – a solution by dissolution in so far
as it erases or whites out everything in aid of a mystical voiding.

A spacing blank between paragraphs follows this rhapsody on 'timeless light' and graphically embodies the point being made. The text of
Dream now challenges the reader to come to terms with a number of
apparent non sequiturs. We are told that 'shortly after this terrifying
experience' of 'albescence' there is a story in the Twilight Herald an-
nouncing the death of Nemo (of whom we have had many reminders
in situ, with Nemo poised on his bridge, ready to jump): 'A finding of
Felo-de-se from Natural Causes was found' (183). Belacqua retires to a
pub to drown his own sorrows and proceeds to convince himself that
Nemo's end was, in fact, 'death by drowning by misadventure' (184).
Suddenly – lightning does strike twice – Belacqua is granted a second
epiphany: 'he felt himself heavenly enflamed as the Cherubim and
Seraphim' (184–5). But just as the experience of Alba's 'whatness' was
termed 'terrifying,' this second 'miracle,' in the final summation, also

constitutes a negative experience, because it does not sustain itself and after its departure Belacqua is worse off than he had been before, 'leaving him bereft and in his breast a void place and a spacious nothing' (185). The first epiphany is *downwards*, the second *upwards*; nevertheless, the result is now felt by Belacqua to be a 'post-evacuative depression' (185), the consequence of the spiritual 'enema' which is the final product of the 'ringing Amen' that initiated his mystical trajectory.

This digressive episode within the series of equivocating delays in actually delivering the full story of Alba and Belacqua on the Silver Strand takes another major detour outside the very confines of the novel we are reading. Supposedly 'years later,' Belacqua and Mr Beckett, our narrator, meet, discuss, and put to rest the whole business of Nemo's death. Belacqua now describes himself as a 'dud mystic' and 'beholds himself' (186) in a way that has given him new knowledge of himself through his reflections on Nemo. The narrator adds that now he was also able to view Belacqua as Belacqua saw himself. What is most interesting here is just how extensive Beckett's reliance on Joycean models is throughout this whole deviation from the supposedly controlling narrative line of the Silver Strand episode, via two different experiences of epiphany and a post-mortem series of reflections on Nemo. Indeed, in the final scene of this extended interlude we are presented with our two gallants (in this instance, Mr Beckett and Belacqua) after the races (in this instance, the equine variety) discussing a painful case, namely, Belacqua's reaction to Nemo's death. The most important analogue, is, of course, with the *Dubliners* story 'A Painful Case,' in which Mr James Duffy in a pub reads in the *Mail* of the death by midadventure, 'with no blame attached,' of Mrs Sinico, his erstwhile soul-companion, whereby he had formerly assumed 'he would ascend to angelical stature.'[53]

Why would Beckett bother to draw out such a detailed rewriting of Joyce's 'A Painful Case' in order to deal with the resolution of Nemo's death? The answer is that the James Duffy-Mrs Sinico relationship in the *Dubliners* story offers a number of telling parallels for the key issues Beckett is exploring in *Dream* as a whole and in respect to Belacqua and Nemo in particular. Mr Duffy is one of Joyce's failed artist figures who is also a miserable failure in life (the two being intimately conjoined). Beckett's Belacqua is another such failure in these two realms, although the Joycean model he is most closely aligned with is Stephen Dedalus of *Portrait*. Throughout *Dream* we have heard the narrator/author heap scorn on Belacqua for his obsession with 'stases,' with this own 'systems' whereby he would have others conform to his wishes, in short, turn

them into idealized symbols (such as Mr Duffy attempted with
Mrs Sinico and Gabriel Conroy with his wife Gretta in the famous 'Distant Music' analogy in 'The Dead'). Such reasoning, such aestheticizing
goes against the grain of the narrator's long-running references to various 'pings' who refused to chime in tune with their would-be orchestra-
tor. It is especially crucial here to keep distinct the points of view of the
narrator/author and Belacqua: the former's critique of the birdgirl epiphany of Portrait as composed of 'gratuitous echolalia and claptrap rhapso-
dies' could, of course, apply equally to Belacqua's waxing lyrical over
Alba's 'whiteness'; indeed, the echolalia here definitely surpasses Joyce's
in the targeted passage. The negative epiphanies experienced by both
Mr Duffy and Belacqua bring them back to the mundane to face their
limited understandings of the unknown depths and fundamental irra-
tionality of those they would all too neatly pigeonhole in their personal
systems. Even the statement in Dream that Belacqua could many years
later meditate on the death of Nemo ('on this emotion recollected in
tranquillity' [185]) and thereby gain some insight into the limitations
and negations involved in his 'theory of the mystical experience' (185) is
indebted to Joyce's short story; Mr Duffy's bookshelf, we are duly informed, contained a complete set of Wordsworth.

After the negative epiphanies induced by Alba and Nemo, the narrator finally gives the reader the much promised but very much delayed
completion of the Silver Strand episode featuring the one and only Alba
and Belacqua. Here the stylistic presentation continues in the mode of a
realistic debunking and rewriting of the romantic excesses of Stephen's
birdgirl epiphany. Neither Belacqua nor Stephen can get away with such
narcissistic rationalizations; for example, the former's statement to Alba
that she is 'white music' (193) is counterpointed shortly thereafter, with
reference to his enquiry as to whether she plans to attend the Frica's
party: '"Hah!" she clapped her hands like a child "hah! the great greedy
wild free human heart of him!"' (196).[54] Such a response is, to be sure, a
far cry from Stephen's religious revelation in which 'no word had broken the holy silence of his ecstasy' (P, 152); in fact, it is as if that remark-
ably self-contained young woman the Alba has read the scene in Portrait
and is mocking young Belacqua in her studied outburst, which ironically echoes effusions such as this from Portrait describing Stephen as
'young and wilful and wildhearted' (P, 151). As in the ending of Joyce's
fourth chapter of Portrait, in Dream the solicitous Belacqua remarks that
the tide is coming in and that it is time to depart, to which replies Alba:
'Are we birds?' (195). And the narrator in his closing remarks adds that

the wooing on the Silver Strand that afternoon had occurred 'with such good auguries, though it broke in no love storm after all' (197–8).

The final thirty-nine pages of *THREE*, like the last section of *TWO*, represent a major decline in the quality and intensity of the writing, for the reason that Beckett is not writing, in a concentrated and critical way, either with or against Joycean models. Certainly, in *THREE* there are some very general correspondences in the Frica's party scenes, which occupy in one way or another most of the remainder of this section of *Dream*, to Joyce's 'The Dead,' the final *Dubliners* story, as well as to the great party scenes at the Guermantes with which Proust concludes his epic work. That beldam Madame Frica who presides with her daughter over this social bedlam of the party terms herself 'a weary exhausted old Norn' (221), the very word used in *Proust* by Beckett to liken the Princesse de Guermantes to one of the three fates of Norse mythology (time past, present, and future).[55] The satirical portraits generated by this carnivalesque comedy of manners possess a certain manic energy at times but do begin to flag badly. By the time the tardy Belacqua arrives, soaked by a pitiless rain, things are looking rather bedraggled at the party itself. To be sure, there is no epiphanic moment when his arrival is trumpeted by the Frica, which earlier had led to the fanfare of Belacqua's first epiphany of the Alba's 'whiteness.' Nor is there any suggestion of a Marcel-like miraculous duplication of 'involuntary memory.' This party isn't going anywhere at this point and neither is *Dream*. The somewhat precipitate departure of Bel and his belle of the ball, Alba, parallels in some revealing ways the poem Beckett wrote in the spring of 1932, 'Home Olga.' The poem's title refers to a husband's shorthand code to his wife when it is time to decamp a tedious social engagement. Beckett's poem, an acrostic that spells out JAMES JOYCE, is at once a critique of Joyce and a homage to him. The last line does, however, seem to turn the criticism against the writer of the poem and away from its target; the reference to a 'pickthank agnus' might suggest that Beckett regards himself as a poseur of sorts who would point out flaws in a great writer without in any legitimate way being worthy of comparison with him.[56] The ending of *THREE* is cued by a veritable 'Home Alba' as Belacqua bellows out: 'Will you come on, for the love of God, away out of this?' (236). So ends *THREE*; but the ending is purely arbitrary at this point and there seems little compelling reason why the final two and a half pages should be given their own section entitled *AND*. These final pages are simply a continuation of the narrative in a linear way. Belacqua accompanies

Alba home, has a drink before her fire, and then is sent on his way alone, the narrator confiding to the reader in an aside: '(you didn't suppose, it is to be hoped, that we were going to allow them to spend the night there)' (240). *AND* also includes the most obvious parodic treatment of Joyce in the whole novel, one which any reader familiar with his work could scarcely overlook: a deflationary naturalistic version of the ending of 'The Dead' in which Gabriel Conroy experiences a mystical identification with the body of humanity. Here, in more realistic Irish fashion, is an all encompassing rain: 'It fell upon the bay, the champaign-land and the mountains, and notably upon the central bog it fell with a rather desolate uniformity' (239). Beckett's own words here fall with a dull uniformity, the intent of the parody being to counterpoint the poetic excesses of the ending of 'The Dead.'

As a hobbling, colicky Belacqua departs Alba, he gazes forlornly into heavens without light, 'no moon was to be seen nor stars' (240). Against this backdrop appears the last reference to Joyce: to the query 'What was that in his lap?' comes the response 'That was his hands' (240–1). The more overt allusion here is to Paul Morel at the ending of *Sons and Lovers* looking at his hands as if they were disembodied fragments of himself, disjointed pieces amidst the cosmic dereliction, just prior to his decision to turn determinedly towards the light of the town.[57] Poor Belacqua's sodden state of disillusionment hardly bears comparison with that of Paul Morel's much more precarious and desperate situation of dissolution. But even here the attempt to get away from Joyce's influence, as we saw was the case from the very beginning of *Dream* in *ONE*, only serves to underline how extensive and deeply felt that influence was: 'That was his hands' is cast in Joycean syntax that echoes 'That was their prayer' (8) from the first pages of *TWO*, and which, in turn, echoes a similar phrase from the opening of *Portrait*, a very young Stephen Dedalus's 'That was his song.' Belacqua's problem is that he wants to be a Stephen Dedalus *redivivus*, but he doesn't know how to go about it; the narrator's problem is that he doesn't want to be James Joyce, but he doesn't know how to avoid this assumed identity except by means of returning with obsessional insistence to a recycling and revising of Joycean materials. Behind them both lies Beckett, who clearly is also of two minds with reference to Joyce's influence but is committed nevertheless to working his way through Joyce to find his own way of going on.

More Pricks Than Kicks, the ten-story collection that Beckett published in 1934, is especially revealing in regard to this question of influence.

Two stories are salvaged from *Dream* – 'A Wet Night' deals with the party scene at the Frica's that concludes *THREE*, and 'The Smeraldina's Billet Doux,' her love letter in mangled German-English to Belacqua – but the overall impression of the collection is fundamentally different than that produced by *Dream*. There are a number of striking reasons for this. First of all, Beckett, in the interests of getting published, has dramatically toned down the extravagant and often arcane language of its predecessor – readability was now clearly a consideration; secondly, this Belacqua is a much less complex character, his theory of 'self-sufficiency' now being based on 'the belief that the best thing he had to do was to move constantly from place to place' (36), as outlined in 'Ding-Dong,' the third story in the sequence; and, most tellingly of all, the Joycean elements that were so extensively developed in *Dream* are now, for the most part, conspicuous mainly by their absence. Belacqua seems to be commenting indirectly on this when he reflects on his earlier behaviour in 'Ding-Dong': 'Was it not from sitting still among his ideas, other people's ideas, that he had come away? What would he not give now to get on the move again! Away from ideas!' (*MPTK*, 39) 'Sitting still' echoes the title of the first section Beckett wrote for what became *Dream* ('Sedendo et Quiescendo') – the section that he had admitted 'stinks of Joyce.' On the move again, figuratively speaking, in *More Pricks Than Kicks*, thereby fulfilling the literal injunction of the voice heard in the last sentence of *Dream* that 'enjoined him to move on,' Belacqua is, however, also fleeing from ideas that would needlessly complicate, in his view, his theory of motion, the most advanced version of which does not proceed beyond an aspiration for 'pure blank movement.'

In reality, however, Belacqua never even approximates this goal of 'a Beethoven pause' (38): the stories, generally speaking, document in painful, sometimes comically grotesque fashion, how Belacqua's various entanglements with women are what really keeps him on the move. But these contingent relationships reveal his solipsistic theory of 'self-sufficiency' to be just that, a theory, one moreover devoid of serious application. This Belacqua, lo and behold, turns out to be that most boring and earnest of all philanderers, the serial monogamist. These relations of short duration (his wives have a surprising habit of dying off) are a far cry from the aesthetic speculations around Beauty with reference to his 'fair to middling women' in *Dream*. 'Away from ideas!' indeed: this is a far cry from Stephen's 'Away! Away!' as he prepares to join the voices that say 'We are your kinsmen' at the end of *Portrait*. Belacqua cannot afford any such grand flight; the Joycean phrasing of the first sentence in the following sequence is negated by his sorry plight: 'Hither and thither on land and sea! He could not afford that, for he was poor' (36).[58] In short, in most of these stories, with the exception of the first (which had already been published in a slightly different version), 'Dante and the Lobster,' and the third, 'Ding-Dong,' Beckett is, as it were, going through the motions in the interval between novels.

The most significant specific references and allusions in *More Pricks Than Kicks* are obviously derived from Dante, as the first word of the title of the first short story announces. Nearly all the stories contain such references. Critics have also pointed out that Beckett's handling of Dantean materials, particularly in 'Ding-Dong,' is, in calculated fashion, meant to engage Joyce in a game of literary one-upmanship as Beckett extends the disjunctions between Dante's vision and contemporary realities, as Joyce had done in the penultimate story of *Dubliners*, 'Grace.'[59] Another way in which it could, however, be maintained that Joyce's influence is still felt throughout *More Pricks Than Kicks* is to argue, as Adrian Hunter does, that 'all Beckett's early stories, in fact, can be read as counterpoints to Joyce.' The counterpointing, according to Hunter, comes into play as Beckett, 'in the treachery of apprenticeship,'[60] reveals and hence debunks the nature of the epiphanic moment by underscoring just how such a privileged illumination is fabricated, either by the author or by the character himself, possibly as a self-deluding rationalization that leads away from any authentic 'sudden spiritual manifestation' of the inherent 'whatness' of the experience in question. One of Hunter's examples focuses on 'Hairy' Capper Quin in the last story in the collection, 'Draff,' who feels, especially as a would-be writer, that he really should have some special visionary insight upon viewing the remains of Belacqua – this might be appropriate since he is making off with the aforesaid's widow: 'For he could not throw off the impression that he was letting slip a rare occasion to feel something really stupendous' (181). Hunter is making the point – and it is one we have encountered in many of our previous discussions – that Beckett adopts a postmodernist type of relationship between the narrator and the narrated in which the former can comment directly on the metafictional goings-on in his narration; a suspension of the suspension of disbelief. For a reader of Beckett this is announced in the second sentence of his first published work, 'Assumption,' in which the author-character relationship is conveyed by the analogy of the 'buffoon in the loft' and 'the organist' and such byplay is, of course, the staple stock-in-trade of the narrator/author of *Dream*, 'Mr Beckett.'

It is not then surprising to see this modus operandi in effect in *More Pricks Than Kicks*. What is particularly interesting, however, is to revisit its use in the final narratorial voice-over of 'Dante and the Lobster'; this is the most dramatic employment of the technique in the collection and is one of the decisive reasons why the first story is regarded by most readers as the best of the bunch. Beckett carefully prepares readers for the epiphany concerning the lobster being boiled alive, which is for Belacqua an unforeseen event that throws into total disarray his earlier academic rationalizations around the 'famous teaser' from Dante about mercy and justice, and which had led to his own query: 'Why not piety and pity together both, even down below?' (21). Here the moments of revelation constitute a palimpsestic double-voicing:

> Well, thought Belacqua, it's a quick death, God help us all.
> It is not. (22)

Hunter's judgment of these two final sentences of 'Dante and the Lobster' is that 'the intrusive "It is not" sums up the break [Beckett] is attempting throughout these early works with the aesthetic of the modernist short story as he inherited it from Joyce.'[61] But, as we have already seen in a host of examples, Beckett's relationship with Joyce is not to be so simply characterized; as *Dream* formulated it, nothing is easier (that is to say, all *too* easy) than setting up a series of antitheses.

That Beckett is intimately acknowledging his debt to Joyce's writing in these early works is, in fact, nowhere else more tellingly demonstrable than in this instance of the narrator's final rebuttal: 'It is not.' Beckett's striking closure is in fact indebted to a particular passage in the aesthetic theory section of *Portrait*'s last chapter. Stephen is telling Lynch how he has defined pity and terror, something which, he asserts, Aristotle has not done. These two terms are certainly relevant to the 'pity' debate in 'Dante and the Lobster' and the sense of 'terror' that Belacqua professes at the thought of the lobster's imminent demise. Stephen repeats the definitions to Lynch: 'Pity is the feeling which arrests the mind in the presence of whatsoever is grave and constant in human sufferings and unites it with the human sufferer,' whereas 'Terror is the feeling which arrests the mind in the presence of whatsoever is grave and constant in human sufferings and unites it with the secret cause' (178). Stephen, the peripatetic philosopher, then offers his student Lynch an exemplum whereby he might fully apprehend the distinctions being made:

– A girl got into a hansom a few days ago, he went on, in London. She was on her way to meet her mother whom she had not seen for many years. At the corner of a street the shaft of a lorry shivered the window of the hansom in the shape of a star. A long fine needle of the shivered glass pierced her heart. She died on the instant. The reporter called it a tragic death. *It is not*. It is remote from terror and pity according to the terms of my definition. (my italics, *P*, 178)

Sorting out the correspondences that Beckett has carefully set up here by means of his appropriation and redistribution of Stephen's 'It is not,' we arrive at the following ironic juxtapositions: the reports of two superficial observers are refuted; the first Joycean example deals primarily with aesthetic matters, the second Beckettian one with ontological matters. That Stephen is mainly concerned with literary affairs here is made perfectly clear in this rephrasing of himself: 'I mean that the tragic emotion is static. Or rather the dramatic emotion is' (*P*, 179). Belacqua will never be able to achieve Stephen's ideal of the mind being arrested by the aesthetic emotion and thereby being transported above the kinetic responses of 'desire or loathing,' which are deemed indicative only of 'improper art.'

The Belacqua of *More Pricks Than Kicks* is no longer the would-be artist-figure of *Dream*. His theory of movement of some sort at all costs is perhaps Beckett's most telling reminder to readers that Belacqua Shuah (finally he has received a surname – a legal requirement, surely, given his numerous marriages) is no longer the Stephen Dedalus redux whom we saw in *Dream*. Hence it is an instance of poetic justice in a story that shows no evidence of God's or man's mercy to invoke Stephen's 'It is not' to revoke Belacqua's self-comforting rationalization. There are, however, a number of other voices that also resonate in the final 'It is not.' We cannot forget that in addition to the narrator's disruption of the text to express his own disapproval of Belacqua's judgment the 'It is not' simultaneously echoes and parodies a Divine riposte mentioned earlier in 'Dante and the Lobster': the spots on the moon were in Dante's reading the branded face of the dispossessed fugitive Cain, 'seared with the first stigma of God's pity, that an outcast might not die quickly' (12). From this perspective, the final 'It is not' is simply a doctrinal repetition of God's judgment as authenticated by Dante. Whereas Dante could reconcile world and book (it was, after all, a *divine* comedy), Stephen can only endorse in his 'It is not' the aesthetic reality, and

Belacqua can only rather lamely attempt to accommodate himself to the ways of the world; even this is categorically rejected by the narrator's final rupturing of such consolatory illusions in his 'It is not.' So it goes in Beckett's literary world.

3 Re-Joyce-ing *Murphy*

One of the commonplaces of Beckett criticism is that *Murphy* (1938) is Beckett's most 'Joycean' work. What exactly this entails is not, however, made fully clear. Harold Bloom's comments in *The Western Canon* might be regarded as a summary of the views of many Beckett critics in this regard. Bloom begins by declaring 'I love best *Murphy*' for it is 'Beckett at his most Joycean,' going on to comment that the 'negative high spirits of *Murphy*' and 'the beauty of the book' are due to its 'exuberance of language,' then concluding with the judgments that this is 'because it is unabashedly Joycean' and the 'purest comedy Beckett ever wrote.'[1] In Bloom's case, and this is characteristic of a great deal of Beckett criticism that would engage the question of Beckett's relationship with Joyce, a logical sleight of hand is discernible: the definition of certain would-be characteristics of *Murphy* as determined by reference to so-called 'Joycean' ones, without ever detailing just exactly what this signifies. The underlying assumption would seem to be that Beckett can in this instance be intimately aligned (indeed identified) with Joyce since both are comic writers who are fascinated by the play of ideas. But we have no real critical sense of what these terms mean. How is Beckett's comic play similar to Joyce's? Joyce is ironic, to be sure, in his early works but is only a full-blown comic writer in *Ulysses* and *Finnegans Wake*, and the humour there is, even for the 'gentle skimmer' of a reader (as *Murphy* puts it), very different, to say the least, than that found in *Murphy*.

Bloom is writing as a generalist when it comes to the Beckett canon; it should, therefore, be particularly revealing to see how his views compare with those of C.J. Ackerley, whose *Demented Particulars: The Annotated 'Murphy'* (1998) is one of the prime examples of the new scholarship in Beckett studies, which avails itself of Beckett's note-books and manuscripts in order to help trace his sources and to recon-struct the fabrication of his works, an area which is particularly rich in terms of Beckett's first two novels. James Knowlson has commented on how Beckett's early writing methods were very similar to those em-ployed by Joyce. Both 'borrowed freely' from their very extensive read-ing for material to be used in their own work. Striking or memorable phrases and quotations from diverse sources would then be spliced into Beckett's works, and, in many instances during this early period, we can see in Beckett's own notebooks that he checked off the use of the particular item obtained through the 'demon of notesnatching,' as *Dream* puts it. Knowlson, in a memorable phrase, calls this 'a grafting technique' and adds that 'at times it almost runs wild' (*DF*, 106). *Murphy* is a text in which this technique is thoroughly in evidence as testified to by C.J. Ackerley's 255 pages of detailed annotations. The technique may run 'wild' in the sense that *Murphy* is supersaturated with references, mostly of the unacknowledged variety, in a number of areas (literary, philosophical, psychological, astrological/astronomi-cal); but the very pervasiveness of this technique of intertextual layer-ing, as we might refer to it today, is also in *Murphy* very much kept in check in so far as this novel is so clearly focused on 'architechtonics,' on Beckett's need to show himself (and any prospective publisher) that he could write a more or less conventional novel that would indeed be recognized as such by its readers, however odd some of its particular features might be. Anyone now working on *Murphy* most certainly does owe a debt of gratitude to C.J. Ackerley's virtually exhaustive cat-aloguing and commentary on *Murphy*'s various strands of source ma-terial. There are, however, a number of caveat emptors: whereas the particular annotations are in most instances illuminating and informa-tive, the generalizations that are enunciated in his seventeen-page in-troduction and echoed throughout his annotations, particularly in the more extensive ones, which are really mini-essays (for example, on the famous chapter 6 in which Murphy's mind is the ostensible subject at hand), are problematical in a number of instances. There is a real dan-ger at times of not being able to see the novel for the annotations.

Ackerley's opening statement in his 'Introduction' contains his most problematical judgment of all since it is a declaration that is never really subjected to critical scrutiny: 'Samuel Beckett's *Murphy* is a vast, rollicking *jeu d'esprit* in the tradition that runs from Cervantes and Rabelais through Burton and Fielding to *Ulysses*; and it can maintain itself proudly in that company.'[2] This might be classified in its own right as a wayward or, in Ackerley's sense, 'demented' generalization; after all, how many readers of *Murphy*, specialist or non-specialist, have actually felt that the mots justes to describe it would be as 'a vast rollicking *jeu d'esprit*'? Harold Bloom, in the midst of the particular judgments about *Murphy* referred to earlier, supplies a very perceptive generalization about the way in which readers might regard Beckett's first published novel in terms of genre classification: 'it is Beckett's only substantial work that is part of a history of representations, the novel as written by Dickens, Flaubert, and early Joyce, rather than the more problematic "anatomy" form (as Northrop Frye liked to call it) of Rabelais, Cervantes, and Sterne. *Murphy* has a surprisingly continuous narrative, and when my two favorite characters, the Dublin Pythagoreans Neary and Wylie, are at hand, sometimes in the company of "Miss Counihan's hot buttered buttocks," Beckett gives them conversations whose vivacity and high good humor he was not to allow us, or himself, again.'[3] Most readers would probably upon reflection tend towards Bloom's position in which *Murphy* is distinguished formally from the anatomy and a strangely mixed number of elements duly acknowledged, particularly the ironic conjunction throughout *Murphy* of an encompassing real and historically situated world that is, however, mediated by the narrator of the novel in such a way that it is highly stylized and patently artificial, distanced from the mire and the dust of the outside world through a process of literary gentrification.[4] The reader is continually reminded of how the various accounts have been 'expurgated, accelerated, improved and reduced.' Such metamorphoses of shape and structure render problematical the whole relationship between various 'inside' and 'outside' worlds well before the encounter with the well-promoted and heavily advertised chapter 6, which 'pictures' the mind of Murphy.

The decisive term in this chain of transformations whereby so-called raw material is processed into the literary is 'reduced.' Beckett in a letter to George Reavey concerning possible cuts to the completed work as requested by publishers complained, 'Do they not understand that if the book is slightly obscure it is because it is a compression and that to compress it further can only result in making it more obscure?'[5] The term 'compression' as a description of Beckett's modus operandi in *Murphy* will help us to see more clearly the nature of Beckett's strategies as employed in terms of the various ontological insecurities his style uncovers in the midst of the very process of covering things up, especially those various unsavoury contingencies of the outside world with its claims to the real. It is the very nature of this complex process of 'reduction'/'compression' that would lead most readers to query, in varying degrees, Ackerley's judgment that Murphy is a 'vast rollicking *jeu d'esprit*.' Not only is *Murphy* a vastly 'reduced' world, the very nature of its comic spirit is perhaps the essential question that must at some point be addressed – 'rollicking' is most definitely not quite the right word.

Ackerley's various comments in *Demented Particulars* on the influence of Joyce in *Murphy* make for an interesting compilation; as with virtually all commentators before him on this subject, Ackerley's judgments are characterized by a certain ambiguity. His opening gambit is to set *Murphy* within a series of particular works that fall into the category of Menippean satire or the 'anatomy' (though he doesn't explicitly employ these critical terms), the last item in the series being Joyce's *Ulysses*: Beckett 'probably believed that his novel should do for his London […] what *Ulysses* had done for Dublin' (xx). Just as *Murphy* is far too 'reduced' and 'compressed' to fit neatly into the more expansive cataloguing of the anatomy form, its limited focus on parts of London and a refugee band of Irish comic characters in search of a 'seedy solipsist' (82), the eponymous hero himself, could by no stretch of the imagination be compared to what Joyce did for Dublin in *Ulysses*, and Beckett could never have seriously entertained such a rivalry in this particular regard. One man's *Ulysses* is not another man's *Murphy*.

In Ackerley's estimation, 'Joyce was a major force, but Beckett's response to the maestro may be defined as much in terms of resistance as influence' (xvi). To support this, he cites Beckett's assessment in 1989, the last year of his life, that Joyce's accomplishments were 'epic, heroic,' a road that Beckett says he couldn't follow, instead choosing what Ackerley calls 'a central theme in *Murphy*, the fundamental unheroic' (xvi). Turning to the actual annotations on Joyce in *Demented Particulars*, Ackerley summarizes the situation in such a way that it makes one wonder to what degree *Murphy* might indeed be written in a 'Joycean manner': 'Borrowings in *Murphy* from Joyce are relatively few, and those from *Ulysses* are mostly from "Ithaca" and "Eumaeus," where style obfuscates certainty' (xvi). Joyce himself figures nowhere in his list of 'big five' sources (Schopenhauer, Geulincx, Burnet, Woodworth, Whitaker).

Mere tabulation of the annotations for *Murphy* will not, however, come anywhere near explaining the novel as a whole. For example, the much-vaunted references to Geulincx (the *'Ubi nihil vales'*) and Democritus (the 'Naught is more real'), which Beckett himself promoted to critics as 'the points of departure' for a study of his work,[6] as well as the host of associated ideas and references, literary and philosophical, which Ackerley has so thoroughly collated and commented on – all are, finally, secondary manifestations of an underlying and more fundamental ongoing debate-cum-dialogue with *Portrait*'s theory of art, which runs through all of these early works, ('Assumption' *Dream of Fair to Middling Women* and *Murphy*), and which Beckett only really begins to move beyond in terms of forging his own way in *Watt*. Many of the so-called determining influences in *Murphy* are really only supplementary for, to adapt Beckett's statement in 'Dante ... Bruno . Vico .. Joyce,' this novel is only *about* something; it is *not* that something itself: in other words, the language of *Murphy* can in no way be said to embody the ideas, for example, of 'naught' and 'nihil.' Here content *is not* form. What *Murphy* is arguably *about* is Beckett's working out of his own aesthetic position vis-à-vis Joyce, who is central to this novel's structure and shaping, in ways very different and much more detailed than those characterized above by Ackerley.

The opening sentences of *Murphy* are derived from a rewriting of the scene that precedes Stephen's encounter with the birdgirl at the end of chapter 4. Stephen muses over his 'strange name,' which echoes the 'fabulous artificer' of Greek myth, and regards this as a 'prophecy' (149) of his own role as an artist-to-be: 'His heart trembled; his breath came faster and a wild spirit passed over his limbs *as though he were soaring sunward'* (149–50, my emphasis). On the other hand, *Murphy* begins perforce with the reader contemplating the most common of all Irish surnames as announced on the cover of the book and repeated on the title page. Far from the sense in *Portrait* of a beckoning destiny to be fulfilled in a host of inspirational ways, *Murphy* opens with the sense of a prescripted and deterministic world: 'The sun shone, having no alternative, on the nothing new. Murphy sat out of it, *as though he were free*, in a mew in West Brompton' (1, my emphasis). Ackerley supplies the anticipated annotation of the well-known reference to Ecclesiastes ('and there is no new thing under the sun'), adds a note on the dictum from Heraclitus of diametrically opposed import ('The sun is new every day'), and then glosses the 'as though he were free' of *Murphy*'s second sentence in terms of the theme of retreating into the 'freedom of the mind' in order to escape the inexorable laws of the big world (1). Ackerley might also have cited Richard Ellmann's description of Joyce's next writing project after

Ulysses: 'It was a wholly new book based on the premise that there is nothing new under the sun' (*JJ*, 545). But his conventional annotation cannot recognize the dialogical nature of Beckett's 'as though he were free' in conjunction with 'as though he were soaring sunward.' The reason for this is that the echolalia of the two clauses doesn't fall neatly into the category of conventional 'allusion'; here is an instance in which the encoded reference does not even register on the annotator's radar screen since it is at once too micro and too macro in nature. Beckett's encapsulation via the two clauses leads to a number of encompassing issues that concern his ongoing debate with Joyce over a number of foundational aesthetic principles, as was the case in 'Assumption' and *Dream*, largely suspended in *More Pricks Than Kicks*, and now in *Murphy* reintroduced, albeit in a way that aims to keep itself out of sight of the reader as 'gentle skimmer.'

Recognition of the detailed referencing of *Portrait* in the opening sentences of *Murphy* does, however, afford a number of significant critical advantages. Firstly, it reminds us yet again how Joyce is the major figure, literary or otherwise, that Beckett is engaged with here, no matter how other more obvious references such as those so thoroughly annotated by Ackerley are foregrounded. The telescoping of 'as though he were free'/ 'as though he were soaring sunward' creates a situation in which both references supply a critical perspective on the two central characters being focused on. 'Soaring sunward,' young Stephen Dedalus is, as we know, more likely to play the role of Icarus than that of the 'fabulous artificer' – the opening chapter of *Ulysses* most decidedly brings down to earth his romantic sense of a great destiny awaiting him. Similarly, Murphy's dramatic reversal of strategy and direction – 'the corner in which he sat was curtained off from the sun' (1) – really amounts to much the same thing: both Stephen Dedalus and Murphy seek, albeit from different ends of the spectrum, to find a means of transcending their worlds. Stephen's romantic flight of fantasy is all too painfully obvious; for example: 'His soul was soaring in the air beyond the world and the body he knew was purified in a breath and delivered of incertitude and made radiant and commingled with the element of spirit' (150). A comic version of this trance-like state of sublimation is presented in *Murphy*'s opening chapter as our 'hero' ties himself up in his rocking chair and strives to set himself 'free in his mind' (2).

Both Joyce and Beckett present critical portraits of their central characters – Joyce implicitly by means of his ironically detached narrative presence, Beckett more explicitly as his narrator interjects direct commentary belittling Murphy's ersatz mysticism (and this is nowhere more in evidence than in the famous chapter 6, which purports to deal with Murphy's mind). Beckett is working with Joyce in the sense that both authors are critically investigating the possibility of a middle ground to put into perspective the extreme positions adopted by their characters. The obvious difference remains, of course, that Dedalus is a would-be artist and Beckett's Murphy is no such thing, a *fainéant* – a 'seedy solipsist' who believes only in his own self-serving 'system' above all other claims of the world at large. Nevertheless, Beckett and his narrator in *Murphy* are, as we will see, very interested indeed in testing out, evaluating, and proposing alternatives to those aesthetic principles formulated by Stephen Dedalus in *Portrait*, which from the very beginning of Beckett's writing career have supplied important touchstone points when it comes to theorizing about the nature of art.

The first two chapters of *Murphy*, which act as a prelude to the work as a whole, plunge the reader into the aesthetic debate that is at the centre of the final chapter of *Portrait*: the nature and art of Beauty and how it constitutes a world unto itself that is distinct from the outside world of the 'marketplace.' In the opening scene of *Murphy*, we are confronted with our protagonist strapped naked in his rocking chair, striving mightily to escape into his mind and hence avoid those contingencies of a capitalistic world of '*Quid pro quo! Quid pro quo!*' and of sundry 'wares [...] being cried' (2). The obvious pun on 'whatness' as commercial exchange (a pound/quid) shows us that we are in these opening pages starting from an origin in the economic world and are far from the more rarified aestheticizing of Stephen Dedalus in the last chapter of *Portrait*. That Beckett, however, expects the attentive reader to identify a series of similarities and differences between his novel and Joyce's is implicit in the narrator's comment in the second paragraph on these various 'sights and sounds' from the outside world that 'he did not like': 'They *detained* him in the world to which they belonged, but not he, as he fondly hoped' (2, my italics). 'Detained' and its various meanings are also foregrounded at the very beginning of the aesthetics section in *Portrait*, Stephen's intellectual skirmishing with the dean of studies and the various verbal contretemps thus encountered: 'One difficulty, said Stephen, in esthetic discussion is to know whether words are being used according to the literary tradition or according to the tradition of the marketplace. I remember a sentence of Newman's in which he says of the Blessed Virgin that she was detained in the full company of the saints. The use of the word in the marketplace is quite different. *I hope I am not detaining you*' (164). For

Beckett's Murphy, of course, the fundamental and abiding problem is his ambiguous fluctuation between these two meanings of 'detained' (not to mention a third meaning that is always in the background: to be 'detained' by the authorities within structures such as those represented in the novel by Pentonville Prison).

Whereas young Stephen Dedalus can pontificate about a theory of Beauty that is self-contained and autonomous, the unfortunate Murphy is caught between definitions, between worlds, and is caught in a tug of war between his physical attractions to the world of quid pro quo (Celia's body, ginger biscuits) and the world of intellectual refuge in his mind, the 'little world' as distinct from the 'big world' of the marketplace, 'where he could love himself' (7). The underlying dramatic contrasts between the world of *Portrait*'s aesthetic sections and that found at the opening of *Murphy* are a key determinant in shaping Beckett's ideas in this novel, and once again, as was the case in 'Assumption' and *Dream of Fair to Middling Women*, the key terms involve 'static' versus 'kinetic' aesthetic responses. Stephen is very clear on his views of this topic: 'The feelings excited by improper art are kinetic, desire or loathing. Desire urges us to possess, to go to something; loathing urges us to abandon, to go from something. These are kinetic emotions. The acts which excite them, pornographical or didactic, are therefore improper acts. The esthetic emotion (I use the general term) is therefore static. The mind is arrested and raised above desire and loathing' (179). Compare this with the lynchpin of the plot of *Murphy* in which the title character's dilemma is cast in these terms: 'The part of him that he hated craved for Celia, the part that he loved shrivelled up at the thought of her' (8). In either case, the action is inescapably 'kinetic' in nature, determined by 'desire or loathing.'

Murphy's situation is definitely of a kinetic nature, through and through, as we first encounter him. Of more import, however, is the even more crucial distinction between himself and a Stephen Dedalus in terms of their vocations: whereas Stephen's whole focus is on his role as artist and the longed-for transformation from would-be status to the artist proper who can reveal the essence of things, their *quidditas* or 'whatness,' Murphy's even more problematical status as a former theological student who is seeking the freedom of the third zone of his mind (as described in section 6 of the novel) is that of an escape artist who would be one with the nihilistic 'flux of forms' (112). Such mystical escapism, openly mocked and scorned by the narrator of *Murphy*, is presented as a paradoxical search for 'pleasure' that entails, however, the very annihilation of self and all egotistic attachments. Despite the obvious differences here between Stephen Dedalus and Murphy, the similarities should also not be lost sight of. Both Stephen and Murphy would prefer to live in the little worlds of their minds within which they would construct their ideal versions of reality and, palimpsestically, impose those views upon the outside world. And it is vitally important to realize that in both works the real testing out of the validity of ideas about art and life has very little to do, in the final analysis, with some doubtful aestheticizing (Stephen) and some even more dubious philosophizing of an obviously ersatz nature (Murphy), but a great deal to do with various images – embodied and disembodied – of women and the ideas of Beauty thereby brought to mind, as well as other more down-to-earth considerations of the complex dialectic between life and art.

In both works these issues are identified with the classical ideal of beauty and creativity/fertility represented by different versions of Venus Aphrodite. Immediately after the passage from *Portrait* cited above dealing with kinetic or 'improper art,' Lynch, Stephen's partner throughout the long section on aesthetics, retorts by reminding Stephen about the time he wrote his name 'in pencil on the backside of the Venus of Praxiteles in the museum' (179). A couple of pages later, Stephen, in full swing now on his thesis that true art involves stasis not kinesis, informs Lynch that he would not have been tempted to write his name in pencil across the hypotenuse of a right-angled triangle. To which Lynch replies: 'No, [...] give me the hypotenuse of the Venus of Praxiteles' (181). In full flight, in conversation now really only with himself, Stephen deigns no reply and moves on to Plato and the idea 'that beauty is the splendour of truth.' Lynch's graffiti story echoes that about the man who was so taken by Praxiteles' likeness of Aphrodite of Knidos that he hid himself in the shrine and at night came out to embrace her and left behind a stain, a souvenir of his lust. Lynch's action serves to bring into ironic juxtaposition high art and popular-culture irreverence. More to the point, it brings into critical focus Stephen's own relationships with women; in the world of his mind and imagination as a creator-figure, he would authorize their being with his own signature. Such fantasies of power via the act of creation (the Pygmalion myth) are evident in Stephen's idealizations with respect to Mercedes, the birdgirl, and the *belle dame sans merci* of his villanelle that follows in the episode after the aesthetic section.[7] Real women who exist autonomously in the world pose more problems for Stephen, whose twenty-five pages or so of critically investigating Beauty are cast aside when Lynch whispers to him, 'Your beloved is here': 'His mind, emptied of theory and courage, lapsed back into a listless peace' (187). Joyce's irony at this juncture is palpable: if Stephen is going to become the artist capable of writing a work such as *Portrait* itself, he will need to find a way of accommodating the ideal *and* the real, particularly when it comes to the question of women and beauty.

Stephen is hence 'detained' among the company of his idealized and stereotyped views of women; since Murphy is, as we have seen, 'detained' in the marketplace and in this world of quid pro quo, it is only fitting that the heavenly body that exercises control over him is that of the prostitute Celia. And when she moves, 'accompanied delightedly by her hips' (11), the result is definitely kinetic – a generation of desire. Chapter 2 opens with a page of measurements, giving her vital statistics for all the various tidbits. This catalogue of various measurements could be regarded as a parodic version of the Bertillon criminal identification system ('identification anthropométrique'), a fitting enough tabulation, realistically speaking, for Celia the prostitute would most certainly 'have form,' possess a criminal record. In Beckett's notebook for *Murphy*, he wrote beside these various measurements: 'Venus de Milo.' As Ackerley comments in his annotation, this is a joke of sorts, since the 'intact' Celia is here depicted complete with missing parts, namely, forearm and wrist (*DP*, 19). The Venus de Milo (so called because it was found on the island of Melos) was a Greek statue of the first century BC that, according to E.H. Gombrich, 'used the achievements and methods of Praxiteles.' Gombrich goes on to add that in the generations after Praxiteles (towards the end of the fourth century) 'artists discovered the means of animating the features without destroying their beauty' and 'they learned how to seize the wakings of the individual soul [...] and make portraits in our sense of the word.'[8] This is exactly what happens when the statuesque measurements of Celia on the first page of chapter 2 are set in motion, 'animated.' But the portrait of that young man Murphy has nothing at all to do with the enterprise of an artist, whether of the visionary sort or not. This is underlined by the ironic echoing in Celia's first meeting with Murphy of Stephen Dedalus's holy encounter with the birdgirl: '[Murphy] arrested the movement and gazed at Celia. For perhaps two minutes she suffered this gladly' (14).[9] Murphy regards Celia as all too real in that she pulls him away from the nether regions of his mind and plunges him into the 'mercantile gehenna' (40) in her demands (backed up by her 'siege' and 'blockade' of Murphy in their sexual warfare) that he get a job so that she can quit hers and then the two of them can make 'music' together. In short, Beckett in *Murphy* is clearly engaged in a dialogue with Joyce over fundamental aesthetic matters, but he approaches the question by reversing the terms in so far as Murphy, against his will, encounters his Beauty in the marketplace where he is a detainee, whereas Stephen Dedalus when we last see him in *Portrait* is 'detained,' in quite a different sense of the word, in the literary realm. He even adds in his final diary section that 'Statues of women, if Lynch be right, should always be fully draped, one hand of the woman feeling regretfully her own hinder parts' (216).

Stephen has a long ways yet to go, but at least there is the chance that he might escape his somewhat priggish aestheticism and move towards a 'new experience' whereby a new synthesis or modus vivendi might be effected. On the other hand, there is no such hope (modernist or otherwise) for Murphy since he is drawn away from the contingent world, the sublunary, towards what he sees as the realm of his true 'escape,' as typified by the third zone of his mind and the self-enclosed world of Mr Endon in the asylum, the Magdalen Mental Mercy Seat. Indeed, at the centre of the novel is Murphy's departure from Celia to take his job at the asylum. Murphy, to his credit, is not even a murphy-artist, that con-man figure who perpetrates with his prostitute girlfriend the fleecing of her clients by nefarious means. This Murphy is a small-time grafter who cooks the books sent to his dutch uncle benefactor Mr Quigley and defrauds Vera the waitress and her employer of a few pence for his tea. The style of *Murphy* is, as always, the decisive factor, suspending this novel between the real world and the ideal world. The mire and dust of the contingent world in time are kept at bay, though we do at times get glimpses, particularly in the subplot shenanigans, of a world of the 'charVenus' and of 'sausage and mash sex' (37). Such unsavoury images (for example, Miss Counihan's 'hot buttered buttocks' – the 'gentle reader' should consult with caution Ackerley's annotation here) are masked by the elevated and wittily 'reduced' style, for the most part. Thus *Murphy* is, however uneasily, more *The Shephearde's Calendar* than *The Newgate Calendar*, more Oscar Wilde than Jonathan Wild; though the shadow of Pentonville Prison is thrown across the novel and there are references at various points to 'touts,' 'twisters,' 'toffs,' 'catspaws,' and 'double-crosses,' the literary idealizations (and those hundreds of references to the literary-cultural tradition tabulated by Ackerley) keep this reality at bay, even if it cannot deny it as the underlying ground for our critical evaluation of this ambiguously suspended novel.

At the centre of this state of 'in-betweenness' is the tug of war in which Celia is caught between the competing needs and demands of her paternal grandfather, Mr Willoughby Kelly, and the other man in her life, Murphy, who seems to have no family to speak of. Celia, the Venus-Muse, the incarnation of both the vulgar and heavenly Venuses referred to by Plato in *The Symposium*, is caught between the differing demands of a Joyce-like figure (Mr Kelly) and a Beckett-like figure (Murphy). A long time ago J.C.C. Mays pointed out in convincing fashion many aspects of Mr Kelly that suggest an identification of some sort with Joyce: for example, 'the yachting cap, the endless work in progress (in bed), the Icaran-kite-flying and the attempts to join heaven and earth.'[10] Mays adds that what is really of greater importance is how 'Murphy's divergences from Mr Kelly coincide with Beckett's divergences from Joyce' and gives the example of how Mr Kelly's Christian name Willoughby sets him clearly in opposition to the will-lessness of the Geulincxian *'Ubi nihil vales, ibi nihil velis.'*[11] (The surname Kelly was presumably adopted as the most recognizably Irish name to follow alphabetically after Joyce.)

But the Joycean dimensions of Mr Kelly and his connection to Murphy can be taken much further than Mays's starting points. One of the defining particularities of Beckett's subtexts in his first three major critical probes into the aesthetic question is how Beckett's encounter with Joyce is mediated by a third party, namely, George Meredith, and, in particular, his masterpiece *The Egoist*. This underlying reference system reaches its most complex and sophisticated form in *Murphy*; indeed, one might go so far as to say 'Meredith, Meredith, Meredith' constitutes another MMM to go along with the three M's of the music Celia and Murphy make, the asylum that draws him away from her (the Magdalen Mental Mercy Seat), and, of course, the most important triad of all, Money, Money, Money, which makes the world go round. Sir Willoughby Patterne, that monumental egoist of a fittingly self-named narrative, who can only see himself in so far as he is reflected by the ideal views he would have others adopt towards him, is, as it were, split in two in Beckett's novel. The Willoughby part becomes a Joyce-like figure and the Patterne becomes Murphy, whose name, as many critics long ago realized, echoes the Greek *morphé*, for form or pattern, as well as suggesting a different type of transformation in the Latin cognate 'Morpheus,' for dream-like changes of form. The pun on Patterne/pattern is also made several times throughout *The Egoist* for, as *Murphy* puts it, 'In the beginning was the pun' (65). Some of the key questions that then begin to proliferate are as follows: can any reconciliation be effected between Willoughby's 'willed' reality, over which certain controls or artistic techniques may be exercised, and Murphy's would-be 'will-lessness' and formlessness, as suggested in the projected image of the third zone of his mind, a 'matrix of surds'; where, finally, does the subject matter for aesthetic expression lie – in the outside world, the inside world, or a combination of the two; and, when these essentially male personified views have had their say and also been tested out in the rest of the novel, where does this leave Celia, the personification of 'Beauty' itself, which is traditionally at the heart of the aesthetic question?

Ackerley has stated that in his view the best short summary of *Murphy* is still Ludovic Janvier's *'Andromaque* jouée par les Marx Brothers' (*DP*, xxiv). The awareness of the underlying Meredithian patterning in *Murphy* affords another phrasing, one which, moreover, addresses the central plot of *Murphy*, that involving Mr Kelly, Murphy, and Celia (and, later, Mr Endon), and not simply the circumferential one of the subplot machinations of Neary and company as Janvier's does. *Murphy* is a rewriting of Meredith's *The Egoist*, Sir Willoughby Patterne having been divided in two as Mr Willoughby Kelly and Murphy, with Celia in the middle as a variation on the Clara Middleton figure of *The Egoist*. What this loses in brevity it gains in an encompassing complexity that will afford a new way of critically engaging *Murphy*. Or, if an attempt at a wittily memorable phrase is de rigueur: *Murphy* is *The Egoist* replayed by Joyce and Beckett, minus the comic resolution.

The most important Joycean characteristic of all that Mr Kelly possesses, and one not mentioned by Mays, is that he actually speaks Joyce's words. While the references to Joyce may be surprisingly small in *Murphy* according to Ackerley, the rider must be added that several of them are, nevertheless, decisive in the plotting and ideational structure of the work (for example, the use of 'detained' in chapter 1). Such is the case also in chapter 2, which focuses on Celia's briefing of Mr Kelly concerning the status and nature of her relationship with Murphy. Mr Kelly quickly becomes very impatient with Celia's recounting of this story and admonishes her to 'be less beastly circumstantial' and shortly thereafter, even more emphatically, commands her to 'lay off' these 'demented particulars' and 'get up to your man' (13). William York Tindall develops in his introduction to *A Reader's Guide to 'Finnegans Wake'* a comparison between Joyce and Beckett that could serve as a veritable gloss on Mr Kelly's objection to Celia's story about

Murphy: 'Joyce lived in a world where accepted frames – Vico, Ireland, the Church – gave meaning to particulars. The particulars of his reluctant disciple [Beckett], who lives in a contingent world, a mess without frames, are meaningless particulars.' Introducing this judgment, Tindall also states how Joyce prepares us for Beckett by his own recognition of 'uncertainties about identity and communication.'[12] And, as Ackerley astutely points out, most of Beckett's references to *Ulysses* in *Murphy* are to 'Eumaeus' and 'Ithaca,' which deal with the erosion of the lines of communication at the end of a very long day, one of the longest in literary history.

Be that as it may, Mr Willoughby Kelly is very explicit in his injunction to Celia after he has determined that in terms of aesthetic apprehension as well as those of the marketplace Murphy is a fragmented nullity, a dud with no prospects to speak of, lacking *integritas* (a 'schizoid spasmophile') and *consonantia* (his irrational heart), it thus being a foregone conclusion that Mr Kelly's query 'What is he?' (17) will offer no glimpse of 'whatness,' of *quidditas*, since Murphy is a seeker of the darkness of the third zone of his so-called mind. Mr Kelly delivers his injunction: '"Sever your connexion with this Murphy," he said, "before it is too late"' (24). These are the very words Leopold Bloom uses (though Joyce's spelling is American and Beckett's British) at the end of 'Eumaeus' in a more diplomatic way (very unlike Mr Kelly's imperative) to suggest discreetly that Stephen Dedalus 'sever his connection' with one Buck Mulligan, who disparagingly mocked the young man and who could do him no good on either the personal or artistic plane. We will, in due course, see two other variations of this 'sever the connexion' motif at key junctures in the novel's structure: at its centre and its conclusion. For here it is enough to chart what parallels are set up by this Joycean patterned echo in *Murphy*:

(i) *Ulysses*: Mr Leopold Bloom counsels Stephen Dedalus 'to sever the connection' with Buck Mulligan.
(ii) *Murphy*: Mr Willoughby Kelly orders Celia to 'sever the connexion' with Murphy.

In this patterning, it is, of course, Celia, surprisingly, who is at the centre and who occupies a position that implies a parallel course to that of Stephen Dedalus, who is teetering on the brink of finding his true subject matter via the 'communion' with Bloom.

Whose story is then really at the centre of *Murphy*? This is a vital question, and its answer is by no means obvious. The novel takes its title from Murphy; the narrator distinguishes the eponymous 'hero' from all the other characters, who are said to be mere 'puppets'; unlike them, Murphy is said not to 'whinge' (122); the minor characters of the subplot all actively pursue Murphy where their 'medians meet' (213). But at the same time the attentive reader does see Murphy 'whinge,' does see him go through the same marionette motions as other characters. And, of course, the most decisive factor of all in this supposed issue of Murphy's centrality is the famous chapter 6 in which, the narrator tells us, against his own will it would seem, that the time has come when 'the expression "Murphy's mind" has to be attempted' (107). Before dealing with how this mind sees itself, the most important point of all to note is the openly scornful dismissal of this topic by the narrator. The narrator himself is clearly of two minds about Murphy, and whether Murphy occupies more than a nominal, titular significance is a moot point to be clarified by the rest of the novel.

Chapter 6 of *Murphy* has almost been done to death by critics.[13] This incredible pastiche of various intellectual systems that has kept so many critics busy for so long is perhaps most sensibly regarded as a particularly Beckettian joke of the Joycean sort about writers supplying an endless work in progress for their critics. J.D. O'Hara's view, for example, is that chapter 6 can be deemed 'irrelevant' once the reader realizes that the proffered structural principles of the novel 'as fragments from one subject, Philosophy' turn out to be just that, fragments which do not cohere into any more significant whole.[14] He then goes on to make a number of distinctions that are important for trying to see what Murphy is indeed really about if the philosophical elements are, in the last analysis, more or less irrelevant since *Murphy*/Murphy does not act upon them. O'Hara's alternative approach is to term *Murphy* a love story and to go on to explore the structural uses of depth psychology in the novel via Beckett's understanding of Freud's discussion of narcissism. However, O'Hara grants in the conclusion to his discussion that 'even when we turn to the Freudian underpinnings of the plot, we must acknowledge that they appear to have been added late and to be rather skimpy.'[15] A more profitable and substantial engagement with the issue of 'self-love,' of egoism, is via the Meredithian mediation of the Joyce-Beckett aesthetic dialogue, for, as we have seen, it has determined in many ways the very structure of the novel and the key ideas that the characters actually embody, as distinct from that in many ways very misleading tour de force that is chapter 6.

In the 'Prelude' of *The Egoist*, entitled 'A Chapter of which the Last Page only is of any Importance,' Meredith acknowledges the governing

influence of the 'biggest book on earth,'[16] whose title is the Book of Egoism, and it is this narrative and its particular spectacles that attract the
Comic Spirit. But since this 'certain big book' is virtually coexistent with
the world itself, the narrator of *The Egoist* maintains 'that to be profitable
to us the Book needs a powerful compression' (33). As we have already
seen, Beckett in his 1936 letter to Reavey on *Murphy* also described it as
'a compression.' Other aspects of the operating principles of *The Egoist* as
set out in the 'Prelude' seem to have determined the very approach to
rendering experience that Beckett adopted in *Murphy*, especially a certain aesthetic distancing from 'the dust of the struggling outer world'
(though as we will see with Murphy's death there are 'violent crashes,'
which are also strictly excluded from Meredith's highly stylized world),
as well as the pursuit of characters within a definite situation that 'rejects
all accessories in the exclusive pursuit of them and their speech' (33). So
much for the techniques that Beckett has clearly adopted and adapted
from Meredith here: they have value only in so far as they make for a
critical illumination of an egoism that no longer functions in a socially
constructive manner and instead brings harm to others and, in the end,
self-destruction to those proponents of egregious self-conceit and utter
self-absorption.

The last words of Meredith's 'Prelude' (and only the 'Last Page' is
supposedly of any 'Importance') underscore the paradoxical nature of
self-love as 'the comic drama of the suicide':

If this line of verse be not yet in our literature,
Through very love of self himself he slew;
let it be admitted for his epitaph. (38)

Or let it also be admitted as a variant form of the epigraph to chapter 6
of Beckett's *Murphy*: '*Amor intellectualis quo Murphy se ipsum amat*' (The
intellectual love with which Murphy loved himself). Spinoza's God as
eternal cause of His own infinite perfections can bestow upon Himself
an 'intellectual love.' By substituting Murphy for God in this version,
Beckett is not simply mocking his title character's self-love; he is also
showing that such incredible hubris can only lead to his own undoing
(an intellectual felo de se, anticipating his actual end) since to end up
in the third zone of his mind 'in the will-lessness, a mote in its absolute
freedom' (113) is to reach an impasse that affords no way out. Simply
put, Murphy can only love himself in this ideal fashion by absolutely
denying the very existence of any such self at all – a veritable dead end.

No wonder the narrator is so contemptuous; only God or a madman could make sense of this patchwork and, alas, Murphy discovers he is neither. There is hence an obvious satirical and comic correction directed against Murphy in chapter 6 by the narratorial commentary. The bathos of chapter 6 will be supplemented later by a certain sense of pathos when Murphy discovers with Mr Endon how his own 'picture' of his mind is, in practice, not reconcilable with any such radical and absolute separation from the social world. As Meredith's narrator says in the 'Prelude': 'The Egoist surely inspires pity. He who would desire to clothe himself at everybody's expense, and is of that desire condemned to strip himself naked, he, if pathos ever had a form, might be taken for the actual person' (36). Yes, Murphy does, indeed, 'whinge': in chapter 6 Murphy tarts up his supposed 'system' by 'clothing himself' in a host of embezzled items from the philosophical tradition. Naked in his rocker, as in the opening of the novel, Murphy's situation is exposed in all its ludicrousness as an 'off his rocker' onanistic fantasy. The only 'form' that Murphy (*morphē*) actually attains is the risibly pathetic.

Chapter 6 of *Murphy* could be regarded as another critique of the Dedalian aesthetic system. The whole philosophical 'compression' could be seen as having as its ultimate goal a comic subversion of *claritas* – the culminating insight of the third phase of aesthetic apprehension as developed in *Portrait* in terms of that 'radiance' which is the *quidditas* or 'whatness' of a thing. The first phase of aesthetic apprehension as outlined in *Portrait* involves a 'luminous' drawing of a boundary line around the aesthetic image that defines it as distinct from 'the immeasurable background of space or time'; the Gestalt references to figure and ground and the various references, ironic and otherwise, to various psychologists of this school show Beckett engaging Stephen's first principles via contemporary developments in new intellectual disciplines such as psychology. What starker contrast could be posed than that between *Portrait*'s 'luminous silent stasis of esthetic pleasure' and *Murphy*'s 'the third, the dark, was a flux of forms'? In Beckett's rendition the decisive qualifications centre around the phrase 'of esthetic pleasure.' First of all, Murphy pictures to himself the third zone as one in which he exercises no will (not to mention aesthetic apprehension), but is 'caught up in a tumult of non-Newtonian motion. So pleasant that pleasant was not the word' (112–13). Again, a central Dedalian aesthetic tenet is being tested out, in this instance by setting it against the cosmology of modern physics, which does, indeed, seem to be light years away from *Portrait*'s Aristotelian and Thomistic revisions. But all of this, of course, goes for naught since these views serve in *Murphy* no aesthetic purpose at all but are merely the narcissistic fantasies of Murphy as escape artist.

The seminal statement in chapter 6 appears in the very middle of the 'bulletin' and concerns the implications of Murphy's view of his mind as 'a closed system' (109): 'Of infinitely more interest than how this came to be so was the manner in which it might be exploited' (110). Who is being spoken of here? Murphy could only be said to 'exploit' this situation in terms of his own self-satisfaction. But, for the narrator, if such an aesthetic exploitation could be somehow effected then there would be the responsibility to find the means to incorporate such new perspectives into the artistic enterprise. Of course, nothing of the sort is more than at most hinted at in *Murphy*; the narrator here can laugh at Murphy and heap scorn on his efforts to escape responsibility for all of his actions, whether in the 'big world' or the 'little world' of his mind. But the narrator's version of *Murphy*, however 'reduced' or 'improved,' does not engage these critical issues either – hence the uneasy laughter of *Murphy* and the difficulty of classifying just what kind of writing *Murphy* consists of in the final analysis.

Joyce gets the last laugh for his works could arguably be said to embody a form of comedy that aims at the condition of stasis by arousing joy – a type of comic *claritas* that led Joyce to term 'comedy the perfect manner in art.'[17] Whereas *Ulysses* could be defined as a 'comic epic poem in prose,' *Murphy* – a novel about the quest for forms, patterns, manners – resists any classification for it is an uneasy mix of various types and theories of comedy. For example, the three zones of chapter 6 could be easily adapted to the three major theories of comedy: in zone one the superiority theory, in which laughter is directed at those inferior specimens who do not quite measure up to the 'standard,' neatly encapsulated in the grotesque 'new arrangement' of Miss Carridge being raped by a Ticklepenny; in zone two the prime characteristics of the incongruity theory, via the grotesque contrasting of the slothful Belacqua dreaming his life away before beginning his ascent up the Purgatorial Mountain; and in zone three a version of the relief theory of comedy as developed by Freud, in which various contradictory impulses and inhibitions find their release through the unconscious and the subterfuges of language play in various forms such as punning associations and witty evasions of conventional pieties,[18] typified by Murphy's incredible sense of the 'self' being freed. The cosmic comedy, if one can call it that, of zone three of Murphy's mind is ultimately of an absurdist nature and a long way from Joyce's 'joy' of the 'perfect manner in art.'

It is the uneasy fluctuation between these various approaches to the comic, without any Joycean sense of an encompassing vision to supply coherence, in the central plot concerning Murphy, Celia, Mr Kelly, and Mr Endon that leads to the conclusion that *Murphy* might best be characterized as having the structure of a 'bad joke.' And it is Murphy's vindictive and self-indulgent telling of one of his favourite jokes that occupies what is, mathematically as well as thematically, the centre of the novel (139–40). Here is the veritable turning point of *Murphy*: Murphy has, at last, landed a job at the asylum, replacing Ticklepenny, and this would seem to have fulfilled Celia's fondest wish. Hence Murphy's dismay when he realizes that Celia, 'so profoundly distressed' (137) by the old boy's suicide, no longer seems to care and now pays scant attention to him. Murphy's response is 'A decayed valet severs the connexion and you set up a niobaloo as though he were your fourteen children. No. I am at a loss' (137–8). Murphy here takes up Joyce's words from *Ulysses* used earlier by Mr Willoughby Kelly in his advice to Celia to 'chuck' Murphy; in Murphy's adaptation at the centre of the novel, the phrase now obviously means to sever the life cord. Then Celia, inadvertently, cues Murphy's joke by correcting him: '"Not valet," said Celia. "Butler. Ex-butler."' Murphy warms up for his joke by responding: '"XX butler," said Murphy. "Porter"' (139). The pun sets the scene for the joke Murphy now tells, after 'a long silence.' It is in this hiatus, which a novel cannot convey dramatically, that one imagines Murphy carefully calculating his joke and how it will affect Celia, and how it will enable him to get back at her for neglecting his 'heroic' success on the job trail. The joke, such as it is, seems a bit of a 'Joe Miller' (mentioned earlier in *Murphy*, 65), a stale old chestnut named after the eighteenth-century jest book that took its name from this actor of farces. Question: '"Why did the barmaid champagne?" Answer: "Because the stout porter bitter."' The joke, we are told, did not amuse Celia and could not possibly have done so 'at the best of times and places'; and this clearly is not one of them, coming as it does when, for various reasons, both Celia and Murphy in their own ways are, not to mince words, 'severing their connexion.'

This joke is not so much addressed to Celia as self-reflexively directed to Murphy, a narcissistic act that is, nevertheless, clearly designed to upset her. His reactions are extreme, to say the least: the narrator allows us access again to Murphy's mind (a further 'bulletin,' of sorts, is indeed being issued); Murphy imagines 'seeing the scene' in detailed cartoon-style, such as might be found in the *Illustrated London News* or a series of seaside postcards, and virtually works himself into an epileptic fit. Murphy is transported to this extreme state by adding a punchline that appears to be completely disconnected from the actual context of the old boy's death, Celia's profound distress, and Murphy's imminent departure for his new position: 'Then the nip, and Tintoretto's *Origin of the Milky Way*' (140). At the end of the joke we get what might anachronistically be termed a 'Woody Allen,' a conjunction of the well-worn popular jest with an upmarket cultural reference. Ackerley's annotation gives a good description of Tintoretto's painting: 'It depicts Jupiter's attempt to guarantee the immortality of his son by the mortal Alcmeme by holding up the infant Heracles to drink from the breast of the sleeping Juno who, waking suddenly, spills her milk in two streams, one falling to form the lilies on the ground, and the other creating the milky way.' He adds that in Murphy's manic response, 'one compatible with the way Jupiter is holding the child and the look on Juno's face, the goddess has been awoken painfully by a nip on the nipple' (129).[19] Why this joke at such an important juncture in the novel's structure, at its very centre? One response might be that the ostensibly irrelevant joke is a Freudian link to Murphy's unconscious and hence an accurate 'bulletin' concerning his anxieties about his relationship with Celia and his 'infidelities' in seeking other 'pleasures,' such as those offered in the third zone of his mind and soon to be proffered by the self-enclosed world of the asylum and the 'closed system' of Mr Endon in particular. Murphy's 'clonic' behaviour, most fitting for a 'schizoid spasmophile,' is at once evidence of a male infantilism (after rolling around on the ground, having laughed himself silly, Celia helps dress him) and a hysterical (almost the right word) anxiety about leaving the room he shares with Celia.

   Be that as it may, it is worth keeping in mind that Celia is left alone at the centre of the novel: she negotiates with Miss Carridge to take over the old boy's room, she replaces Murphy in his chair (though he will return to take it to his garret at the Magdalen Mental Mercy Seat), and in her own way she displaces him 'in the cell of her mind' (149). She approaches a state of 'almost pleasant sensation,' à la Murphy himself. But Celia also does, finally, go out in search of Mr Kelly so as to watch him flying his kite. Mr Kelly, however, fails to show up – the weather is too wet and miserable; Celia continues to move between her inner and outer worlds just as Murphy moves further and further away from such a connection and seeks instead to move solely into his inner world for good. Chapter 8 is clearly a rehearsal for chapter 13, the last chapter, when Murphy will be irrevocably gone and Mr Kelly will get another chance to go fly his kite; Celia will be left afterwards to push him in his chair up the hill and to his home. But in chapter 8 Celia does have some respite from those competing egoists, Murphy and Willoughby Kelly. The latter was described by Celia in chapter 2 as possessing an 'immense cerebrum' into which she believed she could insert a problem and 'the solution would be returned as though by clockwork' (18). Murphy is no better, his overweening Egoism increasingly obvious, painfully and ironically so, the more he supposedly advocates a retreat from the 'big world'; after all, he comes to believe that there is 'no dark quite like his own dark,' that his own 'system' supersedes that of the stars and his horoscope ('So far as the prophetic status of the celestial bodies was concerned Murphy had become an out-and-out preterist,' 183), and so on.[20]

The critical perspective afforded the reader on Murphy's various views of self must be kept in mind at all times. One of the ways in which Beckett has structured this in the 'bad joke' section of chapter 8 is by a series of revealing parallels with a section correspondingly located at the centre of Meredith's *The Egoist*. Once again in Beckett's early works we can see a complex palimpsestic principle at work whereby Beckett identifies his own work with Meredith's in order to work out his relationship with Joyce's aesthetic theory. This literary triangulation involves at the very centre of *Murphy* a doubling or rewriting in which a structural feature of *The Egoist* is recreated in order to suggest a number of critical perspectives implicit in Beckett's novel. The structural features we are about to look at in some detail would not, of course, lend themselves to conventional scholarly annotation in the fashion of Ackerley's *Demented Particulars*. Likewise, such literary referencing goes far beyond what Knowlson has termed Beckett's 'grafting' technique, in which various literary 'borrowings' are woven into his own writing; evident here is a much more complex type of hybridity in which two texts are set in conjunction in order to illuminate each other as well as to afford an indirect relationship to a third.

Briefly outlined here are the parallel sections to *Murphy* as found in *The Egoist*. The twenty-fifth chapter of the fifty chapters of *The Egoist* involves 'The Flight in Wild Weather' of Clara Middleton as she seeks to escape the all-encompassing absorption of Sir Willoughby Patterne's egoistic hegemony. She returns from this would-be flight at the end of chapter 28, persuaded to do so by Vernon Whitford, Patterne's cousin, and rival-to-be for Clara's hand. In chapter 29 Sir Willoughby's ill humour, noted by all, is front and centre as he 'flicked a whip' at Colonel Horace de Craye, whom he accuses of brushing up on 'his book of Anecdotes and neat collection of Irishisms.' The Colonel laughs this off with 'good-humour' only to have the whip flicked again in his face: 'Your laughter, Horace, is a capital comment on your wit' (360). This 'waspish snap' at another perceived rival for Clara is rebuked by Dr Middleton, who says de Craye has not offended and hence doesn't deserve such treatment. Willoughby justifies himself along certain racial lines: '"These Irishmen," Willoughly said, "will play the professional jester as if it were an office they were born to. We must play critic now and then, otherwise we should have them deluging us with their Joe Millerisms"' (361). Again, that arbiter of good taste Dr Middleton intervenes to turn the tables by pointing out that Sir Willoughby's own would-be witty saying, 'the man's laugh the comment on his wit,' is not 'unchallengeably new' and after a mini-lecture chiding him for his own presumption of originality concludes by saying: 'Assuming, then, manslaughter to be your pastime, and hari-kari not to be your bent, the phrase, to escape criminality, must rise in you as you would have it fall on him, ex improviso. Am I right?' (362).

Yes and no: in a novel such as *Murphy*, which announces in its opening sentence that there is 'nothing new,' to escape 'criminality' of the literary sort as outlined by Dr Middleton is virtually impossible. Beckett has embodied this very principle in the quite incredible number of 'borrowings' from various traditions, which Ackerley has annotated in his book-length study. In this sense, all jokes – even including those which were once good jokes, to use another of Murphy's many classifications – are sooner or later bound to become material for the next edition of 'Joe Miller' or the great Book of Egoism as defined by Meredith. In both instances, the joke is a ready-made item that is tactically employed to inflict hurt on another and to satisfy the egoism of the teller. Nevertheless, on another level this is a way in which a certain 'newness' or originality can be achieved: duplicating with significant variations the pattern of the 'bad joke' episode in *The Egoist*, Beckett achieves via this restructuring a 'newness' with a 'nothing newness.' The 'borrowings' have themselves been significantly transformed; Beckett's 'burrowings' into the very structures of works he has incorporated are different in kind from the unacknowledged 'borrowings' of the plagiaristic kind as found, for example, in 'Dante ... Bruno . Vico .. Joyce' and *Proust*, where certain academic conventions do involve the question of a 'criminality' of sorts that is not applicable to writing in a 'novel' form.

Murphy and Patterne are egoists whose comeuppances take very different forms. Both are hoist by their own petard in that the joke is turned against them and neither gets the last laugh. Their epitaph is that found at the end of the 'Prelude' to *The Egoist*: 'Through very love of self himself he slew.' In Sir Willoughby's case it is obvious that his efforts at 'manslaughter' via his witty joking at others' expense are turned against himself as he becomes the object of the Comic Spirit and of man's laughter. The detailed patterning of his comic excoriations as he is humiliated by the refusal of his 'fair to middling' women to have him is mingled with a certain pathos. As Meredith stated in his famous essay on the comic, our life is not by any means a pure comedy, but 'something strangely mixed.'[21] In the end Sir Willoughby is allowed to retain a certain amour propre in order to carry on with his necessary social roles and functions as head of the House of Patterne. While he at times thinks how he would like to escape the social world that has 'slapped him in the face' and caused him to undergo such a monstrous 'self-immolation,' he can in fact only exist in such a social world. Patterne needs these patterns; on the other hand, Murphy in a much more self-contradictory manner seeks to improve 'his system' and yet revel in an asocial formlessness. His amour propre is amorphous. The asylum chapters (9 and 11), which culminate in Murphy's demise, show Beckett pushing his nominal hero into an area that lies distinctly beyond a Joycean world in which a mediation between inside/outside, above/below is if not the very premise of its being at least a legitimate possibility.

Meredith's views on the intimate connection between comedy and a consensus about what constitutes a social sanity capable of confronting a real world are also sorely tested in the asylum section. For Meredith, above all, the comic is the 'perceptive,' 'the governing spirit, awakening and giving aim to these pieces of laughter.'[22] The premise of Meredith's view of comedy is that once you endorse the view that our civilization is based on common sense (and he makes it clear that 'it is the first condition of sanity to believe it'), you will then be able to see the Comic Spirit overhead and perceive those comic discrepancies that deviate from 'common sense,' such as those outlined in the most famous passage in 'An Essay on Comedy,' namely, whenever men's actions 'wax out of proportion, overblown, affected, pretentious, bombastical, hypocritical, pedantic.'[23] The problem in *Murphy* is that in the Magdalen Mental Mercy Seat sections, even if the narrator does supply a modicum of such

Meredithian-type 'perception' by pointing out in many instances in no
uncertain terms that Murphy is only deluding himself in his romanticized views about his supposedly newfound 'kindred,' the reader does
not receive any corresponding assurance that a viable 'common sense'
definition of a social reality does actually exist. Hence the reader (and
the narrator, too) can only laugh uneasily at Murphy's delusions about
his newfound 'brotherhood' with the little race of asylum dwellers; but
there is no sense of our 'superiority' in adopting this comic perspective,
since the reassuring consensus that the world is 'founded in common
sense,' Meredith's 'first condition of sanity,' is indeed missing. This is
certainly no 'rollicking' comedy (Ackerley), and it is anything but 'pure'
(Bloom); as Meredith noted, we know our lives are not a comedy, but
'something strangely mixed.'

Many of the key points in these decisive asylum chapters seem to be
played directly against views and sentiments found in Meredith's
'An Essay on Comedy.' The climactic encounter between Murphy and
Mr Endon ironically makes the point that Murphy's imagined views of
his relationship with the inmates are totally misdirected – 'they wax
out of proportion, overblown, affected, pretentious.' Instead of an ideal
communion, Murphy looking into Mr Endon's cornea can only see 'hor-
ribly reduced, obscured and distorted, his own image' (259). The 'butter-
fly kiss' is never given, for it cannot be received, Murphy 'seeing himself
stigmatised in those eyes that did not see him' (259). Endon has turned
Murphy's world on end. In short, the 'gulf' cannot be broached and
Murphy can no longer pretend to himself that he has found, as indicated in Malraux's epigraph for chapter 9, his 'kindred.' We are a long
way indeed from the romantic euphoria at the end of *Portrait*, when
Stephen Dedalus is drawn to the company of voices of his soulmates:
'We are your kinsmen'; 'We are alone. Come.' For Murphy there is instead only a fractured self-reflexive syntax:

> the last at last seen of him
> himself unseen by him
> and of himself. (250)

This lack of *percipi* is annihilating and this 'guffaw of the Abderite'
(Democritus) would push the comic well beyond the definitions
found in Meredith's essay, written two years before *The Egoist*. However, any careful reader of that novel will know that the common criticism of Meredith's *Essay* that his views are too much in favour of an

endorsement of the status quo does not really hold up in practice. *The Egoist* is full of many acknowledgments of the power of the irrational in determining human actions and, as Dr Middleton, that arbiter of so-called common sense, points out the influence of Sirius, the dog star associated with madness, is often all too painfully obvious.[24]

In Meredith there is still a social matrix of 'sanity' to return to whereas in *Murphy* there is only a 'matrix of surds' (112). Hence in Meredith there is some sense of balance and mediation, as there is in Joyce. Both of these writers share what might be termed a view of comic *claritas*: in 'An Essay on Comedy,' Meredith makes the same distinction that Stephen Dedalus will in his discussion of 'radiance' or *claritas*. It is of *our* world: the Comic 'Spirit overhead' is 'not more heavenly than the light flashed upward from glassy surfaces, but luminous and watchful.' The Comic reveals the 'whatness' of men. The alternative, according to Meredith: 'Not to distinguish it [the Comic Spirit] is to be bull blind to the spiritual, and to deny the existence of a mind of many where minds of men are in working conjunction.'[25] Murphy sees his own mind, his 'own dark,' as separate from all others (an egoism that is at least as great as that of Stephen Dedalus); but in the end Murphy comes to the painful perception (which has a certain comic poetic justice for the reader) that he belongs nowhere, and hence cannot be said to exist; having rejected the marketplace (the world of quid pro quo) and having been rejected by the world represented by Mr Endon and the asylum, he has nowhere to go. After the total impasse with Mr Endon, Murphy makes the only move he can make: to turn back towards Celia and the world he had formerly rejected.

As he leaves the asylum, utterly defeated, Murphy is said to feel 'incandescent,' and as he makes his way to the nurses' quarters he strips himself of his clothes and, to cool himself off, 'lay down in a tuft of soaking tuffets and tried to get a picture of Celia' (251). Murphy, in fact, fails to conjure up any 'pictures' from the world outside the asylum. In a novel that talks endlessly *about* Murphy's mind and its various 'systems' and 'classifications,' we finally get a glimpse of the thing itself, and that brief vision is perhaps the most remarkable sentence in all of *Murphy*: 'Scraps of bodies, of landscapes, hands, eyes, lines and colours evoking nothing, rose and climbed out of sight before him, as though reeled upward off a spool level with his throat' (252).[26] Murphy's reaction: 'It was his experience that this should be stopped, whenever possible, before the deeper coils were reached' (251). This is the decisive encounter of Murphy with himself, and he fails completely to understand the nature of this potential epiphany, of this 'sudden spiritual manifestation,' whereby he could explore in new ways what his mind is really like and how there might be new ways of connecting the various worlds with which he has made only superficial contact thus far. Murphy instead indulges in the narcissistic fantasies of his rocking chair and retreats from any such authentic encounter. No wonder the 'incandescent' Murphy is finally blown up, deus ex machina fashion. The use of Murphy as a critical probe to find new ways, new forms beyond those of Meredith and Joyce, has reached its *terminus ad quem*, a dead end.

There is certainly poetic justice in the fact that Murphy should meet his end due to the malfunctioning of a gas radiator: 'Rusty, dusty, derelict, the coils of asbestos falling to pieces, it seemed to defy ignition' (171). The heavy use of metonymy in the description of the radiator stands out in a novel in which style fends off the messy details of the outside world at the same time that such 'particulars,' 'demented' or otherwise, are perforce acknowledged. Beckett in a letter to MacGreevy talked about how in the last few chapters he had only 'mechanical' writing to get through but that he found himself trapped by the absurdity of details.[27] The haywiring of the radiator by Ticklepenny and the discussions of nozzles and coils is a far cry from the third zone of Murphy's mind and the aphoristic sayings of Geulincx and Democritus. The metonymic details here are the stock-in-trade of the realist writer and distant from the realm of purely mental pleasure. The amateur gas-fitting is simply incompetent: when the gas is errantly turned on in the w.c., Murphy is blown up. That Joyce relished and could recite from memory the passage about the scattering of Murphy's ashes over the floor of the pub due to Cooper's drunken dereliction of duty (the scene that concludes chapter 12) is also poetic justice of sorts (*JJ*, 701). Joyce would have recognized the portrait of himself in Mr Willoughby Kelly and the scene of Murphy's remains being scattered and swept away 'with the sand, the beer, the butts, the glass, the matches, the spits, the vomit' (275) would have certainly fulfilled Mr Kelly's earlier advice to Celia to 'sever the connexion.' It is in this metonymic realm, arguably, rather than in that of metaphorical associations that many of Joyce's most telling epiphanies were to be found. Murphy turned away from any further encounter with epiphanic revelations of his self: no wholeness, no harmony, and no radiance – except for the explosion of the faulty radiator. As the narrator points out, 'it seems strange that neither of them thought of an oil-stove, say a small Valor Perfection' (164).

Exit Murphy; and in the next chapter exit the cast of characters in the subplot, Neary, Counihan, Wylie and Cooper. What is left then? Chapter 13 and the kite-flying scene with Celia and her grandfather Mr Willoughby Kelly. The two obvious set pieces in *Murphy* are chapter 6 and chapter 13; both are very short (six and a half pages each) and are typified by a density of texture, a certain 'compression' – the 'intellectual fireworks'[28] of chapter 6 that Beckett at the time thought justified the work as a whole and what one might call the 'poetic fireworks' of chapter 13. This last chapter is, in fact, the most Joycean in the novel: it is a complex revisioning of the most famous epiphany in *Portrait*, Stephen's vision of the birdgirl at the end of chapter 4. The sighting of the 'mortal angel' is set in contrapuntal opposition to Stephen's visit to the prostitute at the end of chapter 2. In *Murphy* Beckett has drawn these diametrically opposed images together in the figure of Celia, the prostitute/ideal of beauty incarnate. The birdgirl parallel with Celia is, as we have seen, set up in the opening chapter of *Murphy* and the first sighting of her paramour to be by Celia: he 'gazed at Celia. For perhaps two minutes she suffered this gladly' (14). Compare this with the original scene in *Portrait*: 'She was alone and still, gazing out to sea; and when she felt his presence and the worship of his eyes her eyes turned to him in quiet sufferance of his gaze, without shame or wantonness. Long, long she suffered his gaze and then quietly withdrew her eyes from his and bent them towards the stream, gently stirring the water with her foot hither and thither' (151).

The ironic context of *Murphy* is, of course, that Mr Willoughby Kelly, the Joyce figure in the novel, protests against various 'particulars,' some of which are derived from his own very different story in *Portrait*. Murphy's gaze fluctuates between Celia and the firmament as he consults his horoscope: a veritable telescoping of opposing images in a 'whoroscope.' Celia is contemplating the water not in terms of the poetic dallying of the birdgirl's 'stirring,' but as a means of suicidal release. Celia walks away and returns and accosts Murphy and 'they walked off happily arm-in-arm, leaving the star chart for June lying in the gutter' (15). In *Portrait* there is no direct communication, all ecstatic revelations take place in Stephen's head – 'no word has broken the holy silence of his ecstasy' (152). Beckett in *Murphy* executes directly what Joyce ironically implies since his echoing of the birdgirl scene is overlaid with the prostitute scene in which young Stephen is addressed by the prostitute: as 'He stood still in the middle of the roadway [...] [she] laid her hand on his arm to *detain* him and *gazed* into his face' (*P*, 95, my italics). Beckett's palimpsestic strategies here could be regarded as in support of a parody of Joycean themes; but by the time the final chapter is reached there is a complex poetic music of Beckett's own that has grown out of his dialogical engagement with Joycean aesthetics throughout *Murphy*, via the mediating third party with whom they both share strong ties, George Meredith. This connection is particularly prominent in the final episode of *Murphy*, which rewrites Joyce's birdgirl epiphany, for, as Donald Fanger has pointed out, Joyce's 'original' scene is itself a complex refashioning of the 'Ferdinand and Miranda' episode of Meredith's *Richard Feverel*, in particular the passage that begins with the introduction of 'a daughter of the Earth' and ends several hundred words later with the phrase 'she was a bit of lovely human life.'[29]

The Joyce figure, Mr Willoughby Kelly, seems to be on his last legs, at just about the end of the line (figuratively and literally in terms of letting out his kite string); nevertheless, his 'eyes blazed' and he still 'burned with excitement' (276) at the prospect of taking flight again, Daedalian-fashion. He takes flight with his kite after Celia has wheeled him into position, and as she stands on the 'margin of the water' and holds up the kite she is described in terms that echo the birdgirl scene with the wind blowing 'her skirt against her legs, her jacket back from her breasts' (278). Compare with *Portrait*: 'Her slateblue skirts were kilted boldly about her waist […] Her bosom was as a bird's' (151). The key Joycean word 'wild' is prominent as well; the line of the kite is let out in a 'wild rush' (279), similar to the 'instant of wild flight' (150) as Stephen's soul takes flight in the lead-up to the sighting of the birdgirl. The 'enraptured' (280) joining of the heavens and earth in the image of Mr Kelly's kite flying is, however, ruptured when he 'dozes' off and loses control of the winch, thereby causing the string to snap. This is the third 'severing the connection' instance in *Murphy*, preceded by Mr Kelly's injunction to Celia and Murphy's comment on the suicide of the old boy. But all is not totally lost in this instance, even though Mr Kelly now totters to his feet, 'a ghastly lamentable figure' (281–2) who is only saved from an Icaran fall into the pond by Celia: 'The end of the line skimmed the water, jerked upward in a wild whirl, vanished joyfully in the dusk' (282). Mr Kelly might be on his way out, but at the end of his life, assisted by Celia/Beauty, there is still the recognition of the possibility of an idea of pleasure, albeit the phrasing is now, finally, one that can be termed in its own right authentically 'Beckettian,' as in 'vanished joyfully.' A negative positive, with perhaps even a pun on Joyce's name.

What is to be made then of the ending of *Murphy*? Chapter 13 most resembles Beckett's 'Assumption' in that it is focused upon a reconfigured and carefully contrived rewriting of a passage from *Portrait*. In both instances Beckett's intentions are more than merely parody as mockery; there is homage and recognition of Joyce's achievements while at the same time there is a critique of the limitations of the aesthetic of modernist revelation and an attempt to formulate an alternative approach. In both 'Assumption' and *Murphy*, the nominal hero ends up dead and a woman is left grieving in the final scene. But in *Murphy*'s conclusion there is a much more complex rendition of the means, however tentative, whereby the story might continue and a new aesthetic replace the supposedly worn-out one of Joyce that appears on its last legs. Compare Mr Willoughby Kelly's dozing off (even Joyce nods, it would seem), which leads to the snapping of his kite's string, with the poetic dream-sleep of the artist as a young man that envelops Stephen Dedalus after he has walked an unknown distance in a trance-like state after he has experienced the holy encounter with the birdgirl: 'He closed his eyes in the languor of sleep. His eyelids trembled as if they felt the vast cyclic movement of the earth and her watchers, trembled as if they felt the strange light of some new world. His soul was swooning into some new world, fantastic, dim, uncertain as under sea, traversed by cloudy shapes and beings. A world, a glimmer or a flower?' (152). *Murphy* is a novel that consigns itself with rare exceptions (for example, the 'uncoiling' of the minds of Murphy and Celia) to the surface of things, to the superficial. The narrator has 'expurgated' the raw material to give certain stylized form to the novel (a characteristic often notable only by its absence in *Dream*). In *Portrait*'s lyrical effusion above, we are vouchsafed entry into Stephen's mind and the glimpse is of the act of re-creation, of the artist's ability to suggest an alternative reality. Mr Kelly's 'doze' carries no such connotation of course, it is simply a fatigued lapse into unconsciousness. It would be all too easy to see in this comparison/contrast only Beckett's ironical critical assessment of the supposedly exhausted aesthetic credo of Joyce, which is no longer adequate for the world view of a new generation. In the dream passage from *Portrait* cited above, the world-building powers of the imagination in terms of 'an opening flower [...] breaking in full crimson and unfolding' are depicted, whereas in *Murphy* Mr Kelly's crimson kite, which we have seen him folding and unfolding at various points in the novel, breaks free and disappears from sight.

To focus only on ironic aspects would, however, leave out the most remarkable feature of *Murphy* and one that critics have not yet fully appreciated: the role of Celia as a portrait of the artist as a young woman. We have already seen how in Beckett's very careful permutation of Joycean elements in *Murphy*, particularly the 'sever the connexion' motif of *Ulysses*, that it is Celia who corresponds to the figure of Stephen Dedalus. At the end of *Murphy* the eponymous 'hero' is gone and the Joyce figure Mr Kelly is fading out. Celia gets the last sentence of the novel, 'She closed her eyes,' followed by the narrator's recording of the park rangers' shout of '*All out*' (282). Stephen's dream vision following the birdgirl epiphany, as cited above, opens with 'He closed his eyes.' We do not get to see into Celia's mind (and this would indeed be much more interesting than chapter 6's description of Murphy's): she is pausing in the midst of pushing Mr Kelly in his chair up the hill, against the wind. But we know that Celia has come to replace or resemble Murphy in her 'unpicking of the oakum of her history,' a ritual process identified as the reversal of Penelope's unknitting. Furthermore, his removal to the 'garret' at the MMM is paralleled by her move up to the old boy's room. And Celia, however reluctantly, however uncertainly, still moves – unlike Murphy – between the worlds of her mind and the outside world and hence is faced with the challenge of finding some type of modus vivendi between the two realms. Celia, after all, is the one who is caught in the middle, between Murphy and Mr Kelly, and in the end this tug-of-war (won by default by Mr Kelly) should be regarded as the decisive central struggle of *Murphy*, not Murphy's absurd views of his own mind and his deluded views about joining his 'kindred' folk such as that delightfully self-contained gaga Mr Endon. The woman caught between two men is almost geometrically formulated in the romantic triangles of *Exiles*. The last line of the play after Bertha's final plea for the return of her 'wild lover' is a stage direction: '*She closes her eyes.*' What Celia sees behind her closed eyes holds out the possibility of not only a rewriting of Joyce's *Portrait* and *Exiles* but of Beckett's *Murphy* and its portrait in terms of the title character of the confirmed non-artist.

What indeed are we left with then? A feminist reading of *Murphy*? Hardly, though the 'he closed his eyes'/'she closed her eyes' pattern might suggest one of Joyce's great themes, androgyny, which we will see Beckett elaborate on in his own way in later works. The ending of *Murphy* does, however, show a dramatically different view of women, as represented by Celia, than is found in many of the misogynistic portraits in *Dream, More Pricks Than Kicks,* and parts of *Murphy.* In 'An Essay on Comedy' Meredith argues that the Comic Spirit is a particular friend of women and a great ally in their 'battle with men, and that of men with them; and as the two, however divergent, both look on one object, namely, life, the gradual similarity of their impressions must bring them to some resemblance. The comic poet dares show us men and women coming to this mutual likeness.'[30] Meredith also argues in the essay that the Comic Spirit allows for 'fusing the tragic sentiment with the comic narrative' and 'the Comic Spirit is not hostile to the sweetest songfully poetic.'[31] Joyce rewrote Meredith's effusive lyricism with its complex metaphors in the birdgirl epiphany of *Portrait*; Beckett, in turn, rewrote Joyce's scene for the ending of his first published novel, and though the context is very different it still does contain certain passages of real poetry – for example, 'the wind tearing the awning of cloud to tatters, pale limitless blue and green recessions laced with strands of scud, the light failing,' though Beckett simultaneously giveth and taketh away by adding ' – once she would have noticed these things' (281). The conventionally beautiful and the sentimental are very much held in check at the end of *Murphy*, but the quest behind 'closed eyes' to determine what is now regarded as Beauty and the Forms for the expression thereof, the driving force in *Portrait*, is still the vital residual question in *Murphy* and it is tied up with Celia's dual role of Venus Coelestis (Celestial) and Venus Naturalis (Vulgar) and the narrator's unresolved relationships with her.

4 What's What in *Watt*

In *Murphy* Beckett engaged in an aesthetic debate with Joyce, and it was necessary as a prolegomenon to our discussion to deconstruct the assumptions about what constituted the so-called Joycean sources and influences. No such barriers block the critical approach to *Watt*. Indeed, the overwhelming consensus is that Beckett has by now moved decisively beyond Joyce, once and for all. This judgment is echoed even with reference to the one feature of *Watt* that critics from early on did deem to be obviously 'Joycean,' namely, how the maddeningly (pseudo-)logical permutations of inventoried 'items' of all sorts in *Watt* seem reminiscent of Joyce's 'scientific catechism' of the 'Ithaca' section of *Ulysses*. In *The Stoic Comedians: Flaubert, Joyce, and Beckett*, Hugh Kenner proposes that in the logical analyses of possibilities in *Watt* 'Beckett is 'subtracting from the methods of *Ulysses* all the irreducible realities of Joyce's Dublin, and so transposing the novel to a plane of empty but oddly gripping construction.'[1] In Kenner's assessment, the Joycean elements identifiable in *Watt* show Beckett moving from Joyce's comedy of the inventory to Beckett's own comedy of the impasse. As we will see, the Joycean aspects of Beckett's *Watt* are much more extensive, to say the least, than those adumbrated by Kenner in his early study and not significantly added to in subsequent Beckett criticism.

It could in fact be said that *Watt* is in many respects Beckett's effort *in memoriam* Joyce. *Watt* was begun in Paris on 11 February 1941, less than a month after Joyce's death on 13 January of that year. Most of *Watt* was written by Beckett in Roussillon in Vichy France, where he was working as a peasant by day and labouring fitfully on *Watt* by night; in short, *Watt* is a work about fragmentation written in a perforce fragmented manner, and not completed until the middle of 1945.

As *Watt* developed over this long period of time, the Joycean elements clearly became more and more pronounced, and it is no exaggeration to say that Joycean elements haunt *Watt* and are deciding factors in the very shaping and development of the novel's structure and guiding ideas. Simply put, *Watt* is about one man (Watt) replacing another man (Arsene) in attendance at the house of Mr Knott; on another plane, it is about Beckett trying to find his way after Joyce. Beckett's *Watt* is a complex portraiture of Beckett's Joyce, at once a hail and farewell, a homage, and a critique.

In the period after the completion of *Murphy* (1935; published 1938), Beckett explored in more depth the crucial question of art's function and the vehicles for its expression, issues which were raised in *Murphy* but the engagement with for the most part suspended. It is hardly a surprise that in Beckett's investigation of these issues Joyce figures in various ways in a prominent fashion. In the 1937 letter to Axel Kaun, Beckett sets out what sounds like a program for his future writing: 'And more and more my own language appears to me like a veil that must be torn apart in order to get at the things (or the Nothingness) behind it.' Within a few sentences, Beckett repeats this idea of getting behind or beyond language, though now the attack is more calculated: 'To bore one hole after another in it [language], until what lurks behind it – be it something or nothing – begins to seep through; I cannot imagine a higher goal for a writer today.' And in the third phrasing concerning what might be found out as a result of this 'tearing' and 'boring,' to which now is added 'this mocking attitude towards the word, through words,' the 'something or nothing' either/or proposition is itself transformed to 'it will perhaps become possible to feel a whisper of that final music or that silence that underlies All.' Then, dramatically, in the very next sentence of the following paragraph enters Beckett's Joyce: 'With such a program, in my opinion, the latest work of Joyce [*Work in Progress*] has nothing whatever to do. There it seems rather to be a matter of the apotheosis of the word.' Beckett is unable to 'imagine a higher goal for the writer today' than to seek to somehow get beyond the limitations of language, whereas Joyce is said to exalt the very powers of language itself, raising himself on high to god-like status in a veritable 'apotheosis of the word' (*Dis*, 171–2).[2] Beckett's strategic intent here is obviously designed to distinguish his own enterprise from Joyce's in that its 'higher goal' has nothing to do with the supposed omniscience and omnipotence of the Joycean 'apotheosis of the word.' Through the proper arrangement of the right words, Joyce believed significant meanings might be expressed, a Logos validated and sustained, remarking to Beckett that he could 'justify every line' (*JJ*, 702) in his own writing.

That these judgments have more to do with Beckett's own need to claim original points of departure from Joyce, a certain rhetorical distancing ('in my opinion,' 'it seems'), than with any definitive evaluation of the Joycean enterprise is made clear by juxtaposing statements made in the same year (1937) in his German Diaries, which were made available to Knowlson for the work on his biography. Beckett records a heated discussion in which his interlocutor won't even entertain the question of the word's inadequacy (the same topic that the Kaun letter focused upon) and refuses categorically to accept that 'dissonance [...] has become principle and that the word cannot express, because literature can no more escape from chronologies to simultaneities, from Nebeneinander to Miteinander, that [than] the human voice can sing chords.' In the Kaun letter Beckett definitively rejects any identification between Joyce's work and this principle of 'dissonance,' there phrased in terms of the inherent weaknesses of words: 'In this dissonance between the means and their use it will perhaps become possible to feel a whisper of that final music or that silence that underlies All'; in the German Diaries entry Joyce is, however, now identified with Beckett's own avant-garde program: 'As I talk and listen realise suddenly how *Work in Progress* is the only possibility [possible] development from *Ulysses*, the heroic attempt to make literature accomplish what belongs to music – the Miteinander and the simultaneous. *Ulysses* falsifies the unconscious, or the 'monologue intérieur,' in so far as it is obliged to express it as a teleology' (*DF*, 258). A couple of points are worth underscoring here. First, Beckett's sudden insight into Joyce's laudable program of turning 'simultaneities' against the grain of conventional narrative 'chronologies' does indeed seem to leap unannounced off the page – a veritable critical epiphany. Hence the form of Beckett's revelation does poetic justice to this new conceptual vision Beckett has of Joyce's work. Secondly, in both the Kaun letter and the German Diaries entry Joyce's presence suddenly breaks into a discussion that ostensibly has nothing in particular to do with him, his sudden interjection testifying, however, to how Joyce was for Beckett the touchstone figure when it came to the dilemmas and challenges confronting the modern writer.

What then is one to make of these two contradictory views of Joyce's *Work in Progress* voiced virtually simultaneously in 1937, both occurring within a German cultural context? The Axel Kaun letter attempts to establish the nature of the real world of things-in-themselves (what Beckett refers to as something or nothing, music or silence behind the veil of language), resulting, however, in what Kant called 'antinomies,' contradictory conclusions both of which can be reasonably 'proven' to be true. No wonder Beckett later dismissed this letter as 'German bilge'[3] – it contains a number of uncritical judgments and smacks of naive Idealism/Transcendentalism in its portentous references in phrases such as 'that final music or that silence that underlies All.' The probing of the 'dissonance' within language itself comes across authentically, even if the terms in which the consequences of such a program are phrased seem mere metaphysical maundering. On the other hand, the German Diaries entry has the ring of a spontaneous insight, in sharp contrast to the overwrought rhetoric of the Kaun letter. The real antinomy at stake here is the two fundamentally contradictory views of Joyce's work that Beckett puts forward. Decisive here is not the so-called truth value of either judgment (both of which can be 'proven' and 'disproven'), but Beckett's own abiding needs and his conflicted nature: at times identifying with Joyce's work ('to make literature accomplish what belongs to music'), at other times rejecting Joyce's way ('the apotheosis of the word') in order to underscore just how very different his own work is.

The Denis Devlin review (1938) is focused upon seeing art (poetry) in 'its own terms, that is in terms of need' and is hence very much on the way to *Watt*, to be begun in the next few years. The Joycean reference points here are not so explicitly identified but suggested more indirectly. Beckett's argument that art now has to deal with itself on its own terms is further supported by historical circumstance since 'social reality (*pace* ex-Comrade Radek) has severed the connexion' (*Dis*, 91) with art. As we have encountered in *Murphy*, Beckett adapts this phrase from Joyce's *Ulysses* where Leopold Bloom cautions the aspiring artist Stephen Dedalus to 'sever the connexion' with Buck Mulligan (and by implication any of his ilk who would lead him away from the true domain of aesthetic speculations). In 1938, such an injunction is, of course, much more politicized and necessarily generalized in larger societal terms. The consequent development of a theory of art that turns in upon itself is formulated in terms which do, however, appropriate some identifiable Joycean elements: 'On the one hand the "Unbefriedigt jeden Augenblick," the need to need ("aimant l'amour"), the art that condenses as inverted spiral of need, that condenses in intensity and brightness from the mere need of the angels to that of the seraphinns, whose end is its own end in the end and the source of need' (*Dis*, 91–2). The defining quality of this type of authentic need – as distinct from the other kind, 'the need that in its haste to be abolished cannot pause to be stated' – is that it is 'condense[d] in intensity and brightness,' as a variant of *claritas* or radiance.

For Beckett, however, such 'condensation' of 'intensity and brightness' also must, ineluctably, as we have seen in *Dream* and *Murphy*, be intimately conjoined with darkness and issues forth in a paradoxical revision as a 'dark radiance.' This admixture of elements is what the conclusion of Beckett's Devlin review concentrates upon, suggesting that the creative act should not 'burk its own conditions for the sake of clarity.' Beckett's major point is that through poetic images there is a 'minimum of rational interference,' whereby artistic consciousness manifests itself 'with the least loss of integrity.' Such *integritas* in Beckett's world is from 'Assumption' onwards pictured as a multiplicity of selves engendered by the creative act itself: as the first sentence of the Devlin review elliptically announces with reference to the artist's predicament, 'With himself on behalf of himself. With his selves on behalf of his selves' (*Dis*, 91). This 'integrity' is the first mode of apprehension in the theory of aesthetics advanced in *Portrait*, and, in another related ethical sense of the word, it is what Beckett said he learned from Joyce and what was vital for his own development as an artist.[4] Beckett concludes his own manifesto within a review with a mannered repetition of the idea of 'clarity,' which at once seems to endorse an affinity with Joyce while also implying a significant point of departure: 'The time is perhaps not altogether too green for the vile suggestion that art has nothing to do with clarity, does not dabble in the clear and does not make clear, any more than the light of day (or night) makes the subsolar, -lunar and -stellar excrement' (*Dis*, 94). Art's role is not to make clear, just as light does not make clear the various excrementa that encompass us in our various subpositions. Logically conjoined here by their negative functions, 'art' and 'light' can apparently work together to reveal what is, even if they do not make this clear 'in terms of enlightenment' (*Dis*, 94), that is, in a rational, coherent manner, as those terms have been traditionally understood, mockingly referred to earlier in the Devlin review as 'Davus and the morbid dread of sphinxes, solution clapped on problem like a snuffer on a candle' (*Dis*, 92). Hence Beckett reinforces in a more affirmative manner the parallelism of 'subsolar, -lunar and -stellar excrement': 'Art is the sun, moon and stars of the mind' (*Dis*, 94). This 'whole mind' includes the outside world, even if, as Beckett stressed at the beginning of his review, art is likened to an 'inverted spiral of need,' turned in upon itself. But this is not so much an art-for-art's-sake argument as an argument in support of art for life's sake, an acknowledgment of the 'absolute predicament of particular human identity' (*Dis*, 91), as Beckett characterizes the artist's dilemma at the beginning of his review.

Watt is much more fundamentally and directly engaged with Joycean concerns than the much more ballyhooed *Murphy* in this regard. Stephen Dedalus expounds the theory that this *claritas* or radiance is '*quidditas*, the *whatness* of a thing. This supreme quality is felt by the artist when the esthetic image is first conceived in his imagination. The mind in that mysterious instant Shelley likened beautifully to a fading coal. The instant wherein that supreme quality of beauty, the clear radiance of the esthetic image, is apprehended luminously by the mind which has been arrested by its wholeness and fascinated by its harmony is the luminous silent stasis of esthetic pleasure' (*P*, 185). *Watt* could be read as a novel whose founding principles are self-consciously set in some type of conjunction with and opposition to those outlined above in the excerpt from *Portrait*. Watt cannot comprehend or, in the Joycean sense, 'apprehend' the 'whatness' of various things and experiences encountered at the house of Mr Knott (and hence by implication his own 'Watt-ness'). Instead, Watt's predicament consists of the very painful experience of undergoing a whole series of negative epiphanies, as he vainly and futilely tries to draw meaning from a series of inexplicable events. Language and logic seem helpless before a number of experiences that refuse to be fitted into encompassing patterns within a series of similar events.

Beckett's last sentence in the 'review' (more properly viewed as a critical probing into his own aesthetic credo) accords his ostensible subject (Devlin) a memorable endorsement as 'a mind aware of its luminaries' (*Dis*, 94). In *Watt* Beckett himself is indeed just such a mind and the two most important 'luminaries' are Immanuel Kant and James Joyce. Strange bedfellows upon a first consideration, to be sure, but most appropriate in terms of Beckett's overall development of his own aesthetic at the time of writing *Watt*. In an earlier discussion, 'Beckett and the Philosophers,' I argued in detail that *Watt* is a Kantian novel and that for Beckett Kant remains the indispensable philosopher in so far as Beckett used his reading of him to help clarify for himself the boundary lines of the knowable and unknowable.[5] There is no need to rehearse here the details of that argument; specifics as needed will be referred to in the following critique of *Watt*. In effect, what Beckett is doing by bringing these two 'luminaries' into conjunction is testing out the limitations of the aesthetic theories of modernists such as Proust and especially Joyce, whose theorizing turns in Beckett's reading on a mystical transcendence of sorts that is, logically enough, ineffable in that it crosses the boundary lines of that which is comprehensible by 'pure reason' as set out by Kant. Mr Knott embodies this Kantian function of bringing into play the various types of negation encountered under such liminal conditions. Arsene is the Joycean figure whose epiphany temporarily transcends such limitations, but which singularly fails to sustain itself and in time collapses. Watt is the middle-aged man with an imagination that had never been very 'lively' and whose name itself embodies a key aesthetic tenet of *Portrait*, *quidditas*, the testing out of which will determine the directions Beckett's art might take.

These generalized judgments play out in a number of very specific and detailed ways in terms of the actual structure of *Watt*. The pseudo-realistic frame tale of the 'twilighters,' Mr Hackett and Mr and Mrs Nixon, affords us our first glimpses of Watt as he prepares to set off on his fatal journey to Mr Knott's. Speculating about why Watt has got off the train at this particular stop and not simply proceeded on to the train station for his journey out of town, Mr Hackett ventures that Watt was of two minds after his initial departure. Summarizing his view, Mr Hackett says that Watt has been caught up in the impasse of at once wanting and not wanting to go and offers this 'conclusion': 'Too fearful to assume himself the onus of a decision, said Mr Hackett, he refers it to the frigid machinery of a time-space relation' (*W*, 21). This subjection to the Kantian catergories of the knowable – *lo scibile*[6] – echoes another street scene in Dublin as described in Stephen Dedalus's penultimate page of journal entries in *Portrait*, as he readies himself for his departure from Ireland. He runs into his 'beloved' in Grafton Street and changes his tactics from that of indirectly chastising her to one of mocking self-aggrandizement: 'Turned off that valve at once and opened the spiritual-heroic refrigerating apparatus, invented and patented in all countries by Dante Alighieri' (*P*, 217). Stephen's poetic posturing is, of course, in dramatic contrast to the onlookers' speculations about Watt, who is, to say the least, at this point in time anything but a would-be artist joyously on the verge of embracing untold new opportunities of self-discovery. Nevertheless, the embedded terms 'frigid machinery' / 'refrigerating apparatus' are aligned so as to constitute the first allusion to *Portrait* in Beckett's *Watt*, a work which is engaged in an extensive rewriting of its great predecessor text. Support for this contention is found in the description Arsene offers of his negative or reversed epiphany. Arsene as Beckett's version of Joyce describes the experience in specifically Kantian terms: 'I perceived it [the 'slip'] with a perception so sensuous that in comparison the impressions of a man buried alive in Lisbon on Lisbon's great day seem a frigid and artificial construction of the understanding' (*W*, 43). This is a recondite reference to Kant's pre-critical *De Igne*, which commented on the Lisbon earthquake and which Beckett referred to in his poem 'ainsi a-t-on beau' where Kant is depicted as dispassionately viewing the spectacle of destruction: 'sur Lisbonne fumante Kant froidement penché.'[7] The critique of Kant's philosophical sang froid implicit here is not, however, simply an ironic dismissal, for Arsene notably cannot sustain his 'existence off the ladder' and so falls back into the 'old thing where it always was, back again' (44); in other words, back again into the world in which the Kantian distinctions and boundaries between the noumenal and phenomenal do indeed unfortunately apply.

Arsene's frametale opens with him projecting for Watt the experience that he initially had himself upon his arrival at Mr Knott's House – 'The dawn! The sun! The light!' (39) – and via this 'anticipation' Arsene reflects that 'it all comes back to me.' And, lo and behold, the frametale does end twenty-five pages later with the prospect of Watt actually undergoing his own experience of *claritas* or radiance after Arsene has completed his 'short statement' and vacated the premises, leaving Watt in his stead. Arsene's 'statement' is also a 'frame' in the sense that Mary Ann Caws employs the term to describe the experience many readers have of finding that certain passages in works of prose fiction 'stand out' from their surroundings, are foregrounded, particularly in modernist fiction.[8] This is certainly the case with what is in reality Arsene's monologue; it has garnered a great deal of critical attention, even if the set piece as a whole has not yet been thoroughly investigated. The key to this 'outstanding' passage is to trace the process of the epiphanic experience for Arsene and then the process of disintegration whereby this ecstatic experience 'slips' away and is lost. Subsequently, the rest of the novel turns upon a comparative analysis, a contrasting of Watt's experience of the 'radiance' of 'the new day at last' (64) at Mr Knott's with that of Arsene, whose rhetorically powerful first-person rendition is the 'frame,' which does indeed stand out for readers of *Watt*.

As with *Murphy*, Beckett has set up a cunning literary artifice whereby he can test out his views against those of Joyce, here expressed via Arsene, who is, as we will see in many and varied ways, designed as a Joycean figure or surrogate within the novel. The encounter is, however, still mediated or indirect in fundamental ways, for even though an intermediary figure such as Meredith is no longer employed we discover as readers to our dismay that our version of events comes via a narrator named Sam who met Watt while they were both inmates in a mental asylum. Supposedly, Watt experiences and Sam records. Of course, the whole narrative modus operandi of *Watt* is hopelessly riddled with in-built misinterpretation in that Arsene's 'short statement' itself only comes to us via Sam's revision; and this is a riddle compounded by an enigma since we know that at the time Arsene delivered his oration Watt paid virtually no attention, and it is only in the tenth entry in the 'Addenda' that we are told that 'Arsene's declaration gradually came back to Watt' (248). 'Gradually came back,' as in the sense of overcoming an amnesiacal trauma or coma, is a far cry indeed from the very idea of the epiphany's instantaneous nature, as defined by Joyce in *Stephen Hero*. The so-called authenticity of Arsene's vision is obviously open to question, but there is no doubt that Beckett (if not Sam) intends those views to be his own particular version of Joyce's aesthetic credo.

The Joycean echoes and parallels are decisive for a deciphering of *Watt*; hence, it is vitally important in terms of 'source and influence' to set out just how these Joycean elements are crucial and the Swiftian parallels, so often educed by much influential criticism of *Watt*, are, finally, decidedly of secondary importance. Two of the most suggestive arguments for the Swiftian influence in *Watt* are by Francis Doherty, who maintains 'Swift presides over a good deal of *Watt*,' and Frederik N. Smith, who pushes the case even further, arguing that *Watt* 'demonstrates a far deeper Swiftian influence than any text we have discussed so far,'[9] and then proceeds to develop a ten-page comparative analysis of Beckett's novel and Swift's *A Tale of a Tub*. Granting the relevancy of the 'general affinities' and even some of the specific details, correspondences, and allusions still does not, however, constitute a convincing case of 'influence' in the sense that *Beckett's Dedalus* is pursuing; namely, those ideas which determine the very structure and direction of the work itself. Swift has long been rightly regarded, of course, as an important influence on Beckett, and the works of Doherty and Smith certainly do make significant and valuable additions to this tradition. Nevertheless, neither of these more detailed analyses develops a critical engagement with the Arsene tale (itself, of course, a narrative interpolation common to the eighteenth-century novel), which is crucial for seeing the structure and strategic design of this radically fragmented text. Indeed, one might say that Arsene's story, after the 'slippage' that undermines his sense of engulfing 'radiance,' is, in effect, a veritable 'Tale of a Turd,' his disgust with his return to the old world in which subject and object are ruptured and broken apart termed a disgusting excremental vision (variously regarded as 'ordure,' 'excrement,' and 'turd'). But, again, this would be too easy, mere 'analogymongering' of the 'book-keeping' variety: the aftermath of Arsene's experience may indeed contain 'Swiftian' elements, granted; nevertheless, the lynchpin behind the very nature of the Arsenean visionary experience is Beckett's own version-cum-misprision of Joyce's aesthetic theories and his complex and, in so many ways, contradictory attitudes towards it. Joyce's modernist innovations are for Beckett in the foreground; the concerns of Swift's Moderns and the related issues of the general limitations of reason, however congenial to Beckett generally speaking and still obviously relevant to the perplexities encountered in *Watt*, are, in the final accounting, of a secondary, less decisive nature.

The problem of determining what 'sources' are most 'influential' in *Watt* is compounded by the fact that the very lack of any ostensible meaning seems to drive the reader towards discovering (or creating) his own meaning; as David Hesla said a long time ago, 'Every major character, every major scene and incident, invites interpretation based on esoteric intelligence.'[10] Hesla, for example, puts forward the case in some detail that Arsene is really Arsenius, an anchorite and saint, whose whole life was dedicated to escaping from the public world, of being dead to that outside world, so that he could explore in silence and repose identification with the God within.[11] Even if Beckett does 'intend' such an 'esoteric' interpretation in this instance, it can, however, only be meant ironically, for the fundamental reality of Beckett's Arsene is that he is compelled to leave Mr Knott, where he had found a certain type of beatific vision, never to return. Mr Knott is a good master; he compels his servants to leave him to pursue their own lives. Mr Knott's house affords a 'window on refuge,' not that opening of a 'window on the real' (16) that Beckett in *Proust* saw as the vision vouchsafed by the 'suffering' which underlies aesthetic experience.[12] What Beckett seems to be engaged with here is an extended critique of the essentializing nature of the modernist aesthetic of the 'moment' of revelation (which however extended in time will not be able to sustain itself indefinitely) as exemplified in two of its major practitioners, Proust and Joyce. In *Proust*, for example, Beckett points out the logical limitations and existential implications of his author's 'reduplication' or 're-membering': 'But if this mystical experience communicates an extratemporal essence, it follows that the communicant is for the moment an extratemporal being' (56). In experiencing the manifestation of the 'soul' of even the meanest object, it stands to reason that the 'communicant' is partaking of a 'transubstantiation' of sorts whereby he is 'for the moment an extratemporal being.'

This is the case as presented in *Portrait* in the aftermath of the birdgirl epiphany that ends chapter 4; Stephen loses track of time completely, 'What hour was it?' (152) And in his 'brief eternity' of aesthetic revelation he identifies with the cosmos in an oceanic experience that, in many ways, anticipates Arsene's experiences at Mr Knott's *before* his 'fall' off the ladder whereby he has reached a transcendental experience of sorts (an apotheosis – if not of the word – since this experience remains 'ineffable'), a sense of oneness with the universe: 'His eyelids trembled as if they felt the vast cyclic movement of the earth and her watchers, trembled as if they felt the strange light of some new world' (152). At this very juncture, just as he did with Proust, the Beckettian 'But' would critically intervene: how, for example, does 'light of some new world' connect with that radiant 'wholeness' which in theory young Stephen Dedalus asserted is of this world, the secular and profane world that is the artist's workshop? Compare Stephen's transports at this pivotal point in *Portrait* with Arsene's opening description of his own sense of 'whatness' as enveloping 'radiance' at the beginning of his 'short statement': 'The sensations, the premonitions of harmony are irrefragable, of imminent harmony, when all outside him will be he, the flowers the flowers that he is among him, the sky the sky that he is above him, the earth trodden the earth treading, and all sound his echo' (40–1). Stephen's visionary experience is similarly framed by deictics of ascent/descent: 'He felt *above* him the vast indifferent dome and the calm processes of the heavenly bodies'; 'the earth that had borne him, had taken him *to* her breast' – and this scene is framed by Stephen lying *down* in a 'sandy nook' where he closes his eyes and has these visionary experiences of 'the strange light of some new world' described above and later wakes and climbs 'to the crest of the sandhill and gazed about him' (152, my emphasis). The chapter ends at this point, elongating the moment of 'eternity' of Stephen's ecstatic experience (at least until the bathetic opening of chapter 5 with its breakfast scene of 'dregs' and 'yellow dripping' [*P*, 153]).

Contrast these images of 'sandy nook' and 'crest of the sandhill' with Arsene's picturing of the 'change' that undermined, forever, his sense of 'wholeness' ('the long joys of being himself' [*W*, 41]), 'harmony' (the 'irrefragable' will indeed be 'disputed') and 'radiance' (being fully himself in the service of Mr Knott – 'The dawn! The sun! The light!'), whereby a veritable light dawned. Then the 'negative' or reverse epiphany:

when suddenly somewhere some little thing slipped, some little tiny thing. Gliss—iss—iss—STOP! I trust I make myself clear. There is a great alp of sand, one hundred metres high, between the pines and the ocean, and there is the warm moonless night, when no one is looking, no one is listening, in tiny packets of two or three millions the grains slip, all together, a little slip of one or two lines maybe, and then stop, all together, not one missing, and that is all, that is all for that night, and perhaps for ever that is all, for in the morning with the sun a little wind from the sea may come, and blow them one from another far apart, or a pedestrian scatter them with his foot, though that is less likely. It was a slip like that I felt that Tuesday afternoon. (43)

This turning point for Arsene is counterpointed in *Portrait* by Father Arnall's hyperbolic image of a 'mountain of sand' (a million miles high and wide, for starters) as he tries to convey to those young penitents at the retreat the unimaginable awfulness that is 'the eternity of hell' (*P*, 119). The image of a bird coming every million years to carry away one grain of sand rubs in the point that even after 'millions upon millions of centuries' (*P*, 120) virtually nothing would have been changed and 'not even one instant of eternity could be said to have ended' (*P*, 120). It is all a matter of Time – 'that double-headed monster of damnation and salvation' (1), as Beckett characterized the situation in *Proust*. The only permanent 'stasis' is afforded by Father Arnall's Jesuit rhetoric of eternal damnation. On the other hand, Arsene's sense of 'salvation' at Mr Knott's where all is 'forgiving' and 'healed' (*W*, 40) is definitely projected in terms of the paradoxes of a modernist-type transcendence: 'For ever. In a moment' (40). Two sentence fragments juxtaposed. Such an epiphanic 'moment,' however stretched out, is unavoidably subject to change; even if it is impossible to determine in such a case 'the distinction between what was inside and what was outside,' the perception of the 'change' or 'slip' is 'sensuous' (we are back at this point to the Kantian allusion discussed earlier). Here we are back in the mundane via the loss of a 'distended' sense of self ('my personal system' [43]); instead, Arsene is plunged back into the world as characterized by the rupture of the lines of communication, the breakdown of subject and object: 'the reversed metamorphosis. The Laurel into Daphne. The old thing where it always was, back again' (44).

Arsene's monologue is composed of two enormous paragraphs: the first (seven pages long) basically deals with Arsene's visionary experiences and loss thereof; the second much longer one (eighteen pages) consists of a number of discrete topics that increasingly reflect Arsene's anxiety-ridden final efforts to make some sense of Mr Knott's establishment and to pass this information to his successor. (The twenty-five-page total for this interlude is virtually the same as that devoted to Stephen's aesthetic theory in *Portrait*.) These topics consist of a very short anecdote about Mr Ash that is intended as some type of exemplum and bridges the two paragraphs; the famous discussion of the three laughs (the bitter, hollow, and ethical); the eight pages on the 'increeping and outbounding house and parlour maids' (50), followed by five pages on the corresponding set of permutations as applied to the servants who have waited on Mr Knott, up to and including Arsene and Watt; and, finally, the 'hail and farewell' as Arsene, at last, takes his leave of Watt for good. For the further development of the Joyce-Beckett connections, the two most important sections are those that 'frame' this second 'paragraph,' the Mr Ash story and Arsene's 'hail and farewell.' The story of Mr Ash is also 'framed' in Caw's sense: it stands out from the incredibly long 'short statement' as the foregrounded beginning of its second part, and its opening sentence forces the reader (no 'gentle skimming' possible here) to draw out a comparison with the ideas implicit in the concluding sentence of the preceding paragraph: 'But I am worse than Mr Ash, a man I once knew to nod to' (45).

In his summing up at the end of his first paragraph, Arsene says he has 'information of a practical nature to impart.' This consists of his 'opinion' that his visionary experience 'was not an illusion, as long as it lasted, that presence of what did not exist' (45) and, secondly, the tortured question of whether what has happened to Arsene will happen also to Watt, ending with the generalization 'For in truth the same things happen to us all, especially to men in our situation, whatever that is, if only we chose to know it.' So: the question upon which the two disjointed parts of Arsene's celebrated 'short statement' turns is how does a statement of a general principle ('in truth the same things happen to us all') connect with, 'But I am worse than Mr Ash, a man I once knew to nod to.'

Let us briefly suspend the answer until we have summarized the Mr Ash episode and considered the most influential critical interpretations of it. Arsene meets Mr Ash on Westminster Bridge one day when 'it was blowing heavily.' In vaudevillian fashion, Mr Ash unpeels various layers of clothing, extracts his watch ('a gun metal half-hunter') and declares, unsolicited, that the time is 'seventeen minutes past five exactly, as God is my witness'; but, a moment after he has sped away, Big Ben tolls six o'clock. Arsene's summary conclusion follows: 'This in my opinion is the type of all information whatsoever, be it voluntary or solicited' (46). The distinguished Joyce scholar David Hayman has argued that this scene is 'curiously similar' to Joyce's version in *Finnegans Wake* I ii of the meeting of HCE with the Cad:

> Walking across Phoenix park one gusty April morning, HCE was accosted by a stranger, a 'cad with a pipe,' who asked him 'how much a clock it was that the clock struck.' In response, motivated by fear of violence, HCE drew from his 'gunpocket his Jurgensen's shrapnel Waterbury,' but just as he was about to announce the time he heard the 'ten ton tonnant thunderous tenor foller in the speckled church' ring the hour. Promptly he told the 'inquiring kidder' that 'by Jehova, it was twelve of em sideral and tankard time.' The cad's question was suspicious, given the fact that the clock had not yet struck, but so was HCE's response, given the discrepancy between the two times.[13]

Hayman develops in detail a comparison of the two episodes and concludes that it is probably best regarded as Beckett's 'oblique and probably reflexive homage' to Joyce. What is most fascinating here, however, is Hayman's description of Beckett's reaction to this proposed source of influence when Hayman visited him in Paris in 1969. In Hayman's words, Beckett was fascinated by the supposed 'parallel' (took a 'lively interest' in it), denied any such intention, yet during the visit 'returned frequently to the subject, asking first to see the passage, then to hear it, and finally to have the page reference.'[14] Hayman's case that the Mr Ash episode strongly echoes the Cad scene in *Finnegans Wake* is endorsed by another distinguished Joyce scholar, William York Tindall, in his *Reader's Guide to 'Finnegans Wake.'*[15] John P. Harrington in *The Irish Beckett* (1991) simply regards this as an accepted critical judgment and refers to it as '*Watt*'s allusion to Joyce,' along with the apparent assumption that this is the only such allusion in the text.[16]

No wonder Beckett took such a 'lively interest' in Hayman pointing out to him the 'parallel' with Joyce: his persistent questioning for specific details might be explained, at least in part, by the argument I have put forth with respect to *Watt* as a Joycean novel and Arsene a composite Joycean figure. To have a renowned Joyce scholar visit him and point out a supposed analogue to the *Wake* without, however, making any mention at all of the extensive referencing in *Watt* of other Joycean materials would indeed be somewhat surprising. Doubly so, for the Joyce material invoked by Hayman, however interesting in itself, does not address the issues raised and so carefully foregrounded and poised in Arsene's transition between the first and second parts ('paragraphs') of his 'statement' to Watt; in short, that question of linkage between the two parts that we suspended in order to set up the Mr Ash episode in conjunction with the story of HCE and the Cad in the *Wake*.

The link between Mr Ash and Arsene and the critical probing of the way in which, in some particular regard, the latter could be deemed 'worse' than the former has nothing to do with Joyce. It does, however, have a great deal to do with Kant's philosophy, and this can be much more convincingly argued as *intentionally* there than the *Wake* analogue. In his commentary on Beckett's reading and notetaking from Kant in the *Murphy* Notebook, John Pilling supplies hints for a quasi-Kantian reading of the Mr Ash incident, one which can be extended and more directly connected with the linkage between the two parts of Arsene's statement. One of Beckett's notes on Kant conjures up the mise en scène of the Mr Ash story: 'Kant's exact description of Westminster Bridge (having never set foot outside Prussia).'[17] Kant was indeed famous for his precise and exacting schedule: the inhabitants of Königsberg could set their watches by his daily constitutional. Hence there is a grotesque contrast between Kant's ordered world in which various chronologies are synchronized and the very bizarrely detailed description of Mr Ash, which is still somehow lacking in such 'exact[ness]'; and there is a maddening disparity between his time ('as God is my witness') and official authorized time as pounded out by Big Ben. There is obviously no longer any Enlightenment master narrative that can encompass these conflicting perspectives.

There is also present in the Mr Ash story another set of Kantian ideas that would be more accessible to a general reader and do address the link between Arsene and Mr Ash that occurs at an important point both structurally and thematically in Arsene's speech. In the Mr Ash story, Arsene does indeed have 'information' of 'a practical nature to impart,' offering up as he does a version of Kant's famous categorical imperative from the

Critique of Practical Reason. Kant formulated the categorical imperative in several different ways, the first of which is this: 'Act only on that maxim whereby thou canst at the same time will that it should become a universal law.'[18] Arsene's first 'paragraph' ends with his own neo-Kantian version of a universal law, which applies to the servants of Mr Knott: 'For in truth the same things happen to us all, especially to men in our situation, whatever it is, if only we chose to know it' (45). Here, of course, there is an uneasy fluctuation between passive and active roles that undercuts the dynamic 'act' of Kant, which is a declared imperative. Nevertheless, Arsene is putting forth a general law that *could* become the basis for ethical conduct based upon an examination of the existential realities referred to in the following phrases and clauses – 'especially to one in our situation, whatever that is, if only we chose to know it.' Arsene is 'worse than Mr Ash,' therefore, in that he wants to impose a sameness, a number of universalizing factors that lay out a uniform reality or common ground of experience, whereas the story of Mr Ash's own time being out of joint with the big world's reckoning is exemplary of the differences that subvert any general law. Hence Arsene adds the moral to the story: 'This in my opinion is the type of all information whatsoever, be it voluntary or solicited' (46).

Is Arsene's 'information' of a supposedly 'practical nature' then only ironically equivalent to *mis*-information, a *mis*-taking of reality? Not quite. The vital issue upon which the novel pivots, and implicit in the complex connections suggested between the last sentence of Arsene's first paragraph and the first sentence of his second, is whether a series of generalizations based on what happened to Arsene can be legitimately projected to anticipate what will happen to Watt. With reference to this pervasive question of 'influence,' of 'tradition and the individual talent,' to recast the terms, another of Kant's famous formulations of the categorical imperative is also relevant: 'So act as to treat humanity, whether in thine own person or that of any other, in every case as an end withal, never as a means only.'[19] This is, in effect, another way of stating such maxims as 'Do unto others as you would have them do unto you.' That is, each man should be treated as an end in himself; at Mr Knott's house there is only false equality in that all his servants are employed as a means only of testifying to Mr Knott's needs, not to their own. Arsene's compulsive fixation upon the series in which such servants may be slotted (and which Watt will take to an even more advanced state of mania) is pursued in conjunction with the 'practical' (ethical) issue of individuality, of Arsene and Watt, for instance, and how each will have different

experiences at Mr Knott's and afterwards as well, how each will be potentially his own end. This is the decisive question Arsene raises at the
end of the first part of his speech and to which he returns at the very end
of his speech, appropriately enough. Watt needs to be himself, not just a
mimic-man version of Arsene, and the same goes for Beckett in his relationship to Joyce.

Arsene ends his first paragraph with the idea that he has 'information of a practical nature' to impart; he ends his second paragraph with
a paradoxical formulation of his failure to convey his 'quite useless
wisdom so dearly won' during his tenure at Mr Knott's. In Arsene's
monologue the discussion has moved from a consideration of the
boundary lines of 'pure reason' and the two worlds of the phenomenal
and noumenal, to considerations of an ethical nature (what Arsene refers to in Kantian terms as 'practical'), and, finally, in his last words of
advice to Watt, to a consideration of the role of the imagination, to issues of 'aesthetic judgment' (*W*, 165). But such is the angst-ridden nature of Arsene's statement that there is no neat compartmentalization
of these various 'critiques,' for they are all patently self-critiques.

In his pointed questioning of man's conflicted being, Arsene is echoing
Kant's well-known dictum in the *Critique of Judgment* that '*Beauty* is an object's form of purposiveness insofar as it is perceived in the object *without
the precondition of a purpose.*'[20] Arsene is not merely an aesthetician, however, being concerned rather with a number of excruciating questions of
an existential nature as he tries to determine whether in all our comings
and goings there might not be some larger pattern of meaning: 'For what
is this shadow of the going in which we come, this shadow of the coming
in which we go, this shadow of the coming and the going in which we
wait, if not the shadow of a purpose, of the purpose that budding withers,
that withering buds, whose blooming is a budding withering? [...] And
though in purposelessness I may seem now to go, yet I do not, any more
than in purposelessness then I came, for I go now with my purpose as
with it then I came, the only difference being this, that then it was living
and now it is dead' (58). In a footnote example of this 'Beauty,' Kant says
that 'when we are judging the flower, we do not refer to any purpose
whatever.'[21] But Arsene does refer to a purpose, or at least the shadow of
a purpose: man's coming and going is a budding and a withering, not an
aesthetic stasis, and how do we make sense of that? On one level, the answer would be an artistic embodiment that combines stasis and kinesis,
the two defining characteristics of supposedly opposing views of artistic
experience as set out in Stephen Dedalus's theory in *Portrait*.

In an attempt to 'formulate' his 'useless wisdom,' Arsene draws a comparison from classical mythology: he says that he is so totally 'imbued' with this 'useless wisdom' 'that I neither eat nor drink nor breathe in and out nor do my doodles but more sagaciously than before, like Theseus kissing Ariadne or Ariadne Theseus, towards the end, on the seashore' (62–3). The classical allusion is appropriate in a number of ways. First of all, as Arsene is winding up his 'advice' to Watt he is just about to leave Mr Knott's house, which at the beginning of his speech was likened to a labyrinth of sorts: 'All the old ways led to this, all the old windings' (40). He has gained a sort of wisdom, however 'useless,' in that he has now worked his way through the maze of Mr Knott's house and is about to leave it – just as Theseus and Ariadne have gained a new knowledge of the labyrinth by killing the Minotaur and escaping by means of Ariadne's guiding thread. But the ironic connection between Arsene and Theseus and Ariadne in terms of their future situations is also becoming obvious here. What follows the scene on the seashore is, in Ovid's words, described this way: 'but on the shore of that island he cruelly abandoned his companion'[22] (reportedly upon the command of Minerva, who appeared to him in a dream vision). Theseus will abandon Ariadne, just as Arsene will now be 'abandoned,' replaced by another man at Mr Knott's, namely, Watt. Or one could speculate that in a sense Arsene has 'abandoned' Watt, even though there are, we are told, very strict regulations controlling the coming and going of the servants. Did Beckett, on another level, feel 'abandoned' by Joyce's 'departure' just a month before he started work on what became *Watt*? Whatever the case, Joyce's presence is most pronounced in *Watt* at this very end point of Arsene's seemingly endless 'short statement.' The sentence from Ovid's *Metamorphoses* cited above comes only seven sentences before the famous formulation concerning Daedalus's inventiveness, from which Joyce extracted the epigraph for *Portrait*: 'with these words [referring to his means of escape: Minos 'does not possess the air'], *he set his mind to sciences never explored before, and altered the laws of nature*' (epigraph italicized). – '*Et ignotas animum dimittit in artes*' – Ovid, *Metamorphoses*, VIII, 188. Thus, by invoking the Theseus-Ariadne story Beckett also brings into play by association and textual proximity the whole story of the Cretan Labyrinth and Daedalus's construction of it.

Arsene's valedictorian address invokes a number of other famous literary leave-takings. Arsene tells Watt that he has taken him 'as far as it lay in my power to take you, under the circumstances' (63). This echoes that most famous of all 'hail and farewells' in literature, Virgil's guiding of Dante to the point beyond which he must travel on his own. And it is hardly a surprise that Beckett's own doodles in the *Watt* manuscript show him depicting this very scene.[23] There is even a muted echo of one of the most poetic passages in all of Joyce, the very last words of *Finnegans Wake*, in Arsene's last words to his successor: 'And now for a little along the way that lies between you and me Erskine will go by your side, to be your guide, and then for the rest you will travel alone, or with only shades to keep you company, and that I think you will find, if your experience at all resembles mine, the best part of the outing or at least the least dull, even though the light falls fast, and far below the stumbling feet' (63). Compare 'for a little along the way' and 'for the rest you will travel alone' with 'A way a lone a last a loved a long the.' Here are also embedded the famous words of Knowledge when he introduces himself to Everyman: 'I will go with thee, and be thy guide,/In thy most need to go by thy side.' And, in short order, Everyman is led to the realization that at the point of death he will indeed have to travel alone, with only shades for company. The great comic irony is that in Beckett's redaction Arsene is introducing the totally uninformed Erskine to play the role of Knowledge for Watt. Arsene's purported desire to impart his own 'information' of a 'practical nature' has thus turned out to be a sort of literary practical joke.

In a more serious vein, Arsene's final words also focus on the imagination, or 'aesthetic judgment': 'And I think I have said enough to light that fire in your mind that shall never be snuffed, or only with the utmost difficulty' (62). After Arsene departs, Watt resumes his 'innocent little game' (38) of playing with the lamp, covering and uncovering it so the ashes in the fire alternately 'greyen, redden, greyen, redden' (38).[24] The whole monstrously long 'short statement' of Arsene is framed by Watt playing with the light of the fire, which is oddly reminiscent of that section in chapter 5 of *Portrait* when Stephen Dedalus discusses, or rather attempts to discuss, aesthetic matters with the dean of studies. Stephen says he is working 'by the light of one or two ideas from Aristotle and Aquinas' (164) and that they are only 'for my own use and guidance until I have done something for myself by their light' (164). At the end of part 1, we see Watt trying to distinguish whether the dawn of the 'new day' has indeed risen, or whether it is a false light he is seeing; to clarify his vision, Watt turns down the wick of the lamp 'and blew down the chimney, until it was quite extinguished' (64). The sense of the old ending and the new beginning is cunningly woven Dedalian fashion into the beginning and ending of Watt's very long and drawn-out encounter with Arsene. When Watt finally gets into Mr Knott's house for the first time, he encounters a gentleman, who, we learn later, is Arsene: 'The gentleman gazed long at Watt, and then went away, without a word of explanation' (38). The gentleman soon reappears, 'dressed for the road,' and delivers his infamous 'short statement' to *Watt*. The 'gazed long at Watt' echoes the famous birdgirl epiphany of *Portrait*: 'Long, long she suffered his gaze and then quietly withdrew her eyes from his and bent them towards the stream, gently stirring the water with her foot hither and thither' (151). Twenty-five pages later, in his final words of wisdom to Watt, Arsene finally completes the birdgirl epiphany sentence of *Portrait* cited above; Arsene is explaining how difficult – in fact, impossible – it was to express epiphanic moments even when he found himself experiencing 'the pleasant dawdling motion carrying me about in the midst of them, hither and thither, with unparalleled sagacity' (63). Watt's arrival signals Arsene's departure into silence and exile.

It now remains to be seen what Watt can make of his experiences at Mr Knott's without the company of Arsene. The short answer: not very much. Watt is definitely no Arsene – he has no visionary experience to speak of; no epiphany of any discernible import radiates within Watt's mind, the phenomenal world outside, or points betwixt the two. The most obvious reason for this anticlimactic outcome of Watt's 'new day' is that he does not expect or desire any such outcome; he is simply not attuned to such possibilities. To adapt the last words of the novel: 'no [epiphanies] where none intended.' Watt clearly does not 'intend' any such revelations. Instead Watt seeks consolation in a number of pseudo-logical permutations of reality (such as the options inherent in feeding Mr Knott's dogs), finally focusing in the asylum scenes of part 3, where he meets Sam the narrator, on the various permutations that can be applied to language itself in terms of both diction and syntax. In such discussions of language in *Watt*, and they have predictably dominated criticism of the work, parallels with Mauthner and Wittgenstein have often been invoked, as well as with Joyce, as mentioned earlier, particularly to the 'Ithaca' chapter of *Ulysses*. There is no need to rehearse these arguments here; it is, however, worth noting that Beckett's bizarre presentation of Watt's linguistic breakdown probably owes less to *Ulysses* proper and more to Beckett's ironic response to Joyce's statement to him that he had a supreme confidence in making words say what he wanted, that it was a matter of rearranging the right words in the right order to achieve the intended effects: 'I have discovered I can do anything with language I want' (JJ, 702). Watt does implement such tactics in a parodic and demented manner; his imagination, which we are told had never been 'lively' (83), is ostensibly satisfied by surface appearances, as long as they fit neatly into his categories of cognition. He is certainly not looking for any symbols whereby the penetration of the phenomenal by the noumenal might miraculously occur. Hence the appropriateness of Beckett's own judgment that *Watt* was basically a series of 'exercises' whereby he could keep his mind off the chaos of the engulfing war years.[25] Some qualification is, however, needed here: the designation of *Watt* as a series of 'exercises' can only legitimately be applied to the last three sections of the novel, not to the opening part dominated by Arsene's tour de force of the 'short statement.' But Beckett and his fictional probe, the hapless Watt, do not know what to do next, after having paid homage to as well as having proffered a critique of the modernist tenets inherent in Arsene's visionary experience. Not able or willing to repeat Joyce's work and unable to supply at this point a viable alternative to it, *Watt* turns out to be post-Arsene a series of 'exercises' whereby Beckett can begin to work towards what his own aesthetic might entail.

The principal 'incident of note' during Watt's early days at Mr Knott's involves the visit of the piano turners, the Galls, father and son. How Beckett has reframed Stephen Dedalus's central aesthetic tenets is made explicit in the following sentences with their memorable phrases concerning the 'nothingness' rather than the 'whatness' (or *quidditas*) of Watt's processes of apprehension:

(i) 'For the incident of the Galls father and son was followed by others of a similar kind, incidents that is to say of *great formal brilliance* and indeterminable purport' (74, my italics).

(ii) 'Yes, Watt could not accept ... that nothing had happened, with *all the clarity* and solidity of something' (76, my italics).

In the first citation, it might be said that *morphē* has been apprehended, but there is no corresponding revelation of significance as in *Portrait*'s synthesis of the three stages of aesthetic apprehension; in the second example, we do have a sort of 'whatness,' but it is depicted as a 'nothingness,' 'with all the clarity and solidity of something.' Somehow Watt and his narrator Sam need to find a way of reconciling these apparently antithetical elements.

In a sense, Beckett is saying in *Watt* what Stephen Dedalus said at the beginning of his discussion of aesthetics with the dean of studies: he is provisionally using one or two ideas (in Stephen's case from Aristotle and Aquinas; in Beckett's and Watt's case from *Portrait*'s aesthetic), but he needs them for his 'own use and guidance' only until he has done 'something' for himself 'by their light' (*P*, 164). Whereas Arsene could experience moments of transcendence of god-like insight during his time at Mr Knott's ('I was the sun'), Watt is much more down to earth and just wants things to remain as they were before so that he can fit them into preconceived patterns, into certain various habitual configurations. If necessary he will even 'extract' (79) such patterns when they do not exist, as is suggested with reference to the episode with the Galls. This is a 'self-defence' of a Kantian nature since it manipulates a priori categories such as time and space to accommodate something of 'indeterminable purport.' The galling experience is not then totally unmitigated.

That Beckett is grappling with some of the perplexities and aporias of the philosophical problems associated with modernist aesthetics is reinforced in the Gall episode by an excursus on Proust's aesthetic of involuntary memory (a fictionalized version of Beckett's major reservations as voiced in *Proust*):

> But what was this pursuit of meaning, in this indifference to meaning? And to what did it tend? These are delicate questions. For when Watt at last spoke of this time, it was a time long past, and of which his recollections were, in a sense, perhaps less clear than he would have wished, though too clear for his liking, in another. Add to this the notorious difficulty of recapturing, at will, modes of feeling peculiar to a certain time, and to a certain place, and perhaps also to a certain state of the health, when the time is past, and the place left, and the body struggling with quite a new situation. (75)

Sam then compounds this already vexed situation by adding a commentary about the disintegration of Watt's language functions and 'the obscurity of Watt's communications.' Crucial aspects of modernist aesthetics are now even more difficult to apprehend since the very means of conveying them, of expressing them, are now subjected to a radical and sceptical critique.

Such modernist dilemmas are even further compounded with theoretical and existentialist impasses in two other incidents of note, Watt's pots and the picture in Erskine's room. For Watt Mr Knott's pots are no longer pots: word and thing, signifier and signified, are ruptured. However marginal, the gap is nevertheless decisive and the consequences for Watt 'excruciating' – 'this hairbreadth departure from the nature of a true pot' (81).[26] Compare this with Stephen's example in *Portrait* of a basket:

> – In order to see that basket [...] your mind first of all separates the basket from the rest of the visible universe which is not the basket. The first phase of apprehension is a bounding line drawn about the object to be apprehended. An esthetic image is presented to us either in space or in time.
>
> What is audible is presented in time, what is visible is presented in space. But, temporal or spatial, the esthetic image is first luminously apprehended as selfbounded and selfcontained upon the immeasurable background of space or time which is not it. You apprehend it as *one* thing. You see it as one whole. You apprehend its wholeness. That is *integritas*. (184–5)

The situation in *Watt* is indeed inverted: the 'luminous' quality is displaced by an enveloping 'obscurity.' Watt is 'potty,' a basket case, his 'pottiness' consisting of an inability to determine 'whatness' for at Mr Knott's house there would appear to be a proliferation of some things being at once fixed and in flux, in a state of kinesis and stasis.[27]

The traumatic effects on Watt progressively deepen, as with the scene at the centre of the novel, Watt's encounter with the picture in Erskine's room, of a circle 'broken at its lowest point' and 'in the eastern background' a point that might be its centre. This private viewing has an untoward effect on Watt, who has struggled thus far to avoid 'symbols' of anything and to keep his mind only on the surface of phenomena: 'at the thought that it was perhaps this, a circle and a centre not its centre in search of a centre and its circle respectively, in boundless space, in endless time, then Watt's eyes filled with tears that he could not stem' (177). This Watt 'unbounded' who has confronted the Kantian sublime is no longer of sound mind. He has lost his pots and general sense of wholeness and integrity. There is no longer a clearly discerned centre; whereas Lynch can retort wittily 'Bull's eye' to Stephen's pontifical aesthetic pronouncements, Watt can only haltingly admit that he is no longer certain about what to say about himself as a 'man,' no more so than he is certain about the pot's 'whatness.' His only recourse is the idea of a series whereby he can tame such recalcitrant images of this disturbing new reality by pretending that there is indeed an encompassing pattern whereby an *integritas* of sorts might be re-established. Such cataloguings do not in the end convince even Watt and instead of supplying solace are symptomatic of his mental and linguistic breakdown, which leads him to the asylum where he meets our narrator Sam, since he cannot integrate his 'knowledge' of Mr Knott's house with the more ordinary worlds of the frametales.

In the frametale that concludes the novel, Watt makes his way from Mr Knott's house to the train station; one of the incidents of note here concerns Watt's encounter with a chair in the waiting room. Unlike his experiences at Mr Knott's, this particular object seems to meet Stephen's initial requirements in *Portrait* for identifying 'a thing': 'Your mind first of all separates the [object] from the rest of the visible universe which is not the [object]' (184). Watt recognizes 'what seemed an object of some importance' (234), namely, the chair-to-be, and then proceeds to locate it in space by stating further what it is not: 'It was not part of the ceiling, nor of a wall, nor, though it seemed in contact with the floor, of the floor, that was all that Watt could affirm, of this object, and even that little he affirmed with reserve. But that little was enough, for Watt the possibility was enough, more than enough, that something other than he, in this box, was not intrinsic to its limits' (234). Watt is only able to effect Stephen's 'first phase of apprehension' in which 'a bounding line' is 'drawn about the object to be apprehended' (*P*, 184) when the darkness in the waiting room lightened and 'he saw now that his companion all this time had been a chair' (*W*, 235). Watt notes the specifics of his new 'companion': 'a high, narrow, black, wooden chair, with arms, and castors' (235), and 'came to know this chair, so well, that in the end he knew it better than many a chair he had sat on' (235). Outside of Mr Knott's house, objects such as this chair do seem to have regained their conventional status as particular things; whether or not there might be an epiphany that reveals their 'radiance' or 'whatness' is the decisive question. In Beckett's transition scene between worlds at the ending of *Watt*, there are no ex cathedra aesthetic pronouncements in the manner of *Portrait*, only further critical questioning of the relevance of such theories to Beckett's particular predicament in this novel.

In the midst of expounding his theory of beauty to Lynch, Stephen mentions that he has a book at home full of curious questions and that the answers to them have enabled him to formulate his provisional aesthetic theory. Here is the very first question he refers to: '*Is a chair finely made tragic or comic?'* (*P*, 186) Watt's chair has both 'castors' and 'clamp[s]' on its 'feet,' but only one foot is presently 'screwed to the floor'; hence it is not fixed to one set of static points but can potentially move through a fixed circular pattern. Is this 'tragic or comic' or both or neither? Who knows? In Beckett's discussion of Watt's chair 'no symbols' are 'intended,' even if the whole episode seems designed to evoke such aesthetic speculations. At the climax of this discussion in *Portrait*, Stephen likens the moment when the aesthetic image is 'conceived' in the artist's imagination to 'The mind in that mysterious instant Shelley likened beautifully to a fading coal' (185). Beckett also uses similar imagery in Watt's chair episode: 'Through the bars, which were vertical, of the back, Watt saw portions of a grate, heaped high with ashes, and cinders, of a beautiful grey colour' (236). This 'beautiful' sight – by definition an aesthetic experience – is literally viewed through the bars of the chair's back; but the two experiences are not fused into one, are not integrated as they are in Stephen's discussion in *Portrait*. Beckett's fundamentally parodic treatment of these ideas in *Watt* – even though he is nostalgically drawn to them – is emphasized by the comically grotesque images of Watt having often employed chairs for purposes of podiatry: 'or toileted his feet on, one after the other, paring and curetting the nails' (235). This is indeed a far cry from Stephen's idealised image of 'The artist, like the God of creation' as somehow 'above his handiwork, invisible, refined out of existence, indifferent, paring his fingernails' (187). Watt is a mere foot soldier in terms of such avant-garde critical speculations on beauty and aesthetic theories. To make sense of his disparate experiences – in this instance a chair and 'the beautiful grey colour' of the ashes – Watt and Beckett are going to have to find ways of being more directly engaged in the experience of aesthetic apprehension, of finding ways of defining themselves into existence as artist-figures in their own right, acting on their own behalf.

In my discussion in 'Beckett and the Philosophers,' I pointed out that the most important Kantian reference came at the very end of the novel and set up a complex interaction between the final scene and the taunting and tantalizing last entry in the Addenda, 'no symbols where none intended.' Rather than rehearse that argument in detail, its main point can be briefly summarized: Kant's comments in 'On beauty as the symbol of morality' (the conclusion to 'Part I. Critique of aesthetic judgment,' in the *Critique of Judgment*) are treated satirically by Beckett to mock the trite conventional symbolism of Mr Gorman and his ilk, who cannot make any sense of Watt for he obviously doesn't fit into their 'pretty picture' of God's in his heaven, all's well with the world. Beckett's parody in this instance of Kantian aesthetics and morality is, however, critically focused in the very last words of the novel in its second ending, the Addenda: 'no symbols where none intended.' The superficial views of Mr Gorman and company are clearly not 'intended' as any resolution to the dilemmas that Watt has encountered at Mr Knott's. Rereading *Watt* in terms of the Beckett-Joyce question can also throw some new light on the last entry of the Addenda and the relationship of this fragment to the work as a whole. Beckett has played off Kant and Joyce throughout the work, and this carries through to its final words in the last entry to the Addenda.

C.J. Ackerley's annotated version of the Addenda goes beyond earlier criticism by not simply elucidating obscure philosophical and literary references but also setting these thirty-seven unused fragments or leftovers from the novel proper (if such a term may any longer be legitimately invoked in these circumstances) within their original context in the manuscript versions of the novel. The context is revealing in terms of the final entry of the Addenda. The last words of *Watt* appear as a concluding remark to a discussion between Arsene and Watt (then called Johnny Watt) in the darkened bowels of Mr Quin's house (to be renamed soon Mr Knott's) about the issue of illuminating the darkness. Here is Ackerley's citation from the manuscript, accompanied by his summary-cum-gloss:

> on the uttering of the sentiment, 'Each in his own way, all are in the dark,' a match is struck, and burns bravely, until its fire reaches the fingers and it is dropped; whereupon 'it continued for a little while bravely to burn, till it could burn no longer, bravely or otherwise. Then it went out.'
>
> But in that brief light, things are revealed: 'the passage and the stairs, all as we had left them, and the dark in which we were, each in his or her own way, and Eamon [the duck] and Arsene and the passage and the stairs and the bells and newell – and we' [the narrator, Johnny Watt in this instance, refers to himself as 'we']. It is all too easy: a little light in the big dark; a feathered and featherless biped; a dark passage; purgatorial stairs; the hint of eucharist in distant bells, rung by Watt to tell Quin his meal is ready, or by Quin, to tell Watt that he might clear away. But 'we' remains in the dark. In a context so insistently demanding symbolic interpretation, in the presence of details so often used to translate consciousness into meaning, the only thing Watt can say is: 'No symbols where none intended.'[28]

Ackerley's own final annotation says that these words of Watt invoke an 'impossible paradox' about not-knowing in that the text encourages us to deal with it symbolically at the very time its final injunction is to forestall such practices.[29]

The match struck in the dark hallway passage is a vintage example of Beckett revising the modernist aesthetic of the epiphany. (Indeed, the struck match and its brief flare of illumination is also strongly evocative of one of Virginia Woolf's best-known 'moments of being' in her novels.)[30] Arsene as a complex composite of Joycean characteristics would in this scene invoke the 'miracle' of a 'sudden spiritual manifestation.' We have already examined in a number of ways how such 'transports' do not work for Watt. The Kant-Joyce connection that Beckett has employed in a number of ways throughout *Watt* is here used as a sort of double negation: for Watt (and by indirection Sam and Beckett) the Arsene-Joyce symbolic weighting of the dark scene that seeks illumination is just as 'pre-scribed' in its own predictability as is the 'gesture of worship' of Mr Gorman and cohorts as they welcome their new day.[31] Watt's own 'new day' of 'enlightenment' at Mr Knott's has come and gone, and no vision of the Arsenean-Joycean type has been vouchsafed him. Ackerley is dead right, of course; 'it is all too easy' in the dark passage scene to invoke a series of symbolic remedies of an ultimately theological nature. 'No symbols where none intended' is a rejection of such an easy way out; yet to leave the question engulfed only by a series of negatives at this point is also to miss the full import of Beckett's critical strategies in *Watt* and throughout his early works.

The very title of Ackerley's elucidation of the residual materials of Beckett's third and last novel in English is indicative of this bias towards all too easily emphasized negatives in Beckett studies: '"Fatigue and Disgust": The Addenda to *Watt*.' Beckett's (or Sam's) footnoted entry on the Addenda reads in full: 'The following precious and illuminating material should be carefully studied. Only fatigue and disgust prevented its incorporation' (246). The two-part structure here is significant; even if 'precious and illuminating' is saturated with heavy mockery, it does, nevertheless, raise the spectre in its very phrasing of Joyce's description of the epiphany in *Stephen Hero*, which was published posthumously in 1944: 'He believed it was for the man of letters to record these epiphanies with great care, seeing that they themselves are the most delicate and evanescent of moments' (*SH*, 215–16).[32] Beckett handles his leftover fragments with open contempt and simply confronts the reader with the thirty-seven entries, which have been denied entry into the story proper (such as it is), when Sam supposedly came to edit his little notebooks in which he recorded Watt's jumbled narrative.

Yet some of the entries in the Addenda do have the potential for an epiphany or revelation within Stephen Dedalus's own categories whereby such discoveries might occur, 'whether in the vulgarity of speech or of gesture or in a memorable phrase of the mind itself' (*SH*, 215). Most of the entries in the Addenda fall into the third category; they do indeed require 'careful study' so that their significance may manifest itself. One man's epiphany is, however, another man's dud, for there is an absence of the context in which such an illumination might be experienced. From Ackerley's identification of the last entry of the Addenda 'no symbols where none intended' within the context of an earlier manuscript version of *Watt*, we know that these words had originally been attributed to Watt himself. But they have been taken away from him and any such direct attribution withdrawn; Sam doesn't know how to accommodate the caveat and leaves it suspended ambiguously in his final entry. Realization of a potential illumination can only occur when someone takes responsibility for the words and stories being conveyed; as it stands, Watt experiences and Sam records. Somehow or other experiencing and recording must be incorporated within a narrative structure that can validate both of their claims to being – 'somethings' and 'nothings' need to be brought into a new relationship. Mr Knott is indeed a good master; he compels his servants to leave his employ and return to the outside world whence they came, the task then becoming the quest for integration of these two realms in a critical and imaginative fashion. This is the first key step in Beckett's moving forward to find his own way as he rewrites and critiques Joyce, via Kant in particular, thereby clarifying for himself how his own 'a way a lone a last' differs from Joyce's, even as he acknowledges his influence. Beckett and Joyce, Watt and Stephen would all agree on this foundational point: after a certain point of theorizing, a new experience is indeed needed to see the way to an aesthetic of one's own; the 'reality of experience' needs to be 'forged' anew.

Watt is about a middle-aged man who has no pretensions to being an artist. Nevertheless, Watt's various failures do lead him, however unintentionally, towards questions of 'aesthetic judgment' (*W*, 165), such as the rearrangement of words and the selective hearing of various voices. His alter ego Sam is another matter; he clearly has artistic pretensions of a sort, even though they are concealed behind the figure and supposedly originating source of Watt. Sam's own experience needs to come to the fore. The one aesthetic principle of *Portrait* that Beckett never seriously entertains (not even in *Dream* or *Murphy*) is that of a god-like author creator who resides, invisibly, behind his handiwork, 'refined out of existence.' On the contrary, in Beckett's work the central literary-ontological issue is to find out and redefine the very existence of such an entity vis-à-vis the world that is to be represented. Joyce's 'invisibility' allows *Portrait* to end with the semblance at least that Stephen is beginning to take control of his own story, as evidenced in his final twenty diary entries. The ending of *Watt* in the Addenda is no such 'pretty picture.' The leftover dog's breakfast of various elements that could not be incorporated within the boundaries of the work itself do, in however disconnected a fashion, constitute a section unto themselves, the Addenda. The five distinct parts of *Watt* could be regarded as a botched and mangled parody of the five chapters of *Portrait*, which trace at least a chronologically coherent development of one figure, Stephen Dedalus. But *Watt* has also made some major strides forward in foregrounding the issues that must now be dealt with if Beckett is going to be able in his own way to incorporate the various fragments that are left unaccommodated in his last novel in English. Without Joyce's guidance, Beckett could not have reached this point at which the need for new revelations is absolutely critical.

5 The Pseudocouple Dante-Joyce: The Nature of the 'Revelation' in *Mercier and Camier* and *Stories*

This study has thus far shown just how extensively Beckett's works were influenced by a Joyce who exercised a much greater role in determining the structure, style, and aesthetic underpinnings of Beckett's own writing than critics have heretofore recognized and acknowledged. Of course, it is Beckett's own choice of Joyce that is decisive in this regard; from the very beginning in 'Assumption,' Beckett committed himself to an in-depth dialogical engagement with Joyce, in particular his *Portrait*, in order to determine what direction his own aesthetic thinking might take. As we have encountered in a telling number of instances, Beckett's fundamental dilemma might be characterized as a classic case of approach-avoidance: drawn to Stephen Dedalus's aesthetic precepts as an obvious point of departure for his own speculations, Beckett began by formulating his own critique of such modernist theories, only to discover in his early works through *Watt* that he had nothing of substantive import to replace them with. Arsene as a Joycean composite was vouchsafed a visionary experience that could not, however, sustain itself, and its aftermath plunged him back into a world devoid of any transcendental significance. This is Beckett's most powerful critique of the theoretical aporias inherent in the modernist aesthetics that he grappled with in his early fiction and his critical study of Proust. On the other hand, *Watt*'s failure to experience any such revelatory experience results in a series of what might be termed negative epiphanies in which he loses touch with even the most mundane and commonplace of objects, such as Mr Knott's pots. Such failures of comprehension and expression did, however, at least hold out the theoretical possibility of new syntheses whereby various negatives might themselves be transformed into affirmations in the creation of new worlds of the imagination.

Indeed, this is exactly what occurs in Beckett's works after *Watt*; in a miraculously short period of time, in a handful of years between 1945 and 1949, Beckett produced the major works that for many readers still constitute the basis of his reputation as a writer of the first rank, namely, the *Trilogy* (*Molloy, Malone Dies*, and *The Unnamable*) and his most famous play, *Waiting for Godot*. Beckett went to a great deal of trouble to ensure that this outburst of creative production would be regarded as intimately conjoined with, indeed dependent upon, a visionary experience in his own life, what he persistently referred to as the 'revelation.' As the story was told by Beckett to various friends and associates over the years, his quintessential experience of a world-changing shift in perspective came about as a recognition that the 'dark' which he had heretofore tried to suppress was in fact the very area in which he now had to seek the reality of his own artistic explorations and that henceforth he would dedicate himself to contriving means for its expression (*DF*, 352).[1] This 'revelation' – or rather a variant thereof – famously appears in a satirical rendering in *Krapp's Last Tape* (1958) in which the protagonist is much more concerned with locating a recording of a very different kind of epiphany concerning a moment of love in a boat;[2] in passing, Krapp does offer, however inadvertently, a description of the visionary experience he underwent at age thirty-nine (the same age at which Beckett had his):

> until that memorable night in March, at the end of the jetty, in the howling wind, never to be forgotten, when suddenly I saw the whole thing. The vision, at last ... What I suddenly saw then was this, that the belief I had been going on all my life, namely – (*Krapp switches off impatiently, winds tape forward, switches on again*) – great granite rocks the foam flying up in the light of the lighthouse and the wind-gauge spinning like a propeller, clear to me at last that the dark I have always struggled to keep under is in reality my most –[3]

Filling in the blanks involves much more here than simply adding Beckett's own comments to friends such as Ludovic Janvier that the dark he had sought to keep at bay was 'ultimately to become the source of his creative inspirations.'[4] It also entails much more than debunking the crapulent Krapp's romantico-mystical rendering of storms and lighthouses (symbols where intended?).

In the two most suggestive accounts of Beckett's 'revelation' – those of Richard Ellmann in *Four Dubliners* (1986) and James Knowlson in his

Beckett biography (1996) – it is underscored that Beckett's 'vision' is to be sharply distinguished from Krapp's, occurring as it does without a romantic mise en scène in Ireland in the summer of 1946 at his mother's house, New Place, across the road from the old family home, Cooldrinagh (*DF*, 352).[5] This accurate placing of Beckett's 'revelation' is, of course, only a preliminary step – albeit an essential one – in beginning to determine just what significance should be attributed to this self-styled visionary experience, which Beckett has repeatedly proposed as the very basis of his being as a writer. Beckett's own insistence upon the decisive significance of this 'revelation' obviously entails a much more complex investigation of the art-life nexus than that which Beckett peremptorily curtailed in his 'Foreword' to *Proust*: 'There is no allusion in this book to the legendary life and death of Marcel Proust, nor to the garrulous old dowager of the Letters' (followed by three more 'nors' that further 'purify,' supposedly, Beckett's commitment only to the Proustian texts themselves). But in Beckett's particular case his promotion of the 'revelation' as a turning point in his artistic life does indeed necessitate an 'allusion' to his 'legendary life.' To unpack the various critical assumptions that have grown up around the so-called 'revelation' – aided and abetted by Beckett's own propagandizing – is an essential first step in order to see how Beckett's works after *Watt* are of a visionary nature and afford complex readings of 'source and influence' that go well beyond the very often oversimplified versions of a negative world view attributed to him.

Ellmann's first comment on Beckett's 'revelation' implicitly draws a contrast with Dante's *Vision*: 'Unlike most revelations, this one offered no new heaven or new earth. If anything, something like a present hell.'[6] As we will see, *Mercier and Camier* is saturated with Dantean references and the 'vision' afforded can by no means be simply consigned to a 'present hell.' Beckett's own 'revelation' will proceed to a complex purgatorial ascent of its own whereby the Beckettian 'I' is afforded a complex new perspective on the contingent relationship between fiction and reality, life and death. (This remarkable development – one of the most startling in all modern literature – was foreshadowed, as we have already seen, in the very first paragraph of his 'Dante ... Bruno . Vico .. Joyce.') Moreover, from the very beginning of his writing career Beckett has identified Dante and Joyce, reaffirming in the last years of his life how he regarded Dante as a 'Joycean writer.'[7] The reasons for this critical oversight with reference to Beckett's own visionary writing are, however, revelatory of the nature of Beckett studies and the deeply engrained assumptions that have determined so many of its guiding judgments. As Kevin Dettmar has very provocatively argued in 'The Joyce That Beckett Built,' many of Ellmann's views in the late chapters of his *James Joyce* are indebted to a paradigm of Beckett's own devising, as evidenced in his various comments and anecdotal reconstructions when interviewed by Ellmann.[8] Implicit in Beckett's summary reflections on Joyce for Ellmann are the views that were soon to be made explicit in the 'interview' with Shenker, in particular that Joyce's god-like vision afforded him an embarrassment of riches for which he, as a heroic organizer of materials, could and would find the appropriate formal accommodation in language.

For Beckett 'revelation' carries the idea of the imagination making known new worlds; for example, Beckett referred in 1983 to his 'Dante revelation' and added, suggestively, 'This I seem to have managed on my own.'[9] The famous 'revelation' at his mother's could be seen as the creative distillation and synthesis in surprising new combinations of Beckett's understanding of both Dante and Joyce and their influence upon him. And this 'revelation' was indeed something that he was not able to manage solely on his own. Joyce had an integral role to play in Beckett's development throughout his early works; in fact, it would not be an exaggeration to say that without Beckett's long drawn out and in-depth dialogical engagement with Joycean aesthetic theory from 'Assumption' to *Watt* there would not and could not have been the 'revelation.' Hence Beckett's 'dark'-ness is arguably not so much antithetical to Joycean aesthetics as complementary to it; the Beckettian project might then in some important respects be regarded as an extension of the Joycean.

James Knowlson's version of the 'pivotal moment in his entire career' (*DF*, 351) is particularly interesting in terms of the Joycean context of Beckett's work. Like Ellmann, Knowlson begins with Beckett's tendency to speak of his 'revelation' in terms of a preoccupation with impotence and ignorance and tellingly adds that Beckett 'reformulated' this idea 'while attempting to define his debt to James Joyce': 'I realised that Joyce had gone as far as one could in the direction of knowing more, [being] in control of one's material. He was always adding to it; you only have to look at his proofs to see that. I realised that my own way was in impoverishment, in lack of knowledge and in taking away, in subtracting rather than in adding' (*DF*, 352). Here we can see Beckett appropriating his biographer's text, stressing that Knowlson underline how his 'revelation' must be distinguished from Joycean aesthetics.

But any serious appraisal of Beckett's account is bound to make a number of 'subtractions' of its own. The rhetorical sleight of hand of setting up Joyce's work so that it can then be played off to the advantage of the successor's texts cannot be uncritically accepted. Texts such as Jean-Michel Rabaté's *Joyce Upon the Void* and Joseph Buttigieg's study of *Portrait* in a 'different' light are just two obvious examples from a host of recent studies that have dealt with a radically destabilized Joyce. Joyce as 'author-god' is no longer accepted as a matter of course, most notably perhaps in terms of Beckett studies in Daniel Katz's *Saying I No More*, about which there will be more to say in the next chapter. Knowlson does not query Beckett's judgment, returning to this point two more times in his two-and-a-half page discussion of the 'revelation,' repeating Beckett's rejection of 'the Joycean principle that knowing more was a way of creatively understanding the world and controlling it' and concluding with the point that Beckett knew with 'certainty that he had to dissociate himself at an early stage from Joyce's influence' (*DF*, 353).[10] That two such influential scholars, the principal biographers of Joyce and Beckett, should so comprehensively underestimate Joyce's influence and active presence within Beckett's oeuvre, particularly in the early period from 'Assumption' to *Watt*, further reinforces the need to rethink and reconfigure the very assumptions whereby Beckett's work has been read.

The 'revelation' is only of real value if its vision is embodied through access to new worlds of the imagination, or, as Beckett put it in his discussion of the Proustian revelation, the 'assumption' must be accompanied by an 'annunciation' (*Pr*, 51). While this is precisely what has not transpired in Beckett's prose from 'Assumption' through *Watt*, there is in Beckett's early poetry a remarkable anticipation, at least in a paradigmatic fashion, of the forms of representation Beckett's 'revelation' might indeed take. As I argued in *Reconstructing Beckett*, the very first poem of *Echo's Bones and Other Precipitates* (1935), 'The Vulture' (*CP*, 9), has played just such a seminal role in outlining the components of a creation myth that Beckett is only able to put into practice in his prose of the post-'revelation' period.[11] This six-line poem warrants foregrounding in our discussion of this key transition point in Beckett's writing career; the issues, questions, and challenges raised in the poem, taken in conjunction with the lessons learned by Beckett in his often incredibly detailed rewriting and reworking of Joycean works through *Watt*, are vital determinants in his 'original' departures in *Mercier and Camier*, *Stories*, and the famous *Trilogy* itself:

dragging his hunger through the sky
of my skull shell of sky and earth

stooping to the prone who must
soon take up their life and walk

mocked by a tissue that may not serve
till hunger earth and sky be offal (*CP*, 9)

The artist-vulture is depicted in the first lines as weighed down by the material reality of hunger, and the rhythm of the poem conveys a descent into the world ('stooping to the prone'), thus associating the artist in an affirmative way that Belacqua of *Dream* never envisaged with Vega, 'the falling vulture.'[12] The interchange of possessive adjectives in the first lines ('his hunger'/'my skull') also indicates that it is in the art of poetic creation that an authentic relationship of subject and object may take place.

The major achievement of the poem is that Beckett has effected the coincidence of form and content in an ontologically significant way: 'the one is a concretion of the other, the revelation of a world' (42), to adopt Beckett's words from *Proust*, where, as critic, he could only vicariously praise his author's achievement. While the skull of the artist-vulture is hermetically sealed, the correspondence of the outer and inner realms precludes any solipsistic interpretation. The process of transfer is not simply mentalistic: the physical world is not suitable material for the artist until it becomes 'offal' – this is not the superficial art of the naturalists or pseudo-realists whom Beckett scornfully dismissed as 'worshipping the offal of experience' (*Pr*, 59). The artist-vulture cannot feed upon his creatures until living 'tissue' is metamorphosed by the organic cycle of decay, which would strip away the conventional surface and reveal the underlying reality. But, as the second stanza relates, he can, however, still stir them into being ('the prone who must/soon take up their life and walk'). The enigmatic last line suggests that the 'tissue' will not be of use for the artist until 'hunger earth and sky be offal,' which need not imply an extinction of the poetic microcosm; the cyclical structure of the poem and the subsumption of 'hunger earth and sky' by the 'skull' suggests that the final identification of the artistic quest with its appropriate subject matter occurs in the endless rhythm of life, decay, and regeneration.

Read in the context of Beckett's early prose through *Watt*, 'The Vulture' is a remarkable achievement that does supply an at least paradigmatic solution – however abbreviated – to central literary questions Beckett had been struggling with. Long before the well-publicized 'revelation,' it incorporated the idea of an interior world of darkness somehow in conjunction with the light of the world: 'my skull/shell of sky and earth.' Beckett, as a realist of a new sort, will investigate just what is the relationship between 'his hunger'/'my skull'/'their life.' How are they somehow all one, yet things apart? How can this tripartite division of 'the absolute predicament of particular human identity' (*Dis*, 38) be accommodated within a literary whole? Indeed, how might a fictional creation even be legitimately deemed to have 'a particular human identity'? Where does authority for the creative act ultimately reside: with 'his,' or 'my,' or 'their'? An even more fundamental question is what type of stories could these three potentially diverse voices tell that might satisfy their different needs. What words, what type of language, would each need in order to corroborate its claim of a being or a life of its own?

Beckett's artist-vulture figure as the demiurge behind the works after *Watt* is, above all, concerned with determining the nature of the real within literary worlds and finding the appropriate modes of representation. In these works, the most vexed terms of all are 'real,' 'reality,' and its various cognates, and while the problem Beckett has set himself as an extension of his critique of the aesthetics of Joyce and Proust admits of no simple resolution it remains an abiding concern and driving force in his writing. Certainly, any romantic sense of untrammelled joy and religious transcendence is debunked immediately in the image of a vulture slowly circling its prey – no skylarks, nightingales, or, for that matter, hawks or eagles of more conventional poeticizing are invoked here. Beckett informed Lawrence Harvey that the 'starting point' for his poem was the opening stanza of Goethe's 'Winter Journey to the Harz Mountains,' which depicts a vulture ('Geier') seeking its prey.[13] Harvey's commentary on Goethe's poem depicts its author 'in his joyful moment of expectant creativity,' adding that 'Goethe's "Geier" might well be a hawk.'[14] Beckett's depiction reinforces a certain literalism of the imagination: a vulture is a vulture is a vulture, as the three stanzas of Beckett's poem 'stoop' downwards towards its prey.

Beckett is also implicitly drawing a distinction here between Stephen Dedalus's 'fear of symbols and portents, of the hawklike man whose name he bore soaring out of his captivity' (*P*, 195) and his own more down-to-earth and realistic art of hunger as outlined in his own figure of the artist-vulture. Even though Beckett pointed Harvey towards Goethe's poem, Joyce's *Portrait* is arguably the more important background text. Beckett was much more forthcoming about Joyce's influence on his poetry than he ever was about his impact on his prose; in a promotional description of himself for some poems published in *The European Caravan* (1931), Beckett declared that he had 'adapted the Joyce method to his poetry with original results.'[15] This is certainly the case with 'The Vulture,' where Beckett has taken Joyce's use of mythical analogues and realistically adapted them to the contemporary artist's situation. This description of Stephen Dedalus's mythical namesake in *Portrait* is finally much more influential in Beckett's 'The Vulture' than the reputed 'starting point' found in Goethe:

> Now, at the name of the fabulous artificer, he seemed to hear the noise of dim waves and to see a winged form flying above the waves and slowly climbing the air. What did it mean? Was it a quaint device opening a page of some medieval book of prophecies and symbols, a hawklike man flying sunward above the sea, a prophecy of the end he had been born to serve and had been following through the mists of childhood and boyhood, a symbol of the artist forging anew in his workshop out of the sluggish matter of the earth a new soaring impalpable imperishable being? (*P*, 149)

Beckett's central images in 'The Vulture' are indeed formulated as being inherently antithetical to those proposed by Stephen Dedalus, most obviously in the concluding lines of the poem in which the subject matter for the artist is of no use until it has been metamorphosed by the cycle of decay to reveal its underlying nature, until it is 'offal,' whereas for Stephen the artist 'forges' from 'the sluggish matter of the earth a new soaring impalpable imperishable being.'

The artist-vulture has to forage or scavenge for his subject matter. And in this context Beckett is perhaps also implying an ironic indictment of himself, for in 'adapting' Joyce's 'method' Beckett is feeding off scraps of Joyce's great work, even as he is beginning to develop his own aesthetic views, which will allow him after *Watt* to produce works that could be regarded as legitimate rivals to Joyce's. Later in *Portrait*, Stephen laments the fact that 'the monkish learning, in terms of which he was striving to forge out an esthetic philosophy, was held no higher by the age he lived in than the subtle and curious jargons of heraldry and falconry' (158). Stephen's 'monkish learning' refers to his interpretation of Aquinas's theory of the beautiful, which we have seen Beckett's critiques of from 'Assumption' through *Watt*. And the artist-vulture '*stooping* to the prone' (my italics) also invokes the jargon of falconry. It is therefore particularly appropriate that when Beckett is on the verge of translating his own 'revelation' into art his formulations should rely on an adaptation of his own early aesthetic speculations as found in 'The Vulture,' which was in part an adaptation of Joyce's ideas as found in *Portrait*. Stephen's romantic effusions about 'a new soaring impalpable imperishable being' are qualified by the ironic presence of Joyce's invisible narrator, who is recording the young artist's fledgling sense of self. Moreover, it could be argued that Stephen's fundamental mistake in his quest for artisthood is to seek a 'prophetic' or 'symbolic' equation of himself with the 'fabulous artificer' of myth whose name he bears (minus the diphthong). In Beckett's 'The Vulture,' the artist-figure is distinct from the realms of 'my skull' and 'the prone' who will 'soon take up their life and walk.' This complex series of interrelationships whereby the poetic cosmos is sustained is to be distinguished ontologically from Stephen's romantic longings for fusion of subject and object (namely, of himself with his mythical forefather).

Surprisingly, Beckett's commentators have not discussed his next novel, *Mercier et Camier*, in conjunction with his 'revelation.' His biographers have also found it difficult to make any meaningful connections between this novel and Beckett's visionary experience. Knowlson focuses primarily upon Beckett's move to French and various particulars of language play contingent upon this, with no mention at all of the 'revelation' experience that occurred only a couple of months before he started writing the novel (*DF*, 360–1). Anthony Cronin does draw attention to the conjunction of the two events, but only to deny that there is any meaningful interconnection: 'It would be much more dramatic and nicer all round if we could associate this change of language on Beckett's part with the revelation which he seems to have had at Killiney Harbour in 1946. [T]he clean and satisfying pattern we might establish of an immediate change of mode as well as language, and of progress through the *Nouvelles* to the great trilogy of novels, *Molloy, Malone Dies*, and *The Unnamable*, is marred somewhat by the composition of another novel, *Mercier et Camier*, in French in 1946.'[16] On the contrary, *Mercier and Camier* (published in French in 1970, in English in 1974) is a visionary work in a number of seminal ways and preparatory for the great breakthrough in Beckett's writing career that was soon to follow. The word 'vision' itself is prominent throughout the text and in the summaries that follow every two chapters. Most of the novel transpires in shadow or darkness, or in waiting for the same. The very last summary entry for the final chapter 8 reads: 'Dark at its full.' All the key ingredients of the 'revelation' are foregrounded in *Mercier and Camier*. Cronin misreads the very nature of this process of incorporation when he states that there is no 'immediate change of mode as well as language' in *Mercier and Camier*; in fact, over the course of the work there are some dramatic turning points that have proven decisive for all of the later works, foremost of which is a 'fall into fiction' whereby the narrator by the end of the novel becomes his own central character.

Sam in Watt was only a pseudo 'I' in that he wrote on behalf of, and behind, the figure of Watt. Beckett's first authentic 'I' as self-creator appears in the *nouvelle* 'La Suite' (later re-titled 'La Fin'), written two months before *Mercier et Camier* was begun. But it is in the novel that we can actually trace the very means by which such an 'I' as author comes into being within the fiction. The process entails a complex interrelationship of Beckett's two most abiding literary influences – Dante and Joyce. We know from Beckett's manuscript notes for *Murphy* that he initially envisaged a Dantean design for that novel, one which was to be kept 'out of sight' of the reader's recognition.[17] This plan was dropped and what Dantean shaping elements there are in *Murphy* are very clearly signposted, such as 'the Belacqua fantasy.' It is the Joycean elements that are kept 'out of sight' and that, in my reading, prove decisive in the structuring of that work. In *Mercier and Camier*, the Dantean elements are heavily foregrounded for the reader's consideration (multiple references to things 'hellish,' heavy cues such as 'station of the damned' and 'all hope abandoned,' to name only the most explicit); the Joycean ones are much less pronounced but are nevertheless significant in determining the visionary elements in *Mercier and Camier*. This is particularly important for an understanding of Beckett's work after *Watt* since Beckett went out of his way to underline to Knowlson that his new literary program as foreshadowed in his 'revelation' had nothing to do with Joyce's. In the following discussion, we will see that from the very beginning of Beckett's efforts to translate his 'revelation' into his writing practice Joyce still continued to play a number of important roles in determining the shape and direction of Beckett's own work.

The problematical status of the narrator is highlighted in the opening sentence of the novel, an ostensibly third-person narrator, even if he does insist upon preserving his right to the first-person pronoun: 'The journey of Mercier and Camier is one I can tell, if I will, for I was with them all the time' (7). Whose story is this to be, that of the 'I' of the opening sentence or that of Mercier and Camier? The relationship of the latter is finally of secondary importance; the decisive issue con-cerns the relationship between a narrator who progressively defines himself as the 'deviser' of this recounting and not merely its recorder – in short, as the authorial presence within the text – and his two dupes. The presence of a Mr Knott figure in earlier fictions obscured the fact that the central relationship to be deciphered is not Watt-Knott, but that of Watt-Sam. By dispensing with an 'Endon-Knott' figure in *Mercier and Camier*, Beckett takes a major step towards focusing atten-tion upon the 'not-within' – Mercier and Camier have no destination because they are their own goals. Or rather they would be their own goals if they were not the puppets of an author who controls and thwarts their plans in order to further his own ends. The true 'pseudo-couple' (as *The Unnamable* will term them, 297) is not Mercier and Camier, but the narrator-cum-author linked with his two creatures/creations. *Mercier and Camier*'s authentic revelation is the emergence of an 'I' that would disown adherence to fictional creations and the con-ventions of representation that accompany them.

The beginning of the novel returns to the ending of part 1 of *Watt* – a departure into the unknown, only this time there is a couple: 'The day has dawned at last, said Camier, after years of shilly-shally, when we must go, we know not whither, perhaps never to return … alive' (16). While there is no authentic epiphany for this couple that would reveal the nature of their quest and any particular goal, both do experience various 'visions'; for example, Mercier whose inner 'reflections' are characterized as 'a dark torrent of brooding' (32) has what the narrator in the summary for chapters 1 and 2 terms the 'Vision of the canal,' in which he envisages the couple throwing themselves into the canal. Camier's most striking 'vision' is his rejection of that melodramatic old reprobate Mr Conaire, which seems in some ways to be an ironic ver-sion of Beckett's own 'revelation': 'The truth is I suddenly saw my work was over, I mean the work I am famous for, and that it was a mis-take to have thought you might join me here, if only for a moment' (64). Just as the mythical Cartesian 'conarium' could not hold body and mind (let alone soul) together, the stock character Mr Conaire cannot any longer advance the plot of the ostensibly meaningless journey of Mercier and Camier.

The 'visionary' experience of the narrator is, however, quite a different matter; throughout the story he often coyly and ironically exploits the conventions of narratorial omniscience, at times falling back on the role of a mere reporter seeking verisimilitude and such certitudes. At times, however, his vehement denunciation of the horror of existence and the useless and pathetic pretensions of art is such that he speaks out in his own voice. There are minor outbursts along the way, but the major one occurs at the beginning of the last chapter (8), a page-and-a-half or so tirade on the human condition and all the outrageous things that can and ineluctably will happen. This spectacle is framed in terms of the 'dark' Beckett highlighted in his description of his 'revelation': 'But one black beast is hard to keep at bay, the waiting for the night that makes it all plain at last, for it is not every night possesses this property' (109).

The narrator coming out in the open and initiating the quest to find ways of making his way in the darkness can only be understood by realizing what has occurred in the previous chapter in which Mercier and Camier, after having killed the constable, leave the bourgeois necropolis, journey into the countryside and then into the mountains. Mercier and Camier are here led towards what appears to be an austere Beckettian version of Dante's Earthly Paradise, atop the Purgatorial mountain, one of the most visionary moments in all literature. Almost imperceptibly an ascent has occurred: 'All seems flat, or gently undulating, and there at a stone's throw these high crags, all unsuspected by the wayfarer' (97). Beckett's 'last word about the Purgatories' in 'Dante ... Bruno . Vico .. Joyce' helps clarify the relationship between the narrator-cum-author and the characters in this novel:

Dante's is conical and consequently implies culmination. Mr Joyce's is spherical and excludes culmination. In one there is an ascent from real vegetation – Ante-Purgatory, to ideal vegetation – Terrestrial Paradise: in the other there is no ascent and no ideal vegetation. In the one, absolute progression and a guaranteed consummation: in the other, flux – progression or retrogression, and an apparent consummation. In the one movement is unidirectional, and a step forward represents a net advance: in the other movement is non-directional – or multi-directional, and a step forward is, by definition, a step back. (*Dis*, 33)

Beckett's Purgatory in *Mercier and Camier* combines essential characteristics of both the Joycean and Dantean purgatories: for the characters the journey is ultimately multidirectional (they do take one 'step back' to the city), but for the narrator/author a consummation of sorts does take place. The halfway measures of social alienation and madness are finally irrelevant to the strikingly simple equation: art=death. Beckett means this quite literally, just as he had foreshadowed such a transformation much earlier in his poem 'The Vulture.' Mercier and Camier on the mountaintop seem to be no more than spirits, partially purged agents who are susceptible to hallucinations and illusions. While they have penetrated the zone of creative consciousness, this is itself of little importance for they, after all, are not artists. What is important is that the 'narrator' has used them to transport *himself* to this point. The quirky banalities of the opening sentence of the novel thus take on a new and startling significance: he was with them all the time and therefore must also experience death. But for the artist (who must, after all, return to the world for his subject matter) a consummation of sorts has taken place. The consummation is also a transubstantiation in that it involves an apparent fusion of contraries: the mental with the physical, the past with the present (compare 'for I was with them all the time' with the narrator/author's use of the present tense in chapter 7), the ideal and the real. All these changes are contingent upon one fundamental transformation – the narrator's acceptance of the role of author as character. He must soon take up his life as a would-be authentic fiction and explore the paradoxes of language involved in trying to determine just what the being of a fiction might be.

This is also an important juncture in the reconfiguration of the Beckett canon. Those who like Cronin see *Mercier and Camier* as having 'marred' the progression to the great works soon to follow are fundamentally missing the point here; on the contrary, this novel has marked out the means whereby Beckett was able to attain the breakthrough of *Stories* and the *Trilogy.* Moreover, the dramatic turning point in *Mercier and Camier* is indeed a 'revelation' – a revisionist version of Dante's ascent to the top of the Purgatorial mountain. Beckett criticism has been most reluctant to acknowledge this visionary dimension of Beckett's writing. For example, Eric Levy, in an important instance of literary sleuthing in Beckett studies, has educed a host of specific parallels between Beckett's novel and Dante's great *Vision*, especially from the first two realms, foregrounding to just what extent Beckett's text is indebted to Dante. Levy's argument underlines, however, only the negative dimensions of such analogies: 'It is not so much a case here of *Mercier and Camier* paralleling or mimicking the *Divine Comedy* as of the later work being superimposed upon the earlier spiritual voyage. Hence, at every moment we can see, under the wanderings of this Beckettian couple, the Dantean convictions which they cannot even glimpse. The gap between the two works makes *Mercier and Camier* at once pathetic and pointless.'[18] But Levy's identification of various echoes, allusions, and references large and small of various types is really only preliminary to a fully engaged critical analysis; positing an ironic gap between Dante and Beckett as the only mode of interpretation effectively curtails the possibility of seeing in certain instances, most notably the ascent of the mountain in chapter 7, what is actually there.

Daniela Caselli has proposed a much more sophisticated way of reading Dante and Beckett. Rejecting the approach found in most studies of simply identifying fragments of Dante in Beckett's writing and then explicating their function in terms of their roles as so-called quotations, sources, and so on, she is more concerned with determining *how* Dantean intertexts affect the exegesis of Beckett's texts on their own merit and *how* Beckett uses Dantean intertexts in the construction of authority within his own texts.[19] This is much more promising and represents an important theoretical advance, even if Caselli does not seem to recognize the possibility that in privileged instances such as chapter 7 of *Mercier and Camier* Beckett might actually be reconstructing his own version of Dante's visionary synthesis. Beckett's very first paragraph in 'Dante ... Bruno . Vico .. Joyce,' his first piece of published critical commentary, implied and arguably even embodied just such an act of creative reappropriation. Further intertextual support for Beckett's re-creation of Dante's Terrestial Paradise as his favoured trope for depicting the creative zone where the artist tries to make sense of the perplexing questions concerning fiction and being, word and world, will be evidenced as we work our way through Beckett's prose works of the post-'revelation' period.

In *Mercier et Camier*, there is a passage, omitted from the English translation, that refers in more detail to the 'covenant' of Mercier and Camier to forbid 'dreams or quotes at any price' (62):

> Lo bello stilo che m'ha fatto onore, dit Mercier, est-ce une citation?
> Lo bello quoi? dit Camier.[20]

The citation is from the first canto of the *Inferno*, as Dante acknowledges his debt to Virgil:

> You are my teacher, the first of all my authors,
> and you alone the one from whom I took
> *the noble style that was to bring me honour.* (my emphasis)[21]

One might here substitute Joyce for Dante since it was Joyce's style, not Dante's, that was the primary driving force behind Beckett's early explorations, in the same way as Dante acknowledges Virgil as his exemplar in the works preceding his *Divine Comedy*. From the very beginning of his writing career Beckett identified Dante and Joyce, in later years often citing Dante as a 'Joycean' writer. And Joyce's presence is still a significant factor in *Mercier and Camier*, even if it is more obviously saturated with Dantean references. Mercier and Camier's botched meeting at the beginning of their journey is jokingly framed in terms of a modernist aesthetic when the two do finally meet up: 'Their joy was thus for an instant unbounded' (8). This 'epiphany' is indeed short lived. Moreover, the whole sorry tabulation of their earlier failures to behold each other at the appointed rendezvous is dismissed as 'What stink of artifice' (9) in the way that Beckett had to admit that parts of *Dream* were undeniably redolent of Joyce's influence. There are certainly residual traces of the 'fabulous artificer' of *Portrait* as our couple gets tangled up in the 'maze' and 'quincunxes' of the appointed meeting site. These two unfortunate middle-aged travellers still possess memories of when they were young and 'loved art' (11).

Echoes of *A Portrait of the Artist as a Young Man* are numerous and significant, even if not nearly so much in evidence as those derived from Dante. Revealing examples include ironically recast variants of two of the most striking epiphanies in *Portrait*. First, the narrator describes the ranger who has been bought off by Mercier and Camier in these terms: 'The ranger's head appeared in the doorway. Believe it or not, only his head was to be seen' (18), which echoes, however distantly, the reaction of Stephen Dedalus at his aunt's place to the apparition-like appearance of Ellen – 'Suddenly he became aware of something in the doorway. A skull appeared suspended in the gloom of the doorway' (*P*, 69). Second, the odd ritual that Camier goes through before deciding whether to raise their umbrella, in which he 'submitted the sky to a thorough inspection, turning celtically to the north, the east, the south and finally the west, in that order' (73), is strongly reminiscent of Stephen's observation and, memorably, 'short laugh' as 'he thought of how the man with the hat worked, considering in turn the four points of the sky and then regretfully plunging his spade in the earth' (*P*, 144). This latter incident is arguably a decisive epiphanic moment for Stephen in *Portrait* since it marks the vital decision to turn away from the call of the priesthood and instead to embrace his vocation as an artist.

Beckett's distant echoing affords little solace in these instances. Some Joycean echoes are, however, much more musical in nature in *Mercier and Camier*, suggesting a poetic reconstruction in Becket's own terms. The more subtle counterpointing of Joycean musical cadences contrasts with the extensive referencing of Dante's *Comedy*, which tends towards more allegorical identifications of concept and image. Beckett plays off the 'distant music' of Joyce's final story in *Dubliners*, 'The Dead,' by echoing its final words in a complex series of abridgments that have nothing to do with the heavy-handed symbolization Gabriel Conroy had initially tried to deploy when he sought to characterize his wife's listening to the singing as a painting entitled *'Distant Music.'* Camier at the beginning of the journey says that he hears 'singing' (25), a necessarily 'distant music' since Mercier does not hear it at all, and even though Camier adds that it sounds 'For all the world a mixed choir,' Mercier gets the last word in, suggesting 'Perhaps it's a delusion' (25). The 'mixed choir' has been pointed to by several critics as a Dantean reference,[22] hence in this particular instance Joycean and Dantean allusions are in a collaborative relationship. We will see that the poetic investigation of trying to find the right words to illuminate the 'dark' of Beckett's 'revelation' and to give voice to the 'murmurs' owes more finally to Joyce than to Dante.

Here is where Beckett's revisions of the last words of 'The Dead' in *Mercier and Camier* come into play, which is poetically fitting in a novel that is about death and the 'afterlife' of artistic visions in the dark. Fragmented yet recognizable echoes of Joyce's phrasing in the 'death sentence' that concludes 'The Dead' – 'as he heard the snow falling faintly through the universe and faintly falling like the descent of their last end upon all the living and the dead' – are distributed at several junctures in *Mercier and Camier*:

(i)   when Mr Gast takes 'civil leave' of his customers from his bar, who head off into the rain (we have already seen in *Dream* and 'A Wet Night' how Joyce's 'snow' becomes Beckett's 'rain'): 'They were perhaps so pleased, who knows, for professional reasons, to see it fall, that they were pleased to feel it fall, wetting them through' (48).

(ii) in the narrator-cum-author's breaking through the paltry artifice of his story to speak *in propria persona*, near the end of chapter 7: 'all ears for the footfalls, footfalls distinguishable from all the other footfalls, and they are legion, softly falling on the face of the earth, more or less softly, day and night' (104). 'Softly falling' and 'falling softly' are prominent pairings in the last paragraph of 'The Dead.'

(iii) in the very last sentences of Beckett's concluding paragraph of
       Mercier and Camier: 'Alone he watched the sky go out, dark
       deepen to its full. He kept his eyes on the engulfed horizon, for
       he knew from experience what last throes it was capable of. And
       in the dark he could hear better too, he could hear the sounds the
       long day had kept from him, human murmurs for example, and
       the rain on the water' (122).

Listening to the rain (as Gabriel Conroy 'had heard the snow'), Mercier
can give thanks for small mercies, foremost of which is the fact that this
particular story is finally over (even if the formulaic 'Summary of two
preceding chapters' is still to follow). And by the ending of this novel
Beckett has made the 'dark' of his 'revelation' his central subject in a
way that is indeed a major departure from his previous work. The last
paragraph of the novel also illustrates how Beckett's 'debt' to Joyce can
still be recognized, however distant the verbal music is, even as Beckett
has incorporated Joyce's legacy in order to fashion innovative works of
his own.

    Beckett went out of his way to emphasize to Knowlson that his new
'vision' of the 'dark' had nothing to do in his estimation with Joyce's aesthetic program. That this is not the case is indicated by a number of developments in the ending of *Mercier and Camier* that prove decisive for
future developments in Beckett's prose fiction. The sudden appearance
of Watt directly raises two vital questions, those of *quiddity* and artistic
creation. Watt briefly reunites the two central characters, who had gone
their own ways, and over a drink confides, 'I too have sought [...], all on
my own, only I thought I knew what' (113–14); then he adds, propheti-
cally, 'one is born of us, who having nothing will wish for nothing, except
to be left the nothing he hath' (114). This 'one' is no other than the narrator as author, the 'I' who speaks in his own voice at strategic junctures in
Mercier and Camier and who will assume responsibility for the narration in
the three *Stories* that follow and the famous *Trilogy*. But the Geulincxian
aesthetic and ethic of 'for nothing' is immeasurably complicated by the
ontological exigencies that accompany the illumination of new fictional
worlds in the dark. Yes, they are, in some obvious senses of the word,
'nothing'; still they are in some equally self-evident ways a 'something,' a
verbal construct in which questions of being and reality need to be critically illuminated. Mercier's final 'vision' before he is left 'alone,' 'dark at
its full,' in the final paragraph is the 'prospect' in the 'skywrack' of 'The
ancients' Blessed Isles' (121), which for Camier are perceived, if at all,

only as 'a few pale gleams.' Here we are, back again, to Beckett's reappraisal of a major tenet in Stephen Dedalus's aesthetic theory, that *claritas*, the defining quality of aesthetic apprehension, is *not* 'a light from some other world, the idea of which the matter is but the shadow, the reality of which it is but a symbol' (*P*, 185). Beckett agrees with Joyce on this most important issue of all concerning aesthetic judgment: to see the *whatness* of a literary thing is to apprehend its illumination by a light within – from our world here below and not as 'representation of the divine purpose' (*P*, 185).

An in-depth investigation of these and related issues occurs in 'The Calmative' (1946), second in the sequence of three *Stories* first published, but the last to be written. 'The Calmative' is the most complex and developed of the *Stories* for it is more directly engaged than the others with finding a modus vivendi whereby the narrator can deal with a number of perplexing questions concerning his fictional being and its relationship to other worlds and the words that accompany them. What is striking in this story, which is Beckett's most thorough embodiment thus far of the significance of darkness in his artistic vision, is the degree to which it is, nonetheless, punctuated by flashes of a blinding radiance. For example, the narrator at mid-point in his story cannot determine what time it is, day or night, because of 'the extraordinary radiance shed by the street-lamps and traffic-lights' (*CSP*, 70); this shortly thereafter leads him to long for 'the shade of my wood, far from this terrible light' (73); but there is no escaping 'the atrocious brightness' (75), even though he hugs the walls 'famished for shadow' (75). Finally, however, the 'I' does elude the 'brilliancy flooding the boulevard' (76) as, 'in a slow swoon, darkness fell about me' (76), and he then falls first to his knees, then on his face in the midst of a throng of people. Here follows the most complex interrelationship of darkness and light in the whole story: 'It was well with me, sated with dark and calm, lying at the feet of mortals, fathom deep in the grey of dawn, if it was dawn. But reality, too tired to look for the right word, was soon restored, the throng fell away, the light came back and I had no need to raise my head from the ground to know I was back in the same blinding void as before' (76). But this narrator, while tempted to stay where he is, compulsively sets foot uphill and the story ends six sentences later with him unable to take his celestial bearings (literally and figuratively since he is looking for the Bears): 'For the light I stepped in put out the stars, assuming they were there, which I doubted, remembering the clouds' (77). The narrator has experienced at first hand some of the dangers inherent in posing profound questions of aesthetics as outlined by the dean of studies to Stephen Dedalus in *Portrait*: such as 'Many go down into the depths and never come up' (163) and 'It may be uphill pedalling at first' (166).

Throughout this image cluster, the Dantean references stand out; indeed, one might say that such references are overdetermined and constitute a surplus of allusion. All the various degrees of light are measured against the 'little wood' (62) from which the 'I' takes his departure at the beginning of the story. The second reference is even more directly an echo of Dante's first canto of the *Inferno*: 'But it was nothing, mere speechlessness due to long silence, as in the wood that darkens the mouth of hell, do you remember, I only just' (66). This paraphrases Dante's initial encounter with Virgil:

> While I was rushing down to that low place,
> my eyes made out a figure coming toward me
> of one grown faint, perhaps from too much silence.   (*Inferno*, Canto I, 61–3)

The repeated references to a blinding radiance and variants thereof are, on the other hand, most strongly reminiscent of a number of parallel incidents in the *Paradiso* in which the eyes of Dante the pilgrim are opened to the ultimate realities of the universe and God's revelation of the True Light. Whereas Dante in several instances is first blinded and then strengthened in his vision so that he can endure the paradisial radiance, Beckett's 'I' is ineluctably drawn towards a darkness where his hunger for determining his own being might be satisfied. The beatific radiance of the *Divine Comedy* no longer has a role to play. Beckett's story takes its departure from the *Inferno*, and its imagery of a blinding radiance from its mid-point onwards strongly echoes the *Paradiso*; but the story as a whole transpires within the middle-ground of *Purgatorio*. The 'skull' within which we are told this whole fictional process is occurring is yet another variant of Beckett's revisionist reconfiguration of Dante's Terrestrial Paradise at the top of the Mountain of Purgatory as that zone of a critical creativity whereby the artist-figure can explore the connections between fictional being, our world (which is somehow contingent with it), the author-figure responsible for its very being, and, finally, the residual question of the historical author (reputedly one Samuel Beckett) who is ultimately behind it all. Above all, this is a dynamic mixture of elements and is to be distinguished sharply from what

Beckett characterized as the static allegorical representations of Hell and Paradise in 'Dante ... Bruno . Vico .. Joyce.'

Some illumination is needed to see in the dark in which Beckett's 'revelation' determined his authentic vision was to be sought. The very last sentence of 'The Calmative' is, next to the 'little wood' motif, the strongest allusion to Dante's tripartite *Vision* of the after worlds: 'For the light I stepped in put out the stars, assuming they were there, which I doubted, remembering the clouds.' Each book of the *Divine Comedy* ends with a sighting of the stars as emblematic reminders of God's powers. But in Beckett's 'The Calmative' the light into which our author-as-character has 'stepped' emanates from *within* this fictional world itself. The very first reference to the Dantean focal point of the 'little wood' establishes in no uncertain terms that no matter where you stood in this wood, 'you saw on every hand the gleam of this pale light, promise of God knows what fatuous eternity' (62). Shades of Mercier's vision of 'a few pale gleams' (*MC*, 121) of 'the ancients' Blessed Isles.' In both *Mercier and Camier* and 'The Calmative' Beckett redirects the focus away from a supernatural intervention and back to the world at hand. In other words, Beckett once again replaces Dante's Radiance with *Portrait*'s *claritas*. However, the 'whatness' of the reality Beckett is exploring in 'The Calmative' is much more complex than that encountered by that young theoretician Stephen Dedalus, for in this story Beckett is not merely talking about a theory of art but actually embodying its very principles. Beckett is able to implement the epigraph of *Portrait* in a way its protagonist never was really capable of: *Et ignotas dimittit in artes*, translated as 'And he applies his mind to unknown [obscure] arts.' This description of Daedalus in Ovid's *Metaphorphoses* continues, 'and changes the laws of nature.' Beckett's 'obscure' or dark arts in his own brand of visionary writing do indeed change the very laws of nature as evidenced in the complex and ostensibly contradictory admixture of darkness and blinding void in its conclusion, so much so that the very nature of what is being described is only problematically and provisionally termed 'reality, too tired to look for the right word' (76).

The influence of Dante is pervasive in 'The Calmative' while Joyce's is much less obvious even if it also plays an important role. This is most evident in the final visionary experience of the narrator. The 'I' is on his way through 'the brilliancy flooding the boulevard' (76) when 'in a slow swoon darkness fell about me.' He is vouchsafed then a visionary experience: 'I saw a mass of bright flowers fade in an exquisite cascade of paling colours.' He falls into a state of semi-consciousness in the midst of the 'throng' and finally emerges from his swoon, 'sated with dark and calm, lying at the feet of mortals, fathom deep in the grey of dawn, if it was dawn.' The light of the 'blinding void' returns and he is again on his way, the story ending very shortly thereafter with an ironic variation, as we have already noted, on Dante's references to the stars at the end of each part of the *Divine Comedy*. The 'swoon' could be identified with Dante's fall into unconsciousness at the end of Canto III of the *Inferno*, when 'a reddish light' extinguishes his senses and he 'fell as one falls tired into sleep' (134–6). Likewise, the 'cascade' of flowers might be regarded as a reference to Canto XXX of *Purgatory* and the 'nebula of flowers' that 'poured down' (28–30).

At this juncture, one could, however, also argue that the Joycean echoes are of even greater importance and that this visionary passage might best be regarded as a complex palimpsestic layering of Dantean and Joycean elements, whereby Beckett's appropriations enable him to formulate his own vision through the words of others. Beckett's visionary encounter contains strong echoes of the birdgirl epiphany that concludes chapter 4 of *Portrait*, an episode we have seen Beckett turn to again and again in earlier discussions of his fiction. Beckett's visionary experience at the end of 'The Calmative' is preceded by failed attempts to see clearly a number of women; the narrator tries to conjure up Pauline, who had figured prominently in the story told by the man he met in his 'little encounter,'[23] but she 'gleamed an instant and was gone, like the young woman in the street' (75), a reference to an earlier sighting of 'a young woman perhaps of easy virtue' (71). He has to make do with a brief memory of the 'little girl' he had glimpsed earlier (69), a residual image in which she disappears 'without having yielded me her little face' (75). This is indeed a far cry from Stephen Dedalus's encounter with the birdgirl, whose eyes 'turned to him in quiet sufferance of his gaze' (*P*, 151). Denied such an aesthetic reference point in the world without, Beckett's 'I' is perforce drawn to the darkness within in order to pursue his own revelation of new literary worlds. This distinction having been made, there are still a number of striking similarities between the two visionary experiences. The Beckett narrator's 'swoon' and vision of the cascade of flowers are also strongly associated with what Stephen Dedalus experiences after his birdgirl encounter, when he closes his eyes:

His eyelids trembled as if they felt the vast cyclic movement of the earth and her watchers, trembled as if they felt the strange light of some new

world. His soul was swooning into some new world, fantastic, dim, uncertain as under sea, traversed by cloudy shapes and being. A world, a
glimmer or a flower? Glimmering and trembling, trembling and unfolding, a breaking light, an opening flower, it spread in endless succession to
itself, breaking in full crimson and unfolding and fading to palest rose,
leaf by leaf and wave of light by wave of light, flooding all the heavens
with its soft flushes, every flush deeper than other. (*P*, 152)

'The Calmative''s 'swoon' also specifically echoes Joyce's 'fading' and
'palest,' thereby identifying his revision more closely with Joyce's not so
distant music than with Dante's heavenly music of the spheres. Furthermore,'fathom deep' in Beckett counterpoints Joyce's 'as under sea.' Just
prior to entering the interior world behind his eyes, Stephen Dedalus
'felt above him the vast indifferent dome and the calm processes of the
heavenly bodies.' Beckett's 'I' only achieves a comparable sense of oceanic well-being ('It was well with me') when he is transported within
himself and is thereby 'sated with dark and calm.' While Beckett has
gone to considerable lengths to distinguish at times his vision from
Joyce's, it is nevertheless evident that Beckett's vision is still greatly indebted to him. After all, the very first 'calmative' in the Beckett canon –
'Assumption''s 'He thought of George Meredith and recovered something of his calm' – was a surrogate for Joyce himself. Dante and Joyce,
in conjunction, assist Beckett in bringing his own light to bear on his new
worlds of the imagination.

Beckett's originality in this text entails the incorporation of the rewritings of Dante and Joyce within his own aesthetic program as outlined in
'The Vulture.' The aesthetic of death in the poem and implicit in chapter 7
of *Mercier and Camier* now becomes explicit. Only an understanding of
what occurred in the novel prepares the way for the startling first sentence, 'I don't know when I died' (61). By assuming responsibility for the
creative process, this new author-figure undergoes a change that can be
legitimately regarded as a death since it transports him into a new spatio-
temporal zone in which there is no simple objective orientation towards
what passes as the socially accepted definition of reality. This Beckettian
manoeuvre involving the death and rebirth of the author is, needless to
say, a far cry from the Barthesian version in which a *scriptor* or textual ad-
ministrator replaces the traditional view of the author as originator. The
death of the conventional pseudo-identity requires the fabrication of another in the story he tells in order to calm himself. The rebirth in the act of
story-telling creates a new time ('what I tell this evening is passing this

evening'), which causes the speaker, thinking back on his old dead identity, to comment that he is now 'older than I'll ever have been' (62). The 'I' unites two locales, a 'here' and a 'there'; he is at once in his 'ruins,' the 'refuge' of disembodied creative consciousness represented (as in *Mercier and Camier*) by the 'outskirts,'[24] and in the 'city' to which the creative consciousness must return to find the concrete forms for its embodiment: 'I wasn't returning empty-handed, not quite, I was taking back with me the virtual certainty that I was still of this world, of that world too, in a way' (69–70). A novel situation, indeed: where is so-called 'reality' to be located, and is this even any longer the 'right word'?

Beckett would seem to be acknowledging the decisive role Joyce played in his own development in 'Premier Amour' ('First Love'), the third of the four *nouvelles* written during 1946, but held back from publication until 1970. However circuitously, this short story might be regarded as revisionist literary history in which Beckett recasts the most traumatic event in his relationship with Joyce and his family, his expulsion from the family circle over the 'misunderstanding' between himself and Lucia Joyce, who was infatuated with him, as one of her first loves (one of her many dreams of fair to middling young men). The narrator of this story tells us that the events he will be treating belong to a distant time when he was twenty-five years old. This focus on youth is an obvious reason why Beckett chose not to publish it with the other *Stories*, all of which deal with the 'I' character at a much later point in his life-story, or, as in 'The Calmative,' his 'afterlife.' Beckett was in fact twenty-four when the rupture with Joyce took place over Lucia; in 1931 Beckett was in the midst of the excommunication which began in May 1930 and ended in early 1932.

From this revisionist autobiographical angle, the opening sentence of 'First Love' – 'I associate, rightly or wrongly, my marriage with the death of my father, in time' (*CSP*, 25) – might be glossed as follows: Beckett's exile from Joyce, his literary father (in accordance with the fosterage principle of paternity in *Portrait*), is likened to a 'death' and his marriage to Lulu (soon to be renamed Anna) is somehow akin to a poetic compensation of sorts since the woman in 'First Love' is in many ways strongly reminiscent of one Lucia Anna Joyce. Beckett in real life had made it clear to Lucia that he came to the Joyce household to see her father and that her romantic interest was not reciprocated, at which point Joyce, strongly encouraged by his wife Nora, made it all too abundantly clear to Beckett that his family came first and everything else a very distant second. In the aftermath of Lucia's mental deterioration and subsequent confinement,

Beckett felt guilt and remorse over his inability to love, more particularly, to give any love to, Lucia Joyce. In dramatic contrast, the very title of this story announces that the central topic at hand is 'love' and the very last sentence reaffirms the fatalistic nature of such engagements: 'But there it is, either you love or you don't' (45).[25] A certain poetic justice is evident then in Beckett's phantasmagorical composite of his 'break up' with Joyce: it was Lucia Joyce who had made it known to all and sundry that she wanted to marry before her twenty-fifth birthday.

Moreover, specific features of 'First Love' would seem to be derived from Beckett's earlier depiction of Lucia Joyce as the Syra-Cusa in *Dream of Fair to Middling Women* (1932). Joyce's daughter takes her name, as Knowlson has pointed out, from Dante: 'in the *Divina Commedia*, Lucia is one of the "tre donne benedette" (three blessed women) and, one of [Beckett's] student notebooks records, she comes from Syracuse' (*DF*, 151). In the novel, Belacqua bestows a copy of the *Divina Commedia* upon her and she promptly proceeds to lose it in a café. In 'Premier Amour,' there is, ironically enough, an explicit mention of Dante in a context that also mixes up various high-culture/low-culture references, but in the 'First Love' translation the allusion to Dante is completely excised, lost for good, just as Syra-Cusa had lost Beckett's favoured edition of Dante. Other distinguishing features shared by Lucia, Syra-Cusa, and Lulu-Anna are a squint (as the narrator of *Dream* admits, 'Eyes – less good, to be frank, than we make out, our pen carried us away' [50]), musical ability and an affinity for singing, and, above all, a highly sexualized presence, coupled with a persistent pursuit of her amorous prey. The last words accorded her in *Dream* are 'Be off, puttanina, and joy be with you' (51). Two and a half pages earlier at the beginning of the Syra-Cusa passage, the narrator remarks: 'She belongs to another story, a short one, a far far better one' (49). This could, of course, be a jesting reference to such 'short' works as *Ulysses* and the then *Work in Progress* in which Lucia Joyce served as a model for various fictional reincarnations. But it could also be regarded as a self-fulfilling prophecy whereby 'First Love' itself becomes that 'far far better' short story. The farewell to the Syra-Cusa – 'Be off, puttanina' – becomes the basis for the plot, such as there is, in 'First Love' in which Lulu-Anna is a prostitute and supports the narrator by the avails thereof. As in previous Beckett 'whoroscopes,' the underlying issue is an aesthetic one: what is beauty and what is its significance? Trying to decide whether Lulu-Anna is beautiful or not, but admitting 'the eyes were crooked' (37), this narrator confesses that he had no idea at all 'in what beauty was supposed to consist' (38), just as earlier he had not been able to characterize accurately his 'first love' (priapic, platonic, or a 'different variety' [34] altogether). The only affirmation now on such prickly issues would seem to be paradoxical: 'And my father's face, on his death-bolster, had seemed to hint at some form of aesthetics relevant to man' (38). This reference immediately brings to mind Harry Levin's comments on Joyce's death mask and his identification of it with 'the face of his Stephen Dedalus' (*PJJ*, 2).

There is, however, no denying that this fair to middling woman Lulu-Anna is a variant on the Anna Livia Plurabelle of *Finnegans Wake* in so far as various shifting selves return to fundamental questions of beauty, aesthetics and, yes, love. Two scenes – one dealing with Anna's wooing of the narrator, the other detailing his final departure from her – underscore how Joyce's 'music,' however 'distant,' can still be heard, however faintly. In the first scene the 'I' asks Anna to sing him a song:

> I thought at first she was going to refuse, I mean simply not sing, but no, after a moment she began to sing and sang for some time, all the time the same song it seemed to me, without change of attitude. I did not know the song, I had never heard it before and shall never hear it again. It had something to do with lemon trees, or orange trees, I forget, that is all I remember, and for me that is no mean feat, to remember it had something to do with lemon trees, or orange trees, I forget, for of all the other songs I have ever heard in my life, and I have heard plenty, it being apparently impossible, physically impossible short of being deaf, to get through this world, even my way, without hearing singing, I have retained nothing, not a word, not a note, or so few words, so few notes, that, that what, that nothing, this sentence has gone on long enough. Then I started to go and as I went I heard her singing another song, or perhaps more verses of the same, fainter and fainter the further I went, then no more, either because she had come to an end or because I was gone too far to hear her. (36–7)

For Beckett to strike such an allusive chord in a work that seems, among other things, to be a retrospective assessment of his relationship with Joyce and his family is hardly surprising.

Of particular interest here is how we might see via this passage Beckett's own estimation of his relationship with Joyce at this juncture when he has found his own voice, however replete with Joycean echoes, and is no longer essentially rewriting Joyce in the hope of finding his own voice, which was essentially the case from 'Assumption' through to *Watt*. The key for gauging Beckett's sense of his new relationship with Joyce, post-'revelation,' is found in an obscure allusion in the above passage to an even more 'distant music': the song that Anna sings that had 'to do with lemon trees or orange trees' is a reference to a scene in Mozart's life as dramatized by Edouard Mörike in his *Mozart on the Way to Prague,* which occasioned one of Beckett's most savage reviews.[26] Beckett scathingly dismisses Mörike's slight lyrical novel as a dishonest and sentimental travesty that is 'a violation of its subject' (*Dis,* 62), Mozart as musical genius. In Beckett's estimation, Mörike simply lacks the ability to make any sense of the great artist-figure who is ostensibly his subject matter; unlike the lamentable Mörike, Beckett is now able to hold his own with Joyce and is worthy of comparison with the master in that he too has found his own voice. The second scene referred to above, the one with which 'First Love' ends, might be taken as a corroboration of this since it is set in counterpoint to the passage dealing with Anna's singing and creates its own 'distant music,' which is at once indebted to its source and yet also goes beyond it to exist in its own right. As the narrator relives the memory of Anna giving birth to their child, he hears again and yet again the cries that drove him away:

> I began playing with the cries, a little in the same way as I had played with the song, on, back, on, back, if that may be called playing. As long as I kept walking I didn't hear them, because of the footsteps. But as soon as I halted I heard them again, a little fainter each time, admittedly, but what does it matter, faint or loud, cry is cry, all that matters is that it should cease. For years I thought they would cease. Now I don't think so any more. (45)

'Distant music' and 'distant cries' will be powerfully orchestrated in the Joycean counterpoint of Beckett's great *Trilogy.*

6 A Not So *'Distant Music'*: Joycean Counterpoint in the *Trilogy*

The major breakthrough in 'The Calmative' was brought about by Beckett devising his own aesthetic by means of a combination of elements in his poem 'The Vulture' and an appropriation and revision of aspects of Dante's vision concerning the Terrestial Paradise motif as the privileged zone of creative consciousness whereby the artist-figure can reconcile apparently contradictory elements. But the breakthrough in that story almost immediately becomes one of the breakdowns of the *Trilogy* as the issue of multiple subjects generated by the act of writing itself anticipates almost from the very beginning another author figure behind both Molloy and Moran and later Malone as well, resulting in an incredible proliferation of would-be authorities claiming or disowning responsibility, as the case may be, for the very operations of language itself. It has not, however, been noted to just what degree these Beckettian ideas are developed in conjunction with (indeed are counterpointed by) aesthetic arguments of a distinctively Joycean nature. The following discussion will explore how this Beckett-Joyce counterpointing does in fact constitute the formative double-voicing that structures the *Trilogy*, most extensively in *Molloy*, and with a more distant resonance elsewhere.

It is important from the start to draw attention to the complex supporting role Joyce plays in *Molloy* for there is the danger of not seeing the forest for the trees in so far as this work is obviously saturated with allusions from a host of other writers from a number of particular disciplines. As was the case with *Dream* and *Murphy*, there is the possibility of being distracted from the main structuring ideas by the plethora of secondary allusions that riddle the text. Phil Baker in *Beckett and the Mythology of Psychoanalysis* (1997) incisively summarizes this problem of intertextuality: 'In the prose works of the forties psychoanalysis takes its place within the referential glut of literature, philosophy, religion, and psychology.'[1] In this regard, it is worth remembering Molloy's own version of his curriculum vitae: after his studies had progressed through astronomy, geology, anthropology and psychiatry, he concludes that 'in the end it was magic that had the honour of my ruins' (*M*, 30).[2] Baker's study is an interesting case in point when it comes to the difficult question of evaluating the relative importance of various sources: he carefully gauges the claims of his own subject, emphasizing in his very title that psychoanalysis will not be *the key* to interpreting Beckett's oeuvre but only another mythological structure that can be parodically invoked in a number of ways: 'Within its elegantly doubled Oedipal structure, the "knowingness" of *Molloy*'s Oedipal material makes it a form of unstably ironised citation; a mythic borrowing compounded by considerations of polarity and structure along the lines of Beckett's declared interest in the "shape of ideas" rather than their content.'[3] Baker then draws an analogy with Joyce's use of Vico 'as a trellis for *Finnegans Wake*' and goes on to describe the psychoanalytic scaffolding in *Molloy* as functioning in similar fashion.[4]

A complex allusive irony is at play in Molloy's 'magic.' Prior to his revelation that the darkness he had tried formerly to suppress was indeed his true subject, Beckett was the failed sorcerer's apprentice who both as critic and writer could neither understand nor duplicate in his own right the epiphanic moments of his great predecessors Proust and, above all, Joyce. Given the nature of Beckett's revelation of darkness, it is hardly surprising then that his own speciality and that of his principal characters should be of the black magic variety. It is fitting poetic logic that Molloy's catalogue of the various disciplines he has studied and found wanting should mimic Faust's program of study as tabulated in the opening sequence of Goethe's Part I. Faust turns to magic so that he might 'the bitter task forego/Of saying the things I do not know'; instead he seeks to 'detect the inmost force/Which binds the world, and guides its course' so that he need not any longer 'rummage in empty words.'[5] Ironically enough for Beckett's Molloy, his quest for what 'binds the world' necessarily involves further scavenging in the ruins of a host of earlier story-telling models from Homer to Joyce and beyond. Language itself is now the medium to be investigated in order to determine whether what Beckett in the Axel Kaun letter termed 'this mocking attitude towards the word, through words' (*Dis*, 172) might reveal the very nature of things. Beckett added that his program of the 'unword' has nothing to do with Joyce's 'most recent work' (*Work in Progress*) in which 'the apotheosis of the word' is assumed to be the defining characteristic: 'Unless perhaps Ascension to Heaven and Descent to Hell are somehow one and the same' (*Dis*, 172). For Beckett this is most definitely not the case; Joyce is in his 'Heaven' and Beckett in his 'Hell', which is implicit in Beckett's oft-cited statements that Joyce is tending towards omniscience and omnipotence whereas Beckett himself is working with impotence and ignorance. Beckett's ostensibly modest assessment of his own program in the Shenker 'interview' – 'My little exploration is that whole zone of being that has always been set aside by artists as something unusable – something by definition incompatible with art' – echoes the choice made by Milton's Satan: 'Better to reign in [Beckettian] Hell than serve in [Joycean] Heaven.'[6]

But Beckett's word-worlds are not as distinct or distant from Joyce's as he would have us believe, especially if we turn from Joyce's 'latest work' to his earlier work. It might even be argued that Beckett is in some respects more 'Joycean' than Joyce himself. For whereas Joyce made it clear that he had become bored with Stephen Dedalus and was drawn much more to the vitalistic world of Leopold and Molly Bloom and the family romance, Beckett has shown little interest in such a 'middling' solution to the aesthetic question. Beckett has stuck with Stephen Dedalus, and it might even be proposed that the latter only attains the artist-figure status Joyce denied him in so far as aspects of his artistic identity are incorporated into figures such as Beckett's Molloy. Stephen's 'revolt,' his *non serviam*, his risking of his soul if need be to gain artistic knowledge – all of these characteristics can be identified to a certain degree (and not merely ironically as an errant romanticism) with Molloy's dark designs as set forth in his comments on the 'diabolical complexity' (82) of the means whereby he is able to make any 'progress' at all in his efforts to work things out for himself. The Faustian theme has indeed much in common with the Daedalus-Icarus rise and fall, as witnessed in the 'Prologue' of Marlowe's *Doctor Faustus*: 'His waxen wings did mount above his reach/And melting, heavens conspired his overthrow!'[7]

The 'diabolical complexity' of *Molloy* is all too evident in its opening paragraph of a page and a third (which, in turn, is developed in the second 'paragraph' of eighty-three pages). The crux of the matter is the disjunction between the beginning and ending of Molloy's 'story' (his sighting from his vantage point behind a rock, midway up a mountain, of the A and C figures and his subsequent quest to get things settled with his mother) and the beginning and ending of Molloy's writing about this story, which necessarily takes place at some later point, after this story has run its course (whereby Molloy ends up in a ditch at the end of the forest) and Molloy then finds himself – he knows not how – in his mother's room, where, as he tells us, he is now engaged in the act of writing down what he experienced in his abortive journey to locate his mother. What can this provisional 'now' possibly mean in such a riven and riddled context? What are the broader implications for the status of fiction and of language itself in such a situation?

The last seven pages of Daniel Katz's discussion of *Molloy* in *Saying I No More* (1999) focus upon an investigation of the 'distant music' allusion Beckett employs at the outset of Molloy's journey in search of his mother, the point at which he is stopped by a policeman who demands to see his papers:

> I felt the faces turning to look after us, calm faces and joyful faces, faces of men, of women and of children. I seemed to hear, at a certain moment, a *distant music*. I stopped, the better to listen. Go on, he said. Listen, I said. Get on, he said. I wasn't allowed to listen to the music. It might have drawn a crowd. He gave me a shove. I had been touched, oh not my skin, but none the less my skin had felt it, it had felt a man's hard fist, through its coverings. While still putting my best foot foremost I gave myself up to that golden moment, as if I had been someone else. (21, italics mine)

Katz identifies the most obvious instance of 'distant music' in Joyce: Gabriel Conroy watching his wife Gretta pausing on the stairs to listen to the music from the room above, as both are making ready to depart the Morkan sisters' Epiphany celebration in the final story of *Dubliners*, 'The Dead.' Katz's main point in his discussion is that the citation of such an obviously identifiable allusion in *Molloy* leads to a post-structuralist recognition that all allusion is *already* an echo of an anterior reference and that there is hence no sense of an originary voice that could authorize presence; instead, all such referencing points to an indefinite deferral and an indeterminacy of signification. Katz points out that Gabriel's proposed formulation of *'Distant Music'* as the title of the picture he would paint of his wife listening so absorbedly is itself an echo of a much earlier (thus more 'distant') love letter to Gretta: 'Like distant music these words that he had written years before were borne towards him from the past' (*PJJ*, 232). Gabriel's 'distant music' also reverberates with another phrase, 'the thought-tormented music' of his Browning newspaper review. Such multiplicity of sourcing in the would-be primary text leads to Katz's conclusion, a commonplace of post-structuralist criticism, that 'the moment of originary expression is always an echo.'[8]

In terms of the immediate context of the passage, the first point (or, more accurately, counterpoint) to make is that Katz's assertion that the 'distant music' allusion only works in English is open to question. Anyone reading Katz's judgment might at first assume that he means the phrase is simply not present in the French version of the novel, which indeed is not the case: 'Il me sembla entendre, à un moment donné, une musique lointaine. Je m'arrêtai, pour mieux l'écouter.'[9] Surely a bilingual reader with knowledge of Joyce's work would recognize the allusion in the French version; moreover, a French reader of Joyce in translation could also be expected to recognize the allusion. Such pedestrian objections need to be made in order to bring the post-structuralist rhetoric back down to the reality of the textual markings. My original citation of the 'distant music' passage above included the social context of the audience watching Molloy's attempt to pause (to hear the music that they, like the policeman, are deaf to) while at the same time being shoved by the policeman. Shades of Belacqua in *More Pricks Than Kicks*: Molloy is a veritable 'moving pause.' It is at this point that Molloy says 'I gave up myself to that golden moment, as if I had been someone else.' This 'golden moment' might, in one of its manifestations, have been the illusory epiphany that, famously, Gabriel Conroy thought he felt when he watched his wife listening rapt on the stairs. But the real point is that this can only be regarded as ironic counterpoint since Molloy is obviously suggesting that he is *not* that 'someone else' (neither Joyce nor his fictional creations). This is made explicit in the immediate context that follows the 'distant music' allusion; here all the images are of a reprieve for the rest of humanity, as envisaged by Molloy, who distinguishes himself from their contemplative state with an accusation: 'Was there one among them to put himself in my place, to feel how removed I was then from him I seemed to be, and in that remove what strain, as of hawsers about to snap?' (21).

Here Beckett's image is powerfully kinetic and set in dramatic contrast with any traditionalist theory of aesthetic stasis such as that promoted by the young Stephen Dedalus. This underscores just how different Molloy is from the projected Joycean figure straining to hear the 'distant music,' whom he only superficially resembles. Molloy does, however, experience an epiphany of sorts at this junction, one which allows him to blend into the scene in which previously he has depicted himself as an outsider. 'Straining towards' what he terms his 'spurious deeps,' he is miraculously transformed: 'Forgetful of my mother, set free from the act, merged in this alien hour, saying, Respite, respite' (21). This experience of release, however, expires with the formulation of this very sentence; the next begins with him having been mysteriously transported to the police station – we have no accounting for how he got there – the merging having indeed rendered Molloy atemporal during this blanked-out period. Molloy then undergoes questioning and experiences a linguistic epiphany of some sort: 'And suddenly I remembered my name, Molloy. My name is Molloy, I cried, all of a sudden, now I remember' (22–3). Beckett's 'straining' throughout the 'distant music' passage and contextual environs distinguishes itself from Stephenesque aesthetic stasis as the beau idéal at the same time that in counterpoint it resonates with strains of Joycean language. 'My name is Molloy,' for example, is reminiscent of similar scenes in *Portrait* when Stephen Dedalus resorts to such self-reflexive repetitions in order to calm himself down and to get his bearings.

Once we get beyond the conventional assumption of Beckett criticism that Joyce is no longer a significant influence at this point in Beckett's career, and once we can also move beyond the ready-made application of a post-structuralist reading, a quite different picture of the Joyce-Beckett relationship begins to emerge. It is not so much a question of 'overcoming' or 'resisting' Joyce's influence (the mainstream view) or of remaining always in a suspended state of being merely an echo of a Joycean echo (the post-structuralist view); it is a more complex question of appropriation, assimilation, and reconstruction through incorporation and counterpointing within a new structure. A case in point occurs two pages before the 'distant music' allusion. With reference to his mother, Molloy answers the question 'What did I see of her?' with, 'A head always. Veiled with hair, wrinkles, filth, slobber. A head that darkened the air' (19). This echoes one of the most intriguing – because unexplained – epiphanies so officially designated by Joyce in *Portrait*: 'Suddenly he became aware of something in the doorway. A skull appeared suspended in the gloom of the doorway' (19). Both instances involve cases of mistaken identity: that 'mad old woman' (19), Molloy's mother, takes him for his father; the 'feeble creature like a monkey' takes Stephen for Josephine, a mistaken assumption that she repeats several times and at which 'she fell to laughing feebly.' Whereas Stephen is portrayed as a young boy sitting and watching without comment this domestic mini-drama, Molloy and his mother are depicted as a 'couple of old cronies' (17). What then is Beckett suggesting when he has Molloy see his mother through the refracted reference to *Portrait*? One aspect might be the rueful recognition that it has taken Beckett so very long to get to his own portrait of the artist that the counterpart to Joyce's young boy is now Beckett's old man Molloy. Shortly after the Josephine-Mother Molloy reference, Molloy comments on his mother's 'odour of antiquity' and admits that he too does not exactly exude 'the perfumes of Araby' (19). 'Araby' is also the third and final story of the opening childhood sequence of *Dubliners*. Beckett's reference here is Joycean in another obvious sense as well: Joyce's multitudinous references to other writers often made superficial play with their names and the titles of their works, whereas Beckett, in addition to this, often more deeply embeds his textual allusions, such as with the Josephine epiphany. Beckett might indeed still be said to 'stink of Joyce,' but unlike the mimicking of some passages of *Dream of Fair to Middling Women*, Beckett now has not only adopted but more fully adapted the reference to his own ends.

Moreover, the 'distant music' reference in *Molloy* is not quite so obvious or quite as 'distant' as Katz would have it. Molloy underlines that he was 'far removed from him I seemed to be.' The more appropriate and arguably more illuminating parallel here is with the 'distant music' that Stephen Dedalus hears in *Portrait*. The scene in which this occurs is at the beginning of chapter 3 (Hell Fire Sermons) and develops in the aftermath of his visit to the prostitute that ends chapter 2 (and which Beckett took as the focal point for his first major rewriting of Joyce in 'Assumption'). Stephen's mathematical calculations in the classroom blossom into a complex cluster of imagery of a cosmological nature as worlds are created and destroyed:

> The equation on the page of his scribbler began to spread out a widening tail, eyed and starred like a peacock's: and when the eyes and stars of its indices had been eliminated, began slowly to fold itself together again. The indices appearing and disappearing were eyes opening and closing; the eyes opening and closing were stars being born and being quenched. The vast cycle of starry life bore his weary mind outward to its verge and inward to its centre, a *distant music* accompanying him outward and inward. What music? The music came nearer and he recalled the words, the words of Shelley's fragment upon the moon wandering companionless, pale for weariness. The stars began to crumble and a cloud of fine stardust fell through space. (97, italics mine)

Such passages in *Portrait* foreground the lacunae and ruptures that go with the cycle of cosmic creation and disintegration.[10] A kindred passage that we have already discussed in detail is the aftermath of the birdgirl encounter that concludes chapter 4. Here inchoately are the elements for new worlds of the imagination, of 'some new world, fantastic, dim, uncertain as under sea, traversed by cloudy shapes and beings. A world, a glimmer or a flower?' Whereas in *Dream* Beckett parodied this passage – in large part because he could not realistically at that stage hope to emulate it, let alone compete with it – in part *I* of *Molloy* such passages of poetic suggestiveness and heightened ontological insecurities are rife and arguably constitute its most distinctive as well as most disruptive textual feature. Such passages are perhaps best regarded as a type of Bakhtinian *parodia sacra*, to be distinguished from the postmodernist variety, making claims in their own right that extend beyond the dialectic of negation and affirmation proposed by Hutcheon in her discussion of parody.

Compare the passages from *Portrait* referred to above with this representative one in which Molloy recounts how he listens and 'the voice is of a world collapsing endlessly':

> Yes, a world at an end, in spite of appearances, its end brought it forth, ending it began, is it clear enough? And I too am at an end, when I am there, my eyes close, my sufferings cease and I end, I wither as the living can not. And if I went on listening to that far whisper, silent long since and which I still hear, I would learn still more, about this. But I will listen no longer, for the time being, to that far whisper, for I do not like it, I fear it. But it is not a sound like the other sounds, that you listen to, when you choose, and can sometimes silence, by going away or stopping your ears, no, but it is a sound which begins to rustle in your head, without your knowing how, or why. It's with your head you hear it, not your ears, you can't stop it, but it stops itself, when it chooses. It makes no difference therefore whether I listen to it or not, I shall hear it always, no thunder can deliver me, until it stops. (40)

There are a number of similarities with the passages cited from *Portrait*, foremost of which is that of two worlds which are presented as occupying distinct realms yet at the same time suggestive of some type of identification or at least necessary connections between them. Beckett's situation is typically cast in more extreme terms than Joyce's, an abiding characteristic of his rewriting of Joyce from 'Assumption' onwards.

Molloy's transportation to this other world would appear to be a variation on the vulture aesthetic of 'The Calmative''s opening sentence, 'I
don't know when I died,' in that this is a world in which 'its end
brought it forth.' Another plane of meaning implied here is that of fictional being; once Molloy's abortive quest for his mother supposedly
ends in a ditch it all begins again in a different temporal and ontological sense in his recounting of it in his narrative version of events.

The 'far whisper' that Molloy cannot evidently exercise any choice
over listening to echoes Beckett's comments in the Axel Kaun letter
where he proposes that by investigating the 'dissonance' inherent in
language, 'it will perhaps become possible to feel a whisper of that final music or that silence that underlies All' (*Dis*, 172). This 'dissonance'
or clashing of sounds and sense is fundamentally related in the *Molloy*
passage to the unsettling and disorienting reference to two worlds, resulting in the deferral of any ultimate meaning with reference to 'All.'
What Beckett later came to dismiss as pretentious 'German bilge,'[11] the
striving for some sort of transcendental illumination, is replaced in
Molloy by a profound ambiguity: the 'far whisper' does not lead to any
'final music,' but instead a 'distant music' interspersed with a 'silence'
that is itself not in any way 'final.' In the Kaun letter Beckett opined
that such a multifaceted investigation of 'dissonance' had nothing at
all to do with 'the latest work of Joyce.' Such a belief is re-echoed in the
'world collapsing endlessly' passage when Molloy affirms, however
paradoxically, that he will continue to hear the whispering and that 'no
thunder can deliver me.' This oddly interjected reference resonantly alludes to the ten Vichian thunders of *Finnegans Wake*, which mark the
stages of the cyclical progression that deliver the various figures to the
next developmental phase. Even if Joyce's 'latest work' does indeed
have nothing to do with the situation in which Molloy finds himself,
his earlier work certainly does, particularly the 'distant music' of *Portrait*. Even if in the final accounting the differences outweigh the similarities, it should nevertheless be recognized that such counterpointing
of Joycean materials plays a significant role in Beckett's progression towards an aesthetic distinctively his own.

A whole series of Joycean allusions and echoes are associated with
Molloy's various scattered remarks on the aesthetic principles guiding
his writing. In the forefront of these speculations are the paradoxical
formulations concerning beginnings and endings with which the first
paragraph of part *I* of *Molloy* is primarily concerned, and which is
most fully developed by Molloy after he finally manages to escape the

clutches of the policeman and the social worker. The aesthetic of death in one world as the means of rebirth in another, which appeared first in *Mercier and Camier* and proclaimed in the first words of 'The Calmative,' is explored in much more depth in *Molloy*. The eponymous hero tells us that since he has 'ceased to live' he is able in 'the tranquillity of decomposition' to recollect his life and hence 'judge it': 'To decompose is to live too, I know, I know, don't torment me, but one sometimes forgets' (25). Indeed, it is just such a suspension of disbelief about that doubling displacement which ineluctably accompanies representation (perforce always a 're-presentation') that most novelistic conventions gloss over by relieved mutual consent of writer and reader. Molloy may 'sometimes forget' this, but he always returns to this fundamental disruption of reference in which there are two worlds – the most striking feature of his story and the one most disconcerting for most readers. For example, in Beckett's revision of Wordsworth's famous characterization of poetry as 'the spontaneous overflow of powerful feelings,' which are 'recollected in tranquillity' (now recast as 'the tranquillity of decomposition'), it is the experience of life being over that affords him the critical perspective on 'the long confused emotion which was my life' (25). But such recollection does not yield a privileged 'spot of time' whereby the various selves can be harmoniously integrated and illuminated. For Beckett these two worlds and the perplexities thereby foregrounded are not amenable to resolution by purported literary 'miracles' of the Wordsworthian, Proustian, and Joycean variety.

Nevertheless, 'vestiges' (39) of such magical transformations still riddle the text of *Molloy*, and the Joycean traces, particularly from *Portrait*, play an especially important role. One of the most salient Joycean clusters in *Molloy* – one pointed to in passing by many critics – indirectly makes this point: 'I who had loved the image of old Geulincx, dead young, who left me free, on the black boat of Ulysses, to crawl towards the East, along the deck [...] And from the poop, poring upon the wave, a sadly rejoicing slave, I follow with my eyes the proud and futile wake.' (51) References to Joyce's *Ulysses* in *Molloy* are virtually non-existent in any specific sense, and broadly generalized views that, for example, regard Molloy's narrative as derived in some way from Molly Bloom's stream of consciousness in the concluding 'Penelope' section of *Ulysses* are unconvincing. Moreover, most of Beckett's references to the Ulysses story are derived from *The Odyssey*, not from the Joycean rewriting of it. Parallels are much more convincing with reference to the classical text, as K.J. Phillips has demonstrated.[12] References to *Finnegans Wake* are also few and far between and, as with the instance of the thunder cited earlier, are primarily designed to distinguish Beckett's work from Joyce's 'proud and futile wake' – 'futile,' that is, for anyone who might attempt to emulate it, as Beckett discovered very early on in his *Dream of Fair to Middling Women*.

There are, however, a number of telling images and allusions from *Portrait* on matters aesthetic. Molloy's comment that he saw the world 'in a way inordinately formal,' even though he insists on asserting 'I was far from being an aesthete or an artist' (50), in conjunction with his various remarks on how he is attracted to 'pure sounds' for their own sake and harmony, echoes Stephen Dedalus at several junctures in *Portrait* where he wonders whether it is the formal patterns or the 'legends' and associations of words that attract him the most. An ironic reference to the very beginning of the aesthetic discussion in *Portrait* seems to be alluded to in Molloy's comment that while at Sophie Lousse's he could remember in detail the tray he was served with whereas 'the basket made no impression on me, good or bad, and I could not tell you what it was like' (55). Stephen Dedalus, on the other hand, did indeed tell Lynch about the basket – 'what it was like' – describing how its 'wholeness' and 'harmony' combined to reveal its 'whatness' (*P*, 184–5). But what is one to make of Beckett's micromanagement of more elliptical, seemingly minor echoes, such as those that link Davin's story about the 'strange thing' that happened to him in the country one night with Molloy's story of his 'stay' at Sophie Lousse's? Davin is returning home late at night, having missed his ride, and says 'and only for the dew was thick I'd have stretched out there and slept' (*P*, 160). A young woman, in response to his knock at her door, brings him 'a big mug of milk' and invites him in for the night. The innocent Davin refuses her sexual proposition. In the Sophie Lousse episode, Molloy is *already* in her house (having replaced the late Teddy, Sophie's dog, whom he had run over) and is seeking a way of escaping. Molloy comes out when it is dusk to look for his bicycle; when Sophie sights him, she comes 'warmly' towards him and gives him food and drink. Molloy finds his bicycle but it no longer is working and he cannot take his leave of this 'accursed place' (47). Then, overcome by 'a great weariness,' Molloy lies down and, in this comment on doing so, seems to be directly engaging in an intertextual exchange with Davin's 'strange story': 'and lay down on the ground, on the grass, careless of the dew, I never feared the dew' (47). At this point

Lousse squats down beside him and begins 'to make propositions.' What indeed is one to make of these similarities, which are too many in number and too detailed in specifics to be dismissed out of hand as mere 'coincidence'? Davin is afraid to cross the threshold afforded by the young peasant woman (who is 'carrying a child,' he believes); even though Stephen Dedalus says the words of Davin's story 'sang in his memory,' he too does not know how to appropriate and reconstitute Davin's story for his own development as an artist (he is definitely more at home with theoretical discussions of a basket's 'whatness'). It is that very Johnny-come-lately of an artist-figure Molloy who does cross the threshold and does try to write about the experience; how successfully is another question.[13] In short, Beckett is again rewriting *Portrait* via a detailed counterpointing as he seeks to formulate his own version of what an artist is like.

After Molloy finally manages to depart Sophie's, there is an odd scene, a sort of *mise en abîme*, as Molloy encounters what could be regarded as a prototype of himself, a version, admittedly somewhat the worse for wear, of one Stephen Dedalus. Molloy sights a 'young old man of wretched aspect, shivering all alone in a narrow doorway' (62) and, as a result of this 'encounter' (a good Joycean word), experiences an epiphany of sorts: 'I suddenly remembered the project conceived the day of my encounter with Lousse and her dog and which this encounter had prevented me from carrying out' (62). Molloy then goes on to draw attention to the necessarily duplicitous nature of his narrative via references to *Portrait*: 'Thus from time to time I shall recall my present existence compared to which this is a nursery tale' (61), adding almost immediately: 'Or again, Oh it's only a diary, it'll soon be over' (62). *Portrait*, of course, begins with the nursery tale of baby tuckoo and ends with Stephen's diary. Molloy then comments 'and I set off, believe it or not, towards the sun' (62). Molloy, limping along towards his mother's place – a far cry from his earlier Hamlet-like invocation that once he had found his 'reasons' for doing so he 'would sweep, with the clipped wings of necessity, to my mother' (27) – is a fallen Icarus who still traces as best he can the sun's trajectory.

Beckett's acknowledgment of indebtedness in conjunction with a distancing from the Joycean project is most evident in the concluding movement of *Molloy I*, in which the word 'progress' is prominently displayed in a number of contexts. Progress is indeed so impeded that it virtually comes to a standstill: 'Yes, my progress reduced me to stopping more and more often, it was the only way to progress, to stop'

(78). Soon the whole question of Molloy's 'progress' is of a 'diabolical complexity' as his various 'weak points' are compounded with the problems with his legs. This is obviously not an 'esthetic stasis,' 'prolonged and at last dissolved' by what Stephen Dedalus termed 'the rhythm of beauty' (*P*, 180). Beckett likened the experience of writing *Molloy* to taking a walk,[14] and the prose of the novel does at times have a distinctively flowing rhythm absent from much of Beckett's earlier work. Beckett's 'rhythm' in *Molloy* critically engages Stephen's definition of it as 'the first formal relation of part to part in any esthetic whole' (*P*, 180), most obviously in that it is indeed difficult, if not impossible, to describe just how *Molloy I* and *II* might be said to constitute a whole. Beckett's 'progress' is not the confident cycling towards beginning and ending that held Joyce's *Work in Progress* together until it became *Finnegans Wake*. Nor is this Bunyan's *Pilgrim's Progress*, despite some obvious echoes such as a double journey and wicker gates, nor a picaresque tale of unfortunate travellers, nor any of the many other pointed references to the novel's history scattered throughout *Molloy*. Or, for that matter, to the prehistory of novelistic discourse. At the end of his inconclusive journey in search of his mother, in the ditch, Molloy invokes Chaucer's 'General Prologue' to *The Canterbury Tales*, citing a spring day replete with showers and bird melody; but whereas Chaucer's characters 'longen' then 'to goon on pilgrimages,' Molloy 'longed to go back into the forest. Oh not a real longing' (91). Of course not: at this stage of the game, it can be nothing but a literary longing.

In the concluding passage of *Molloy I*, Molloy comments on the odd fact that whereas now he hears birds he had not heard any while in the forest. This judgment is (again) strongly reminiscent of Beckett's concluding remarks to a paragraph in the Axel Kaun letter in which he has posed the question of whether the 'boring' of holes in language will reveal the 'something or nothing' that lies behind it – the 'music' or the 'silence.' Beckett's idea of 'silence' is rigorously pursued here; he dismisses the views of those ostensibly 'sensitive and intelligent people' who believe there is no shortage of silence, dismissing them as 'hard of hearing': 'For in the forest of symbols, which aren't any, the little birds of interpretation, which isn't any, are never silent' (*Dis*, 172). The remarkable double-voicing of this sentence needs to be carefully unpacked; subtracting the two clauses of negation, we are left with a Baudelairean 'forest of symbols' in which the 'little birds of interpretation [...] are never silent.' Such is the conventional nature of literary language, and there is no possibility in this view of experiencing anything like Beckett's authentic sense of silence. The birds were silent in Molloy's journey through the forest since it was not intended as a 'forest of symbols.' The birds are, however, heard once Molloy is outside the forest, but it is no longer a question of an 'interpretation' of 'symbols' that point to alternative or higher realms of meaning in which a 'correspondence' might be located.

Instead of these traditional approaches, Beckett is proposing an examination of language *in itself*: how its terms operate as signs within its own system; how its exchange of terms can create its own modes of being. The last sentence of *Molloy I* reads: 'Molloy could stay, where he happened to be' (91). But we know he is in two places (at least) at the same time: in his mother's room and in the ditch. In the opening sentence of the novel, Molloy pointedly questions how he got to his mother's room and, while he is not sure whether it was by ambulance, maintains it was 'certainly a vehicle of some kind.' The vehicle is language itself as the very medium of *Molloy*. More specifically, it is via the process of metaphor ('a carrying across'), and 'vehicle' in this context means the literal meaning of words used metaphorically, as was the case with Molloy's opening comments on ambulances and various means of transport. The 'tenor' is the subject to which metaphor refers, and in terms of bridging the gap between the beginning and ending of *Molloy I* this entails the issue of language itself and, more particularly, the various selves brought into play when authorship is a fundamental concern. Molloy's first memory after noting the birds' music is of the two travellers, A and C, perhaps as signs of Author and Character functions, both roles having been played by himself, as necessarily required by the doubling inherent in the 're-presentation' of narrative. 'The Vulture' aesthetic that led to the breakthroughs in *Mercier and Camier* and *Stories* whereby the writing self and the fictionalized self can critically probe the question of being in literature is strained to the breaking point as the number of selves behind each would-be self begins to proliferate.

Enter Jacques Moran. The appearance of this new narrator in *Molloy II* is the most startling and challenging development in the novel as a whole and immediately raises the question of significant or revealing connections between Moran's narrative and his predecessor's. Moran himself is a great let-down after Molloy's mythological journey in search of his mother and the recording of the same. He is an apparatchik, a petty functionary who as a detective of sorts (namely, the defective kind) is ordered by his boss Youdi, via the messenger Gaber, to find Molloy and to take his own son Jacques Jr along on the mission. A petty bourgeois tyrant, he would initially appear to be the very antithesis of the troubadour Molloy.

A great deal of criticism has been devoted to the question of determining the nature of the Molloy-Moran relationship. A useful summary of the symmetries between the two halves is supplied in *The Grove Companion to Samuel Beckett*, by Ackerley and Gontarski. Of greater critical interest, however, is their interpretation of these various parallels between *Molloy I* and *II*: 'It is not so much that Moran has become Molloy, or that the second half should precede the first, but that Molloy was always part of Moran, as were Gaber and Youdi, agents of a superego: "For who could have spoken to me of Molloy if not myself and to whom if not to myself could I have spoken of him" (112). What the Moran section offers, and why it follows the Molloy section (and why the novel is called *Molloy*, not *Moran*) is a fiction written by Molloy of Molloy as Moran encountering Molloy.'[15] Such a reading greatly oversimplifies the question of voice and authorial origins in *Molloy*. The self-reflexivity of Molloy writing Moran's narrative does make for tidy packaging, to be sure, but it can hardly be credited with a thorough critical engagement of the question of who is speaking in the two parts of *Molloy*. The opening paragraph of *Molloy* provocatively raises the spectre of another 'I' behind our ostensible narrator, and we know that the diptych *Molloy* is not sufficient unto itself and that Malone's emergence in the next work necessitates a re-examination of all conventional assumptions about who is speaking.

The whole entry on *Molloy* in *The Grove Companion* fluctuates in a critically divided manner between aspects of a liberal humanist reading and those of a deconstructionist bent. For example, Freud and Jung are invoked in the discussions of the two parts of the novel as if they are representatives of truth bearing discourses capable of deciphering the riddles of oedipal conflict, the law of the father, and so on; at the same time, however, the argument is forwarded that 'there is no truth to discover, save that the journey has been fictive.'[16] I would agree in this regard with Katz that it is simply not possible to resolve the voice-origins-authority issues of *Molloy* as posed by its two-part structure; such integrative readings are 'inextricably bound to a hermeneutics of causality, primacy, and determination' whereas 'both stories in *Molloy* foreground and parody just this sort of interpretive quest and the assumptions that go with it.'[17] In the final analysis, the elliptical nature of the narratives precludes any such neat reduction.

Molloy I shows that the counterpointing of elements from *Portrait* is still relevant to the development of Beckett's art. Gontarski and Ackerley have categorically excluded any such consideration: '*Portrait* does not figure in SB's postwar writings, as its aesthetic concerns and affirmation (however ironic) of the artist as hero had become irrelevant and out-dated.'[18] Beckett's level of engagement with Joycean aesthetics is far too complex at this point to be so comprehensively and prematurely dismissed. Our earlier discussions of *Mercier and Camier* and *Stories* have already demonstrated that this is not the case in the postwar writings. Molloy is Beckett's most fully developed portrait of the artist, and, in the second half of the novel that bears his name, there appears the figure of Moran, who undergoes a series of transformations that make him appear more Molloy-like, without, however, attaining the end result of actually becoming Molloy. The basic question posed is whether or not Moran's will as personified by his bourgeois identity is weakened to such a degree that he actually does experience creative consciousness in his own right. The references to *Portrait* are significantly fewer in *Molloy II*, and those that are invoked tend to focus primarily on the question of what is art and underline the degree to which Moran's transformations have still not fully effected an authentic sense of what being an artist entails.

The most obvious difference between Molloy and Moran is that the latter lacks an appreciation of music, 'distant' or otherwise. The short, jerky sentences of the opening of his report fall flat in comparison with the flowing rhythms of Molloy's narrative. On a more literal level, Moran declares that 'If there is one thing gets on my nerves it's music' (105). Later he congratulates himself on having an 'extremely sensitive ear,' adding the rider 'Yet I have no ear for music' (121). Instead, he claims to be particularly attuned to detecting 'the silence of which the universe is made' (128). These self-appraisals ironically enough again echo Beckett's critical comments in the Axel Kaun letter on those who lack an authentic perception or understanding of what lies behind (or within) language – 'a whisper of that final music or that silence.' Moran is one of those 'sensitive and intelligent people' Beckett scorns; he is prone to melodramatic statements such as that the universe is composed of silence when his own report on his journey in pursuit of Molloy is all too obviously entangled in a 'forest of symbols' with their accompanying 'little birds of interpretation' in a way that Molloy's narrative critically resists or interrogates. A case in point is Moran's account of killing off his double in the forest, during which he does 'give way to literature' (151) in a much more self-conscious and contrived

manner than the corresponding scene in *Molloy I* in which the eponymous protagonist kills the charcoal burner. The clamour of such 'artful'
and 'crafty' interpretations precludes any serious engagement with the
'silence.' Moran is 'hard of hearing' in Beckett's critical sense of the
word. It is fitting that after he has killed off a repugnant earlier version
of himself he should come across an ear, which he then throws away.
The 'little birds of interpretation' are never silent.

Similarly, Moran's speculations about beauty, which lies at the heart
of traditional aesthetics, begin with a number of trite and conventional
views that he has still not fully overcome by the end of the novel.[19] For
example, before his midnight departure, and in the midst of the appall-
ing comedy of manners that characterizes his relationship with his son
Jacques Jr and his housekeeper Martha, Moran offers the following
homily upon the vista offered up by his window: 'A great joy, it is
hardly too much to say, surged over me at the sight of so much beauty,
so much promise. I turned away with a sigh, for the joy inspired by
beauty is often not unmixed' (116). *Molloy* contains more references to
'joy' and cognates thereof than any other Beckett work,[20] such references sometimes seeming to play on Joyce's name as Joyce himself was
prone to do. A case in point is Gaber's diktat to Moran from Youdi:
'home, instanter'; Moran then prods Gaber into remembering what
Youdi had told him the other day: 'He said to me, said Gaber, Gaber, he
said, life is a thing of beauty, Gaber, and a joy for ever. He brought his
face nearer mine. A joy for ever, he said, a thing of beauty, Moran, and a
joy for ever' (164). Youdi's words of wisdom add a crucial existential
dimension to Keats's opening line of 'Endymion': 'A thing of beauty is
a joy for ever.' Keats's opening stanza sets forth the identification of the
aesthetic and human realms: 'Some shape of beauty moves away the
pall/From our dark spirits.'[21] Youdi's explicit emphasis on 'life is' suggests a similar identification. What Youdi 'means' is, to say the least,
moot; what Joyce thought on such issues is, however, well known.
Joyce's 'perfect manner in art' he termed 'comedy' for it 'embraced the
whole of life, including even its tragedy, and because it contemplated it
steadily, in a spirit of "joy."'[22] This is a more fully developed exposition
of the 'some form of aesthetics relevant to man' that the narrator of
'First Love' says his father's death mask alluded to.

Beckett's own professed vision of Joyce as Artist-God is another reason for associating the Youdi (Jehovah) figure of *Molloy II* with Joyce.
Additional support of the Youdi-Joyce identification is Beckett's use here
of a technique that we examined earlier in 'Assumption' and *Murphy*: a

literary triangulation whereby a third party mediates between two others, only one of which, however, is openly identified. Here Keats is that intermediary whereby Beckett formulates his points of departure from Joyce, who is a powerful presence here, even though not openly identified. From as early as *Murphy*, Beckett has associated Keats and Joyce: Mr Kelly, the Joyce-figure, is depicted, as he flies his kite in the final chapter of the novel, as focused 'with his eagle eyes' at a spot in the heavens where he thought his kite would 'swim into view' (280). This echoes, most appropriately, Keats's sonnet 'On First Looking into Chapman's Homer,' in which the poet describes how his reading made him feel 'like some watcher of the skies / When a new planet swims into his ken' or like Cortez, gazing at the Pacific 'with eagle eyes.'[23]

The Youdi-Joyce-Keats connection is further reinforced by three references to Keats's opening of 'Endymion' in *Ulysses*, the most important of which is Molly Bloom's adaptation in 'Penelope.' She remembers Bloom's 'mad crazy letters' in which he glorifies her body and claims all 'that comes from it is a thing of beauty and of joy for ever something he got out of some nonsensical book' (*U*, 721). Body and book, in different ways, are identified by Bloom and Molly as they were for Joyce, who famously said of *Uylsses* that 'if it isn't fit to read, life isn't fit to live.'[24] Yes, Joyce could be said in his own way to affirm that 'life is a thing of beauty and a joy' – if not 'for ever,' at least in the sense of *Portrait*'s everliving 'mortal beauty' (151). Moran subversively challenges this proposition by questioning whether it applies to the domain of 'human life,' but his report shows that he is himself scarcely human in many regards. He pictures himself as at best a mere functionary in what he presumes to be Youdi's vast organization. He is a mere contrivance; as his own fictional construct, he is at best a third-rate version of the mythical Molloy he has so vainly sought. As a human construct, he is an even greater failure, as witnessed by his authoritarian treatment of his son, which is predicated upon a horror of the body and a brutal repression of any real sense of beauty and joy. On the other hand, Molloy incorporates in his own narration a number of visionary insights about the darkness in which he investigates his own sense of what life and, yes, even beauty might mean. It remains to be seen whether Moran in the final reckoning has gained enough insight into himself and the act of writing to be seriously regarded as a portrait of the artist in his own right.

The opening paragraph of Moran's narrative is, like Molloy's, a fictional reconstruction of his journey ex post facto: 'It is midnight. The rain is beating on the windows. I am calm. All is sleeping. Nevertheless I get up and go to my desk. I can't sleep. My lamp sheds a soft and steady light. I have trimmed it' (92). Implicit here is a founding aesthetic principle of Moran's narrative, which will not become fully apparent until the last four sentences of his report, some eighty-four pages later, as a final accounting that leaves hanging the question of whether Moran is any freer now than he was before: 'Then I went back into the house and wrote, It is midnight. The rain is beating on the windows. It was not midnight. It was not raining' (176). Whereas young Stephen Dedalus tells the dean of studies that he is presently working 'by the light of one or two ideas of Aristotle and Aquinas' (164) and that he will use them until he has achieved something in his own right, adding, moreover, that he will not hesitate to 'trim' these ideas 'if the lamp smokes or smells,' now an older and supposedly somewhat wiser Moran will adjust the lamp under which he does his writing by means of one specific idea from Hegel's *The Phenomenology of Mind*: 'A. Consciousness, 1. Certainty at the Level of Sense-Experience – The "This," and "Meaning."' Here Hegel undertakes a critique of empiricism, which naively takes the immediately given as the source of all knowledge:

> Sense-certainty itself has thus to be asked: What is the This? If we take it in the two-fold form of its existence, as the *Now* and as the *Here*, the dialectic it has in it will take a form as intelligible as the This itself. To the question, What is the Now? we reply, for example, the Now is night-time. To test the truth of this certainty of sense, a simple experiment is all we need: write that truth down. A truth cannot lose anything by being written down, and just as little by our preserving and keeping it. If we look again at the truth we have written down, look at it *now, at this noon-time*, we shall have to say it has turned stale and become out of date.[25]

It is as if in the writing of his report Moran has become fully aware of Hegel's truth and how the 'simple experiment' can reveal the complex duplicity inherent in the art of recounting an extended narrative. Hegel goes on to explain that when we say 'now' we may mean to refer to the particular now which is present, but, in fact, we say something universal, since the word 'now' expresses not this or any particular 'now,' but applies to all 'nows' in general. Nevertheless, for Moran the painful discovery is that he is caught between his various 'nows': 'For describing this day I am once more he who suffered it' (122); 'For it is one of the features of this penance that I may not pass over what is over and straightway come to the heart of the matter [...] I am far more he who finds than he who tells what he has found, now as then ...' (133). Moran has made some significant progress towards an understanding of the novel situation he now finds himself in; nevertheless, the extent of his awareness is still a far cry from Molloy's much more adept and insightful display of how such narrative perplexities might be exploited. Moran's statements concerning his newfound sense of identity are all too painfully self-conscious, an obvious inversion of his original bourgeois conformity, bearing too many traces of strain, too many whiffs of midnight oil.

The Hegel allusion that frames the opening and closing of *Molloy II* can be made to serve double duty: in addition to the critical appraisal of Moran's progress in his own writing, it also serves at this crucial juncture to suggest a number of vital differences between Beckett's vision and Joyce's. The Hegel passage from *The Phenomenology of Mind* cited above goes on to extend the critique of language as being fundamentally incapable of expressing a sensuous immediate reality since it belongs to a consciousness that is inherently universal. Hegel underscores that language possesses a nature that reverses the meaning of what is ostensibly said and thus prevents what is meant from ever getting into words. This is a focal point for one school of Hegel interpretation that has had a profound influence on French thought from Kojève through Derrida and helps to explain the interest of contemporary French philosophers in Beckett's work. The common point of interest takes up the various divisions revealed within the 'unhappy consciousness' in its futile search for unity. This is the French Hegel interpretation that would dominate from the 1960s onwards in various permutations and revisions; however, as Bruce Baugh so lucidly explains in *French Hegel*, this movement was preceded by another French Hegel, which took the 'anthropological turn': 'it was a historicist philosophy of existence that saw the end goal of the dialectic as a harmonious and organic totality that would transcend and reconcile all oppositions.'[26] Jacques Aubert states time and again in his study of Joyce's aesthetic that it was formulated within neo-Hegelian terms that were very influential at that time.[27]

In an overall assessment, then, *Molloy* is a complex and climactic coming to terms with Joyce's influence on Beckett's writing through his early and middle period. *Malone Dies*, the 'middling' novel in the *Trilogy*, moves from a series of calculated aesthetic stratagems towards the emotional outpouring that drives the tortuous and tortured rhetoric of *The Unnamable*. Revealed as the figure behind both Molloy and Moran,

Malone's own 'full programme' (182) is projected as 'Present state, three stories, inventory,' with the possibility of an 'occasional interlude,' as he fills up the time before his imminent demise. Or so he promises. We will see at the end of his story that he has harboured a much more desperate and daring stratagem whereby he might transcend the dilemmas posed by writing, being, and fiction-making. What is most notable in *Malone Dies* prior to its remarkable conclusion is the very paucity of references to Joyce's work. When in his opening paragraph Malone states 'I shall be natural at last' and adds that since he has not complained throughout his life there is no reason to 'rejoice now' (179), an obvious rejoinder is in order. Beckett can indeed 'rejoice' that Joyce is now no longer the determining force he was in his earlier work. Most tellingly, references to *Portrait* appear to be absent and references to other Joyce works function primarily as secondary echoes rather than the determining principles behind the narration. For example, Malone's anticipation of his death as a departure 'from the world that parts at last its labia and lets me go' (189), as a veritable birth into death, and later his impression 'that his feet are clear already, of the great cunt of existence' (283), might be regarded as echoes of *Ulysses'* 'grey sunken cunt of the world' (59). The elaborate play on 'little cloud' in the story of Sapo points to the *Dubliners* story of the same title. The naturalistic as well as ironical elements in this episode do seem to owe something to that baffled sense of entrapment so strongly felt in 'Little Cloud' and many of the other stories in *Dubliners*. These are admittedly minor points, whereas a dominant refrain throughout *Malone Dies* is of a particular Beckettian type of 'rejoicing,' one which intimately conjoins joy with darkness and suffering, for example, 'waiting for them to end, for my joy to end, straining towards the joy of ended joy' (206–7).

Two other Irish writers do, however, play principal roles in the structure and design of *Malone Dies*. In the 'interlude[s]' Malone refers many times to his own 'earnestness' as he toils to return to what he conceives as his authentic self, which is believed to reside somewhere behind the effigy his writing has portrayed: 'What I sought, when I struggled out of my hole, then aloft through the stinging air towards an inaccessible boon, was the rapture of vertigo, the letting go, the fall, the gulf, the relapse to darkness, to nothingness, to *earnestness*, to home, to him awaiting for me always' (195, my emphasis). The link to Wilde is flaunted in Malone's phrase 'within me the wild beast of earnestness padded up and down' (194). The image conjures up Wilde caged in his cell at Reading Gaol, a world away from the brilliant wit of *The Importance of Being Earnest*'s comedy of manners. For Malone it is most definitely not a question of art for art's sake, but of art for his own sake, how he might extricate himself from his terminal situation. There is, admittedly, a comedy of manners of sorts in the story of Sapo and his earnest petit bourgeois parents, but this quickly deteriorates into a brutalized human comedy in the story of Big Lambert and his family. At the end of the novel, elements of a comedy of manners are combined with a savage Swiftian satire in the outing of Lady Pedal with the asylum inmates from the House of St John of God, among whom is Macmann (formerly Sapo) and their keeper Lemuel: 'Come, Ernest, said Lady Pedal, let us find a place to picnic [...] The voice of Lady Pedal, calling. She appeared, joyous. Come along, she cried, all of you, before the tea gets cold. But at the sight of the late sailors she fainted, which caused her to fall. Smash her! screamed the Saxon. She had raised her veil and was holding in her hand a tiny sandwich' (286–7). If we recall 'Assumption,' the buffoon in the loft and the organist both now seem to have gone mad: Lemuel, the buffoon, runs amok with his hatchet, while Malone, the organist, scribbles frantically with his dwindling stub of a pencil (a Venus, no less).

There is, however, as I argued in *Reconstructing Beckett*, a method behind Malone's madness. The concluding ten pages of the novel contain another of Beckett's reinterpretations of Dante's Terrestial Paradise, a revision which is very different from that found in chapter 7 of *Mercier and Camier*, where the motif was employed in order to enable the author to enter the zone of creativity in which he could become an artist in his own right. The striving for an absolute transcendence in *Malone Dies* transforms the Terrestial Paradise locale so that it is no longer the point at which the artist might integrate the ideal and the real, but a would-be point of departure for a Paradise beyond. Malone tries to sweep away the terrible confusion surrounding the terms 'real' and 'ideal,' 'human' and 'fictional,' by a daring assault on the Absolute, on the 'Paradise' that lies beyond the Terrestial Paradise he has suddenly transported his dupe Macmann to, the House of St John of God, located on top of a mountain plateau. Malone's statement, 'Let us try another way' (277), signals the concentration upon the Terrestial Paradise theme. The 'pure plateau air' (277) echoes the first Canto of *Purgatory* in which Dante and Virgil experience the exhilarating contrast between the 'dead air' of the *Inferno* and this new 'pure air.' The 'fine view [...] of the plain, the sea, the mountains, the smoke of the town' (277) also parallels Dante's reaction to his new viewpoint. Malone is definitely not an artist-vulture seeking to integrate various aspects of the real and ideal; instead he seeks an identification with the ideal by 'hoisting the real unjustifiably clear of its dimensional limits,' to use the words Beckett employed to criticize both Vico and Proust. For Malone the Terrestial Paradise is only a penultimate step; his death and the departure of his creatures for the island will, he hopes, lead to a Paradise that is not terrestial, and a consummation beyond the boundaries of art.

The progression towards this consummation is, however, by no means guaranteed, as Beckett termed the situation at the end of Dante's Purgatory. In his 'last word about the Purgatories,' Beckett had clearly distinguished Joyce's world vision from Dante's: 'Mr Joyce's is spherical and excludes culmination' (*Dis*, 33). Beckett's vision in *The Unnamable* is closer to Joyce's *ricorso* in so far as it does have some 'spherical' qualities, even if they are by no means as systematized as in Joyce: 'I have said that all things here recur sooner or later, no, I was going to say it, then thought better of it' (299). *The Unnamable* is one of Beckett's most original works and propels him into an area of exploration that has come to be regarded as distinctively his own. In the next chapter our discussion will consider how *The Unnamable* presents Beckett with a host of new problems in the wake of his *Molloy*, in which he finally was able to write his own version of *A Portrait of the Artist* and to come to terms with the Joycean legacy of his earlier works.

In the midst of seemingly interminable opening comments, the Unnamable notes that even while preoccupied with his 'troop of lunatics' (308), all those Murphys, Watts, Molloys, Morans, and Malones, he heard 'murmurs' concerning 'a certain number of highly promising formulae and which indeed I promised myself to turn to good account at the first opportunity'. He goes on to add that he was 'sufficiently impressed by certain expressions to make a vow (while continuing my yelps) never to forget them – and (what is more) to ensure they should engender others' (308). His conclusion is posed as yet another version of 'distant music': 'For if I could hear such a music at such a time (I mean while floundering through a ponderous chronicle of moribunds in their courses, moving, clashing, writhing or fallen in short-lived swoons) with how much more reason should I not hear it now, when supposedly I am burdened with myself alone?' (308). One way of interpreting this 'confession' is in terms of Beckett's relationship with Joyce. The 'highly promising formulae' could ironically refer to the contestation of the aesthetic theory put forward by Stephen Dedalus that so sufficiently impressed Beckett that he never forgot 'certain expressions,' which in turn engendered others of his own devising. This is the abridged version of the development of Beckett's prose from 'Assumption' to the *Trilogy*. But the twist that the Unnamable's retrospective summary draws attention to is that Beckett always did have his own stories to tell, and the various 'yelps' sounded therein needed to modify and finally dramatically transform the Joycean 'music' in order to find their own expression. And now that the Unnamable believes (albeit mistakenly) he is alone there is hope that finally he should be able to hear that 'music' purely on its own terms, and that this would allow for 'another and less unpleasant method of ending my troubles' (308), of ending the civil war within the language he has to learn to live with. What the Unnamable has not fully apprehended is that for him (and for Beckett, who is somehow behind all these fictions) the cries need to be incorporated into the music. On the very last page of his final will and testament the Unnamable's torrent of words features 'murmurs' and 'silences,' punctuated by 'distant cries' (414).

7 Critical Beckett: Incorporating Joyce in the Post-*Trilogy* Works

The closing words of the *Trilogy* pose a perplexing challenge: how to proceed when an ethical imperative is set in direct opposition to a negative that decries any such action and then, contrariwise, accedes to that very directive – 'you must go on, I can't go on, I'll go on.' This final 'sentence,' over three thousand words long, fittingly begins 'Enormous prison,' an apt structural description of what becomes in the process of articulation an embodiment of a veritable life sentence. The impasse of this would-be closure is inherent in the Unnamable's desperate opening decision to 'stay in,' to shut out the world: 'you think you are simply resting, the better to act when the time comes, or for no reason, and you soon find yourself powerless ever to do anything again' (291). But words, as if by tropism, drag the self irresistibly towards fiction and the world. The decision to 'stay in' has become a part of a much larger question about the nature of language and the culturally sanctified fictions it engenders, such as the individuation of the 'I,' a God-figure, and the twin ideas of guilt and innocence (the 'Enormous prison' is, for example, immediately likened to 'a hundred thousand cathedrals').

The Unnamable does not try to make these existential fictions real because he does not want to accept being in time and, moreover, does not have a language whereby he can speak of himself without being entangled in a world of deceit and illusion. The truly remarkable feature of Beckett's prose fiction in the last forty years of his writing life (1949–89) is the unprecedented investigation into the very syntactical foundations of language as he attempts to forge what he termed 'the proper syntax of weakness' which would let 'being into literature.' I regard the impasse with which the *Trilogy* brings itself to a provisional close as the starting point for Beckett's search for the means of finding a way out of the dilemmas that confound the language of *The Unnamable*. In Beckett's prose from 'Texts for Nothing' to 'Stirrings Still,' there is a turning towards the world and the underlying problem of relocating and reconfiguring the self that has fallen into the no-man's-land of fictional non-being. These post-*Trilogy* works will, I believe, come to be recognized as Beckett's most important and original contributions to the literary tradition. In this pursuit, Beckett is paradoxically the most derivative of writers and the most original. We have seen how in the extensive and wide-ranging network of allusions in Beckett's work Joyce occupies a privileged position of influence in terms of Beckett's own aesthetic development. Joyce is still present in a number of important echoes and contrapuntal patternings, even if these intertextual references now function primarily as a means of counterpointing Beckett's departures from Joyce. The controlling strategy now is one of incorporation as Beckett has assimilated particular aspects of Joyce's work and adapted them to his own writing.

Beckett's major challenge is to formulate a new language of his own that will allow for a way out of the rhetoric of failure surrounding the dislocated and dysfunctional pronouns of *The Unnamable*. Beckett has disclaimed any connection between his own work and that of later Joyce in which he saw an 'apotheosis of the word.' Indeed, Joyce's 'revolution of the word' stems from a veritable cornucopia of lexical inventiveness, morphological and phonological.[1] On the other hand, Beckett's project in his post-*Trilogy* works turns decisively upon the forging anew of a 'proper syntax of weakness.' Whereas Joyce could claim to have 'split the etym,' it is Beckett who dismantles the conventional syntax of the English (and French) sentence. A commonplace of Joyce criticism is that one of the frames Joyce left intact in *Finnegans Wake* was the standard syntax of the English sentence. Thus when it comes to an ontological investigation of the very foundations of language in terms of subject-object (predicate) relationships, it might now more accurately be stated of Beckett himself what he had earlier said of Joyce: 'His writing is not *about* something; *it is that something itself*' (*Dis*, 27). Beckett's 'forgings' may indeed still echo a Joycean usage in which wordsmithing and counterfeiting are both implied, but it is Beckett who, beginning with *How It Is*, adopts 'a revolutionary attitude toward word *and* syntax' (my emphasis), thereby fulfilling one of the precepts of the manifesto 'Poetry Is Vertical' (1931), to which he was a signatory. In the following discussions of the post-*Trilogy* prose, the main focus will be on those Joycean elements which counterpoint Beckett's attempts to formulate a new language for being that would let being into literature. The fully detailed analyses of these works were the subject of my earlier study, *Reconstructing Beckett*; here the primary emphasis will necessarily be on the Joycean elements as a supplementary feature challenging more traditional readings of Beckett and thereby enriching our understanding of the development of his fiction.

The first of the 'Texts for Nothing' shows Beckett's 'I' dialogically engaging earlier formulations of the 'voice' as well as entering into an intertextual dialogue with Joyce. The first sentence of 'Text 1' virtually recapitulates the last phrases of the *Trilogy*, 'I couldn't any more, I couldn't go on,' and this narrator seems to be answering the Unnamable, 'I can do nothing any more, that's what you think' (*CSP*, 100), even affirming that 'we seem to be more than one, all deaf, not even, *gathered together for life*' (100–1, italics mine). But this intended escape from what Beckett termed the 'attitude of disintegration' that characterized the status of language at the end of *The Unnamable* 'failed in 'Texts for Nothing.'[2] To substantiate the claims for being enunciated in 'Text 1,' a new language is needed to corroborate a vision redirected towards the world. And, in this regard, Beckett is engaged in a dialogue with Joyce in which the underlying import is to distinguish this new perspective from Joyce's; in short, to echo Joyce and then to reply in his own voice: 'All mingles, times and tenses, at first I only had been here, now I'm here still, soon I won't be here yet, toiling up the slope, or in the bracken by the wood, it's larch, I don't try to understand, I'll never try to understand any more, that's what you think, for the moment I'm here, always have been, always shall be, *I won't be afraid of the big words any more, they are not big*' (102–3, my italics). This echoes Stephen Dedalus's comment to Mr Deasy in the 'Nestor' chapter of *Ulysses*: '– I fear those big words, Stephen said, which make us so unhappy' (*U*, 31). 'History' is, of course, another such 'big word' that Stephen is afraid of – a 'nightmare' from which he is trying to awake. Beckett, on the other hand, is not afraid of the 'big words' because 'they are not big.' Like Joyce, Beckett is concerned with history ('times and tenses.') Moreover, he is in ways very distinct from Joyce also focused on the ontological dimensions of language whereby such a self (or selves) might come into being by integrating its various 'times and tenses.' Moreover these 'big words' are indeed 'not big': the key words are 'here' and 'be.' The little words of language, the deictics such as 'above' and 'below,' 'here' and 'there,' constitute on the linguistic plane 'all my little company' (103). The 'here,' however, varies, as the narrator is all too painfully aware, and any clarification of the mingling of tenses and times necessarily depends 'on what I meant by here, and me, and being' (101).

For Beckett the specifics of how these terms are connected necessitate a reconfiguration of the syntactical foundations of the sentence. For Joyce the mingling of times and tenses is celebrated as a joyful multiplicity of selves; for example, in that principal figure and function HCE (Here Comes Everybody), replete with the virtually endless metamorphoses of the words that constitute the all-including, all-encompassing 'farraginous chronicle' that is *Finnegans Wake*. For Joyce the chronicling can proceed as expansively as it wants on the assumption that the conventional syntax of the English sentence allows for the registering of events, however palimpsestically overlaid with the echoing effects produced by morphological and phonological play with the fluidity of words within that syntactical frame. For Beckett, however, the inability to determine who is who, what is what, and – above all – who is speaking results in a linguistic impasse; as 'Text 6' puts it, 'this farrago of silence and words, of silence that is not silence and barely murmured words' (125). The question of to whom the voice belongs is raised in the first sentence of 'Text 4': 'Where would I go, if I could go, who would I be, if I could be, what would I say, if I had a voice, who says this, saying it's me?' (114). A perfectly balanced formal construct, any content it might express is drained away by the final query. The last sentence of this 'Text' pretends to resolve this problem: 'That's where I'd go, if I could go, that's who I'd be, if I could be' (116). But the pronoun 'that' is no longer demonstrative since it lacks any clear antecedent. The reasonable 'I' is the common term that relates 'he who neither speaks or listens' and 'he who moves.' As a consequence, this 'I' becomes literally an 'excluded middle,' not refined out of existence as in the Joycean ideal of the artist propounded in *Portrait*, but simply reasoned away as a logical impossibility.

Another reason for misreading the direction and import of Beckett's post-*Trilogy* writings is the quite incredible way in which Beckett's 'Three Dialogues' (with Georges Duthuit, 1949) has been adopted by many Beckett commentators as if it were a programmatic description of Beckett's guiding principles. Whereas the manifesto speaks of the 'dream of an art unresentful of its insuperable indigence and too proud for the farce of giving and receiving' (*Dis*, 141), 'Text 13' speaks of the 'end of dream [...] the end of the farce of making and the silencing of silence' (154). Beckett declared at the end 'Three Dialogues' that he would not circumvent the 'fidelity to failure' by turning it into 'an expressive act, even if only of itself, of its impossibility, of its obligation' (*Dis*, 145). Yet this is arguably what he has done in the 'silencing of the silence' in 'Texts for Nothing.' The studied variation on the phrase from 'Three Dialogues' in 'Text 13' is dialogical in the critical sense and is a recognition on Beckett's part of the rhetoric of failure in 'Texts for Nothing' and the degree to which this undercuts his 'fantastic theory' (as Duthuit terms it) of an art that is no longer 'expressive.'

Another instance of Beckett's third-party triangulation between himself and Joyce is lodged in the midst of the second dialogue on Masson and the critique of that artist's 'concern with the amenities of ease and freedom': *'The stars are undoubtedly superb, as Freud remarked on reading Kant's cosmological proof of the existence of God'* (*Dis*, 141). This reference is an echo with variation of an anecdote about Joyce that Ellmann cites in his biography (the source is identified in the endnotes as Samuel Beckett): 'Joyce attended a party in Zurich where the guests were brought out on the balcony to look at the stars, and a priest who was present embarked on a cosmological proof of the existence of God, adduced from the intricate order of the starry heavens. Joyce interjected *"Schade dass alles von der gegenseitigen Zerstörung abhängt"* ("What a pity that the whole thing depends upon reciprocal destruction")' (*JJ*, 648). Here Joyce is just as attuned to various dissonances in the music of the spheres as Beckett.

Later in the Masson dialogue D. puts forward a view of painting, of art, that strongly evokes Joyce's view of history, minus the Vichian framework: 'But must we really deplore the painting that admits "the things and creatures of spring, resplendent with desire and affirmation, ephemeral no doubt, but immortally reiterant," not in order to benefit by them, not in order to enjoy them, but in order that what is tolerable and radiant in the world may continue?' (*Dis*, 141).[3] D's final sentence in the Masson section concludes rhetorically, 'Are we really to deplore the painting that is a rallying, among the things of time that pass and hurry us away, towards a time that endures and gives increase?' (*Dis*, 141–2). B. cannot answer this and exits weeping. Joyce's vision is obviously more openly affirmative than anything in Beckett, particularly around the time of the *Trilogy* and 'Texts for Nothing.' Nevertheless, we will see in our discussion of Beckett's final works that as a result of the radical reconfiguration of syntax that begins with *How It Is* (*Comment c'est*) he also manages in his own way to portray a number of startling visions of a more affirmative nature.

The short story 'From an Abandoned Work,' Beckett's only published prose work between 'Texts for Nothing' and *How It Is*, warrants a brief comment for it alludes to *Portrait* in a way that anticipates Beckett's handling of Joycean materials in *How It Is*. This most recent avatar of the Beckettian portrait of the artist as an old man states: 'Over, over, there is a soft place in my heart for all that is over, no, for the being over, I love the word, words have been my only loves, not many. Often all day long as I went along I have said it, and sometimes I would be saying vero, oh vero' (*CSP*, 162). This is a geriatric updating of a very young Stephen Dedalus's much earlier statement: 'Words which he did not understand he said over and over to himself till he had learned them by heart: and through them he had glimpses of the real world about him' (*P*, 64). For the Beckett narrator, it is the failure to 'take his part in the life of that world' (to transpose Stephen's words in the sentence which follows that cited above) that has led him to fixate on the very word 'over' itself and the concept of 'being over' rather than the repetition of words in order to commit them to memory, to learn them by heart. For the narrator in Beckett's tale the only truth to tell would appear as the result of an ana-grammatical reshuffling in which 'over' becomes 'vero.' The obvious dif-ferences between the Joycean 'original' and Beckett's rewriting should not, however, prevent us from seeing a number of similarities, which, in any overall assessment of Beckett's appropriation of Joyce, need to be taken into account. In both there is a love of words, even if the number of words might be greatly reduced in Beckett's case – 'words have been my only loves, not many' – and many of these originate from *Portrait*, words which Beckett seems to have learned by heart.

The lifelong referencing of *Portrait* is again in evidence in 'The Im-age,' the first published piece en route to *Comment c'est* (*How It Is*). Written in 1956, it was first published in French ('L'Image') in the jour-nal *X* in 1959 (Edith Fournier has translated it for S.E. Gontarski's *The Complete Short Prose*). 'The Image' is not divided into the versets of *Comment c'est*; it is one continuous block of prose without punctuation, beginning with 'The tongue gets clogged with mud' and ending with a full stop to the 'sentence' well over twelve hundred words later. In a re-vised and reformatted version, 'The Image' is incorporated into the middle of part 1 of *How It Is* (28–31). Even when absorbed into the larger work, the original title is still appropriate since this develop-ment of an image from adolescence is the single longest and most ex-tensively detailed portrayal of the 'I''s life above in the light to be found in the whole novel. The memory-image vouchsafed in the mud of this underworld depicts the 'I,' aged about sixteen, at a racecourse with a young girl and an 'ash coloured terrier' (*CSP*, 166); it is glorious spring weather (in April or May, the narrator is not exactly sure which month), and the couple is drawn towards mountains of 'modest elevation' (166) where they picnic. All three principals – the dog gets equal billing in this regard – are grotesquely depicted in this parody of a pastoral young love.

The scenes elaborated upon in Beckett's 'The Image' strongly echo a number of features in a memory that an adolescent Stephen Dedalus suddenly experiences in the midst of the tram scene in *Portrait*'s second chapter in which 'a voice within' questions whether he ought to reach out for a kiss from E–C– (Emma Clery): 'And he remembered the day when he and Eileen had stood looking into the hotel grounds, watching the waiters running up a trail of bunting on the flagstaff and the fox terrier scampering to and fro on the sunny lawn, and how, all of a sudden, she had broken out into a peal of laughter and had run down the sloping curve of the path. Now, as then, he stood listlessly in his place, seemingly a tranquil watcher of the scene before him' (70; an earlier variant is found on 49). In addition to similar characters and settings, both scenes refer to an inner voice and, most importantly, a detached sense of watching an earlier version of the present self. Joyce's vignette occurs in the midst of a complex web of micro-narratives beginning a few pages earlier with the visits he and his mother pay to various relatives, one of which depicts the senile Ellen mistaking Stephen for Josephine (a scene which we saw Beckett rewrite in *Molloy I*); and, in the scene following the intercalated memory of himself with Eileen and the fox terrier, Stephen is shown trying to transform the tram scene and the kiss not taken incident into a poem in which 'all those elements which he deemed common and insignificant fell out of the scene' (*P*, 71) (whereas in Beckett's redaction in 'The Image' such elements are heaped on to the point of caricature). The rewriting is extensive in the elaboration of details, many of which, such as the racecourse (Leopardstown), refer to fixtures of his own Foxrock childhood. An obvious point of difference between Joyce and Beckett is underscored through the comparison of 'The Image' with its seminal starting points in *Portrait*; the fragmented and interpolated narratives in the *Portrait* segment challenge Stephen Dedalus (and the reader) to integrate the bits and pieces and are representative of that fracturing of the conventional linear narrative of *Stephen Hero* whereby Joyce transformed himself into a modernist writer. The temporal disjunctions still, however, hold out the possibility of a sense of wholeness, possibly even of an epiphanic experience that would reveal how the disparate points in time might be integrated. But in Beckett's 'The Image' and throughout *How It Is* there is a radical ontological rupturing as evidenced by the dualism of a world above in the light and a world below in the excremental underground. The sense of a detached observation of self is taken to an extreme point at which there appears to be absolutely no means by which this absurdly contrived fictional underworld can ever be reconnected with any anterior life above.

Beckett's major problem is that the 'I' of 'The Image' and *How It Is* does not exist in time and can only authenticate his claims to being if he can find a way to return to the world above, where time is truly to be located. The 'good moments' – a veritable refrain throughout the novel – are drained of any ontological significance; these momentary illuminations of the world above puncture the world below but are then engulfed by the mud. Hence the obvious echoes of Vico's cycles of history,[4] and by association Joyce, are only a source of ironic mockery since the defining characteristic of *How It Is* is of a timeless realm. Such Joycean echoes as 'abject ages each heroic seen from the next' (*HII*, 10) serve primarily to underline the fundamental differences between his work and Beckett's or to show how Beckett has incorporated Joycean elements for his own purposes. An example of the former is the reference to the Ballast Office in part 1 of *How It Is* (44). In Beckett's reference it resolutely remains 'an item in the catalogue of Dublin's street furniture' and is not revealed in its 'whatness' – 'epiphanised' (218), as Stephen Dedalus phrases it in *Stephen Hero*.[5]

Phyllis Carey has compared Shem the Penman in *Finnegans Wake* with Beckett's Pim in *How It Is*: both writers employ Eucharistic imagery and both 'find the common denominator of their respective approaches to artistic creation in the paradox of the cross.'[6] These provocative points give way, however, to a series of statements in which Beckett's use of Eucharistic imagery is termed 'antithetical' to Joyce's and his handling of it labelled with a litany of negatives that echo the ready-made rhetoric of so much Beckett criticism. Beckett is deemed to have reduced life in the Pim episode to 'meaningless words in a text,' and, in terms of the vision afforded by the work as a whole, the illusory temporal divisions of past, present, and future are thought by Carey to 'mask the unchanging, static paralysis of universal human impotence.'[7] This last judgment could be taken, for example, as an accurate summary of many of the situations Joyce portrayed in *Dubliners*. But no one would seriously venture the naive critical judgment that because Joyce depicts this situation he must therefore be endorsing it; why then should such judgments be so uncritically applied to Beckett's work?

Carey proposes that whereas Joyce emphasized 'the sacramental quality of the Eucharist, Beckett focuses on the underlying sacrifice it represents,' and the ending of *How It Is* 'contextualizes the novel as a seemingly endless ritual of crucifixion.'[8] As I argued in *Reconstructing Beckett*, a much more affirmative reading of the novel is possible if we consider how Beckett's 'proper syntax of weakness' in this work allows for the possibility in the final pages of the 'I' (which Beckett referred to as 'the narrator/narrated') forging for himself 'weak as me a voice of my own' (*HII*, 35).[9] If we trace the various contestations between the authorial self in *How It Is* and the 'other' in the excremental underworld, a dramatically different interpretation of the novel's ending could be projected. The vulture aesthetic is vitally present in the last pages and helps the reader to realize imaginatively that the voice now also belongs to the narrator and is not solely at the disposition of the authorial self who has contrived the absurdly logical and grotesque literary paraphernalia of a great chain of being of torturers and victims, each supplied with his own sack of provisions. The 'I' narrator likens himself to the 'prone who must soon take up their life and walk' (in the words of 'The Vulture'): 'flat on my belly yes in the mud yes the dark yes nothing to emend there no the arms spread like a cross no answer LIKE A CROSS no answer YES OR NO yes' (*HII*, 146). Christ on the cross is the human being moving towards the divine. The narrator with his cross of words is the fictional being moving towards historical being. In the former, the flesh is becoming word; in the latter, the word is becoming flesh. It is as if Beckett had to write in a radically different manner than Joyce before he could move towards an affirmation in his own way of a number of telling points about humanity and fiction-making that he shared with him.

How It Is is the major breakthrough text in Beckett's post-*Trilogy* prose. Its quest for a 'proper syntax of weakness' enables Beckett in later works such as 'Lessness,' 'Still,' *Ill Seen Ill Said*, *Worstward Ho*, and 'Stirrings Still' to develop some startling affirmations of the connections between language and being. However, in tandem with these radical innovations there is another line of development in Beckett's later work in which the failure to determine a means of accommodating the conflicting claims of the authorial voice and the 'someone' discovered in the 'place' of the imagination results in the authoritarian imposition of restrictive forms that silence the struggle for voicing by this 'other' presence. Beckett's first work after *How It Is*, 'All Strange Away' (written in 1963 but not published until 1976), falls in this latter category.

The 'he' and 'she' (and multiples thereof) discovered in the 'place' of the imagination are never substantiated as images of a living reality; instead, they are reduced to mere figures, abstracted personifications at the disposal of the authorial consciousness that rules this timeless zone of fiction-making. These images are avowedly not 'real' and are manipulated in a highly ritualized manner obsessed with geometrical and pornographic details, none of which conjures up a sense of an authentic 'other.'

There are a number of ironic echoes of early Joyce in the sighting of the character Emma in the closed place of the imagination and the poking and prying that the author-narrator imagines the 'he' subjecting her to: 'Imagine him kissing, caressing, licking, sucking, fucking and buggering all this stuff, no sound' (*CSP*, 171). The sentence 'Imagine lifetime, *gems*, evenings with Emma and the flights by night, no, not that again' (171, my emphasis) harks back to that scene in *Stephen Hero* when Stephen Dedalus makes his 'mad' proposal to Emma Clery, whose eyes 'shone like gems': 'Just to live one night together, Emma, and then to say goodbye in the morning and never to see each other again!' (202). It is hardly a surprise that Stephen's passionate espousal of the dictates of romantic youth is so unceremoniously rebuffed; as Emma walks away 'with her head slightly bowed he seemed to feel her soul and his falling asunder swiftly and for ever after an instant of all but union' (203). In Beckett's revised version the 'evenings with Emma and the flights by night' sentence is followed by a description of Emma's 'vague *bowed* body' (*CSP*, 171, my emphasis). Beckett's Emma cannot, however, walk away or express her views for she is trapped in the crucible of the authorial voice's own self-serving imaginings: her body is 'bonewhite when light at full, nothing clear but ashen glare as imagined, no, attitudes too with play of joints most clear more various now' (171–2). No wonder the flesh is 'quite expressionless, ohs and ahs copulate cold' (175); Beckett's portrayal is soulless – there is no 'whatness' or *claritas* to be revealed when Emma (or her male counterpart Emmo) is merely 'meat' or 'stuff' at the disposal of the 'deviser' of this piece as a pornographer-cum-vivisector. There cannot be any 'instant of all but union' since time itself is devoid of any significance in this zone of fictional non-being. There will be no Mr Knightley for this Emma, no suggestion of a Flaubertian 'c'est moi.' In a post-mortem assessment of Stephen's mad proposal to Emma, Lynch states 'you went about the affair so strangely' (204). Later Stephen concludes that she only turned down his proposal because of a 'menial fear,' adding that her eyes 'just look strange when upraised to some holy image' (214). All 'strange' away, indeed.

Beckett employs a much more readily identifiable allusion to *Portrait* in the final sentence of 'All Strange Away': 'Fancy dead, to which now add for old mind's sake sorrow vented in simple sighing sound *black vowel a*' (181, my emphasis). Compare this with Stephen's thoughts about Emma (who in this work has been reduced to a set of initials or to simply 'she') as he watches her pass through the dusk after she leaves the library; Stephen feels 'a trembling joy' and wonders why this is so, whether it is because of her presence or because of the line of poetry running through his head (*'Darkness falls from the air'*): 'Her passage through the darkening air or the verse with its *black vowels* and its opening sound, rich and lutelike?' (*P*, 201, my emphasis). Stephen admits that his desire for her conjures up memories of lubricious women, but affirms that 'the images he had summoned gave him no pleasure' and that 'her image was not entangled by them' (201). On the other hand, Beckett's images of Emma in 'All Strange Away' strip away all mystery and call attention to their patent falsity, to sounds divorced from living sense – such as the 'black vowel a' in 'Fancy,' which Joyce borrowed from Rimbaud and which Beckett in turn adapted from Joyce.

'Enough,' originally written in French ('Assez') in 1965, is an anomaly in terms of the development of Beckett's prose after *How It Is*. While it belongs to that sequence of works that deals with a modus vivendi between the competing interests of author/other, 'Enough' effects these new relationships not via experiments with a 'syntax of weakness' but by affording a vision which proceeds on the assumption that such reciprocal exchanges are possible. The story does not, however, begin this way; initially, the narrator is in a totally subservient position to the old man and 'only had the desires he manifested' – 'When he told me to lick his penis I hastened to do so' (*CSP*, 186). Over the course of their time together, the first-person narrator reflects movingly on travelling with the old man until one day ordered to depart; she now is also old and thinking back on the relationship with the old man pays homage to the fact that 'all I know comes from him' and that it was the time with him ('Ten years at the very least') that 'I shall have lived then or never' (*CSP*, 189). The story ends with a memory-image that is antithetical to the clinical debauchery of 'All Strange Away': 'Nothing but the two of us dragging through the flowers. Enough my old breasts feel his old hand' (192).

The tracing of Beckett's relationship with Joyce affords another way of elaborating upon the situation depicted in 'Enough.' First of all,

Beckett's startled reaction – 'I don't know what came over me'[10] – might in part be explained by synchronizing the biographies of Joyce and Beckett: Beckett wrote 'Assez'/'Enough' when he was fifty-nine, the age at which Joyce died. As we have seen throughout this study, Beckett has from the very beginning measured himself against Joyce's corpus. The old man is on his last legs while the 'I' narrator 'belonged to an entirely different generation' (187) and 'had only to straighten up to be head and shoulders above him' (188). But now the narrator is also old and is 'entering night' (187), and, on another plane, Beckett and Joyce are meeting at a point of equilibrium that will soon be enshrouded by the passing of time. 'Enough' is in this sense both a homage to and a requiem for Joyce. There are a number of other factors that point to the Beckett-Joyce relationship as the underlying source for this text: for example, the reference to the narrator fulfilling the desires the old man 'manifested' (repeated twice) crudely and ironically brings down to earth the concept of the Joycean epiphany as a 'sudden spiritual manifestation'; the 'ten years at the very least' they spent together is virtually the same time Beckett spent with Joyce (minus the period of 'exile' over the Lucia Joyce imbroglio and the period apart precipitated by the German invasion of France); indeed, the very phrasing of the narrator's departure upon the old man's command – 'we were severed' (188) – echoes Joycean phrasing we have seen Beckett employ in *Murphy*; 'the notion of calm' (192) that comes from the old man is indeed an accurate retrospective assessment, for we saw in 'Assumption' that the first 'calmative' in Beckett came, however circuitously, from Joyce; moreover, the Terrestial Paradise motif in which the weather 'was eternally mild' (191) and 'we lived on flowers' (192) might be regarded in some respects as a nostalgic reminiscence of Beckett's 'salad days' when he first met Joyce in Paris in 1928. In short, we have in 'Enough' a balancing of the creative experience – an 'assumption' of the Joycean old man in conjunction with the 'annunciation' of the Beckettian narrator.

The gender ambiguity of the first-person narrator might also be regarded as an acknowledgment of Joyce's theme of androgyny, which runs throughout his writing. And the many silences that punctuate their years of walking and talking together cannot help but bring to mind Richard Ellmann's memorable references to similar encounters between Joyce and Beckett (*JJ*, 648). Images of sharing and communion are further suggested by the depiction of the old man looking at the constellations with his 'little round mirror' and ejaculating with joy when he spots the Lyre or the Swan. (Shades of Mr Kelly in the last chapter of *Murphy*.) The Lyre is the constellation of Orpheus and contains Vega, a syzgetic or paired star. Beckett certainly shares Joyce's interest in Vega, as further evidenced by references in 'Assumption' and *Dream*. The scene in 'Enough' strongly echoes the 'Ithaca' chapter of *Ulysses* in which Stephen and Bloom scan the heavens as they relieve themselves in Bloom's backgarden:

> What celestial sign was by both simultaneously observed?
> A star precipitated with great apparent velocity across the firmament from Vega in the Lyre above the zenith beyond the stargroup of the Tress of Berenice towards the zodiacal sign of Leo. (*U*, 656)

The oddly catechismal nature of 'Enough' and its use of mathematical calculations recall the format of 'Ithaca.' 'If the question were put to me suitably framed I would say yes indeed the end of this long outing was my life' (*CSP*, 188); this is followed by calculations that do indeed confirm that they 'took flight in arithmetic': 'Say about the last seven thousand miles. Counting from the day when alluding for the first time to his infirmity he said he thought it had reached its peak' (188–9).

Beckett's short story is also characterized by a poetic apprehension of life in time, most obviously in '*I see the flowers at my feet* and it's the others I see. Those we trod down with equal step. It is true they are the same' (189, my italics). Here Beckett is rewriting the first line of the fifth stanza of Keats's 'Ode to a Nightingale': 'I cannot see what flowers are at my feet.' The fifth stanza effects a vital transition in which the 'I' enters a death-like state in an unsuccessful attempt to become one with the 'immortal Bird.' Beckett's variant in 'Enough' is actually more affirmative in this regard than Keats's original. As we have seen at several junctures in our discussion, Beckett has used allusions to Keats in order to refer indirectly to Joyce. Within the sense of loss and death, there is, nevertheless, a countervailing sense of reclaiming time lost by means of the duplicating and recreative powers of memory. The old man adopts the role of a mentor to the narrator, and because the vision passed on is a poetic one, it is necessarily depicted as sensual in terms of the love of words and the flowers of rhetoric, the 'love of the earth and the flowers' thousand scents and hues' (190). Such an emphasis upon a series of Orphic affirmations of the living connections between word and world is perhaps poetic justice since Joyce had at one time considered naming the hero of *Portrait* Stephen Orpheus.[11] Beckett in

'Enough' offers an alternative to Harold Bloom's thesis that the new-comer's anxiety of influence entails a repression of various ways and solutions arrived at in the tradition the newcomer must strive to re-write. 'Enough' modifies in dramatic fashion the sixth and final phase of Bloom's paradigm for dealing with the anxiety of influence: the *apophrades*, or return of the dead. Bloom depicts this phase as the 'most cunning of revisionary ratios' in which 'strong poets' make it appear that they are in fact 'being *imitated by their ancestors*.'[12] Instead of such retroactive appropriation, the overall impression in 'Enough' is of having certain experiences in common, even as each figure develops its different ways of combining words. Moreover, the discussion does not seem in the end to have been solely literary in nature. Ellmann records an instance of how Joyce 'made clear to Beckett his dislike of literary talk. Once when they had listened silently to a group of intellectuals at a party, he commented, "If only they'd talk about turnips!"' (*JJ*, 702).[13] There is perhaps a nostalgic echo of this sentiment in the penultimate paragraph of 'Enough': 'What do I know of man's destiny? I could tell you more about radishes' (192).

'The Lost Ones' (Le Dépeupleur) was written in 1966, but it was only with the addition of the fifteenth and final section in 1970 that the work was completed. This fable depicts a sealed cylinder, a veritable prison, from which 205 inhabitants, the 'little people,' vainly seek to escape by exploring with their ladders the various tunnels that are arranged quincuncially in the walls of their abode. 'The Lost Ones' is worlds apart from the vision vouchsafed in 'Enough'; in dramatic contrast, it falls into the category of those writings in which Beckett critically reveals that if there is no accommodation possible between the needs of the author and his 'others' – those figures or characters discovered in the place of the imagination – then the authorial presence will impose his will upon them and shape them to meet his own requirements. In short, this is the argument I pursued in *Reconstructing Beckett*, with primary reference to the quincuncial patterns developed in Sir Thomas Browne's *The Garden of Cyrus*.[14] Browne educed a host of telling correspondences between such patterns and God's intelligent design of the world; Beckett's fundamental strategy entailed cutting the cylinder off from any connections with an outside world, thereby forcing the reader to deal with the ontological status of the inhabitants trapped within the lost world. They have no independent status and the narrator has adapted the reality of the cylinder to his own system, a move that leads directly to allegory, which Beckett in his early essay on Joyce pejoratively termed 'a threefold intellectual operation: the construction of a message of general significance, the preparation of a fabulous form, and an exercise of considerable technical difficulty in uniting the two' (*Dis*, 26).

Focusing on the Joyce-Beckett connection can add a number of supplemental considerations to our understanding of 'The Lost Ones.' The various references to 'abode' and the pervasive carceral imagery of the work bring to mind the hellfire sermons of chapter 3 of *Portrait* as an added dimension of the Dantean mise en scène,[15] but the most telling references are to Joyce's *Dubliners*. Joyce added the fifteenth and final story 'The Dead' to the collection during the period in which its publication had been delayed over a number of objections raised by his printers, foremost of which were the references to specific places and actual personalities. This additional story was also to make up for what Joyce deemed his insufficient acknowledgment of Irish hospitality in the preceding stories (*JJ*, 230–1). Beckett added his fifteenth and final section to 'The Lost Ones' after a self-imposed four-year delay, a hiatus brought about by the fact that the only way out of the textual world in which the narrator was trapped along with the inhabitants was to impose an allegorical final solution whereby his need for order superseded all other considerations. In this fifteenth section, the very last searcher is depicted as coming to his end: 'There is nothing at first sight to distinguish him from the others dead still where they stand or sit in abandonment beyond recall' (*CSP*, 222). After examining the face and eyes of one of the vanquished women, this hypothetical last searcher then enters the realm of the vanquished and 'after a pause impossible to time finds at last his place and pose whereupon dark descends and at the same instant the temperature comes to rest not far from freezing point' (223).

Beckett's vision of the dead here could be compared with the great poetic vision in all its ambiguity with which Joyce concludes 'The Dead': the snow 'faintly falling like the descent of their last end, upon all the living and the dead.' In 'The Lost Ones' there are no living left, *only* the dead. Joyce moved dramatically from the ironic allegorical equations of his fourteenth story, 'Grace,' in which Mr Kernan and his friends settle down in church 'in the form of a quincunx' (*PJJ*, 187) to hear a comforting sermon from Father Purdon on how, without too much trouble, they, worldly-wise businessmen all, might put to rights 'with God's grace' their accounts, the books of their spiritual life. Beckett in his fifteenth section moves towards allegory to resolve a host of complexities that cannot any longer be adequately managed or controlled; on the other hand, Joyce in his fifteenth story of *Dubliners* moved from a crass allegorical accounting to a complex poetic rendition of human realities encompassing the quick and the dead, thereby allowing for the possibility at least of a way out of the state of moral paralysis conveyed in *Dubliners* 'for the most part in a style of scrupulous meanness' (*JJ*, 210). The narrator/deviser's vision of ultimate stasis as the only abiding reality in the abode is, however, meant to be regarded critically. For the vanquishing of all the 'little people' is ultimately not only self-defeating but self-cancelling; without them the observer is also rendered null and void.

In the last twenty years of Beckett's writing life there is a fundamental reconfiguration of modernist assumptions that Beckett from the very beginning has identified primarily with Joyce. Beckett in these later works finds new ways of accommodating stasis and kinesis, of temporalizing the moment of the modernist revelation. With the forging of various versions of a 'proper syntax of weakness,' Beckett is able to corroborate a vision of a subject-self co-existing in conjunction with an authorial self. From the very beginning, Beckett has contested the traditional distinction that Stephen Dedalus makes in *Portrait* between 'proper' art as 'static' and 'improper art' as 'kinetic' (whether pornographic or didactic). For Beckett, aestheticizing the experience of living (whether rejoicing or suffering) risks anaesthetizing it. 'Fizzle 7: Still' (1975) is a remarkable reconciliation of contraries such as motion and stillness, sound and silence, light and darkness by means of a syntax of weakness. It is the most recognizably human of Beckett's works since 'Enough' and much more realistic in representation. There is no longer the complex and vexed questioning of the 'something' located in the room, box, rotunda, cylinder, et cetera, which has been the hallmark of many of Beckett's writings since the *Trilogy*. By dispensing with the conventions of both first-person and third-person narration in 'Still,' Beckett is able to achieve a modus vivendi between the claims of the author and the other. The text opens with the sun going down at 'close of a dark day' (*CSP*, 240). Unlike Murphy, this protagonist does not sit out of the sun 'as though he were free.' The nothingness associated with the closing of his eyes must not be identified with a Murphean quest for the so-called inner void of the self. 'Still' involves aperception, the mind's perception of itself as part of the 'outside' against which it can never be hermetically sealed. We saw earlier that the opening of *Murphy* could be seen as a complex rewriting of the passage preceding the birdgirl encounter of *Portrait* in which Stephen feels a sense of an impending transcendence: 'His heart trembled; his breath came faster and a wild spirit passed over his limbs as though he were soaring sunward' (*P*, 149–50). Over forty years later Beckett is again revising and incorporating this scene: 'But casually in this failing light impression dead still even the hands clearly trembling and the breast faint rise and fall' (*CSP*, 240). No matter where the man in 'Still' directs his sight, total absence of perceiving or being perceived is not possible: 'Or anywhere any ope staring out at nothing just failing light quite still till quite dark though of course no such thing just less light still when less did not seem possible' (241). Even the climactic meeting of head and hand in which they are brought into a tremulous equilibrium is not merely self-reflexive but recognizes a need for being that requires a relation of both inside and outside worlds: 'As if even in the dark eyes closed not enough and perhaps even more than ever necessary against that no such thing the further shelter of the hand' (242). However much this figure tries to cut himself off from the external world, such futile actions serve only to underline the impossibility of such escapism. The subject-self must come face to face with its bodily reality and with the world of nature outside the window.

Beckett has finally attained a version of the Joycean epiphany, but in a way that deals with the impasses inherent in the modernist moment. Foremost among these reconfigurations are the avoidance of a syntax that enshrines subject-object divisions and the underlining of how the 'presence' depicted is ineluctably positioned in time. The meeting of hand and head in 'Still' could, for example, be regarded as Beckett's fulfilment, in his own terms, of *Stephen Hero*'s definition of the epiphany as a 'sudden spiritual manifestation' realized by a perception, a gesture or a 'memorable phrase of the mind itself.' In 'Still' one such phrase might be found in 'staring at some point on the hillside such as that beech in whose shade once' (241). The phrase alludes to the first line of Virgil's first eclogue ('The Dispossessed'), 'under the awning of a spreading beech,' as well as perhaps bringing to mind the 'beechen green, and shadows numberless' of the first stanza of Keats's 'Ode to a Nightingale,' or possibly even a more personal reference to Sylvia Beach and her bookstore and the time of Beckett's first meetings with Joyce in Paris.[16] Beckett works the miracle by reconfiguring the words whereby a world can come into being in which a human subject can substantiate claims to being. Foremost among these is a sense of the temporal, however fragmented, in which such 'moments' persist within an existentialist continuum.[17] Even though the often mis-cited passage from *Finnegans Wake* beginning 'Sam knows miles bettern me how to work the miracle' (*FW*, 467) has definitively been proven not to be a reference to Beckett since the passage was published in *transition* before Beckett even met Joyce,[18] it could now be argued, over a half-century later, that Beckett has appropriated these words and indeed fulfilled their prophecy.

Beckett's trilogy of works in the early 1980s – *Company* (1980), *Ill Seen Ill Said* (1981), and *Worstward Ho* (1983) – offer significant variations on this process of world creation and acceptance of being in the world, however attenuated that residual 'leastness' might be. *Company* is a great summary work in which Beckett orchestrates the various perplexities of competing selves and voices that the act of writing has always engendered for him. In many ways it might be regarded as Beckett's own literary autobiography in so far as the text incorporates fifteen memories of a 'you"s life above, many of which were easily recognizable as Beckett's own in light of the then recently published biography by Deirdre Bair. *Ill Seen Ill Said* and *Worstward Ho* do, however, make significant breakthroughs in the types of being possible for both the 'deviser' and the 'devised.' While references to Joyce in *Company* are few and far between, this is itself indicative of a counterpointing of the much more pervasive presence of Joycean materials in the unpublished manuscript 'The Voice' (1977), which is a forerunner of that work.[19] Joycean elements still resonate powerfully with Beckett, as is underscored in the play *Ohio Impromptu* (1981), which Beckett wrote for a conference in celebration of his seventy-fifth birthday.

In *Company* Joycean allusions are strictly limited and the controlling pattern of reference as I pointed out in *Reconstructing Beckett* is Shakespearean.[20] The early episodes of the 'you"s life above focus on how the hunger for communication and for love is continually frustrated, driving this self inwards to the light of his own imagination, in the dark of his own mind. There is, however, one major exception to this pattern of negation in paragraph 40, which deals with 'Bloom of adulthood' (*NO*, 28). In this Joycean paean of accommodation, two 'memories' are incorporated, that of the young boy in the summerhouse chuckling along with his father who retreats there 'on summer Sundays after his midday meal,' and that of the adult meeting his lover in the summerhouse: 'you sit in the bloom of adulthood bathed in rainbow light.' There is a bizarre communion of creator/created in the grotesque yet compelling coupling of 'Dissolve to your father's straining against the unbuttoned waistband. Can it be she is with child without your having asked for as much as her hand?' (30–1). The juxtaposition of male and female pregnancy – a dimension of the androgynous theme developed by Joyce throughout his writing – suggests that they are both metaphors for literary creation as the privileged means of mediating the irreconcilable dualities of life in the world. So this anomalous episode – by far the longest single section in *Company* – is, like 'L'Image'/'The Image' in *How It Is*, strongly flavoured with Joycean associations. The scene closes with 'you' going back in his mind to remember – imagine sitting face to face with his lover 'In that rainbow light. That dead still' (31). The ending of *Company* – and indeed the work as a whole except for paragraph 40 and a last glimpse of an ideal unity between lover and loved in paragraph 40: 'eyes in each other's eyes' (35) – embraces the negative world of loss, the foremost casualty of which is 'love': 'And how better in the end labour lost and silence' (46), the penultimate sentence of paragraph 58, which in turn is followed by the single word 'Alone' centred in the middle of the page.

It would seem that even when Beckett is focusing on his own life his lifelong tendency to compare himself to Joyce will often make its presence known. There are fifty-nine paragraphs, including the final 'Alone,' in *Company*, a number that corresponds to Joyce's age when he died. Perhaps there is even a suggestion at the end of *Company* that Joyce's name is being 'whispered.' Joyce's poem 'Alone' in *Pomes Penyeach* sets up a romantic mise en scène in its first four-line stanza, and in the second stanza nature 'whisper[s]' in the dark 'A name – her name – /And all my soul is a delight' (*PJJ*, 654). Such sentimentality, except for the love scenes dealt with above, is rigorously repressed in *Company*. But in the play *Ohio Impromptu* (1981) Beckett does find 'relief,' an outlet for this Joycean material, and accompanying it is a very personal and highly emotional response to a lost lover, 'the dear name,' with whom once this 'he' was 'so long alone together.'[21] This lost one has, however, sent a messenger to read to her former companion to comfort him and it is within this framework that a number of specific allusions to the Joyce-Beckett relationship are developed.

Ohio Impromptu was commissioned for the Columbus, Ohio, Beckett Conference of 1981 by S.E. Gontarski in celebration of Beckett's seventy-fifth birthday (and a year in advance of the forthcoming Joyce centenary). Those of us who were there for the premiere shared the frisson of recognition that this play was not only written for us but was also about us as critics. A gathering of Beckett scholars would be particularly attuned to issues such as Beckett's relationship with Joyce – an issue about which

Beckett was often questioned and with which Beckett criticism had often concerned itself. Beckett plays with such issues in a metafictional manner (the 'Sad tale' is read from the last pages of a well-worn but unidentified book) that is also metatheatrical as L (= Listener) and R (= Reader) confront each other across a table, as veritable mirror images (with the suggestion that L might be encountering his doppelgänger). Specific details identify the pair as latter-day versions of Beckett and Joyce. Beckett and Joyce used to take long walks to the Isle of Swans; the 'old world Latin Quarter hat' is, of course, a synecdochic reference to Stephen Dedalus in the 'Proteus' chapter of *Ulysses*. Most interesting in this regard is the fact that it is not clear to whom the hat belongs in this re-enactment. Beckett had been heralded as 'the new Stephen Dedalus' by Adrienne Monnier when he made his debut as a writer, and our study has shown in a host of hitherto unexpected ways just how seriously and thoroughly Beckett played out this role in his own writing, arguably becoming more 'Joycean' in this regard than Joyce himself. In *Ohio Impromptu* the two have grown 'as one.' More to the point, their bodies of work are also identified in a number of intriguing ways. For example, R's 'sad tale' relates how the protagonist in his Latin Quarter hat would pause at the tip of the Isle of Swans: 'How in joyous eddies its two arms conflowed and flowed united on. Then turn and his slow steps retrace' (286). This could be taken as a minimalist Beckett summation of the ending of *Finnegans Wake*, 'joyous eddies' echoing Joyce's name whereas the image of retracing or following in the steps of neatly summarizes Beckett's early engagement with Joyce before he found his own way. The following description of 'his old terror of night' is a very strong reminder of what Beckett insisted on calling his 'revelation,' that self-declared turning point in his career when he discovered that the 'dark' he had formerly tried to suppress was in fact the real source of his own creativity, if only he could overcome, in the words of the play, his 'fearful symptoms.'

R states that the 'fearful symptoms' are 'described at length on page forty paragraph four' (286). Joyce devised the publication of *Ulysses* on his fortieth birthday and in the 1922 Shakespeare and Company original edition (which by the time of *Ohio Impromptu* would indeed have been 'well worn') the reference to 'My Latin quarter hat' appears on page 41. A scholarly reader of *Ohio Impromptu* might be duly prompted to look this up, at which point the reader's eyes might then turn to page 40 and in particular paragraph four in which there is the discussion of what could be termed 'fearful symptoms' and indeed 'with redoubled force.' Literally so, to begin with: the 'Dringdring' depicts the simultaneous elevations of the host in different ceremonies and how 'their two bells [...] twang in diphthong'. Stephen Dedalus speculates that despite the number of such celebrations there is 'still only one body of Christ.' We have traced how Beckett could not accept Joyce's theory of the epiphany and that through his critique of it he finally discovered in works such as 'Still' the means whereby fictional selves could lay claim to a language that would substantiate and manifest their being. In *Ohio Impromptu*, L and R do 'communicate' in the various senses of the word. There is more than one way of doing or being, and in the end the two may seem 'as one.' And the one who draws the two male figures together is the woman – 'the dear name,' 'the dear face.' In his dreams we are told that Listener 'heard the unspoken words, Stay where we were so long alone together my shade will comfort you' (286), suggesting that the dearly missed is a Beatrice-type figure (or *Everyman*'s Knowledge as a Woman),[22] as well as echoing the ending of part 1 of Beckett's *Watt* in which the Joyce-Arsene composite takes his leave of Beckett-Watt. Here in *Ohio Impromptu* the two are united by the woman's compassion. This is a 'sad tale,' not the *Divine Comedy*, and R tells L that he has had word from the 'dear name' and heard the 'unspoken words,' 'No need to go to him again, even were it in your power' (287), and the possibility of any future 'reawakening' is profoundly doubtful.

Ill Seen Ill Said (*Mal vu mal dit*) is in my estimation Beckett's masterwork of the post–*How It Is* period, as well as the culmination of his incorporation-cum-collaboration with Joyce. The text is fabricated under the sign of Venus as announced in its opening sentence: 'From where she lies she sees Venus rise' (*NO*, 49). Although the old woman whose sighting is at the centre of this ontological fable initially 'rails at the source of all life' (49), her story as it unfolds is about her love and devotion for a lost one whose tomb she regularly visits. The opening invocation of Venus also announces the aesthetic dimensions of this fable: what is Beauty and how is it to be expressed? These were, of course, the guiding questions behind the aesthetic theory passages of *Portrait*, and we have seen how from the very beginning Beckett challenged the static nature of this formulation and sought instead to accommodate the kinetic and the static; in short, a painful Beauty, or in *Ill Seen Ill Said*'s allusion to Yeats' 'Easter 1916' in regard to the old woman's appearance being 'unchanged. Utterly' (*NO*, 79), a 'terrible beauty' of a particularly Beckettian variety 'is born.'[23]

The other constant feature of Beckett's critical approach to the aesthetic question is to foreground the recognition of the role played by the authorial self vis-à-vis the depiction of the 'other,' in this instance the old woman in her zone of stones and in her cabin who makes the pilgrimages to the tomb. The opening of *Ill Seen Ill Said* depicts, yet again, the 'hovering eye' (76) of the 'imaginary stranger' (53) 'stooping to the prone who must/soon take up their life and walk,' in the words of 'The Vulture.' Conjured into being by the hungry eye, she nevertheless pursues an existence that is independent of the searching eye, which is variously 'glutted' or left to 'digest its pittance.' *Ill Seen Ill Said* is the story of the relationship between this insatiable 'relentless eye' and the other it seeks to fathom in an act of creation, which is, paradoxically enough, based on the death of a 'figment' who no longer had 'the misfortune to be still of this world' (50). This perceiver as narrator is led by his own self-interests to speculate 'How simple all then. If only all could be pure figment. Neither be nor been nor by any shift to be' (58). But the images of the old dead woman are anything but 'pure figments.' All would indeed be very simple if this were the case: she could then be manipulated for the narrator's convenience, as was the case in authoritarian texts such as 'The Lost Ones.' There is, however, in *Ill Seen Ill Said* an ineluctable 'shift to be' – she is not a still life but a moving portrait. Once the figure is sighted, even though acknowledged as dead, it comes to life in the eye's recounting of her in the present tense. In the final paragraph of this text, the 'radiant haze' of ambiguity about her status (fictional and real, dying, dead, yet alive, and so on) seems the only certainty to acknowledge about her 'whatness.' She most definitely does not possess either 'the luminous silent stasis of esthetic pleasure' or 'the clear radiance of the esthetic image,' as theorized by young Stephen Dedalus in *Portrait* (185).

In *Ill Seen Ill Said* there is, however, a remarkable incorporation of Joycean elements, in particular from the ending of 'The Dead,' a revisioning which might more accurately be characterized as Beckett collaborating with Joyce. Not only is the physical geography of *Ill Seen Ill Said* obviously set in the Joyce country of western Ireland, but its literary topography is also Joycean for it retraces Gabriel Conroy's 'journey westward' in the famous final paragraph of 'The Dead.' This 'journey westward' is represented both literally – the snow was falling on 'the lonely church yard where Michael Furey lay buried' – and figuratively – 'his [Gabriel's] soul had approached that region where dwell the vast hosts of the dead' (*PJJ*, 241). The last sentence of the penultimate paragraph effects the crucial translation to this other 'region' in which Gabriel was 'conscious of, but could not apprehend their wayward and flickering existence' (241): 'His own identity was fading out into a grey impalpable world: the solid world itself which these dead had one time reared and lived in was dissolving and dwindling' (241–2). Where Joyce's journey leaves off, Beckett's begins. From the 'vast hosts of the dead,' the 'imaginary stranger' (*NO*, 53) will try to seize 'the wayward and flickering existence' of the old woman among the stones, try to find a means of accommodating their coexistence in this afterlife.

There is an echoing and reconfiguring of the most striking and resonant images of 'The Dead,' particularly its ending, in *Ill Seen Ill Said*. Most notably and most obviously, there is the snow which upon its introduction blanks out the vision of the authorial presence: 'Where nothing to be seen in the grazing rays but snow. And how all about little by little her footprints are effaced' (55). Whereas the climax of the snow imagery in 'The Dead' occurs in the poetic repetitions of 'It was falling' in the final paragraph, in *Ill Seen Ill Said* Beckett locates his at the very centre of his text:

> Winter evening in the pastures. The snow has ceased. Her steps so light they barely leave a trace. Have barely left having ceased. Just enough to be still visible. Adrift the snow. Whither in her head while her feet stray thus? Hither and thither too? Or unswerving to the mirage? And where when she halts? The eye discerns afar a kind of stain. Finally the steep roof whence part of the fresh fall has slid. Under the low lowering sky the north is lost. Obliterated by the snow the twelve are there. Invisible were she to raise her eyes. She on the contrary immaculately black. Not having received a single flake. Nothing needed now but for them to start falling again which therefore they do. First one by one here and there. Then thicker and thicker plumb through the still air. Slowly she disappears. Together with the trace of her steps and that of the distant roof. (67–8)

The essentially unrealistic nature of Joyce's final paragraph is also much more foregrounded in Beckett's revision in which it begins snowing heavily right on cue.

Then follows Beckett's most telling and resounding allusion to Joyce – his own version of Joyce's uncanny opening sentence of the last paragraph of 'The Dead,' 'A few light taps upon the pane made him [Gabriel] turn to the window' (242): 'Silence but for the imaginary murmur of flakes beating on the roof' (68). As John Paul Riquelme has underscored, 'the snow that Gabriel is said to hear at the end is clearly not literal snow [...] such language, which is figurative, not referential, strenuously resists being translated as a single meaning.'[24] In his heavy-handed naturalistic parody of this last paragraph of 'The Dead' at the end of *Dream of Fair to Middling Women*, Beckett resorted to a bathetic reduction since he could not hope to emulate in any convincing manner the poetically charged vision of the Joycean original. Now, a half-century later, he is able to not only incorporate Joyce's original but to rival it. Beckett's revisioning of Joyce here is an incorporation that is truly a re-creation: a veritable *parodia sacra*.

Beckett also distinguishes his writing from Joyce's in the closing movements of *Ill Seen Ill Said*. 'Winter night. No snow. For the sake of variety. To vary the monotony' (73) could be regarded as Beckett's intertextual disengagement from the snow of 'The Dead' descending 'upon all the living and the dead.' Beckett is no longer pursuing the 'mocking attitude towards the word' and the resultant 'dissonance' so that it might 'become possible to feel a whisper of that final music or that silence that underlies All' (*Dis*, 172). In *Ill Seen Ill Said* a new harmony is now possible: 'The silence merges into music infinitely far and as unbroken as silence. Ceaseless celestial winds in unison. For all all matters now' (*NO*, 74). What is this? Is this another version of the Joycean epiphany? Not quite. Wholeness ('unbroken'), and harmony ('in unison') are prominently foregrounded, to be sure; but their synthesis does not issue forth in any definitive revelation of 'radiance.' Here the 'radiance' is 'haze' enshrouded. This is because the dead and dying old woman is not and cannot be an object of aesthetic stasis. There is hence no defining moment, Joyce's 'sudden spiritual manifestation.' Time is not frozen in a moment of modernistic revelation; instead, however fluctuating and intermittent, time is still current, as in the old woman's reappearance at evening: 'Slowly with fluttering step as if wanting mass. Suddenly still and as suddenly on her way again' (61). She cannot be reduced to a merely static picture by the self-serving gaze of the hungry eye of the narrator/author any more than Gretta Conroy could be reduced to the pictorial plane of *'Distant Music.'* Here the silence and music merge and stasis and kinesis are brought into trembling equilibrium. The true revelations in Beckett are the glimpses of a world, however unstable, coming into being, dissolving, reconfiguring itself, and so on as the fading self of the authorial presence and the flickering existence of the old woman are somehow identified.

This situation is perforce 'ill seen' and bound also to be 'ill said' since words cannot hope to stabilize such a situation or impose any aesthetic stasis upon it. Instead of the perfectly balanced chiasmus of the final paragraph of 'The Dead' – 'falling faintly [...] faintly falling' – we have the more typical Beckettian double-cross of 'The mind betrays the treacherous eyes and the treacherous word their treacheries' (78). Hence the observing eye (or implied 'I') in order to escape this impasse and to deny his interdependence with the old woman invokes a mock-apocalyptic closure in the last paragraph of *Ill Seen Ill Said*: 'Grant only enough remain to devour all. Moment by glutton moment. Sky earth the whole kit and boodle. Not another crumb of carrion left. Lick chops and basta. No. One moment more. One last. Grace to breathe that void. Know happiness' (86). The 'sweet foretaste of joy at journey's end' (84) fails, however, to materialize. The very question of 'to what journey's end – what heart? – bearing what tidings?' is posed in one of Stephen's last diary entries in *Portrait* (217). Joyce is certainly present in a number of specific correspondences and revisions concerning 'The Dead,' and this homage to a literary lost one has produced one of Beckett's most remarkable achievements. In the final reckoning, 'deposition done' (84), the situation remains a uniquely Beckettian one: how in the end to be. Joyce has collaborated as ghost writer on this question, but the means of going on are distinctively of Beckett's own devising. Beckett's very last prose work, 'Stirrings Still' (1988), in the last sentence of part 1 evokes this stoical sentiment: 'And patience till the one true end to time and grief and self and second self his own' (*CSP*, 261). We have traced in *Beckett's Dedalus* the truly startling degree to which Beckett's 'second self,' his various writing selves, have been indebted to Joyce. In arguably the most important as well as the most comprehensive case of literary influence in twentieth-century literature, Beckett, whose work mentions a host of writers whose work he admired and in varying degrees assimilated, almost always turned to Joyce as the writer who undeniably played the most important role in helping him to find his own way.

Beckett's final work, the poem 'Comment dire' ('What is the word'),[25] can be read as a coda or postscript to our discussion of his relationship with Joyce. 'What is the word' is an enueg, that troubadour poetic form of which there are two long examples in *Echo's Bones* ('Enueg I' and 'II' follow the opening poem 'The Vulture'). According to Lawrence Harvey, the enueg deals with a number of vexing issues in a form that stresses the discontinuities of the various thoughts about them. The main unifying feature is the frequent repetition of a set word or phrase that conveys the writer's attitude towards his subject.[26] In Beckett's enueg the perplexing issue to be commented on is the 'folly' of trying to find the word or words that would name a world and our presence in it. The discontinuities are evident in a number of ways: in the stuttering fragmentation characteristic of certain aphasic disturbances, in the dash that functions as a questioning mark at the end of the first fifty-two lines (only the final line 'what is the word' is exempt from this pattern and these last words are also further distinguished from the rest of the poem by a two-line blank spacing). These discontinuities do, however, manage to formulate themselves into an answer to the opening queries of 'folly-/folly for to-' by the midpoint of the poem (the twenty-sixth line): 'folly for to need to seem to glimpse –.' The 'what –' so 'glimpse[d]' must be the 'world' or 'being' or some such facsimile. The frequently repeated phrase 'what is the word' (seven times) supplies a counterpointing sense of some potential linkage of the disparate elements. The fiftieth line is the longest in the poem, and while it is still grammatically and ontologically incomplete, it does come closest to articulating the scope of the issues vexing the poet in his dying words in this his funeral elegy: 'folly for to need to seem to glimpse afaint afar away over there what –.' Within this phrasing can be detected the incorporation of Joycean echoes in 'afaint afar away,' poignantly reminiscent of both the endings of 'The Dead' and *Finnegans Wake*. The final response to this question of 'what –' is 'what is the word,' without a dash. We have here arguably Beckett's most revealing comment on his debt to Joyce and how through his critique and revision of Joyce's aesthetic he found his own ways and means to explore his own 'folly.' In this strangely beautiful incantation, the final revelation is that for Beckett the 'what'-ness is the word itself as a process of saying ('comment dire') and making. Both Joyce and Beckett as word men would have associated 'faint'/'afaint' with 'feign' as the imaginative faculty, with 'fiction' as the activity of making or forming.[27] Beckett's last words as a writer are – after the pause, after the blank spacing – in the declarative mode: 'what' is indeed 'the word.' In the ending was the word …

Notes

Prolegomenon to Any Future Beckett Criticism

1 Beckett's comment to Lawrence Harvey; see *Samuel Beckett: Poet and Critic* (Princeton, NJ: Princeton UP, 1970), 247–9.
2 Umberto Eco, ed., *History of Beauty*, trans. A. McEwen (New York: Rizzoli, 2004), 415.
3 Wendy Steiner, *Venus in Exile: The Rejection of Beauty in Twentieth-Century Art* (Chicago: U of Chicago P, 2001), xvi.
4 The term 'epiphany' does not occur in *Portrait*; there are numerous references, however, to the term – both parodic and serious – in *Ulysses*; for instance, Stephen's exemplum of Mr Deasy's 'manifestation of God' as a 'shout in the street' (34).
5 Linda Hutcheon, *A Theory of Parody: The Teaching of Twentieth-Century Art Forms* (Champaign: U of Illinois P, 2000), xii; this dual function is developed throughout her study.
6 Kevin J.H. Dettmar, 'The Joyce That Beckett Built,' in *Beckett and Beyond*, ed. B. Stewart, Princess Grace Irish Library Series 9 (Gerrards Cross, UK: Colin Smythe, 1999), 81.
7 Ibid.
8 James and Elizabeth Knowlson, eds., *Beckett Remembering Remembering Beckett* (New York: Arcade, 2006), 47. Beckett then goes on to critique the ending of *Portrait*: 'He got pompous about his vocation and his function in life'; this ambiguous 'he' is another example of Beckett's conflation of author-character roles in *Portrait*.
9 Paul Jay, *Being in the Text: Self-Representation from Wordsworth to Roland Barthes* (Ithaca, NY: Cornell UP, 1984), 122.
10 The epigraph 'E fango è il mondo' ('the world is mud') is taken from Leopardi's 'A Se Stesso' ('To Himself').

11 Jacques Aubert, *The Aesthetics of James Joyce*, rev. English language edition (Baltimore: Johns Hopkins UP, 1992), 109.
12 Ibid., 122.
13 Ibid., 125.
14 Cited in John Pilling, *Beckett before Godot* (Cambridge, Cambridge UP, 1997), 36, from Beckett's letter to Charles Prentice, 17 February 1931.
15 Hutcheon, 110.
16 Ezra Pound, 'Joyce,' in *Literary Essays of Ezra Pound*, ed. T.S. Eliot (New York: New Directions, 1918), 410. Beckett would also have been attracted to what Pound termed in this essay Joyce's 'swift alternation of subjective beauty and external shabbiness, squalor, and sordidness' (412).
17 Lois Gordon, *The World of Samuel Beckett* (New Haven, CT: Yale UP, 1996), 58. Gordon refreshingly concludes her third chapter, 'James Joyce,' with the judgment that 'Beckett and Joyce have much more in common than Beckett's comments suggest' (81).
18 M.M. Bakhtin, *The Dialogic Imagination: Four Essays*, ed. M. Holquist, trans. C. Emerson and M. Holquist (Austin: U of Texas P, 1981), 74.
19 Samuel Beckett, letter to Sighle Kennedy, in *Disjecta*, ed. Ruby Cohn (New York: Grove, 1984), 103.
20 Beckett critics have not recognized the importance of *Portrait* in Beckett's early works. One obvious reason for this is the fact that Beckett's own work is contemporaneous with Joyce's *Work in Progress* and there is hence a tendency to identify the two, a linkage aided and abetted by Beckett's efforts in *Dream* to imitate Joyce's new style. Vivien Mercier's judgment in *Beckett/Beckett* (New York: Oxford UP, 1977), is representative in this regard: 'His greatest folly consisted in attempting to imitate James Joyce: not the earlier work, either, but *Work in Progress*, the drafts of *Finnegans Wake*' (36).
21 Cited in James Knowlson, *Damned to Fame: The Life of Samuel Beckett*, London: Bloomsbury, 1996, 351–3.
22 Knowlson, *Damned to Fame*, 44; John Pilling, *Companion to 'Dream of Fair to Middling Women,'* special issue of *Journal of Beckett Studies* 12, nos. 1 and 2 (2004): 366–7; C.J. Ackerley, *Obscure Locks, Simple Keys: The Annotated 'Watt,'* special issue of *Journal of Beckett Studies* 14, nos. 1 and 2 (2005); C.J. Ackerley and S.E. Gontarski, *The Grove Companion to Samuel Beckett* (New York: Grove, 2004), 451.
23 Barbara Gluck, *Beckett and Joyce: Friendship and Fiction* (Lewisburg, PA: Bucknell UP, 1979); Gluck also develops a number of more detailed structural comparisons, for example, her discussion of Beckett's first story in *More Pricks Than Kicks* ('Dante and the Lobster') and Joyce's last story in *Dubliners* ('The Dead'), 57–60.

24 Ed Jewinski, 'James Joyce and Samuel Beckett: From Epiphany to Anti-Epiphany,' in *Re: Joyce 'n Beckett*, ed. Phyllis Carey and Ed Jewinksi (New York: Fordham UP, 1992), 160.

25 Ibid, 170.

26 Friedhelm Rathjen, ed., *In Principle, Beckett Is Joyce* (Edinburgh: Split Pea Press, 1994), 100 (in his own chapter 7, 'Maximal Joyce Is a State of Beckett: Joyce, Beckett, and Bruno's *Coincidentia Oppositorum*').

27 Ibid., 101.

28 X.J. Kennedy et al., *Handbook of Literary Terms* (New York: Pearson Education, 2003), 6.

29 Kevin J.H. Dettmar, 'The Illusion of Modernist Allusion and the Politics of Plagiarism,' in *Perspectives on Plagiarism and Intellectual Property in a Postmodern World*, ed. Lise Buranen and Alice M. Roy (Albany: State University of New York Press, 1999), raises a number of provocative questions about the function of modernist allusion that stem from T.S. Eliot's famous justification of the practice: 'The poet must become more allusive, more indirect, in order to force, to dislocate if necessary, language into his meaning' (99).

30 Israel Shenker, 'Moody Man of Letters,' *New York Times*, 6 May 1956, sec. 2, x, 1, 3.

31 Dettmar, 'The Joyce That Beckett Built,' in *Beckett and Beyond*, ed. B. Stewart, Princess Grace Irish Library Series 9 (Gerrards Cross, UK: Colin Smythe), 85.

32 Daniel Katz, *Saying I No More* (Evanston, IL: Northwestern UP, 1999), 186. Katz's argument is discussed in more detail in my chapter 6. An interesting variation on this identification of Beckett and Joyce approach is Eyal Amiran's argument that both writers appropriate the Neoplatonic tradition, in *Wandering and Home: Beckett's Metaphysical Narrative* (University Park: Pennsylvania State UP, 1993), especially the last chapter. Both approaches are, in my opinion, too reductionist in nature.

33 See Barbara Gluck, *Beckett and Joyce*, 12; Hugh Kenner, *The Stoic Comedians: Flaubert, Joyce, and Beckett* (Berkeley: U of California P, 1962): chapter 2, 'James Joyce: Comedian of the Inventory'; chapter 3, 'Samuel Beckett: Comedian of the Impasse.'

34 Colleen Jaurretche, ed., *Beckett, Joyce and the Art of the Negative*, European Joyce Studies 16 (Amsterdam: Rodopi, 2005), 11.

35 Ibid.

1. Portraits of the Artist as a Young Critic

1 The opening sentences of Beckett's Joyce essay and his short story 'Assumption' neatly complement each other: 'The danger is in the neatness of identifications.'/'He could have shouted and could not.'

2 John Pilling, *Beckett before Godot* (Cambridge: Cambridge University Press, 1997), 15.

3 Beckett states of Joyce in 'Dante ... Bruno . Vico .. Joyce': 'He is conscious that things with a common numerical characteristic tend towards a very significant interrelationship' (32). Beckett would seem to be employing this concept in his five-paragraph version of the five chapters of *Portrait*.

4 Beckett's postcard response to Terence McQueeny's queries concerning the writing of 'Dante ... Bruno . Vico .. Joyce' reads: 'The subject was suggested by Joyce. He had no part in the writing. The texts were available in the Library of the Ecole Normale. He found me short on Bruno.' In Terence McQueeny, 'Samuel Beckett as Critic of Proust and Joyce,' unpublished PhD dissertation, University of North Carolina, 1977.

5 Beckett employs this term in his discussions of the nature of the purgatorial at the end of 'Dante ... Bruno . Vico .. Joyce' (33). 'Obligation to express' is an echo of Beckett's 'Three Dialogues with Georges Duthuit' (1949); for Beckett the boundaries between the critical and the creative (so called) are freely crossed.

6 Terence McQueeny discusses in detail the major 'borrowings' of Beckett from the above-named critics, and it would be a great service to Beckett criticism if that part of his dissertation dealing with 'Dante ... Bruno . Vico .. Joyce' could be published in the *Journal of Beckett Studies* (the section on Proust has been in part superseded by discussions by Nicholas Zurbrugg and others, but the lack of a detailed commentary on the 'Joyce essay' is still one of the most glaring omissions in Beckett studies). The particular page references for my citations from McQueeny run from page 57 to the end of his first chapter on page 81.

7 McQueeny points out that Beckett here adopts Joyce's own characterization of Vico as 'roundheaded' (10). McQueeny goes on to point out that Beckett was original in his identification of Bruno and Vico, that in this instance he is not indebted to his 'sources' (16). It is, however, interesting to note that in *Portrait* Stephen wrangles with 'the plump roundheaded professor of Italian' (168) and later in his concluding diary entries mentions another dispute with 'little roundhead rogue's eye Ghezzi. This time about Bruno the Nolan' (215).

8 John Pilling, *Beckett before Godot*, 23.

9 'Prospects' is a key cue word for Beckett in describing or alluding to the Terrestial Paradise; for example, the ironic uses in the first of the 'Texts for Nothing,' 'glorious prospects,' and in *Waiting for Godot's* 'inspiring prospects' (not to mention the ironically dubbed Dublin cemetery mentioned in the 'Hades' chapter of *Ulysses*).

10 The sonnet paradigm is perhaps not so far-fetched when the Joyce essay and 'Assumption' are read in tandem; Beckett rewrites his short story in part as a burlesque Shakespearean sonnet no less in *Dream of Fair to Middling Women* (70). Prominently displayed is 'the birdless cloudless colourless skies' of 'Assumption.'

11 Beckett might be making play with this question in the first two paragraphs of 'Assumption,' if we extend my 'bifocal' critical reading of them as in virtual conjunction: 'Assumption' consists of 51 sentences – 14 in the first paragraph, 13 in the second, 21 in the third, dwindling dramatically to 2 in the fourth and 1 in the fifth.

12 The references from which Beckett paraphrases here are found on 187 of *A Portrait of the Artist as a Young Man*. Note the Joycean punctuation in Beckett's paraphrase: the ': and' construction is a stylistic feature of *Portrait*.

13 *Portrait*, 213.

14 *Portrait*, 169.

15 *Portrait*, 184. Terence McQueeny also points out this 'error' and deems Beckett's interpretation at best 'questionable' (44).

16 The only two critics I am aware of who have drawn parallels between *Portrait* and 'Assumption' are David Hayman, who in 'A Meeting in the Park and a Meeting on the Bridge: Joyce and Beckett,' *James Joyce Quarterly* 8, no. 4 (1971): 373, refers to the echoes from the end of chapter 2 in 'Assumption' and James Acheson, who in 'Beckett and the Heresy of Love,' in *Women in Beckett*, ed. Linda Ben-Zvi (University of Illinois Press, 1990), also briefly mentions a few echo phrases (69–70). Neither sees the centrality of Joyce's text to Beckett's.

17 Childhood or early adolescence doesn't seem to particularly interest Beckett, hence the lack of references to Joyce's first chapter of *Portrait*. Compare this absence, however, with the opening of *Dream of Fair to Middling Women* and the images of a very young Belacqua. The hellfire sermon of chapter 3 is not directly referred to, but the prison imagery and the 'irruption of demons' could be seen as Beckettian adaptations.

18 'Apostolic fervour' would also seem to be another of Beckett's muffled echoes of *Portrait*. In chapter 5 the dean of studies, just before he asks Stephen, 'When may we expect to have something from you on the esthetic question?' (163), has been described by Stephen as lacking a soul fired 'with the energy of apostleship.' Beckett's narrator in 'Assumption' and, of course, Stephen Dedalus himself are indeed fired by 'apostolic fervour'/ 'energy of apostleship' when it comes to aesthetic questions.

19 See particularly chapters 2 and 5 on 'Texts for Nothing' and 'Enough.'

20 John Pilling in *Beckett before Godot* cites Massimo Verdicchio's argument on this point: 'In *The New Science* the conception of poetry that Beckett valorizes

is only a moment, and a primitive one at that, of history in progress. Vico views the poetic languages of the first peoples as a lack, a defect of the primitive intellect incapable of expressing itself in concepts' (20).

21 Note also the ironic parallels here with the last sentence of chapter 3 of *Portrait*: 'The ciborium had come to him' (131).

22 John Pilling in *Beckett before Godot*, 30, also makes this point. This is the determining factor distinguishing Beckett's seminal critical probe from Joyce's masterpiece: Joyce's third-person narrator creates an ironic ambiguity throughout, but also generates a sense of control behind the scenes (compare Beckett's statement to Shenker that 'the more Joyce knew the more he could do' and that in his view Joyce was moving towards 'omniscience' with the first sentence of 'Assumption,' 'He could have shouted and could not').

23 Claude Melnotte is the hero of Bulwer-Lytton's romantic drama *The Lady of Lyons*.

24 George Meredith, *The Egoist*, ed. with an introduction by George Woodcock (London: Penguin Books, 1968), 43.

25 *The Egoist*, chap. 50, 'Upon Which the Curtain Falls,' 602.

26 George Meredith, 'An Essay on Comedy and the Uses of the Comic Spirit,' in *The Egoist: An Annotated Text*, ed. Robert M. Adams (New York: Norton, 1979), 446. The Joyce-Beckett relationship as mediated by Meredith warrants further investigation; in *Murphy* Mr Willoughby Kelly borrows his first name from Meredith's central character in *The Egoist*, and the famous epigraph for chapter 6, '*Amor intellectualis quo Murphy se ipsum amat*' (adapted from Spinoza), would also seem to echo as ironic counterpoint the 'epitaph' of the 'comic drama of the suicide' with which Meredith concludes his 'Prelude' to *The Egoist*: 'Through very love of self himself he slew.'

27 'Absorption' is a key Lawrentian word and is prominent in the 'Strife in Love' section of *Sons and Lovers* in which Paul Morel sees Miriam as trying to 'absorb' him. 'Absorption' is also a key word in the sexual power politics of *The Egoist*.

28 P.J. Murphy, *Reconstructing Beckett: Language for Being in Samuel Beckett's Fiction* (Toronto: U of Toronto P, 1990), 8.

29 See John Pilling, *Beckett before Godot*, 26–33; Phil Baker, *Beckett and the Mythology of Psychoanalysis* (London: MacMillan, 1997), 110–12; Laura Barge, *God, the Quest, the Hero: Thematic Structures in Beckett's Fiction* (Chapel Hill: U of North Carolina P, 1988), 76–88; Lois Gordon, *The World of Samuel Beckett* (New Haven, CT: Yale UP, 1996), 42–5; Murphy, *Reconstructing Beckett*, 7–9.

30 J.D. O'Hara, "'Assumption''s Launching Pad,' *Journal of Beckett Studies* 8,
    no. 2 (Spring 1999): 42. O'Hara's interpretation emphasizes the mystical ele-
    ments in Beckett's story, via references to Balzac's 'Etudes Philosophiques'
    and their Swedenborgian elements; hence O'Hara asserts *'Louis Lambert* is
    Beckett's basic structural model for "Assumption"' (31). The textual evi-
    dence indicates that the Balzac work should be regarded as distinctly sec-
    ondary to *A Portrait of the Artist as a Young Man.*
31 There are a number of other reasons why Beckett might have been particu-
    larly attracted by the Battle of Vimy Ridge. One is the Joycean obsession
    with dates and numbers: the Battle of Vimy Ridge took place on 9–14 April
    1917 (some historians regard the battle as completed by April 12) and hence
    encompasses Beckett's own birthdate. Another is that the stunning victory of
    the Canadian Corps bears a number of uncanny resemblances to Beckett's
    protagonist being 'pitched breathless on the peak of a sheer crag.' See Pierre
    Berton, *Vimy* (Toronto: Anchor Canada, 2001), 131–2.
32 James Knowlson in *Damned to Fame* identifies the green eyes and hat of the
    Woman with Peggy Sinclair, Beckett's cousin and early love (110). The refer-
    ences to Peggy Sinclair are, as I have suggested, mediated by references to
    Meredith's *The Egoist*; more simply, Beckett's whore/Madonna imagery ap-
    pears to be a play on 'Sinclair' as conjoining two distinctly contradictory el-
    ements – 'sin' and 'clair.' The admixture prevents any clear-cut conception
    of *claritas* or 'radiance'; instead, there are 'pools of obscurity.'
33 The first major series of entries in Beckett's *Dream* Notebook are from J.G.
    Lockhart's *The History of Napoleon Bonaparte* (1829). See 1–11 (entries 2–78)
    of *Beckett's 'Dream' Notebook*, ed. John Pilling (Reading, UK: Beckett Interna-
    tional Foundation, 1999).
34 Lawrence Harvey, *Samuel Beckett: Poet and Critic* (Princeton, NJ: Princeton
    UP, 1970), 3. Cohn supplies a useful survey of major critical analysis in *A
    Beckett Canon* (Ann Arbor: University of Michigan Press, 2001), 13–15.
35 Cohn, *A Beckett Canon*, 5.
36 Ibid., 6.
37 Linda Hutcheon, *A Theory of Parody: The Teaching of Twentieth-Century Art
    Forms* (Champaign: U of Illinois P, 2000), xiii. This homage/critique double
    structure of parody is developed throughout her study.
38 Allan Pasco, *Allusion: A Literary Graft* (Toronto: U of Toronto P, 1994), 183.
39 George Meredith, 'An Essay on Comedy and the Uses of the Comic Spirit,'
    in Adams, *The Egoist: An Annotated Text*, 433.
40 *Portrait* is riddled with parodic structures of all sorts, drawn from various
    high and low cultural references. Stephen, who bears the brunt of the narra-
    tor's cunning silence, which virtually implies a parodic rewriting of all his

youthful effusions, is a talented mimic in his own right; Heron suggests
that Stephen in his role of the 'farcical pedagogue' in the school play should
'imitate' the rector since 'you can take him off rippingly' (75).

41 The introduction and notes to 'A Portrait of the Artist' are by John Whittier-
Ferguson. Joyce requested a copy of the essay from his brother Stanislaus in
1928 to present to Sylvia Beach. It is therefore not inconceivable that Beckett
might have seen a copy of the essay. In any case, there are indeed a number
of striking similarities between Joyce's essay and Beckett's short story that
are worthy of further investigation.

42 Gordon, *World of Samuel Beckett*, 49.

2. Dreams of a Fair to Middling Critic-Artist

1 Paul Goring, J. Hawthorn and D. Mitchell, eds., *Studying Literature: The
Essential Companion* (New York: Oxford UP, 2001), 303, 295–6.

2 Joseph Frank, *The Widening Gyre* (New Brunswick, NJ: Rutgers UP, 1963).
See pages 16–19 for Frank's critical estimation of *Portrait* in these terms.

3 Harold Bloom, *The Anxiety of Influence: A Theory of Poetry* (New York:
Oxford UP, 1973). Bloom emphasizes throughout his influential study 'that
anxiety and desire are the antinomies of the ephebe or beginning poet.
The anxiety of influence is an anxiety in expectation of *being flooded*' (57).

4 Ruby Cohn, *A Beckett Canon* (Ann Arbor: U of Michigan P, 2001), 18.

5 The three descriptors derived from Shelley's 'To the Moon' are italicized
in my citation of the first stanza of the fragment:
    Art thou *pale* for *weariness*
    of climbing heaven and gazing on the earth,
    Wandering companionless
    Among the stars that have a different birth, –
    And ever changing, like a *joyless* eye
    That finds no object worth its constancy?
'Constancy' might also be included in the list since the negative framing of
the question suggests the moon being 'inconstant.' That Beckett is playing
off Joyce's references to the poem in *Portrait* is underlined by the appearance of the adjective 'cruel' in the sentences leading up to Joyce's citation of
the first three lines of Shelley's poem: 'Nothing stirred within his soul but a
cold and *cruel* and loveless lust' (*P*, 92, my emphasis). The repetition of
'ands' in lieu of punctuation is also reminiscent of Joyce in Beckett's cataloguing of adjectives in *Proust*. This is yet another example of the often incredibly detailed and micro-level echoes of Joyce that Beckett has gone to
the trouble of incorporating into his own writing.

6 This rivalry is most explicit in the pub scene in the trip to Cork that Stephen takes with his father: 'His mind seemed older than theirs [his father and his cronies]: it shone coldly on their strifes and happiness and regrets like a moon upon a younger earth' (*P*, 91).

7 Richard Ellmann, *James Joyce*, new and rev. ed. (New York: Oxford UP, 1982), 485. Joyce's misprision of Dostoyevsky's classic is most likely based on his adoption of Raskolnikov's point of view, which maintains that since there was no real crime no punishment could ensue. This is interesting in terms of the Joyce-Beckett relationship for Beckett at times writes also as if Stephen Dedalus's views could be identified with those of his creator.

8 It is indeed Beckett's emphasis upon still somehow maintaining the material connections that distinguishes his engagement with the theory of symbolism from that espoused by Arthur Symons in *The Symbolist Movement in Literature* (New York: Dutton, 1958): 'It is all an attempt to spiritualise literature, to evade the old bondage of rhetoric, the old bondage of exteriority' (5).

9 Rupert Wood, 'An Endgame of Aesthetics: Beckett as Essayist,' *The Cambridge Companion to Beckett*, ed. John Pilling (Cambridge: Cambridge UP, 1994), 5.

10 Ibid.

11 See my "Beckett and the Philosophers," in *The Cambridge Companion to Beckett*, particularly 229–37.

12 Deirdre Bair, *Samuel Beckett: A Biography* (London: Jonathan Cape, 1978), 109. Bair writes: 'several years ago, a copy surfaced in a second hand bookstore in Dublin with comments and emendations in Beckett's handwriting scattered throughout.' Beckett wrote on the title page the comment I have cited: 'I have written my book in a cheap flashy philosophical jargon.'

13 Samuel Beckett, 'Le Concentrisme,' in *Disjecta*, ed. Ruby Cohn (New York: Grove, 1984), 42.

14 See John Pilling, 'Beckett's *Proust*,' *Journal of Beckett Studies* I (1976): 24.

15 John Pilling, *Beckett before Godot* (Cambridge: Cambridge UP, 1997), 36. Pilling documents that Beckett on 14 October asked Charles Prentice of Chatto and Windus 'if it would be possible to add some five or six pages at the end.' This supplement would have dealt with Dostoyevsky.

16 For a complex variation on this argument see Michael D'Arcy, 'The Task of the Listener: Beckett, Proust, and Perpetual Translation,' *Samuel Beckett Today/Aujourd'hui* 12 (2002): 35–52. D'Arcy argues that the 'conception of music as intrinsically other than phenomena or representation that Beckett derives from his reading of Schopenhauer and Proust' is 'important for his indictment of notions of the symbol descending from eighteenth and nineteenth century literary aesthetics' (35).

17 Nicholas Zurbrugg, *Beckett and Proust* (Gerrards Cross, UK: Colin Smythe, 1988), 3. This point is pervasive throughout Zurbrugg's analyses. With regard to the issue of how effective Beckett's study is as introduction, it would be interesting to compare it with Edmund Wilson's contemporaneous chapter in *Axel's Castle* (1931), which is approximately the same length and focuses on Proust as 'the first important novelist to apply the principles of Symbolism to fiction' (131).

18 John Fletcher, 'Beckett et Proust,' *Caliban* I (January 1964), 95; Terence McQueeny, 'Samuel Beckett as Critic of Proust and Joyce,' unpublished PhD dissertation, University of North Carolina, 1977, chapter 2 'Proust.'

19 Ruby Cohn, *A Beckett Canon*, 20.

20 Michel Foucault, *Discipline and Punish: The Birth of the Prison*, trans. A. Sheridan (New York: Vintage Books, 1995), 18.

21 Cited in John Pilling, *Beckett before Godot*, 36, from Beckett's letter to Charles Prentice, 17 February 1931.

22 Samuel Beckett, 'Poetry Is Vertical,' in Sighle Kennedy, *Murphy's Bed: A Study of Real Sources and Sur-Real Associations in Samuel Beckett's First Novel* (Lewisbury, PA: Bucknell UP, 1971), 304.

23 Sighle Kennedy, *Murphy's Bed*, 'Appendix A, Text of Samuel Beckett's Letter,' 300. Beckett's letter to Kennedy is also to be found in *Disjecta*, 113.

24 Ibid., 205.

25 Ibid., 206.

26 Ibid., 301, 302. Kennedy's letter to Beckett is reprinted as the second entry in 'Appendix A,' 301 and 302.

27 Geoffrey Hartman, *The Unmediated Vision: An Interpretation of Wordsworth, Hopkins, Rilke, and Valéry* (New York: Harcourt Brace, 1966 [originally published by Yale UP, 1954]), 128–9.

28 Ibid., 129.

29 Ibid., 173.

30 John Pilling, *Companion to 'Dream of Fair to Middling Women,'* special issue of *Journal of Beckett Studies*, 12, nos. 1 and 2 (2004): 366–7.

31 Linda Hutcheon, *A Theory of Parody: The Teaching of Twentieth-Century Art Forms* (Champaign: U of Illinois P, 2000), 26.

32 Ibid., 110.

33 The reference is, of course, to Bakhtin's theory of the dialogical nature of literary forms, the novel in particular. Hutcheon points out how Bakhtin rejected much of modern parody, which he saw as derivative in a limiting manner, seeking instead, in Hutcheon's words, 'a deep or true parody of a genuinely revolutionary nature' (26).

34 Ruby Cohn, *A Beckett Canon*, 19.

35 *The Portable James Joyce*, ed. Harry Levin (New York: Viking Penguin, 1975), 663. 'Ecce Puer' is the last entry in *Collected Poems*, under the subheading 'Other Poems.'

36 John Pilling, *Beckett's 'Dream' Notebook*, Reading, UK: Beckett International Foundation, 1999, entries 335 (47) and 410 (57); see also the entry in *Companion* to *'Dream of Fair to Middling Women,'* 17.

37 James Joyce, *Exiles*, in Levin, *Portable James Joyce*, third act, 605. Note also the echoing of scenes in *Portrait* such as: 'Stephen sometimes went round with the car which delivered the evening milk and these chilly drives blew away his memory of the filth of the cowyard and he felt no repugnance at seeing the cow hairs and hayseeds on the milkman's coat' (66); and Stephen's refuge when he flees the school theatrical: 'That is horse piss and rotted straw, he thought. It is a good odour to breathe. It will calm my heart' (84).

38 Two of the four chapter headings of Nietzsche's *Ecce Homo* are 'Why I Am So Clever' and 'Why I Write Such Excellent Books.' Nietzsche's mocking self-interpretations capture one aspect of Beckett's attempts to declare his credentials in *Dream* by challenging Joyce.

39 Norma Bouchard in 'Rereading Beckett's *Dream of Fair to Middling Women,'* *Samuel Beckett Today/Aujourd'hui* 6 (1997) also argues that Beckett's first novel 'champions an alternative model of symbolization'; more particularly, 'since the Beckettian literary space is kept in a constant state of over determination and regress, it clearly makes a departure from the stability of sedentary symbolization in forming the epiphanic moments of Modernist narratives' (137).

40 Beckett's rewriting of Stephen Dedalus's statement in *Portrait* is so much longer and convoluted than the original because it develops at length the 'true scholastic stink' (186), as Lynch puts it in *Portrait*, replete with mock-philosophical categories and rhetorical gambits. Even Belacqua's attempts to revise Stephen's views are indebted to characteristics attributed to him in *Portrait*. S.E. Gontarski's view that *Dream* aims for an enunciative voice 'diametrically opposed to the one Joyce expresses through Stephen Dedalus' is far too neatly antithetical; the reality entails a much more complex intertwining of voices. See Gontarski, 'The Intent of Undoing in Samuel Beckett's Art,' *Modern Fiction Studies* 29 (1983): 28.

41 James Knowlson, *Damned to Fame: The Life of Samuel Beckett* (London: Bloomsbury, 1996), 148–56 ('real life' characters in *Dream*); 175 (Lucia Joyce).

42 John Pilling, *Beckett before Godot*, 56.

43 In *Proust*, Beckett refers to this concept in the midst of a discussion detailing the limitations of 'voluntary memory': 'It insists on that most necessary, wholesome and monotonous plagiarism – the plagiarism of oneself' (20).

'Self-plagiarism' as I am employing the term here implies a much more creative employment of various parodic functions.

44 In his *Companion to 'Dream,'* John Pilling points out that the Italian phrase (translation: 'reading Meredith by candlelight') is adapted from line 115 of Leopardi's poem 'Le Ricordanze' (48). Pilling's further annotation suggests that the text to be read here might be Meredith's sonnet sequence *Modern Love* (1862) and adds that Beckett's 'youthful interest in Meredith' is 'apparently not maintained in later life.' As we will shortly see, however, Beckett's interest in Meredith is still maintained in a very significant way in *Murphy*. Just as the Meredith references in 'Assumption' were an indirect way of approaching Joyce, the reference in *Dream* to 'supposititiously, in Dickens's striking adverb' (95) seems to be an indirect reference to Meredith, which Beckett has gone to a lot of trouble to concoct for his own amusement. Whereas Pilling's annotation gives several probable sources in Dickens for this word, he has to admit that the word was 'never used by Dickens in this adverbial form' (189). But the word is indeed used in this very adverbial form in Meredith's *Diana of the Crossways* (New York: Quality Paperback Book Club, 2003), 39: 'But supposititiously?'

45 John Pilling, *Beckett before Godot*, 64 and 65.

46 Beckett's self-critique in his letter to Charles Prentice, cited in John Pilling, *Beckett before Godot*, 64.

47 James Joyce, 'Anna Livia Plurabelle,' in Levin, *Portable James Joyce*, 725.

48 John Pilling, 'A Mermaid Made Over: Beckett's "Text" and John Ford,' in *Beckett and Beyond*, ed. B. Stewart (Gerrards Cross, UK: Colin Smythe: 1999), 212.

49 Linda Hutcheon, *A Theory of Parody*, 45.

50 John Pilling's commentary on the epigraph in *Beckett before Godot* (58–9) points out how Beckett substitutes after the first two lines ('A thousand sythes have I herd men telle/ That ther is joye in heven, and peyne in helle;') his own 'But – ' for Chaucer's 'And I acorde wel that hit be so.' Pilling's main point is that the 'But – ' leads to the purgatorial world of *Dream*, the space for which has been opened up by Beckett's word-wrenching rejection of conventional pieties in the Chaucer citation. The epigraph could, however, be regarded in a potentially more affirmative way. Beckett's 'But –' might be viewed as an echo of Carlyle's last word in the chapter on 'The Hero as Man of Letters' in *On Heroes, Hero-Worship and the Heroic in History*; such heroes may illuminate, punctuate the darkness of the night: 'But – ! –'

51 See Eoin O'Brien, *The Beckett Country* (Dublin: Black Cat Press, 1986), 106–9 for a description of Jack's Hole and a picture of the place where Belacqua and Alba were uneasily positioned (beached?) throughout so much of

Dream THREE. O'Brien clarifies the actual siting of this scene: 'At first it seems that the location for this love scene is the Silver Strand, a golden strip of sand and sea to the south of Wicklowtown, but on deeper scrutiny we find it is the small cove known as Jack's Hole, further south again, closer to the popular resort of Brittas Bay' (107). In 'Gas from a Burner' (1912), Joyce has his narrator comment on the use of actual place names: "It's a wonder to me, upon my soul/He forgot to mention Curly's Hole' (*PJJ*, 661).

52 Ruby Cohn in *A Beckett Canon* supplies a useful charting of where some of Beckett's early poems appear in *Dream* (40).

53 James Joyce, 'A Painful Case,' in *PJJ*, ed. Harry Levin, 122. Compare this with Belacqua's *downward* experience of the epiphany when he hears the word 'Alba': 'It was the descent and the enwombing, assumption upside down' (181).

54 This phrase is recorded in *Beckett's 'Dream' Notebook*, ed. John Pilling, item 281 (39), extracted from Thomas Carlyle's *On Heroes, Hero-Worship and the Heroic in History*. In the context of the actual passage in which it is inserted in *Dream*, the echoing of similar phrasing in Joyce's *Portrait* seems to have been Beckett's primary reason for deploying it in this instance.

55 Thomas Carlyle, *On Heroes, Hero-Worship and the Heroic in History*, ed. Carl Niemeyer (Lincoln: U of Nebraska P, 1966), refers to the 'Three *Nornas*, Fates, – ' in Lecture I, 'The Hero as Divinity' (20).

56 Beckett's conflicted response to Joyce is insightfully investigated in John Pilling's 'A Mermaid Made Over: Beckett's "Text" and John Ford,' 211–12.

57 D.H. Lawrence, *Sons and Lovers*, ed. H. and C. Baron (Harmondsworth, UK: Penguin Books, 1994), 464.

58 The birdgirl in *Portrait* is described as 'gently stirring the water with her foot hither and thither' (151). It is her inspiration that helps transport Stephen Dedalus, in visionary terms at least, across the seas in the final words of the novel.

59 Kelly Anspaugh's '"Faith, Hope, and – What Was It?": Beckett Reading Joyce Reading Dante,' *Journal of Beckett Studies* 5, nos. 1 & 2 (Autumn 1995/Spring 1996): 19–38, explores in greater detail than previous commentators Joyce's role as a mediator between Dante and Beckett.

60 Adrian Hunter, 'Beckett and the Joycean Short Story,' *Essays in Criticism* 51, no. 2 (2001): 241.

61 Ibid, 238.

3. Re-Joyce-ing *Murphy*

1 Harold Bloom, *The Western Canon* (New York: Harcourt Brace), 1994, 494–5.

2 C.J. Ackerley, *Demented.Particulars: The Annotated 'Murphy'*, special issue of *Journal of Beckett Studies* 7, nos. 1 & 2 (Autumn 1997/Spring 1998), ix. Subsequent references to this book will appear in the text.

3 Bloom, *The Western Canon*, 495.

4 Critics have begun to consider more seriously and in more depth the problematic nature of the real in socio-cultural terms in *Murphy*. For example, David Weisberg in *Chronicles of Disorder: Samuel Beckett and the Cultural Politics of the Modern Novel* (Albany: State U of New York P: 2000) states, 'Beckett's ambivalence toward the terms social realism offered, and toward political definitions of the outer world, lead him to an impasse. Aesthetic autonomy, imagined as a closed, self-sufficient system of mind and language, blocks rather than provides access to the liberation of the "real" (as he put it in *Proust*) from habituated modes of perception' (41); Tyrus Miller in *Late Modernism: Politics, Fiction, and the Arts Between the World Wars* (Los Angeles: University of California Press, 1999) begins with a similar assumption: 'Beckett situates Murphy within a definite ensemble of social institutions and forces, and his regressive withdrawal can be seen as a response to increasing pressures threatening the presumably autonomous subject of consciousness' (186).

5 Samuel Beckett, letter to George Reavey (excerpt), 13 November 1936, in *Disjecta*, ed. Ruby Cohn (New York: Grove, 1984), 103.

6 Samuel Beckett, letter to Sighle Kennedy, 4 June 1967, in *Disjecta*, 113.

7 For a feminist critique of Stephen Dedalus's assumptions about the power of the male artist's gaze, see Bonnie Roos, 'Refining the Artist into Existence: Pygmalion's Statue, Stephen's Villanelle and the Venus of Praxiteles,' *Comparative Literature Studies* 38, no. 2 (2001): 95–117.

8 E.H. Gombrich, *The Story of Art* (London: Phaidon, 1972), 70–1.

9 The studied incorporation of key references to *Portrait* in *Murphy*'s opening chapters most likely explains Beckett's comment in his letter to Thomas MacGreevy that the concluding Round Pond scenes of chapter 13 were 'Very early on […] in my mind' (*Dis*, 102); that is, the planting of the bird-girl parallels so early on in the story could have suggested to Beckett that his conclusion would be a rewriting of that scene in a much more complex way than was undertaken in *Dream*.

10 J.C.C. Mays, 'Mythologised Presences: *Murphy* in Its Time,' in *Myth and Reality in Irish Literature* (Waterloo: Wilfrid Laurier UP), 1977, 210. Mays reinforces the rider that ' Endon is no more Thomas MacGreevy, nor is Mr. Kelly Joyce, than Murphy himself is Beckett. But it is true to say that each of the first two characters in the novel embodies values coincident with Beckett's estimation of the two writers, as well as embodying a number of curious shared details' (211).

11 Ibid.

12 William York Tindall, *A Reader's Guide to 'Finnegans Wake'* (New York: Farrar Straus and Giroux, 1969), 22.

13 Chapter 6 of *Murphy* remains, of course, a rite of passage for any would-be Beckett critic. In this regard, see my 'Beckett and the Philosophers,' in *The Cambridge Companion to Beckett*, ed. John Pilling (Cambridge, Cambridge UP, 1994), 224–9.

14 J.D. O'Hara, *Samuel Beckett's Hidden Drives: Structural Uses of Depth Psychology* (Tallahassee: UP of Florida, 1997), 54.

15 Ibid., 68.

16 George Meredith, *The Egoist: A Comedy in Narrative*, ed. George Woodcock (New York: Penguin Books, 1968), 33. All references are from this edition and are given in the body of the text.

17 *The Critical Writings of James Joyce*, ed. Ellsworth Mason and Richard Ellmann (Ithaca, NY: Cornell UP, 1959), 144 (from the 'Paris Notebook').

18 For a more thorough discussion of these three theories of comedy, see the entry on 'Humour' in *The Encyclopaedia of Philosophy*, vols. 3 and 4, ed. Paul Edwards (New York: Macmillan, 1967), 90–3.

19 Sighle Kennedy in *Murphy's Bed: A Study of Real Sources and Sur-Real Associations in Samuel Beckett's First Novel* (Lewisburg, PA: Bucknell UP, 1971), does offer an explanation in terms of the mythological and astronomical analogues for the characters: 'No joke about Hera, wife of Zeus and therefore Queen of Heaven, would ever "at the best of times and places" have amused Artemis [Celia is identified as a moon-goddess figure], who in her own way was also a Queen of Heaven' (101). Ackerley dismisses somewhat too peremptorily Kennedy's achievement and her particular insights, acknowledging, however, that she was the first to refer to Whitaker's *Almanac* and Beckett's use of it in *Murphy* (x).

20 The question of egoism and its value in terms of the Joyce-Beckett relationship could be discussed in broader philosophical terms by building upon the contexts laid out by Jean-Michel Rabaté in 'Joyce the Egoist,' *Modernism/Modernity* 4, no. 3 (1997): 45–65. Of particular relevance to my more narrowed focus in this chapter is the concluding section of his essay: 'The Book of Egoism: "Cribbed out of Meredith."' In term of egoism writ large, the very young Stephen Dedalus's acknowledgment in *Portrait* of a Higher Authority, 'Only God could do that' (27), is cribbed out of Joyce with studied irony in *Murphy*'s questioning of who could 'turn a neurotic into a psychotic': 'Only God could do that' (175–6).

21 George Meredith, 'An Essay on Comedy and the Uses of the Comic Spirit,' in *The Egoist*, ed. Robert M. Adams (New York: Norton, 1979), 434.

22 Ibid., 444.

23 Ibid., 446.

24 Meredith composed a sonnet, 'The Star Sirius,' which emphasized his identification with this bright star that illuminated the darkness: 'Be thou my
star, and thou in me be seen/To show what source divine is.' The poem is
printed in the critical edition of *The Egoist*, ed. Robert M. Adams, 450.
25 George Meredith, 'An Essay on Comedy,' 447.
26 Compare this sentence in which Murphy's life unravels before him with the
passage in *Portrait*, chapter 2, in which a young Stephen Dedalus also suf-
fers a loss of self: 'The memory of his childhood suddenly grew dim. He
tried to call forth some of its vivid moments but could not'; the extenuation
of the sense of self is then summarized in an image that might be regarded
as the forerunner of the cinematic montage of the sentence in *Murphy*: 'He
had not died but he had faded out like a film in the sun. He had been lost or
had wandered out of existence for he no longer existed' (89).
27 Samuel Beckett, letter to Thomas MacGreevy (17 July 1936, excerpt), *Disjecta*, 102.
28 Brian Coffey, 'Memory Murphy's Maker: Some Notes on Samuel Beckett,'
Threshold 17 (1963): 33. Meredith also uses the phrase 'intellectual fireworks' in his 'An Essay on Comedy,' 437.
29 Donald Fanger, 'Joyce and Meredith: A Question of Influence and Tradition,' *Modern Fiction Studies* 6 (Summer 1960): 126.
30 George Meredith, 'An Essay on Comedy,' 433.
31 Ibid., 447.

4. What's What in *Watt*

1 Hugh Kenner, *The Stoic Comedians: Flaubert, Joyce, and Beckett* (Berkeley: U of
California P, 1962), 81.
2 Samuel Beckett's letter to Axel Kaun is labelled 'German Letter of 1937' in
Disjecta, ed. Ruby Cohn, 51–4; an English translation is given in the 'Notes,'
170–3. My citations are from 171–2.
3 Cited in Ruby Cohn's introductory comments in the English translation of
the letter to Axel Kaun, *Disjecta*, 170.
4 Israel Shenker, 'Moody Man of Letters,' *New York Times*, 6 May 1956, sec. 2, 1.
5 P.J. Murphy, 'Beckett and the Philosophers,' *The Cambridge Companion to
Beckett*, ed. John Pilling (Cambridge: Cambridge University Press, 1994),
222–41; 229–41 focus on the Kantian dimensions. The very much neglected
Kant-Beckett relationship is beginning to receive more critical attention. John
Pilling's 'From a (W)horoscope to *Murphy*,' in *The Ideal Core of the Onion: Read-
ing Beckett Archives*, ed. John Pilling and Mary Bryden (Reading, UK: Beckett
International Foundation, 1992), documents Beckett's reading of Kant in the
Murphy notebook, 15–18. In *Beckett and Philosophy*, ed. Richard Lane (London:

Palgrave, 2002), Steve Barfield in his introduction to his essay on Beckett and Heidegger acknowledges that in *Reconstructing Beckett* and *The Cambridge Companion* chapter 'the thrust of both these works by Murphy is in uncovering a relationship between Beckett and Kant (much of which is persuasive) and in arguing that Beckett's main theme is the way language relates to the world, rather than that of an emptying of meaning from language' (155). Recently, John Wall's 'A Study of the Imagination in Samuel Beckett's *Watt*,' *New Literary History* 33, no. 3 (Summer 2002) 533–58, argues that Beckett adapts Kant's transcendental imagination 'and puts it to work in an exploration of the corporeal dimension of the generation of symbols' (534); he concludes that 'there is no reason to limit the ontological explication of the symbol in Beckett to the linguistic model, the basis of the theoretical notion of the self-consciously superficial imaginary of postmodernism' (556). This approaches from a different angle some of my views on the symbol in Beckett, particularly as developed in chapter 2 of this study.

6 Interview with Michael Haerdter, cited in Dougald McMillan and Martha Fehsenfeld, *Beckett in the Theater* (New York: Riverrun, 1988), 230–1. Beckett also refers to *lo scibile* in his review of Pound's *Make It New* (*Dis*, 78).

7 The poem is quoted in toto in Lawrence Harvey, *Samuel Beckett: Poet and Critic* (Princeton, NJ: Princeton UP, 1970), 208.

8 Mary Ann Caws, *Reading Frames in Modern Fiction* (Princeton, NJ: Princeton UP, 1985). See in particular 'V/High Modernist Framing,' with its discussions of the later James, Proust, and Woolf.

9 Francis Doherty, '*Watt* in an Irish Frame,' *Irish University Review* 21, no. 2 (1991): 190; Frederik N. Smith, *Beckett's Eighteenth Century* (New York: Palgrave, 2002), 38. It is revealing to compare Doherty and Smith in terms of their views on Joyce's influence/presence in *Watt*. Doherty only mentions a minor detail, suggesting that Mr Case the signalman might be intended to echo Joyce's 'A Painful Case' – 'a courteous and little jocular benediction to Joyce' (197); but he concludes his discussion with a very strong reference to Joyce in terms of negative influence, arguing that Beckett's refusal to be restricted to realism resulted in his 'scrupulously avoiding the Joycean way or its path to the truly Beckettian use of Irish background and experience' (203). On the other hand, Smith makes extensive reference to Joyce throughout his study and concludes that 'Beckett's embracing of the writers of the eighteenth century enabled him to escape the burden of Joyce and served in a sense to legitimize his own writing by connecting him to a long literary tradition' (8). While acknowledging such influences, I argue that they are, however, still secondary to Joyce's influence.

10 David H. Hesla, *The Shape of Chaos: An Interpretation of the Art of Samuel Beckett* (Minneapolis: U of Minnesota P, 1971), 63.

11 Ibid.

12 'Refuge' suggests a flight from 'suffering – that opens a window on the real and is the main condition of the artistic experience' (16).

13 David Haymann, 'A Meeting in the Park and a Meeting on the Bridge: Joyce and Beckett,' *James Joyce Quarterly* 8, no. 4 (1971): 376.

14 Ibid, 384.

15 William York Tindall, *A Reader's Guide to 'Finnegans Wake'* (New York: Farrar, Straus and Giroux, 1969), 64.

16 John P. Harrington, *The Irish Beckett* (Syracuse, NY: Syracuse University Press, 1991), 119. Harrington does not present Joyce as a pervasive and abiding presence in *Watt* or in the oeuvre as a whole; he sees W.B. Yeats as a more extensive influence on Beckett. Harrington's major discussion of Joyce and Beckett focuses on how Beckett's 1934 short story 'A Case in a Thousand' can be compared to 'A Painful Case' of *Dubliners* (70–2), an instance, in my judgment, of a 'false positive' in terms of influence.

17 John Pilling, 'From a (W)horoscope to *Murphy*,' 15.

18 Immanuel Kant, *Critique of Practical Reason*, cited in 'Immanuel Kant,' *The Encyclopaedia of Philosophy*, vols. 3 and 4 (New York: Macmillan, 1967), 317.

19 Ibid, 318.

20 Immanuel Kant, *Critique of Judgement*, trans. and intro., Werner S. Pluhar (Indianapolis, IN: Hackett, 1987), 74.

21 Ibid.

22 *The Metamorphoses of Ovid*, trans. and intro. Mary M. Innes (New York: Penguin, 1955), Book 8, lines 175–6.

23 See plate 1 in Frederik N. Smith's *Beckett's Eighteenth Century* (New York: Palgrave, 2002), 118 (facing). Smith adds: 'This relationship between Beckett and past authors is comparable to that between Dante and Virgil, caught in a doodle in the *Watt* manuscript; illustrating Canto 1, line 82 of *The Inferno*, Beckett shows Virgil and Dante locked in a sort of yin-yang figure. He even quotes Dante's telling words: "Tu se' lo mio maestro e il mio autore."' (9). My Joyce-Arsene/Virgil analogies give another critical dimension to Beckett's graphic depiction of the end of the first part of *Watt*. Richard Begam in *Samuel Beckett and the End of Modernity* (Stanford, CA: Stanford UP, 1996) also invokes the Dante-Virgil relationship at this juncture in *Watt* (71).

24 Watt's playing with the lamp is said to make a 'pretty picture,' with 'Watt's scalp and the red-grey tufts, and the floor burning up, from below' (37). These images bring to mind scenes in the Clongowes School Infirmary, where Brother Michael, who had 'reddish hair mixed with grey and a queer look' (*P*, 32), tended the feverish Stephen Dedalus. He is also 'queer' in Stephen's estimation since he 'would always be a brother' and he

wonders 'why could he not catch up on the others?' Brother Michael is bound to the Jesuit order by vows but not educated as a priest and hence usually would be assigned housekeeping duties. Beckett is by analogy perhaps implying that Watt also will never be fully initiated into the mysteries of Mr Knott's house. Keith Haughton first drew my attention to these shared synecdoches.

25 Cited in John Pilling, *Beckett before Godot* (Cambridge: Cambridge UP 1997), 182. Interview with Beckett, Paris, August 1969.

26 Richard Ellmann reports how Joyce was interested in variation and sameness in time: Leopold Bloom, for example, consoles himself with the thought that every betrayal is only one of an infinite series. He then adds that Joyce was 'interested also in variation and sameness in space, the cubist method of establishing differing relations among aspects of a single thing, and he would ask Beckett to do some research for him in the possible permutations of an object' (*James Joyce*, 551). Ellmann's comments occur in a complex discussion stemming from the idea of coincidence residing at the base of Joyce's ideas of reality 'as a paradigm' (as stated to Ellmann by Beckett). Whereas for Joyce, according to Ellmann, reality 'can only assume certain forms,' Beckett's research in *Watt* on the permutations of objects would reveal that at times, in a certain place, a pot is also not a pot, and that placing objects in a series (infinite or not) is not always all that comforting.

27 There is perhaps a suggestion of just such a post-Dedalian aesthetic, which would combine stasis and kinesis in Watt's sighting of the strange figure who approaches him as he waits at the train station, after having left Mr Knott's, and who then suddenly disappears. This doppelgänger is described as having for a hat 'the likeness of a depressed inverted chamberpot' (226), which is a doubling of the image of the boy who 'had slung inverted on his head' (184) a basket and to whom Stephen points in his development of his aesthetic theory.

28 C.J. Ackerley, '"Fatigue and Disgust": The Addenda to *Watt*,' *Samuel Beckett Today/Aujourd'hui*, 2 (1993): 187.

29 Ibid.

30 See, for example, chapter 4 on Virginia Woolf: 'Matches Struck in the Dark,' in Morris Beja, *Epiphany in the Modern Novel* (London: Peter Owen, 1971), 112–47.

31 Mr Gorman might be an ironic reference by Beckett to Herbert Gorman, who wrote the 'authorized' Joyce biography that was published in 1939 – a hagiographic work that Joyce controlled ventriloquist-fashion. Richard Ellmann in his Joyce biography states that the effect of Joyce's editing of Gorman's manuscript was 'to curb a sporadic cheeriness in Gorman's book, and to render more solemn and sardonic its picture of the persecuted artist' (726).

32 The Ballast Office epiphany follows immediately after the above citations; Beckett refers to it in *How It Is*, 44.

5. The Pseudocouple Dante-Joyce

1 Finding means to explore the 'darkness' is, of course, the focus of a great deal of twentieth-century literature, perhaps most strikingly announced in Joseph Conrad's *Heart of Darkness* (1901). Beckett has likened the act of writing fiction to 'trying to find your way through a jungle, an area of utter lawlessness where no rules of any sort apply.' Cited in Alec Reid, *All I Can Manage, More Than I Could* (Dublin: Dolmen, 1968), 20.

2 'Krapp's Last Tape,' in *Collected Shorter Plays of Samuel Beckett* (London: Faber and Faber, 1984), 60–1. The great irony here is that Krapp is searching for a romantic memory that is strongly reminiscent of Bloom's memories of Molly's first kiss (*U*, 167–8). Krapp's memory reproduces a number of images from this scene in 'Laestrygonians,' particularly those of eyes. However, in Krapp's memory it is the ending and not the beginning of the romance that is foregrounded: 'I said again I thought it was hopeless and no good going on.'

3 Ibid., 60.

4 Deirdre Bair, *Samuel Beckett: A Biography* (London: Harcourt Brace Jovanovich, 1978), 351.

5 Anthony Cronin in *Samuel Beckett: The Last Modernist* (London: Harper Collins, 1996), 361, mistakenly identifies the 'revelation' as having occurred at Killiney harbour. Neither of the two major studies focused on this period of Beckett's life makes mention of the 'revelation': John Pilling's *Beckett before Godot* and Lois Gordon's *The World of Samuel Beckett: 1906–1946*.

6 Richard Ellmann, *Four Dubliners* (Washington, DC: Library of Congress, 1986), 82.

7 Ruby Cohn, *A Beckett Canon* (Ann Arbor: U of Michigan P, 2001, 4.

8 Kevin H. Dettmar, 'The Joyce that Beckett Built,' in *Beckett and Beyond*, ed. B. Stewart, Princess Grace Irish Library Series 9 (Gerrards Cross, UK: Colin Smythe, 1999), 85–90.

9 Cohn, *A Beckett Canon*, 389.

10 Knowlson is reaffirming here a point made throughout his biography: he concludes his brief discussion of 'Assumption' by stating that the 'young disciple' is 'perhaps already trying to distance himself from the master' (111).

11 *Reconstructing Beckett: Language for Being in Samuel Beckett's Fiction* (Toronto: U of Toronto P, 1990), 15–19. The later discussions of *Mercier and Camier* and 'The Calmative' also build on discussions from my earlier study.

12 Compare with *Dream*, 16.

13 Lawrence Harvey, *Samuel Beckett: Poet and Critic* (Princeton, NJ: Princeton UP, 1970), 113.

14 Ibid.

15 Cited in John P. Harrington, *The Irish Beckett* (Syracuse, NY: Syracuse UP, 1991), 8; the irony here is that Beckett has also 'adapted' Eliot's description of Joyce's 'mythical method' in his famous essay '*Ulysses*, Order and Myth' (1923).

16 Cronin, *Samuel Beckett: The Last Modernist*, 361.

17 See Ackerley, *Demented Particulars: The Annotated 'Murphy'*, special issue of *Journal of Beckett Studies* 7, nos. 1 & 2 (Autumn 1997/Spring 1998), xxiii.

18 Eric Levy, *Beckett and the Voice of Species* (Dublin: Gill and MacMillan, 1980), 41.

19 Daniela Caselli, 'Dante and Beckett: Authority Constructing Authority' (PhD diss., University of Reading, 1999), 12–15. I am indebted to Caselli's identification of Dantean allusions throughout my discussion of *Mercier and Camier* and *Stories*.

20 Cited in Caselli, 'Dante and Beckett,' 186. Her chapter is entitled '"Lo bello quoi?": Dante as (in)visible auctoritas in *Mercier et Camier* and *Mercier and Camier*.'

21 Dante Alighieri, *The Divine Comedy*, 3 vols. trans. Mark Musa (New York: Penguin Books, 2003), *Inferno*, Canto I, lines 85–7. All future citations are from this edition.

22 Ibid., 177. Note also the more explicit reference in *Portrait* to Stephen's siblings taking 'up the air until a full choir of voices was singing'; the choir is indeed mixed and Stephen 'took up the air with them' (145). This scene occurs shortly after his rejection of the priesthood as his vocation.

23 Compare the homosexual nature of this 'encounter' with Joyce's second story of *Dubliners*, 'An Encounter.'

24 Compare with Beckett's attempts to place Proust in a particular literary tradition: 'Proust's point of departure might be situated in Symbolism or on its *outskirts*' (my emphasis, *Pr*, 60). Beckett is perhaps echoing *Proust* in recognition of the difficulty he is having in 'The Calmative' in terms of designating his own new 'point of departure.' Note also that just before Marcel receives the 'oracle,' his 'revelation,' Beckett describes him as being on the 'outskirts' of the 'futility' (51) that is society.

25 Beckett told Peggy Guggenheim years later 'he was dead and had no feelings that were human and that is why he had not been able to fall in love with Joyce's daughter.' Cited in Carol Loeb Schloss, *Lucia Joyce: To Dance in the Wake* (New York: Farrar, Straus and Giroux), 2003, 194–5. Schloss also adds that 'Beckett was to remain Lucia's most loyal friend' (195).

26 Beckett's summary of Mörike's plot mentions how Mozart 'helps himself (with a pensive smile) to an orange' (*Dis*, 61), later adding that a 'number of passages' – 'the orange exhaling its aria' being one – 'would be pleasant enough in a less pretentious context' (62).

6. A Not So *'Distant Music'*

1 Phil Baker, *Beckett and the Mythology of Psychoanalysis* (London: MacMillan, 1997), xii. A revealing contrast with Baker's study is J.D. O'Hara's *Samuel Beckett's Hidden Drives*, also published in 1997. O'Hara has a tendency to equate correspondences between Beckett's work and 'depth psychology' in a one-to-one manner as the key to unlocking interpretations.

2 In *Proust*, Beckett characterized Marcel's evaluation of art prior to his mystical experience in the Guermantes library as overwhelmingly negative in nature, regarding 'the materials of art – Beatrice and Faust and the "azur du ciel immense et ronde" and the seagirt cities – all the absolute beauty of a magic world, as vulgar and unworthy in their reality' (50). Molloy as artist is able to redeem some of these elements in his own way in his 'magic world,' even if it is obviously devoid of 'absolute beauty.'

3 Baker, xiv.

4 Ibid.

5 J.W. Goethe, *Faust Parts 1 and 2*, trans. B. Taylor (London: Sphere Books, 1969), 'First Part of the Tragedy, I, Night,' lines 380–5, 36.

6 Milton, ed. Maynard Mack (Englewood Cliffs, NJ: Prentice-Hall, 1964), *Paradise Lost*, Book I, line 263, 111.

7 Christopher Marlowe, *Doctor Faustus*, ed. S. Barnet (New York: New American Library, 1969), 23–4, lines 20–1.

8 Daniel Katz, *Saying I No More: Subjectivity and Consciousness in the Prose of Samuel Beckett* (Evanston, IL: Northwestern UP, 1999), 92.

9 Samuel Beckett, *Molloy* (Paris: Les Éditions de Minuit, 1951), 29.

10 *Portait*'s 'distant music' is much more central to Joyce's method and vision than the version identified with Gabriel Conroy. John Gordon in *Joyce and Reality: The Empirical Strikes Back* (Syracuse, NY: Syracuse UP, 2004) discusses the importance of the 'nebular hypothesis' throughout Joyce, returning to it in his concluding remark: '*Finnegans Wake*, like *Portrait*, appears to instantiate a universal protocol of creation and destruction that applies equally to the formation of thoughts and the formation of stars' (259).

11 Cited in Ruby Cohn's introduction to Martin Esslin's translation of the Kaun letter in the 'Notes' for *Disjecta*, 170.

12 K.J. Phillips, 'Beckett's *Molloy* and *The Odyssey*,' *International Fiction Review* 11, no. 1 (Winter 84): 19–24. Although Phillips does point out some parallels between *Molloy* and Joyce's *Ulysses*, his main emphasis is upon how Beckett 'deepens many of the implications already present in Odysseus's shifting identities' (19) as found in Homer.

13 An interesting and provocative discussion of the Davin episode in terms of the Irish writer coming into being through a consciousness of desire (both erotic and political) is developed by Marian Eide in 'The Woman of the Ballyhoura Hills: James Joyce and the Politics of Creativity,' in *James Joyce's 'A Portrait of the Artist as a Young Man': A Casebook*, ed. Mark A. Wollaeger (Oxford UP, 2003), 297–318.

14 Beckett's description of the writing of *Molloy* that he made to John Pilling. See his *Samuel Beckett* (London: Routledge and Kegan Paul, 1976), 53.

15 C.J. Ackerley and S.E. Gontarski, *The Grove Companion to Samuel Beckett: A Reader's Guide to His Works, Life, and Thought* (New York: Grove, 2004), 378.

16 Ibid.

17 Katz, *Saying I No More*, 73.

18 Ackerley and Gontarski, *The Grove Companion to Samuel Beckett*, 451. Beckett's observation to Knowlson about how the ending of *Portrait* was 'pompous' about the artist's 'vocation and his function in life' (in Knowlson and Elizabeth Knowlson, eds, *Beckett Remembering Remembering Beckett* [New York: Arcade, 2006], 47) cannot, of course, be applied directly to Joyce himself and hardly does justice to the depth and complexity of Beckett's own relationship with the novel.

19 Note, however, that Stephen's list of aesthetic questions is paralleled in *Molloy II* by Moran's two lists of 'certain questions of a theological nature' (166–8). One of Stephen's questions – '– *If a man hacking in fury at a block of wood* […] *make there an image of a cow, is that image a work of art?* (186) – might be echoed in Moran's attempts to ease the growing anxiety of the Molloy affair by 'hacking madly at an old chopping block that lay there' (127). Moran's narrative in a sense poses the same questions: namely, will his hack writing end up producing an actual work of art?

20 For statistical confirmation of this, see Michèle Barale and Rubin Rabinovitz, *A KWIC Concordance to Beckett's 'Trilogy*,' 2 vols. (New York: Garland, 1988).

21 John Keats, *The Complete Poems*, ed. J. Barnard (London: Penguin Books, 1981), 'Endymion,' lines 12–13, 107.

22 Cited in S.L. Goldberg, *Joyce* (London: Oliver and Boyd, 1965), 69.

23 John Keats, *Complete Poems*, lines 9–11, 72.

24 Cited in Goldberg, *Joyce*, 81.

25 G.W.F. Hegel, *The Phenomenology of Mind*, trans. J.B. Baillie (New York: Harper Torchbooks, 1967), 51.

26 Bruce Baugh, *French Hegel: From Surrealism to Postmodernism* (London: Routledge, 2003), 176.

27 Hans-Joachim Schulz in *'This Hell of Stories': A Hegelian Approach to the Novels of Samuel Beckett* (The Hague: Mouton, 1973) juxtaposes a strong critique of Joyce's Hegelianism of the idealist system-builder (Author-God) with an endorsement of Beckett's Hegelianism, which he reads in existentialist terms.

7. Critical Beckett

1 Anne Banfield also makes this basic point in 'Beckett's Tattered Syntax,' *Representations*, no. 84 (2004): 6. My reading of Beckett's 'syntax of weakness' is more affirmative than hers with reference to various ontological issues of expression.

2 Shenker, 'Moody Man of Letters,' *New York Times*, 6 May 1956, Sec. 2, x, 1, 3.

3 The 'beautiful sentence' of Edgar Quinet, which Ellmann says 'was one of the very few passages from other authors which Joyce honoured by quoting in *Finnegans Wake* in its original as well as in appropriately distorted form' (664), is similar in import and sentiment to Duthuit's sentence in this instance. The sentence translation from the French is given in Ellmann: 'Today as in the time of Pliny and Columnella the hyacinth disports in Wales, the periwinkle in Illyria, the daisy on the ruins in Numantia and while around them the cities have changed masters and names, while some have ceased to exist, while the civilizations have collided with each other and smashed, their peaceful generations have passed through the ages and have come up to us, fresh and laughing as on the days of battles' (664).

4 The 'mute language' theme of *How It Is* may also be indebted to Vico's theory of the evolution of languages: 'the language of the gods was almost entirely mute,' that of the heroes 'an equal mixture of articulate and mute,' 'the language of men, almost entirely articulate and only very slightly mute' (446, 'Book II, Poetic Wisdom'), in *The New Science of Giambattista Vico*, rev. trans. of 3 ed. (1744), ed. T.C. Bergin and M.K. Fish (New York: Cornell UP, 1961).

5 'L'Image' was published in 1959 and the first impression of *Comment c'est* is dated 6 January 1961. Cited in Edouard Magessa O'Reilly, *Samuel Beckett 'Comment c'est 'How It Is' and/et 'L'Image: A Critical Genetic Edition Une Edition Critico-Génétique* (New York: Routledge, 2001), xi. Beckett, of course, would have noted the irony that this was the Feast of Epiphany, Joyce's day of 'The Dead.'

6 Phyllis Carey, 'Beckett's Pim and Joyce's Shem,' *James Joyce Quarterly* 26, no. 3 (Spring): 435.

7 Ibid., 438.

8 Ibid.

9 Beckett used the phrase 'narrator/narrated' with reference to *How It Is* in a letter to Hugh Kenner. See his *A Reader's Guide to Samuel Beckett* (New York: Farrar, Straus and Giroux, 1973), 94.

10 Cited in John Fletcher, *The Novels of Samuel Beckett* (London: Chatto and Windus, 1971), 235.

11 Julia Kristeva, 'Return of Orphéus,' in *James Joyce: The Augmented Ninth*, ed. Bernard Benstock (Syracuse, NY: Syracuse UP, 1988): 'Joyce hesitated over calling his hero Orpheus rather than Dedalus' (179).

12 Bloom, *The Anxiety of Influence: A Theory of Poetry* (New York: Oxford UP, 1973), 141.

13 Ellmann, 702. Compare this with a much earlier statement in *Portrait* when Stephen in the midst of his aesthetic disquisition is interrupted by some students who are discussing exam results and career prospects (and are also self-declared members of the field club): 'Bring us a few turnips and onions next time you go out, said Stephen drily, to make a stew' (183). Compare also with the radishes and turnips of *Waiting for Godot*.

14 See my *Reconstructing Beckett: Language for Being in Samuel Beckett's Fiction* (Toronto: U of Toronto P, 1990), 99–102.

15 Compare, for example, the following statements from the hell-fire sermons in chapter 3 of *Portrait* with Beckett's imagery in 'The Lost Ones': 'The particular judgment was over and the soul had passed to the abode of bliss or to the prison of purgatory or had been hurled howling into hell' (105); 'Hell is a strait and dark and foulsmelling prison, an abode of demons and lost souls, filled with fire and smoke' (110); 'Consider finally that the torment of this infernal prison is increased by the company of the damned themselves' (112). Beckett's 'abode' is definitely of a hellish nature in 'The Lost Ones.'

16 In *How It Was: A Memoir of Samuel Beckett* (London: Faber and Faber, 2001), Anne Atik notes that at her last meeting with Beckett at the nursing home, 16 December 1989, 'We saw the paperback he'd been reading, on a chair, *Sylvia Beach and the Last* [sic] *Generation* by Noel Riley Fitch' (127).

17 With reference to this key question of time and the moment of revelation, critics such as Lois Oppenheim in *The Painted Word: Samuel Beckett's Dialogue with Art* (Ann Arbor: U of Michigan P, 2000) focus upon *ekphrasis* as a verbal representation of 'a visual moment stopped in time' (137). Since Beckett is, I believe, trying to bring kinesis and stasis together, this traditional trope does not seem fully appropriate in this critical context. In my

argument, Beckett has reconceived the nature and function of the modern-ist epiphany. Ashton Nichols in *The Poetics of Epiphany* (Tuscaloosa: U of Alabama P, 1987) points towards this reconfigured sense of the epiphany in contemporary writing: 'The concept of epiphany becomes a way of mo-mentarily balancing the dynamic opposition between the closure called for by traditional theories of literary interpretation and the openness de-manded by recent approaches to verbal discourse. As the epiphany closes in on the determinate moment of verbal power, it opens out onto multiple manifestations of meaning' (xii).

18 See the introduction to *Re: Joyce 'n Beckett*: 'Puzzled by the seeming applica-bility of the passage to Beckett, Carey [co-editor Phyllis Carey] wrote to Beckett, asking him to solve the mystery. He replied in his usual succinct fashion: "I first met Joyce late 28. The passage cannot refer to me"' (xvii).

19 'The Voice' is Reading University Library MS2910, consisting of seven man-uscript pages and dated 'Paris Jan. 77.' See my 'On First Looking into Beckett's "The Voice",' in *The Ideal Core of the Onion: Reading Becket Archives*, ed. J. Pilling and M. Bryden (Reading, UK: Beckett International Founda-tion, 1992), 75.

20 See chapter 10 of my *Reconstructing Beckett*, 'Shakespeare and *Company*: Beckett's *As You Like It*,' 144–53.

21 Beckett, *Collected Shorter Plays* (London: Faber and Faber, 1984), 286. Further references are to this edition. Joyce may figure as a character in Beckett's drama and there are indeed a number of echoes of Joyce's work in Beckett's drama; nevertheless, Beckett's full engagement with Joycean aesthetics oc-curs only in his prose. An obvious reason for this is that Joyce was not a dramatist, publishing but one play, *Exiles*. It is interesting to note, however, that when Beckett wrote his first play, *Eleutheria*, he started with a strategy similar to that which we have discussed with reference to his first prose fic-tion, 'Assumption,' namely, a rewriting of *Portrait*. Richard Ellmann in *Four Dubliners* (Washington, DC: Library of Congress, 1986) stated of Beckett's first dramatic venture: 'Beckett put the play aside, perhaps because it was too much a counterstatement to Joyce's *A Portrait of the Artist*' (92).

22 Knowlson in *Damned to Fame* reports Beckett's statement to him about the identity of the 'dear face': '"It's Suzanne," he replied. 'I've imagined her dead so many times. I've even imagined myself trudging out to her grave"' (665).

23 W.B. Yeats, 'Easter 1916,' *Collected Poems of W.B. Yeats* (London: MacMillan, 1969), 203. Compare with Patrick J. Keane's *Terrible Beauty: Yeats, Joyce, Ireland and the Myth of the Devouring Female* (Columbia: U of Missouri P, 1988). Beckett's old woman in *Ill Seen Ill Said* is an intriguing counterpoint to the deadly arche-type of Cathleen ni Houlihan as femme fatale, a seductive mother-lover.

24 John Paul Riquelme, 'For Whom the Snow Taps: Style and Repetition in "The Dead,"' in *James Joyce: 'The Dead': Case Studies in Contemporary Criticism*, ed. D.R. Schwarz (New York: Bedford Books of St Martin's Press, 1994), 224.

25 The poem was first published in limited and trade editions in 1989. I refer to Beckett's English translation in the *Beckett Circle* in the year after his death (Spring 1990). Frederik N. Smith in *Beckett's Eighteenth Century* (New York: Palgrave, 2002) suggests that the stuttering attempts to articulate the nature of 'folly' in Beckett's last work could be an echoing of Swift's dying words, 'It is all folly' (109).

26 Lawrence Harvey, *Samuel Beckett: Poet and Critic* (Princeton, NJ: Princeton UP, 1970), 80–2.

27 John Paul Riquelme discusses in detail the etymological linkage of these words in 'For Whom the Snow Taps,' 225–6.

Bibliography

Acheson, James. 'Beckett and the Heresy of Love.' In *Women in Beckett*. Edited by Linda Ben-Zvi. Urbana: U of Illinois P, 1990, 68–80.

Ackerley, C.J. '"Fatique and Disgust": The Addenda to *Watt.*' *Samuel Beckett Today/Aujourd'hui* 2 (1993): 175–88.

– *Demented Particulars: The Annotated 'Murphy.'* Special issue, *Journal of Beckett Studies* 7, nos. 1 & 2 (Autumn 1997/Spring 1998).

– *Obscure Locks, Simple Keys; The Annotated 'Watt.'* Special issue, *Journal of Beckett Studies* 14, nos. 1 & 2 (2005).

Ackerley, C.J., and S.E. Gontarski. *The Grove Companion to Samuel Beckett*: *A Reader's Guide to His Works, Life, and Thought*. New York: Grove, 2004.

Amiran, Eyal. *Wandering and Home: Beckett's Metaphysical Narrative*. University Park: Pennsylvania State UP, 1993.

Anspaugh, Kelly. '"Faith, Hope, and – What Was It?": Beckett Reading Joyce Reading Dante.' *Journal of Beckett Studies* 5, nos. 1 & 2 (Autumn 1995/Spring 1996): 19–38.

Atik, Anne. *How It Was: A Memoir of Samuel Beckett*. London: Faber and Faber, 2001.

Aubert, Jacques. *The Aesthetics of James Joyce*. Revised English-language edition. Baltimore: Johns Hopkins UP, 1992.

Bair, Deirdre. *Samuel Beckett: A Biography*. London: Harcourt Brace Jovanovich, 1978.

Baker, Phil. *Beckett and the Mythology of Psychoanalysis*. London: MacMillan, 1997.

Bakhtin, M.M. *The Dialogic Imagination: Four Essays*. Edited by M. Holquist. Translated by C. Emerson and M. Holquist. Austin: U of Texas P, 1981.

Banfield, Ann. 'Beckett's Tattered Syntax.' *Representations*, no. 84 (2004): 6–29.

Barale, Michèle A., and Rubin Rabinovitz. *A KWIC Concordance to Beckett's 'Trilogy.'* 2 vols. New York: Garland, 1988.

Barfield, Steve. 'Beckett and Heidegger: A Critical Survey.' In *Beckett and Philosophy.* Edited by Richard Lane. London: Palgrave, 2002, 154–65.

Barge, Laura. *God, the Quest, the Hero: Thematic Structures in Beckett's Fiction.* Chapel Hill: U of North Carolina P, 1988.

Baugh, Bruce. *French Hegel: From Surrealism to Postmodernism.* London: Routledge, 2003.

Beckett, Samuel. *Collected Shorter Plays.* London: Faber and Faber, 1984.

Begam, Richard. *Samuel Beckett and the End of Modernity.* Stanford, CA: Stanford UP, 1996.

Beja, Morris. *Epiphany in the Modern Novel.* London: Peter Owen, 1971.

Berton, Pierre. *Vimy.* Toronto: Anchor Canada, 2001.

Bloom, Harold. *The Anxiety of Influence: A Theory of Poetry.* New York: Oxford UP, 1973.

– *The Western Canon.* New York: Harcourt Brace, 1994.

Bouchard, Norma. 'Rereading Beckett's *Dream of Fair to Middling Women.*' *Samuel Beckett Today/Aujourd'hui* 6, no. 11 (1997): 137–47.

Bürger, Peter. *Theory of the Avant-Garde.* Translated by M. Shaw. Minneapolis: U of Minnesota P, 1984.

Buttigieg, Joseph A. *'A Portrait of the Artist' in Different Perspective.* Athens: Ohio UP, 1987.

Carey, Phyllis. 'Beckett's Pim and Joyce's Shem.' *James Joyce Quarterly* 26, no. 3 (Spring): 435–9.

Carlyle, Thomas. *On Heroes, Hero-Worship and the Heroic in History.* Edited by Carl Niemeyer. Lincoln: U of Nebraska P, 1966.

Caselli, Daniela. 'Dante and Beckett: Authority Constructing Authority.' PhD diss., University of Reading, 1999.

Caws, Mary Ann. *Reading Frames in Modern Fiction.* Princeton, NJ: Princeton UP, 1985.

Coffey, Brian. 'Memory Murphy's Maker: Some Notes on Samuel Beckett.' *Threshold* 17 (1963): 28–33.

Cohn, Ruby. *A Beckett Canon.* Ann Arbor: U of Michigan P, 2001.

Cronin, Anthony. *Samuel Beckett: The Last Modernist.* London: Harper Collins, 1996.

Dante Alighieri. *The Divine Comedy.* 3 vols. Translated by Mark Musa. New York: Penguin Books, 2003.

D'Arcy, Michael. 'The Task of the Listener: Beckett, Proust and Perpetual Translation.' *Samuel Beckett Today/Aujourd'hui* 12 (2002): 35–52.

Dettmarr, Kevin J.H. 'The Joyce that Beckett Built.' In *Beckett and Beyond.* Edited by B. Stewart. Princess Grace Irish Library Series 9. Gerrards Cross, UK: Colin Smythe, 78–92.

– 'The Illusion of Modernist Allusion and the Politics of Postmodern Plagiarism', in *Perspectives on Plagiarism and Intellectual Property in a Postmodern*

World. Edited by Lise Buranen and Alice M. Roy. State University of New York Press, 99–120.

Doherty, Francis. '*Watt* in an Irish Frame.' *Irish University Review* 21, no. 2 (1991): 187–203.

Eco, Umberto, ed. *History of Beauty*. Translated by A. McEwen. New York: Rizzoli, 2004.

Eide, Marian. 'The Woman of the Ballyhoura Hills: James Joyce and the Politics of Creativity.' In *James Joyce's 'A Portrait of the Artist as a Young Man': A Casebook*. Edited by Mark A. Wollaeger. Oxford: Oxford UP, 2003, 297–317.

Eliot, T.S., ed. *Literary Essays of Ezra Pound*. New York: New Directions, 1918.

Ellmann, Richard. *Four Dubliners*. Washington, DC Library of Congress, 1986.

– *James Joyce*. New York: Oxford UP, 1982.

Encyclopaedia of Philosophy. Vols. 1–4. New York: MacMillan, 1967.

Fanger, Donald. 'Joyce and Meredith: A Question of Influence and Tradition.' *Modern Fiction Studies* 6 (Summer 1960): 125–30.

Fletcher, John. *The Novels of Samuel Beckett*. London: Chatto and Windus, 1971.

– 'Beckett et Proust.' *Caliban* I (January 1964): 89–100.

Foucault, Michel. *Discipline and Punish: The Birth of the Prison*. Translated by A. Sheridan. New York: Vintage Books, 1995.

Frank, Joseph. *The Widening Gyre*. New Brunswick, NJ: Rutgers UP, 1963.

Garrett-Petts, Will, and Donald Lawrence. *PhotoGraphic Encounters*. Edmonton: U of Alberta P, 2000.

Gluck, Barbara. *Beckett and Joyce: Friendship and Fiction*. Lewisburg, PA: Bucknell UP, 1979.

Goethe, J.W. *Faust Parts 1 & 2*. Translated by B. Taylor. London: Sphere Books, 1969.

Goldberg, S.L. *Joyce*. London: Oliver and Boyd, 1965.

Gombrich, E.H. *The Story of Art*. London: Phaidon, 1972.

Gontarski, S.E. 'The Intent of Undoing in Samuel Beckett's Art.' *Modern Fiction Studies* 29 (1983): 25–41.

– *The Intent of 'Undoing' in Samuel Beckett's Dramatic Texts*. Bloomington: Indiana UP, 1985.

Gordon, John. *Joyce and Reality: The Empirical Strikes Back*. Syracuse, NY: Syracuse UP, 2004.

Gordon, Lois. *The World of Samuel Beckett, 1906–1946*. New Haven: CT: Yale UP, 1996.

Goring, Paul, J. Hawthorn, and D. Mitchell, eds. *Studying Literature: The Essential Companion*. New York: Oxford UP, 2001.

Gruen, John. 'Samuel Beckett Talks about Beckett.' *Vogue*, February 1970.

Harrington, John P. *The Irish Beckett*. Syracuse, NY: Syracuse UP, 1991.

– 'Joyce and Beckett: A Preliminary Checklist.' Chapter 13 in *Re: Joyce 'n Beckett*. Edited by Phyllis Carey and Ed Jewinski. New York: Fordham UP, 1992, 185–93.

Hartman, Geoffrey H. *The Unmediated Vision: An Interpretation of Wordsworth, Hopkins, Rilke and Valéry*. New York: Harcourt Brace, 1966.

Harvey, Lawrence E. *Samuel Beckett: Poet and Critic*. Princeton, NJ: Princeton UP, 1970.

Hayman, David. 'A Meeting in the Park and a Meeting on a Bridge: Joyce and Beckett.' *James Joyce Quarterly* 8, no. 4 (1971): 372–84.

Hegel, G.W.F. *The Phenomenology of Mind*. Translated by J.B. Baillie. New York: Harper Torchbooks, 1967.

Hesla, David H. *The Shape of Chaos: An Interpretation of the Art of Samuel Beckett*. Minneapolis: U of Minnesota P, 1971.

Hunter, Adrian. 'Beckett and the Joycean Short Story.' *Essays in Criticism* 51, no. 2 (2001), 230–44.

Hutcheon, Linda. *A Theory of Parody: The Teaching of Twentieth-Century Art Forms*. Champaign: U of Illinois P, 2000.

Jaurretche, Colleen, ed. *Beckett, Joyce and the Art of the Negative*. European Joyce Studies, 16. Amsterdam: Rodopi, 2005.

Jay, Paul. *Being in the Text: Self-Representation from Wordsworth to Roland Barthes*. Ithaca, NY: Cornell University Press, 1984.

Jewinski, Ed. 'James Joyce and Samuel Beckett: From Epiphany to Anti-Epiphany.' In *Re: Joyce 'n Beckett*. Edited by Phyllis Carey and Ed Jewinski. New York: Fordham UP, 1992, 160–74.

Johnson, George. *Dynamic Psychology in Modernist British Fiction*. London: Palgrave, 2006.

Kant, Immanuel. *Critique of Judgment*, trans. with an introduction by Werner S. Pluhar. Indianapolis, IN: Hackett, 1987.

Katz, Daniel. *Saying I No More: Subjectivity and Consciousness in the Prose of Samuel Beckett*. Evanston, IL: Northwestern UP, 1999.

Keane, Patrick J. *Terrible Beauty: Yeats, Joyce, Ireland and the Myth of the Devouring Female*. Columbia, SC: U of Missouri P, 1988.

Keats, John. *The Complete Poems*. Edited by J. Barnard. London: Penguin Books, 1981.

Kennedy, Sighle. *Murphy's Bed: A Study of Real Sources and Sur-Real Associations in Samuel Beckett's First Novel*. Lewisburg, PA: Bucknell UP, 1971.

Kennedy, X.J., et al. *Handbook of Literary Terms*. New York: Pearson Education, 2002.

Kenner, Hugh. *A Reader's Guide to Samuel Beckett*. New York: Farrar, Straus and Giroux, 1973.

– *The Stoic Comedians: Flaubert, Joyce and Beckett*. Berkeley: U of California P, 1962.

Knowlson, James. *Damned to Fame: The Life of Samuel Beckett*. London: Bloomsbury, 1996.

Knowlson, James, and Elizabeth Knowlson, eds. *Beckett Remembering Remembering Beckett*. New York: Arcade, 2006.

Kristeva, Julia. 'Return of Orpheus.' In *The Augmented Ninth*. Edited by Bernard Benstock. Syracuse, NY: Syracuse UP, 1988.

Kroetsch, Robert. 'Voice/in prose: effing the ineffable.' *freelance* 8, no. 2 (November 1976).

Lawrence, D.H. *Sons and Lovers*. Edited by H. and C. Baron. Harmondsworth, UK: Penguin Books, 1994.

Leopardi, Giacomo. *Poems and Prose*. Edited by A. Flores. Bloomington: Indiana UP, 1966.

Levy, Eric P. *Beckett and the Voice of Species*. Dublin: Gill and MacMillan, 1980.

Marlowe, Christopher. *Doctor Faustus*. Edited by S. Barnet. New York: New American Library, 1969.

Mason, Ellsworth, and Richard Ellmann, eds. *The Critical Writings of James Joyce*. Ithaca, NY: Cornell UP, 1959.

Mays, J.C.C. 'Mythologised Presences: *Murphy* in Its Time.' In *Myth and Reality in Irish Literature*. Waterloo, ON: Wilfrid Laurier UP, 1977, 197–218.

McMillan, Dougald, and Martha Fehsenfeld, eds. *Beckett in the Theater*. New York: Riverrun, 1988.

McQueeny, Terence. 'Samuel Beckett as Critic of Proust and Joyce.' Unpublished PhD dissertation. University of North Carolina, 1977.

Mercier, Vivien. *Beckett/Beckett*. New York: Oxford UP, 1977.

Meredith, George. 'An Essay on Comedy and the Uses of the Comic Spirit.' In *The Egoist: An Annotated Text*. Edited by Robert M. Adams. New York: Norton, 1979.

– *Diana of the Crossways*. New York: Quality Paperback Book Club, 2003.

– *The Egoist*. Edited by with an introduction by George Woodcock. London: Penguin Books, 1968.

Miller, Tyrus. *Late Modernism: Politics, Fiction, and the Arts Between the World Wars*. Los Angeles: U of California P, 1999.

Milton, John. *Milton*. Edited by Maynard Mack. 2nd ed. Englewood Cliffs, NJ: Prentice-Hall, 1964.

Murphy, P.J. 'At Beckett's Grave (or why Jacques Derrida has given up on writing in the direction of Beckett – for the moment)'. Photo essay. *Textual Studies in Canada*, no. 6 (Spring 1995): 55–8.

– 'Beckett and the Philosophers.' In *The Cambridge Companion to Beckett*. Edited by John Pilling. Cambridge: Cambridge UP, 1994, 222–40.

- 'On First Looking into Beckett's "The Voice."' In The *Ideal Core of the Onion*. Edited by John Pilling and Mary Bryden. Reading, UK: Beckett International Foundation, 1992, 63–78.
- 'Portraits of the Artist as a Young Critic: Beckett's "Dante ... Bruno . Vico .. Joyce" and the Rewriting of Joyce in "Assumption."' *Journal of Beckett Studies*. 9, no. 1 (Autumn 1999): 26–52.
- *Reconstructing Beckett: Language for Being in Samuel Beckett's Fiction*. Toronto: U of Toronto P, 1990.

Murphy, P.J., Werner Huber, Rolf Breuer, and Konrad Schoell. *Critique of Beckett Criticism: A Guide to Research in English, French, and German*. Columbia, SC: Camden House, 1994.

Nichols, Ashton. *The Poetics of Epiphany*. Tuscaloosa: U of Alabama P, 1987.

O'Brien, Eoin. *The Beckett Country*. Dublin: Black Cat Press, 1986.

O'Hara, J.D. *Samuel Beckett's Hidden Drives: Structural Uses of Depth Psychology*. Gainesville: UP of Florida, 1997.
- "Assumption"'s Launching Pad.' *Journal of Beckett Studies* 8, no. 2 (Spring 1999): 29–43.

O'Reilly, Edouard Magessa. *Samuel Beckett 'Comment c'est' 'How It Is' and/et 'L'Image': A Critical-Genetic Edition Une Edition Critico-Génétique*. New York: Routledge, 2001.

Oppenheim, Lois. *The Painted Word: Samuel Beckett's Dialogue with Art*. Ann Arbor: U of Michigan P, 2000.

Ovid. *The Metamorphoses*. Translated by Mary M. Innes. New York: Penguin Books, 1955.

Pasco, Allan. *Allusion: A Literary Graft*. Toronto: U of Toronto P, 1994.

Phillips, K.J. 'Beckett's *Molloy* and *The Odyssey*.' *International Fiction Review* 11, no. 1 (Winter 84): 19–24.

Pilling, John, ed. *Beckett's 'Dream' Notebook*. Reading, UK: Beckett International Foundation, 1999.
- 'A Mermaid Made Over: Beckett's "Text" and John Ford.' In *Beckett and Beyond*. Edited by B. Stewart. Gerrards Cross, UK: Colin Smythe, 1999, 211–16.
- 'From a (W)horoscope to *Murphy*.' In *The Ideal Core of the Onion*. Reading, UK: Beckett International Foundation, 1992, 1–20.
- *Beckett before Godot*. Cambridge: Cambridge UP, 1997.
- *Companion to 'Dream of Fair to Middling Women.'* Special issue, *Journal of Beckett Studies* 12, nos. 1 & 2 (2004).

Rabaté, Jean-Michel. 'Joyce the Egoist.' *Modernism/Modernity* 4, no. 3 (1997): 45–65.
- *Joyce Upon the Void: The Genesis of Doubt*. New York: St Martin's P, 1999.

Rathjen, Friedhelm, ed. *In Principle, Beckett Is Joyce*. Edinburgh: Split Pea Press, 1994.

Reid, Alec. *All I Can Manage, More Than I Could*. Dublin: Dolmen, 1968.

Riquelme, John Paul. 'For Whom the Snow Taps: Style and Repetition in "The Dead."' In *James Joyce: 'The Dead': Case Studies in Contemporary Criticism*. Edited by D.R. Schwarz. New York: Bedford Books of St Martin's P, 1994, 219–33.

Roos, Bonnie. 'Refining the Artist into Existence: Pygmalion's Statue, Stephen's Villanelle and the Venus of Praxiteles.' *Comparative Literature Studies* 38, no. 2 (2001): 95–117.

Schloss, Carol Loeb. *Lucia Joyce: To Dance in the Wake*. New York: Farrar, Straus and Giroux, 2003.

Schulz, Hans-Joachim. *'This Hell of Stories': A Hegelian Approach to the Novels of Samuel Beckett*. The Hague: Mouton, 1973.

Shenker, Israel. 'Moody Man of Letters.' *New York Times*, 6 May 1956, sec. 2, x, 1, 3.

Smith, Frederik N. *Beckett's Eighteenth Century*. New York: Palgrave, 2002.

Steiner, Wendy. *Venus in Exile: The Rejection of Beauty in Twentieth-Century Art*. Chicago: U of Chicago P, 2001.

Symons, Arthur. *The Symbolist Movement in Literature*. Introduction by Richard Ellmann. New York: Dutton, 1958.

Tindall, William York. *A Reader's Guide to 'Finnegans Wake.'* New York: Farrar, Straus and Giroux, 1969.

Vico, Giambattista. *The New Science of Giambattista Vico*. Revised translation of 3rd ed. (1744). Edited by T.C. Bergin and M.K. Fisch. Ithaca, NY: Cornell UP, 1961.

Virgil. *The Pastoral Poems (The Eclogues)*. Translated by E.V. Rieu. London: Penguin Books, 1954.

Wall, John. 'A Study of the Imagination in Samuel Beckett's *Watt.' New Literary History* 33, no. 3 (Summer 2002): 533–58.

Weisberg, David. *Chronicles of Disorder: Samuel Beckett and the Cultural Politics of the Modern Novel*. Albany: State University of New York P, 2000.

Wilson, Edmund. *Axel's Castle*. New York: Scribner's, 1931.

Wood, Rupert. 'An Endgame of Aesthetics: Beckett as Essayist.' In *The Cambridge Companion to Beckett*. Edited by John Pilling. Cambridge: Cambridge UP, 1994, 1–16.

Yeats, W.B. *The Collected Poems of W.B. Yeats*. London: MacMillan, 1969.

Zurbrugg, Nicholas. *Beckett and Proust*. Gerrards Cross, UK: Colin Smythe, 1988.

Index of Works

Index of Names